THE COMPLETE SURVIVAL GUIDE

Edited by
Mark Thiffault

DBI BOOKS, INC., NORTHFIELD, ILLINOIS

PUBLISHER
Sheldon Factor

EDITORIAL DIRECTOR
Mark Thiffault

PRODUCTION DIRECTOR
Sonya Kaiser

ART DIRECTOR
Dana Silzle

ASSOCIATE ARTISTS
John Vitale
Kristen Tonti

PRODUCTION COORDINATOR
Betty Burris

COPY EDITOR
Chris Wilson-Skinker

PHOTO SERVICES
Cynthia Forrest

Produced by

Charger Productions

ISBN 0-910676-53-4   Library of Congress Catalog Card Number 83-70141

CONTENTS

INTRODUCTION

THIS IS *NOT* the only book you'll ever need to keep yourself and your loved ones alive following a natural or manmade disaster. This is *NOT* the most complete and exhaustive work ever done on the subject. This is *NOT* the last word on survival.

Rather, it's an attempt to inform you of the many perspectives in the industry. My perspective is that survival preparedness is preferable to an unprepared reaction to a natural or manmade disaster. I feel you should accumulate what you can afford and learn those skills you see necessary before you need them. Yes, you can survive without modern equipment and products — but why would you want to?

There are other perspectives in this industry and this book introduces many, authored by acknowledged experts. *Duncan Long* has authored numerous books and articles on a wide range of survival topics. *Don* and *Barbie Stephens* are authors and consultants. *Bob Zwirz* is a fishing hall of famer with many world records. *Dean A. Grennell* is a prolific author and firearms authority who edits, with help from knife authority *Roger Combs, Gun World* Magazine. Shooter-writers *Claud S. Hamilton* and *Gerald FitzGerald* and firearms/archery expert *C.R. Learn* combine talents in the extensive "Armory After Doomsday." Hunter/shooter/radioman *William E. Haynes* discusses his interests. Handgunner *Jack Mitchell* writes of personal protection devices. *Grace Calcagno* grows and preserves for our benefit, and *Louis Bignami* is a big name when it comes to smoke cookery. *Bill Ungerman* and *Ray Dorr* are in the business of training survivalists, both expert at their tasks. And if the chapter has no byline, it was penned by me — a mountain-raised sportsman, author of five books and hundreds of newspaper and magazine articles, and an editor for fifteen years.

It is hoped that this book will start you on the road to survival preparedness — the real form of life insurance. And like insurance, we hate to pay those premiums...until we need it! I hope you never do.

Mark Thiffault
Capistrano Beach, California

Chapter 1

SURVIVAL IN THE WILDERNESS

While you can rely on woodcraft skills to find shelter in the wilderness, it's easier with good equipment!

Learn The Elemental Requirements Of Continued Survival, Regardless of Clime

CARL McCUNN was six feet two inches, 240 pounds, with a shock of curly red hair and an easy-going manner. He was no stranger to the Alaskan wilderness, having spent months alone in various remote areas, during which he foraged off the land to supplement his packed-in provisions.

But when a state trooper cut open McCunn's tent near a nameless lake in a nameless valley of the Brooks Range, he found McCunn's corpse wasted by starvation. Carl McCunn had killed himself after an eight-month ordeal which began

with the melting of winter snows in spring of 1981. McCunn left behind a one hundred-page diary from which others entering the wilderness can learn.

McCunn had been flown into the remote valley about seventy-five miles northeast of Fort Yukon, 225 miles from Fairbanks. He intended to photograph the natural beauty and mysteries of the tundra. He had taken five hundred rolls of film, photo equipment, firearms and 1400 pounds of provisions. He went into the valley in March, figuring to emerge in mid-August. McCunn had spent 5½

Alpha 2 and 4 tents from the Peak 1 line of Coleman Co. are lightweight for portability, can hold four people.

Initially, McCunn's diary entries detailed his awe of nature: fascination with the wail of loons and detailed descriptions of swans and other waterfowl. He wrote of the return to summer breeding grounds of migratory creatures.

"Humans are so out of their 'modern day' element in a place like this," he wrote in tidy block letters that were later to become almost illegible — the life record of an abandoned soul crippled by frostbite and hunger.

Rice and beans were his staples and he didn't worry until stocks began shrinking with no word of departure. By August the entries were undated, as he spent most of his time searching for food.

McCunn supplemented his starchy diet with ducks. He caught fish with a net weighted with pieces of chain. Winter was approaching, the temperature dropped and the leaves changed color. It rained constantly.

"Am down to beans now," he wrote. "Just over a gallon. Finished off the rice yesterday...

"I keep thinking of all the shotgun shells I threw away about two months ago," he wrote in another entry when supplies were nearly exhausted. "Had five boxes and when I kept seeing them sitting there I felt rather silly for having brought so many. (Felt like a warmonger.) So I threw all away...into the lake...but about a dozen...real bright."

Sheltered camp beside Icelandic lake is out of the wind, important when temperatures are dropping.

months in the area in 1976 and was no stranger to living alone.

But the redhead hadn't confirmed his exit plans with Rory Cruikshank, a bush pilot. Cruikshank told investigators that McCunn had given him money to repair his plane and fly him into — not out of — the bush. But then McCunn flew in with another pilot without advising Cruikshank where he was or when he wanted to come out. Diary entries concede McCunn "should have used more foresight about arranging my departure" and "After we later got together and I'd decided to come here, he (Cruikshank) told me not to count on his help as he may be in Anchorage."

McCunn had left three maps with friends, his destination circled and indicated with the words, "Carl's Puddle." He had told his father he might winter over if he had enough provisions and discouraged him from contacting authorities if he was late getting out. "Carl had been late on a previous excursion and I contacted police who began checking with Carl's friends," said Donovan McCunn of San Antonio, Texas. "He told me not to do that again. Besides, some of his friends heard he'd come out and was working in Paxson."

Beach camping in Oregon is more comfortable with tent and windbreak. If you don't have these aids, you often can seek shelter in wind-eroded caves.

The Navy veteran fought scurvy by eating rose hips — when he could beat birds to them. Biting insects feasted on the wearying adventurer. "Had trouble getting to sleep," his diary records. "Almost cried, these bug bites itch and sting and the pain from the swelling is terrible."

For a short time, fate shone no kindness on him: With a half-gallon of beans left, he heard a caribou thrashing in the lake. He hungrily watched it die. "Fresh caribou meat! Just hope to God that it's not wormy," he wrote before wading chest-deep into the frigid water to recover the prize.

He gorged himself on the lean meat. "I couldn't stop eating today...three large meals...first the liver, then a couple of steaks off the hindquarter, then the rest of the liver. I'll bet I ate six or seven pounds of meat today. I feel stuffed."

McCunn dried much of the caribou meat and supplemented the lean ration with more ducks and fish. The nights were getting colder. Winds began gusting from the north — "A bad sign."

And then the plane came. Concerned friends asked Alaska State Troopers to check on him, and Trooper David Hamilton was one of two who flew over McCunn's tent camp. "We saw McCunn waving a red bag," Hamilton said later. "We circled and McCunn waved in a casual manner and watched us fly by. On the third pass, he turned and walked back toward the tent, slowly, casually. No wave, no nothing. We surmised there was no immediate danger or need for emergency aid."

McCunn relates the airplane incident in his diary. He was elated about sighting the plane, but realized later he'd given the pilot the wrong signal. "First I waved my orange sleeping bag cover, then I saw the plane had wheels and quit waving. I recall raising my right hand shoulder high and shaking my fist on the plane's second pass. It was a little cheer — like when your team scored a touchdown or something. Turns out that's the signal (or very similar) for 'ALL OK...DO NOT WAIT!' They probably blew me off as a weirdo...Man, I can't believe it!"

With a five-gallon bucket of dried meat, twenty caribou ribs and a handful of dried beans, the adventurer began to prepare for winter. He dug a four-foot hole into the ground in which to pitch his wall tent. The snow came and the lake

A-frame tents from Peak 1 are for two or four persons and can be closed against severe weather by zipper.

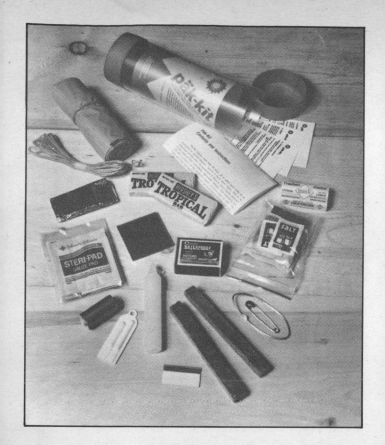

Pak-Kit contents are displayed above, and include all you need for immediate survival in adverse situation. Above right: Packs sized for youngsters increase carrying capacity of your survival group or family. Below: Coleman's best-selling white gas stoves have cooked innumerable outdoor meals. When the gas runs out, you will need natural fuel.

Contents of Pak-Kit are packaged in unbreakable plastic tube that's also waterproof. It's light enough to find a place in your camping gear. It's manufactured by Alpine Map Co. of Boulder, Colorado.

Page 11 Photo: Richard Frear, National Park Service

Left: Well-prepared cross-country skier carries camping supplies — true survival items! — on her back. If you're stranded in the wilderness with this equipment, your chances of living through the experience are good — especially if you seek shelter and warmth. Above: Lightweight and compact is the backpacker stove from Peak 1 line. It fits inside its own cooking accessories. Great for emergencies. Opposite page: Surviving in the arid regions puts different weights on the three requirements listed in text. There should be no problem producing water in this area, with growing plants and solar still.

froze, meaning no more fish. He found a jar holding a few bits of candle, rabbit snares, and some soggy cigarette papers and tobacco. "Dried out the papers and tobacco a while ago and am smoking my first cigarette in about six months," he wrote.

The cold was inescapable and McCunn missed a chance for added warmth when he shot prematurely at a wolf he describes as looking "like a giant husky...shot at it with the .22 and heard it yelp and disappear crashing through the brush. Bad shot and bad show of patience. Hell, it came to me to begin with...I bet with a few moans or the like I could've gotten it closer."

By October, McCunn was driving ravens from partially decomposed kills. "Now I'm a scavenger! Bad as the jays and ravens," he wrote. His rabbit snares were raided by foxes and wolves. Frostbite began to limit his movement and, in an effort to conserve firewood, he tried getting up early in the morning. "I can't do it! I can't do it!" he wrote.

It got colder. "It's been a terrible day for me and I won't go into it," he scrawled in his loose-leaf notebook. "Hands getting more frostbitten every day...fingertips and edges of hands numb and stinging. Feet as well. It's only minus five degrees on the thermometer, but seems colder. Have only one meal worth of beans left. Honestly, I'm scared for my life. I don't feel there's much hope I'll even be alive in a week. But I won't give up."

At this time, McCunn began to dwell on death. "I've never thought of God so much. Or death. Or of suicide... weird," he wrote.

In November, McCunn's food ran out. All he had left were some spices. "I feel very down, but not quite out. Damned close, however," he wrote.

He ran his snare line and set out fishhooks baited with rabbit heads, hoping to catch a fox or wolf. He managed to catch a squirrel, "but that's only a tease, even when you chew up and swallow all the bones, too." He ate "palms full of ground red pepper, thyme and salt, just to let my stomach know I'm still here." He nibbled on the rabbit and fishheads he used for bait.

"I'm frightened my end is near..." he wrote. "If things get too miserable, I've always got a bullet around. But think I'm too chicken for that! Besides, that may be the only sin I've never committed."

By Thanksgiving, McCunn had little to be thankful for. Time and again he found the snares had been raided by other predators. All that was left were "hair and guts and four feet." McCunn at the feet.

He began having dizzy spells. "I feel miserable," he wrote as the end closed in. "Have had the chills upon awakening for the past three days...I can't take much more of this...Can't stop thinking about using the bullet, either."

Occasionally, McCunn would rail in his diary against the friends he felt had let him down. "Certainly somebody

THE COMPLETE SURVIVAL GUIDE

11

Succor Creek winds through rugged canyon it's cut through Owyhee Mountains of southeastern Oregon (above). Hills serve to catch precipitation, then channel it toward base. Below: If stranded in this spot with no particular direction of travel, make for the hills. Water tends to accumulate at the base. Look for vegetation.

Rocky, scorching Twentynine Palms, California, is godforsaken place during summer. Scan the hills for signs of growing plants that indicate presence of water — none! If you do find waterhole, look for animal bones.

in town should have figured something must be wrong — me not being back by now. But then again, there's probably no one in town who gives a ----. What in the hell do those people think I gave them maps for? Decoration?"

The desperate adventurer tried eating spruce shoots. "Some meal, but supposed to be excellent emergency food. My mouth tastes like I ate a bucket of spruce pitch."

He pleaded with God. "God, if you don't bring me a moose, please bring me a plane overhead...one with some peanut butter!"

McCunn dreamed of food, but said he didn't feel hungry — "just tired and weary and very dull-like...and empty, hollow in the gut."

He described his feelings as he neared the end. "It's weird to feel on death's threshold. When's it going to end? One way or the other, I keep telling myself, 'Hang in there, man...somebody will fly over!' But I'm beginning to believe I'm just lying to myself."

Finally, on the last page of his diary, McCunn wrote: "Am burning the last of my emergency Coleman light and just fed the fire the last of my split wood. When the ashes cool, I'll be cooling along with them...

"My nose stings sooooo bad, my fingers a little less, my toes hurt, my feet are swollen...

"I chickened out once already, but I don't want to go through the chills again. They say it (death) doesn't hurt.

"Dear God in Heaven, please forgive my weakness and my sins. Please look over my family."

He wrote a separate note, instructing that his personal effects be sent to his father. Whoever found his body was bequeathed his rifle and shotgun. He signed this "will" and attached his Alaska driver's license. "The I.D. is me, natch," he wrote. Carl McCunn then shot himself.

This story shows the grim consequences which can befall even an experienced outdoorsman if he violates some of the cardinal rules of wilderness life. We can learn much from Carl McCunn's mistakes — so that his death will have benefit.

Carl's problems began with his planning. Whenever you go away from home you should file your travel plans with relatives, friends or authorities. You should tell them your destination, expected route and duration of your trip. If you fail to turn up on the appointed date, help will be dispatched along your projected route. It's certainly preferable to be found slightly embarassed and alive than to suffer Carl's fate. Carl should not have chastised his father for sending out help on the previous late trip, which prevented him from doing so again when help was desperately needed. A second flyover would surely not have elicited the same incorrect response from Carl.

So you've logged your trip plans and are headed into the wilderness, or on a fishing trip, or backpacking, or rock climbing in the desert, or whatever. Regardless of where you go, your survival depends on three essential factors: Food (including water), shelter, and warmth (including clothing). If you satisfy these biological necessities, you can survive in any clime, even with minimal equipment.

Of course, you don't have to worry about living off the land if you have rations with you. There are many companies like Bolton Farms producing lightweight, balanced, nutritional meals which you can pack along. Water can likewise be carried in canteens, or be made safe to drink with the products mentioned in the chapter on Food Preservation & Storage. Water can be procured from a variety of sources, even in the desert, as will be shown later.

Shelter, the second biological requirement, can be pro-

Photo: Michael Jensen, Australian Information Service

Cattle station in Australia's parched Northern Territory is 4730 square miles — but supports just one head per 60 acres. Like wild animals in barren country, these Santa Gertrudis cattle make for water daily. Look for signs of game travel and follow them downhill to water. Below: Australian Aborigines are adept at surviving in hostile desert country. Note weapons — they regard everything as food source.

vided by the tents you see illustrating these pages. Lightweight, compact and portable, they are rated for varying environmental conditions including rain, snow and cold. What to do without such self-contained shelter will be outlined later in this chapter.

What about warmth? It's so easy to supply fire that it's nearly incomprehensible you'd be without "the makin's." However, we'll deal with starting fires in the wilderness in due course. But if you've ever tried to start a fire with bow-drill and fireboard, you'll appreciate what a little planning and foresight can mean!

And that's the thrust of this chapter and this book: to make preparations now, before you need them. Yes, it's great to have woodcraft skills that enable you to survive with nothing more than a pocket knife for equipment, but isn't it easier and more comfortable to not need these skills? To have planned ahead and assembled the equipment you need for a more civilized life? If you plan and prepare properly, you'll not likely face a "reactionary" scenario of alone in the wilderness with just a pocket knife.

If this transpires, however, what you don't have in your hand should be stored in your head: the knowledge of what to do and how to satisfy the three necessities of life. There

Photo: J. Tanner, Australian Information Service

Animal bones and lack of green plant life around waterholes are indicators the water may be poisonous.

are hundreds of books devoted to these topics, many published by the same firm responsible for this book. You should read them and apply what you've read to acquire the skills on which your life may one day depend. It can't hurt, but surely can help.

What follows in this chapter is a short discourse on these subjects. In no way is it complete. The goal is just to introduce the topics, to throw a stone into your placid consciousness, in hopes that the ripples will lead you to further study and master woodcraft.

CARING FOR YOUR KILL

Hopefully, you've been successful at dispatching a large game animal that you've shot cleanly and without a chase. Remember, the animal's state of excitement at time of death dictates his future palatability. A deer killed after a long hard chase will be tougher than one taken while bedded.

It's expected that you were prepared with the needed implements for caring for your killed game at the time you went afield. This includes at least one sharp knife (some hunters carry two, for reasons to be told presently), a rope or towing harness usually fitted with nylon webbing that fits over the hunter's shoulders, and plastic bags suitable for carrying the heart and liver after disemboweling the carcass. Moore Supply Company's Big Buck Field Dressing Kit, which retails for about $2.50, contains a plastic bag, arm-length poly gloves, a sealed moist towelette, large drying towel, a game tag holder and complete field dressing instructions. It weighs an ounce and easily fits inside a hunting coat or folds into a pocket. Once you're back in camp, you make life easier with a game hoist, gambrel, deer bag and a meat saw.

But back to the field. You've downed a deer, elk, moose or goat — field dressing directions are altered mainly by the size of the animal, not the procedure. The most important step you take to ensure good-quality meat is to cool the meat rapidly. This is done by gutting the kill and draining all body fluids.

First, if it's a large animal and he's dropped on a hill, position him so that his head is at the lowest point. It's unwise to behead large animals, especially males, since the antlers are frequently used to help drag the carcass to camp or your transportation. Therefore, you can cut the jugular vein that's at the base of the neck, just to the left of center. Ensure the blood is flowing freely, assisted by gravity. Pumping a hind leg may help speed flow and assure thorough drainage. If the animal was shot or arrowed in a vital organ, there may be little blood drained from the severed jugular — it may have drained off into the abdominal cavity. Get it out quickly to avoid spoiling the meat. (If you're planning to mount the animal's head, don't cut the jugular; it'll give the taxidermist fits and increase the cost of the job!)

Roll the animal onto its back and support it with rocks or logs on either side of the body. This prevents movement when you're making a critical cut. If you prefer, you now may remove a buck's musk glands located inside both hind legs at the hocks. There is some disagreement over the need for doing this, because supposedly the glands cease secretion of meat-tainting fluid upon death. If you do cut off these musk glands, don't use that knife for further work on the deer; you'll taint the meat for sure. This is possible even through your hands, so be careful or be sorry!

To begin opening the abdominal cavity, either make a three-inch slit at the breastbone (sternum) or pinch up the loose skin at the abdomen and, using just the tip of your sharp knife, make an incision three or four inches long. Reach inside with your empty hand and separate the skin from the viscera, that thin layer of skin covering the abdominal structures. Turn your knife blade upward, away from

Once you've bagged game animal, you must know how to gut, hang, skin and cut up meat. See the text.

the internal organs. Making your cuts as shallow as possible, use your free hand under the knive blade or to press down on internal organs, to ensure they aren't cut. Reverse direction and slit down to the vent or anus. If you're gutting a doe, her udder will obviously have to be removed at this time. As you're cutting, pull back the skin for three to four inches away from the incision, to prevent hair from falling inside. Do not yet cut the genitals or anus free.

You make field dressing easier and cleaner by using your knife sparingly at this point. You want to remove the intestines and organs *en masse,* not in messy bits and pieces. Use your knife to sever connection points within the cavity only. This calls for patience and careful observation, which isn't as easy as if the breastbone already were cut and spread open, which is how some hunters begin field dressing. The novice may slip in attempting to cut through the breastbone, however, resulting in a real mess.

If you severed the jugular, chances are you cut through the windpipe. If not, reach inside and sever the esophagus, extracting it through the abdomen and with it will come the lungs, heart and liver. Save the heart and liver for a real feast after soaking in salt water for twenty-four hours.

To remove the viscera intact, carefully cut around the anus, being careful not to cut the rectum. As you pull the

Continued on page 18

Photo: Michigan Conservation Dept.

Steven T. Henson, a woodcraft instructor with California Survival Training Center, samples a thistle root during foray into wilds during which he lived off the land. He advises homework to recognize plant species. Healthy idea!

FOOD & WATER

The major problem with food isn't its lack, but our prejudices regarding what we'll eat. Insects, for example, aren't big on the dinner menu of the average American, even if hungry, yet are delicacies in many foreign countries. Neither are frogs, trash fish, fish-eating ducks, lizards and many types of wild plants. Snails aren't eaten by most of us, while in France they're expensive dinner fare. While we don't hesitate to gulp down raw oysters, many of us balk at the rubbery flesh of an octopus. And eat a big, fat, juicy grub out of a rotting log? Forget it!

That's the type of attitude that'll kill you in the wilderness. The prejudices we have against foods must be eliminated. There's a big difference between inedible and palatable: In the latter case we may not like the taste or idea, but it can keep us alive.

So that's rule number one: Treat everything as having food value. Whether we ingest it will depend largely on the desperateness of our situation.

Steven T. Henson, live-off-the-land expert of California Survival Training Center, lumps wild plants into four categories: edible, poisonous, medicinal, and accommodation (uses for clothing, bedding, tools, etc.). Of the edible wild plants, Steve has the following four rules:

If it grows, it's edible. Jungle combat survival courses add "unless it's bitter to the taste" or "emits a milky substance." These conditions don't always apply to North America. All wild plants can be inedible, he says, depending on the allergies of the person and how much of the plant he ingests.

Eat small amounts of unknown plants. It's preferable not to eat any plant you can't recognize, but circumstances may force you to. Wait with calm detachment for up to twelve hours before ingesting any more. If there are no out-

ward effects, eat a little larger quantity and wait again. Keep in mind poisons may take a long time to work.

It's better to identify an edible plant than to risk rule two. So do some homework and learn to recognize edible or poisonous plants. Good books are available.

Photo: Wyoming Travel Commission

Treat all food as having value. Carl McCunn ate entire squirrel near end of his ordeal, but described meal as "only a tease." Don't let taste decide the menu!

CARING
Continued from page 16

genital organs loose from the body, you'll discover they're attached to the pelvic bone with a strong ligament. Be extra-careful in severing this ligament that you don't cut the urethra, which would permit urine to flow into the cavity from the bladder. Some hunters use string to tie off the urethra and intestines near the colon to prevent feces from soiling the meat. By cutting through the cartilage of the pelvis, the colon can be removed with the genital organs.

Hopefully, you've removed the viscera in a clean and careful manner so that all you need do is wipe the cavity dry. If fluids remain, turn the animal on its stomach for draining, then transport to your vehicle or campsite for further processing. (If you've bagged an elk, bear or moose, you'll probably quarter the animal before transporting). Dusting the cavity with black pepper or powdered charcoal will dissuade these maddening meat bees that seem to appear immediately.

Back at camp or in the garage, you want to hang the meat quickly, remove the skin and begin the aging process. Leaving the deer on the ground prevents rapid dissipation of heat, which leads to souring of the meat.

First, slit the thin skin of each hock, being careful not to cut the musk glands if you've elected to leave them alone. Insert either a commercial gambrel or stiff stick to which your rope or hoist is attached. Run the free end of the rope over a stout tree limb or rafter and hang the carcass completely suspended. If you'll be moving the deer to your home for skinning under more sanitary conditions, you should now encase the carcass in some type of deer bag to prevent insects and dirt from contaminating the meat while it's cooling with a stick propping open the ribs. If you're going to skin on the spot, take pains to keep insects away.

To skin, sever the legs at the second joint. Using your sharp knife, slit the skin along the inside of each hind leg, from the leg joint to the previous cut in the abdomen. After starting the skin with your knife, take a firm hold on the hide and thrust your fist between the hide and the carcass, then pull downward with your hand. According to the Big Buck Field Dressing Kit, this will usually remove the skin cleanly, without any strips of hanging flesh. Use your knife only where the skin clings to the tendons around the legs or hide. Do not allow hair to cling to the meat. Also, you should cut away all bloodshot meat at this time.

Whereas beef needs to be chilled just two or three days to ensure rigor is complete, deer should age a week at about 35F (1.5C) degrees before butchering. If the weather is warmer, deer ages faster; at 70F (21C) degrees, aging may take place in just two days.

The first step in butchering a deer or other large game animal is to cut in halves the entire length of the spine. A good meat saw is the ticket here. More than half of the meat you'll get from a deer is best-suited to stewing. Moore Supply Company says the loin of a 150-pound (72kg) deer will yield about twenty delicious sirloin steaks, and the ribs will account for another two dozen T-bone steaks cut three-fourths-inch thick. Top round cuts can be used for steaks and the bottom round makes a wonderful roast. Shoulders and rump make fine pot roasts; the neck, flanks, breast and shanks are ordinarily used as stew meat or hamburger.

Many cookbooks advocate larding — inserting beef fat in chunks into the venison. Much depends on the quality of the game animal, and what he's been eating. It's wise to trim off all fat, which goes rancid quickly. Moose, which is closest of all animals to beef, is prepared like pork. Venison makes excellent jerky, salami or sausage when mixed with pork suet.

Regard all wild mushrooms as poisonous. This is a better-safe-than-sorry idea. Remember that wild creatures may eat with impunity species that would kill us.

According to Ray Dorr of Adobe Fort, mentioned in the chapter on Survival Schools, more people die from scurvy than from starvation. However, this vitamin C deficiency can be prevented by drinking "tea" made by steeping evergreen needles in water, or by eating rosehips, or eating fresh meat or fish.

Meat is important and the most-hunted animal is the rabbit. He's plentiful and easy to shoot or snare. The lean meat is tasty and his fur has many uses. Rabbit fever (tularemia) is a remote risk that's eliminated by using

Photo: Dept. of Indian Affairs

Native Alaskans have survived for centuries on the flesh and hides of seals, and one man dresses fresh kill near Igloolik. Seals provide sufficient fats.

gloves until the meat is cooked; heat destroys the germs.

A steady diet of rabbit or other game will lead to trouble because the lean meat provides insufficient fat which we need. Our modern diet provides fat in many processed foods like bread, margarine, dairy products, even nuts and candy. Lack of fat causes diarrhea and is fatal unless fat (as from an old buck or doe during the rut) are introduced.

So when it comes to meat, consider fat over flesh. A fawn will have tender meat, but older doe during the rut will provide more fat.

Fish if not overcooked provides sufficient fat, but lacks calories sufficient to maintain good health. As Bradford

Deer is the primary target for wilderness hunters, but in a survival situation, which would you shoot? If you selected a buck or old doe during the rut, you'd be right. They have sufficient fat for human diets.

Angier noted in his excellent and recommended *Living Off The Country*, a one-pound fish provides on average two hundred calories. But an office worker burns 2000 to 2500 calories per day, a figure at least doubled by someone living in the outdoors. You'd have to eat six pounds of fish to meet your daily caloric needs, or your body begins to steal calories from muscle tissue. As this "cannibalization" continues, your strength declines. So figure on supplementing your fish diet with meat.

Birds can be trapped or snared — not sporting or pretty,

Squirrels are avidly sought in many areas of the country. They are readily taken with snares or baited hooks — not pretty, but effective if needed.

unless you're hungry. You can rob nests of eggs or young, or catch adults during a moult. Scavengers can be readily hooked by hiding a small sharpened stick inside your bait. The stick is attached to line or a rope. The gull, crow, raven, hawk, owl or other meat-eater swallows the baited stick and cannot fly away.

Reptiles and snakes, if fresh-killed, are usually edible. Poisonous snakes have poison glands or sacs that must be removed to eliminate toxicity.

While the methods for putting fish on the bank are given in a following chapter, what about hunting game? As with fishing, you must be familiar with game behavior if you're to be successful in even seeing any, let alone downing them. This requires that you study hunting books and magazines, and spend time in the woods or deserts where the game lives. Once you've learned to recognize game-holding areas and understand your quarry's behavior patterns, you can devise a plan for bagging them.

Your hunting method is determined by your equipment. If you have a firearm, you could try still-hunting — waiting for animals to walk within range; "driving" game toward a prepositioned hunter; or stalking — quietly moving through game-holding areas — and hoping for a jump shot or shot at bedded game.

If you have archery tackle, your best success will lie still with hunting. Your range is less than fifty yards, and it's difficult to stalk this closely.

If you have no offensive weapon, you can rig deadfalls or snares that hunt "on their own." You again must know something of animal behavior, or where will you rig a rabbit snare? Where will you position a figure-four deadfall?

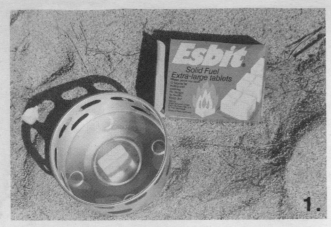

1.

2.

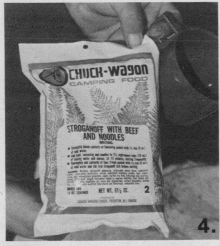

3.

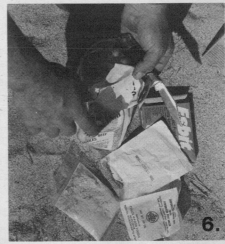

4.

5.

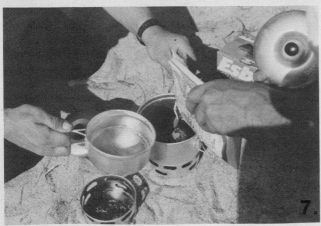

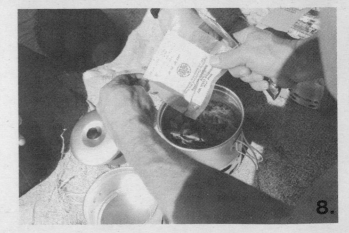

7.

8.

9.

10.

12.

1. Esbit tablet with cooker means hot cooking fire.
2. Magnesium Fire Starting Tool guarantees hundreds of fires can be started. 3. Magnesium shavings and tinder catch flame to ignite Esbit fuel tablet. 4. Dehydrated food is lightweight, nutritious, tasty!
5. Potable water is measured into Esbit cooking pan.
6. Contents of Chuck-Wagon meal are packaged in pre-measured pouches. 7. Following directions, spices are mixed. 8. Noodles and beef chunks are next. 9. Boiling water is added as directed. 10. Steaming contents are stirred with Imperial Frontier folder to prevent sticking. 11. Sour cream is next as hungry "assistant chefs" look on. 12. Occupational hazard of cooking in desert — blowing sand has "peppered" beef stroganoff, served here in Mirro aluminum plates.
13. Undaunted, Dean Hawkins "chows down" — good!

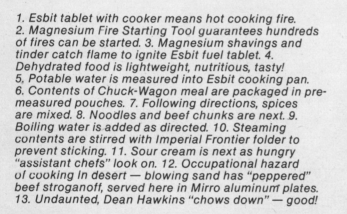

11.

13.

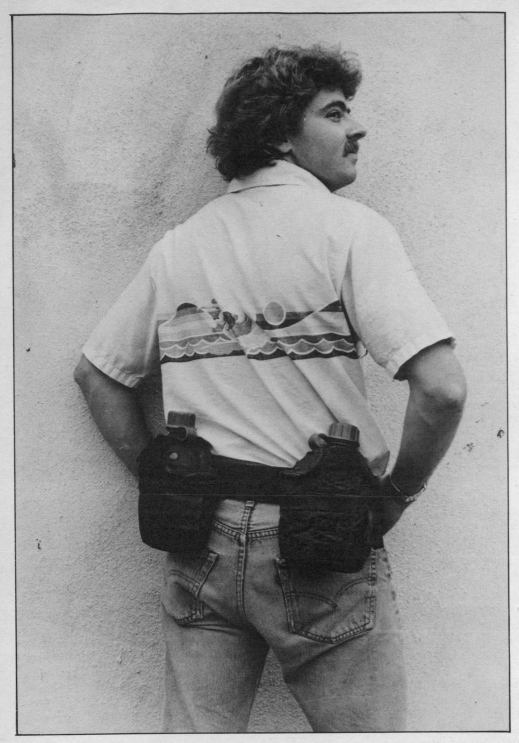

Web belt sporting two canteens inside canteen covers — Paul Arsenault is ready. Small pouch on canteen covers hold GI openers furnished with field rations. Hands are left free when water supply is so carried. Belt supports back.

Water is more important than food, because man can live for up to ten days without food — but just three days without water. There are telltale signs of the presence of water, regardless of geographic region.

Keep in mind that water flows downhill, and therefore you'll tend to find it in larger quantities at the base of a hill. Snow runoff at higher elevations feeds creeks or streams, which then flow downward to this "catch basin."

The best indicator of water is vegetation. Where there's moisture, there will be green plants. You can distinguish creeks above the tree line by glassing for ribbons of green. In flat country, search the horizon for signs of trees, brush or shrubs. Game trails nearly always lead downhill to water, since game drinks daily. This is especially true in arid climates.

In the desert, waterholes may contain poisonous alkali or arsenic. Boiling or purification with a Katadyn Pocket Filter, as discussed later in this book, does not eliminate the toxins. So how can you tell if the water is safe to drink? The best indicator will be an absence of lush plant life. If

Reliance Products sells two-quart canteen (above), made of heavy plastic with screw-on lid secured with lanyard chain. Carry pouch is nylon, as is adjustable strap. Easily attached to saddles, packs. Right: The conventional Desert water bag — familiar trademark of the West. Evaporation cools the canvas bags and water inside. Enhance cooling by hanging from moving car.

there's water and hardly any plants growing around the site, it's probably poisonous. You may find animal bones in the immediate area, too.

If you're in the desert with insufficient water and have no particular direction in which to head, make for any visible hills or high spots. You're more likely to find water near the bases of these hills.

If you encounter a dry stream or creekbed, take a minute to dig a hole. If there's subsurface water, the sand will darken in color. You can continue digging until you strike moisture in drinkable quantities, or construct a solar still.

A solar still is made by digging a hole two feet deep by four feet in diameter. In the center of the hole place some type of recepticle to catch water the sun's heat will extract from the soil. Place a sheet of plastic over the hole, covering the edges carefully. Position a rock in the center of the plastic, directly over the catch recepticle. That's it!

As the sun heats the plastic, moisture in the ground is sucked out and evaporated. It rises and condenses on the plastic. Droplets form and run to the low point of the plastic, formed by the rock. When sufficient droplets converge, gravity pulls them downward and into your catch container. You can improve the efficiency of the solar still by adding bits of vegetation or even urine in the hole; the mois-

ture produced is purified, even if derived from urine or other contaminated sources. To eliminate the need for uncovering the still each time you want a drink, run a rubber tube from catch basin to the edge of the plastic.

In the mountains or swampland, finding water usually isn't the problem, but purification is questionable. Methods of purification are discussed later in the book.

But what about other forms of precipitation like snow and ice? Snow is pure but it takes a lot of quantity to produce much moisture. You'll have faster output if you slowly melt snow enough for two or three inches of water in the bottom of your cup. Be prepared to refill your container several times. Snow can, of course, be consumed in its frozen state.

Ice is simply frozen water and it contains the same impurities as the liquid. It can be melted, but then must be purified or you risk illness. Saltwater becomes desalinated when it freezes. Frozen sea water is as pure as river water after two years, but safe enough for emergency use immediately after freezing.

If you're in a swamp with no means of purifying water, you may obtain water from fish. Either cut up chunks and suck moisture from it, or put the chunks in a cloth and wring out moisture. You won't escape the fishy taste, however.

Page 24 Photo: Redwood Empire Association

Some of the first shelters available to man were caves, which could be heated readily with small fire at mouth that also discouraged predators. This is Colossal Cave in the Rincon Mountain Range in Arizona. Below right: Shady grove of Alabama pines makes idyllic setting. Watch out for poisonous plants here!

SHELTER

Natural shelters in the form of caves have been used by man since time began. It's a place to get out of the elements and, with a fire at the mouth, discourage animal predators. A small cave is relatively easy to heat, too, which makes it a good choice for anyone today. Be sure there's a vent for smoke and gasses, however, or you could poison yourself. Before you "move in," look for animal occupants!

During a summer shower in the forest, where did you seek shelter? Under the thick boughs of a grove of trees, right? That will do for emergencies, and you can improve the shelter with simple woodcraft like constructing a lean-to and covering it with boughs or bark.

If you're caught in a snowstorm, you can tunnel into snowbanks on the windward side (not the the leeward side, as we normally seek shelter, since drifts accumulate there and could suffocate you). You can construct ice houses or modified igloos by piling snow into a mound shape, then burrowing into it from right angles to the wind. Hollow out the inner part of the mound as much as possible without threatening collapse. Poke a ventilation hole for your very

Giant redwoods hundreds of feet tall (opposite page) provide shelter from heat, but can lead to dampness.

small fire and you'll last out the storm well. Try to keep from getting wet by reclining on boughs, plastic, mittens, or similar material.

Depending upon your woodcraft, you can build all manner of natural shelters. Three poles lashed together at the top and draped with either natural or synthetic material becomes a tipi. You can use three or more poles to build a three-sided structure, mouth facing away from the wind, atop which you can layer bark, boughs, ferns, etc., for a comfortable refuge, especially with a reflecting fire against the open side. You can even use saplings to form the frame of your temporary shelter, tying the tops together and applying your siding from bottom to top. Why from bottom to top? Consider the shingle or shake roof: It's attached from the eaves to the peak so that any moisture traveling downward will not back up and find entrance within.

If you're really in a jam, you can crawl next to a fallen log, or burrow beneath it. Much of what you'll do for shelter depends on the conditions you're facing.

If you're in the desert, relief from precipitation isn't your main worry — it's reducing exposure to the sun, which robs your body moisture. Resist the urge to remove your clothes, since they prevent burning and, if worn loosely, help regulate your body temperature. Unlikely as it sounds, you can chill even in the hot sun — perspiration cools the skin as it evaporates and too-rapid cooling isn't healthful.

It's smartest to move at night in summer desert heat, and seek shelter from the sun. If you can spare the expenditure of effort, digging a foxhole in which you can seek relief from direct sunlight is a possible answer to barren country. Your imagination is your greatest asset — use it to solve your problems!

But you don't require much imagination if you take your shelter with you. A trip to your sporting goods store will show a variety of tent configurations suitable for varying numbers of occupants, rated for different climates. Weigh your needs with your pocketbook and you'll inevitably make a choice. New fabrics are emerging and the manufacturers listed in Survival Sources will happily tell you what they offer.

Dampness is feature of Oregon Caves National Monument, seen is stalactite and stalagmite formations. Water accumulated here is high in mineral content and may not be drinkable.

Opposite page: Crescent City on California coastline was ravaged by tidal wave generated by huge earthquake in Alaska. See the chapter on earthquakes for more.

Photos: Redwood Empire Association

*While geothermal application for electricity generation on large scale may rest in the future, could you
think of reasons to stay near Castle Geyser if stranded in Yellowstone? Heat is present just below surface.*

WARMTH

It is almost incomprehensible that anyone could lack
fire-starting capability today. There are so many products
available at such low cost as to make the idea of traveling
into the woods without one remote to the extreme.

What are the types? Waterproof matches are old standbys,
inexpensive, usually packaged in a waterproof container of
some sort that attaches to your clothing with a lanyard.
Another type is the magnesium match, from which you
shave slivers of magnesium into your kindling, then ignite
with sparks made by slashing the match with your knife. Of
course, you can pack a piece of flint and strike it with your
steel knife blade for spark, although iron will substitute for
steel. A magnifying glass held rock-steady will concen-
trate sunlight on tinder until the latter ignites, as many
schoolboys know. You can fall back on a bow and drill if
you have nothing else, but a short session of this labor will
convince you of your folly at forgetting a simpler means.

Besides the fire-starting mechanism, you need tinder
and longer-lasting fuel. Synthetic tinder in the form of fire
tablets like those from Esbit are fast starting and burn hot
enough to ignite larger pieces of wood. If you lack these,
you can use papery wisps of birchbark or slivers of thicker
birchbark pieces. Dry pine needles abundant beneath spreading boughs make good tinder, too. Small twigs carefully
heaped atop fragile moss, birchbark or pine needles will
encourage the blaze to grow, especially if shielded from
prevailing breezes by cupped hands or even your body.

Which wood burns best? There is no difference between
the burning capabilities of either softwoods (pine, aspen,
etc.) and hardwoods (oak, hickory, etc.), although the
amount of heat produced and burning rates do vary. You're
wise to avoid dead timber laying on wet ground — it
absorbs some moisture and is difficult to start. Better to
find a dead snag and use its wood.

The size of the fire and shape will depend largely on

Therapeutic benefits of hot springs have made them popular places; this could be so with you after "the end."

what your use. A hunter's fire is a simple V formed by two logs or rocks, with the open end of the V facing prevailing wind. Cooking pans are then placed atop rocks or logs when fire has burned to embers. (Hint: Coat bottom of pans with detergent before placing them in contact with flames. Black soot is then easily removed.) You can reflect heat by using rocks or even several green logs stacked atop each other and supported by rocks or carved sticks. This helps keep you warm, or reflected heat can gently toast biscuits if you aren't using a dutch oven buried in coals. Of course, since there are such handy, portable and inexpensive units as the Coleman backpacker stoves or those by Primus, you may confine fire chores only for atmosphere and warmth, not for cooking.

Warmth also is supplied by your clothing, which should be matched to the terrain and environmental conditions. You are encouraged to review any of the numerous publications which deal with this topic, and the suppliers in Survival Sources will happily send catalogs arguing strongly for their products. Budget and need then take over, but as a general rule it's wisest to purchase the best-quality attire you can afford; price and quality are usually synonymous when it comes to outdoor apparel and footwear.

Chapter 2
SURVIVAL GROUPS FOR YOU?

Personal Protection & Home Security Are Just Two Arguments For Companionship

Hong Kong is world's most densely populated real estate. Would survival groups function here?

Photo: Tenn. Tourist Dev.

It takes many hands to farm large tracts like this in Tennessee, especially without motorized equipment.

VIRTUALLY EVERY author discusses the breakdowns of social structures like the police force that will probably follow some social disruption. If you lack law enforcement, then you're on your own and that applies to security for your person and property.

Most people, who lack infinite resources, won't have a choice but to remain in their homes or apartments. Transportation will be difficult and dangerous, and where will you go, anyway? Unless you've established a rural retreat, which takes both time and money, you have no real haven.

So you'll stay home. Protecting your stock of food, water and valuables will be important, but how to do it? The idea of stringing concertina wire and floodlights around your residence to discourage visitors is something out of Hollywood. The last time you saw barbed wire was topping a high fence, and what good will floodlights be if there's no electricity and/or gasoline to power the generator?

Same thing with electric burglar alarms. These are fine personnel detectors, but that's all they'll do — they won't summon police help, since there's no police force. But is your greatest threat from the single burglar, the thief in the night who stealthily approaches and attempts to abscond with your possessions? Hardly! The only reason a thief

slinks today and attempts to avoid detection is because a policeman or two may soon arrive to interrupt his life of crime. Without the worry of police intervention, you likely won't face single thieves. Rather, they'll band together in roving gangs of thugs who use force to take what they want. They won't be trying to hide their intentions. You know they're coming and they know you know. So your burglar alarm or deadbolt locks, or foiled window do no good. If they want inside, they'll come through the just-broken window, drive a car through a wall, or break down the door with a ram.

If it's you against the world, the world probably is going to win. But if there's a bunch of you with the intestinal fortitude to exhale, hold, and squeeze one off in the direction of another human being, that's another story!

Defense of life and property is one basis for banding together with pre-selected neighbors and friends into a survival group. All must share your commitment and have demonstrated it by assuming a functional role within the group and stockpiling accordingly. Other bases for formation of survival groups are: psychological benefit — being alone is hard on the psyche; accumulation of skills, discussed further in the chapter on Survival Tools; shared tasks — with more people, there are more hands to help with the work required to keep the group going; fighting, if need be, although the presence of a large group has a

Photo: Nitin Lal

Fire-walking Fijians continue tradition important to their culture. Social bonds are strong, needs few.

deterrent effect on would-be attackers; and more supplies, since everyone will pool goods.

So how do you go about forming a survival group? Don Stephens, who is perhaps more independent than most of us, tells of a risk in his chapter on Survival Structures: Recruiting neighbors has the double-barreled liability of labeling you a crackpot, plus tipping your hand — neighbors will damn sure remember you as a source of sustenance "after the fall." Another value of being discreet is that stockpiling, also called hoarding, may be branded illegal, so the fewer who know about it, the better. Remember, during World War II it was illegal to hoarde certain commodities, so this is a real concern. And even for those in the survival group who are familiar with your stockpiling work, they don't need to know exactly where and how much you've laid-by. "All for one and one for all" goes only so far.

It may take many years to assemble your survival group, and you may begin by carefully probing the attitudes of your friends and neighbors during casual conversation. Never get too specific, but information about the economy, perceived problems in the world, etc., can illuminate attitudes of your target members. Look for people who have skills they can bring to your group — carpentry, plumbing, firearms, cement worker, etc. Consider their geographical location — no good recruiting your best buddy from Texas

Continued on page 32

Photo: Australian Information Service

Safety in numbers applies to survival groups on the move, as are these Tasmanian bushwalkers. Numbers discourage attack and provide psychological relief.

Cajun communities surviving in swamps are different than other Louisiana groups, and aim to stay that way.

STAYING IN TOUCH WITH YOUR SURVIVAL GROUP

By William E. Haynes

YOU'LL need to communicate when away from your group and also want to know what the rest of the world is up to. Because there'll likely be at least a temporary loss of electricity, your radio equipment must be battery-powered to receive information via the Emergency Broadcast System (standard radio) or to communicate with each other. You need portable gear suitable for wear with other survival equipment. Because batteries wear out — even rechargeable nickel-cadmium (called nicads) — you need a good supply of quality batteries or a means of charging nicads to stay on the hit parade; one of the biggest problems you'll face.

SELECTING THE RADIO

Low-power radios are best and have a larger range and frequency capability. Speaking generally, the lower the frequency, the longer the expected range. Unfortunately, much of the available and inexpensive equipment is high frequency (HF) Citizen's Band (CB) stuff. CBs can make good short-range gear, but when the CB band "lengthens out," you might reach Australia but can't talk to a friend a mile away, due to interference from other stations or the skip of your signal off the ionosphere. While CBs beat smoke signals or semaphore flags, I don't want anyone listening in on my conversations!

What about VHF gear? To prevent trouble with the FCC, get your Amateur Radio License before buying any of a number of handi-talkies that are small, easy on batteries and which cover the entire available frequency range in the two-meter band. My Icom puts out 1.5 watts with a power setting of .5 watts and it always amazes me. Its factory-supplied nicad will run ten to twelve hours, and AA battery pack makes a nice backup, all for about $275. Accessories such as a telescoping antenna extend its range beyond present three- to five-mile distance.

The MX-49ET from Maxon Electronics is a small, battery-powered transceiver dubbed the Easy Talk'r. This $50 unit has a range of a quarter- to a half-mile with fresh 9-volt transistor radio battery. Even at 7 volts it gave good comm at four city blocks. I communicated through houses and across a freeway three-quarters of a mile. In unobstructed terrain, range was close to three miles. The transmit mode is FM, which makes for clear audio. The built-in squelch eliminates noise while listening. The MK-49ET has VOX

Continued on page 33

if you live in California. This is an advantage of enrolling neighbors in your group. Group members who live away from your neighborhood or where you intend to headquarter may take over residences abandoned in the area, provided they can overcome the distance and transportation problems.

The long-range prognosis for survival of a group that stays in the city on a block of tract homes may not be so high as in rural areas where there's more land available for food production. Remember, most of the group's time will be spent producing food. Turning backyards of tract homes into food-producing units is possible, but large-scale farming methods — furrows that stretch to the horizon, for example — can't be used. You might be able to use nearby plots of vacant land for supplemental food production, but unless you have some way of securing the crops, you could be raided by hungry passers-by.

Consider the problems facing apartment dwellers in typical inner-city areas. It's tough even meeting neighbors in an apartment building, let alone making friends! How you can recruit for a survival group in this transient community is a good question, equaled by "How will the group survive?" You may have a wonderful citadel from which to repulse armed invaders — reminiscent of English castles — but it's difficult to plow cement for food production. Even if your group raided every food store in reach, there's the question of how long it would last and what you figure to do afterward? If there are hostile groups in your areas, will they permit safe passage to parks or other food-growing sites you've targeted for produce? (See Jack Mitchell's dis-

Winter transport of hay-burning variety. With one person responsible for horses, others can do work.

cussion of bullet-proof vests immediately following — the group should seriously consider them now.) Again, how will you "maintain ownership" of the plots?

The average apartment dweller lacks huge amounts of capital it requires to purchase and stockpile freeze-dried food, seeds, grains, water, and so forth. He also has a lack of storage space. Clearly, survival groups in apartment buildings face many obstacles. They can, however, promote harmony now and help fend off criminals who prey on apartment dwellers...sort of a pre-nuclear Neighborhood Watch program.

The key to a survival group is the skill brought to it by each member. Everyone will be asking themselves who's contributing what, and those who don't will not be tolerated for long just on the basis of past friendship. That's a simple fact of life: Even today, humans willingly sacrifice friends for something they perceive as wanted or needed. This will not change when times *really* get hard.

ICOM walkie-talkie easily attaches to pack strap for low-sound monitoring while moving. Leaves both hands free for other tasks, too. Just one example.

If it's you against the world, the world is going to win. But are survival groups the answer for you?

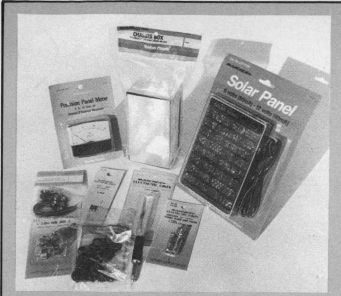

All you require to create solar battery charger for 9-volt batteries. Sun is inexhaustable resource.

transmission capability — the transmitter is keyed simply by talking into the boom mike. (Of course, you can also work on a push-to-talk basis.)

Handi-talkies designed for the business band are low-power and thus have low current requirements. Usually they have a single channel or perhaps two. The usable frequency range is broad and they can be "crystalled" to match with little effort. These were designed for daily use by police and fire departments, and are very tough and weather-resistant.

What about government surplus? Lots of gear designed and built to take a helluva beating is available, but caution is the byword on this equipment. An awful lot of military gear is turned to HF spectrum and shares the CB's problems. VHF and UHF surplus gear is around and some is very good. You don't need a high-power transmitter, again because of current requirements. In many cases this gear is designed for 117-volt operation or for voltages common to aircraft usage or semi-fixed operation. The military depends on an almost-limitless logistical support element to keep themselves in batteries — we won't be so lucky.

POWER SOURCES

To support a control radio station and recharge batteries, you can store a portable generator like those by Honda and fuel to supply electricity — if you can tolerate the noise and odor. (Even if you can supply power at camp, you still need batteries for radios in the field.) What about wind-powered generators? These might work, but there's a visibility factor and eventually parts will wear out. Still, a zillion windmills must prove somthing.

A standby system is a hand-crank generator. You've seen them on the midnight movie. A radioman is sitting at a monster, tube-type radio that would make a good boat anchor, using radio procedures out of the Dark Ages, while a poor soul on a three-legged contraption cranks with both hands to power the transmitter. Don't laugh too hard: It works and is still being made today. Surplus versions from the Korean bash also are around and can charge your batteries (or run drills, electric fans, saws, and even harvest earthworms). They're from Core Resource of Mountain View, California, or Ruvel & Company, Incorporated, of Chicago.

Solar power is a better alternative. Small solar panels are available at low cost from Radio Shack or other retailers. This solar panel is fairly new in the Radio Shack product line and will recharge batteries or can be used directly

Easy Talk'r attaches to belt suspenders and boom mike has Vox and push-to-talk capability. Note antenna on lightweight headset. (Below) Radio Shack's solar panel can provide direct operation of walkie-talkie through 9-volt circuit.

to power the Maxon MX-49ET. It produces 12 volts under load during most of the daylight hours. Even in winter, the panel will easily charge a "dead" 9-volt nicad. For a 12-volt, deep-draw nicad, it functions as a trickle charger.

The panel and charging circuit are small and light. It's not waterproof like the large, roof-mounted units, so keep a plastic bag handy on rainy days. It can be adapted to backpack mode of operation to charge and/or supply current for direct operation while on the move. I found the rear junction of my belt suspenders for my cartridge belt to be ideal. Mounting was easy with Velcro, and the angle to the sun is almost perfect for maximum current generation. It's also out of the way and at least partially protected. Faultwise, reflection could give away your position.

BODY ARMOR

By Jack Mitchell

Author models eight-layer vest from Stay Alive, Inc. It's designed for continuous wear and is effective against most handgun ammunition. Moisture affects effectiveness.

Left: Current manufacturers of body armor vest realize wearer will be in public eye. Designs of protective vests are highly fashionable, as is this safari coat with concealed Kevlar panels from Emgo U.S.A. Ltd.

An Overview Of What's Available, How Good It Is, And Who Should Use Which

BODY ARMOR of some sort has been used since ancient time, but until recently almost exclusively by the military. With today's world situation of rampant kidnapping, terrorist activities and threat of nuclear war, civilians have begun seeking efficient self-protection.

There are several misconceptions about body armor.

One is that it's foolproof protection against any and all fired bullets. The state of the art "bulletproof" vests use Dupont's Kevlar yarn invented in the early 1970s. This Space Age product's remarkable strength makes it ideal for race car bodies and white-water canoes, but when used in the manufacture of bulletproof vests, effectiveness is governed by external conditions: type of fabric weave;

Author tests different swatches of Kevlar with handguns ranging from .22 caliber to .357 and .45 automatic. He found eight layers of Kevlar consistently stopped bullets.

number of plies (layers); amount of moisture from perspiration or rain; and type, size and velocity of the projectile.

A vest must offer two types of protection: prevent a projectile from entering the body, and deal with "blunt trauma." Simply, this describes the effect on that section of the body hit by the bullet. Although body armor may stop the projectile, the tremendous impact of the blow upon one small area of the body can severely bruise or even rupture a vital organ. Fortunately Kevlar, and particularly one type called Kevlar 49, has the high-tensile strength to both stop high-speed projectiles and to dissipate the impact energy over a wider area, greatly reducing the injurious effects of blunt trauma.

Body armor vests consist of multiple layers of woven Kevlar material which are housed in a fabric shell. The shell fabric material functions to prevent chafing, make a single unit of the vest layers for quick removal or wearing, and absorb perspiration. Water is the Achilles' heel of all ballistic tests, as water significantly decreases penetration resistance. Once dried, ballistic properties return to normal. It's believed that a jet of water forms between plies of fabric during ballistic impact. The jet penetrates the fabric and the bullet simply follows after. A small amount of moisture will not allow this situation to occur, but if the jacket is soaked, it should be considered inoperative.

The more layers in a body armor vest, the better its effectiveness against high-power projectiles. Unfortunately, more layers equal more weight.

The most popular vest worn by law enforcement officers during normal duty hours contains eight layers. The principal objective for lightweight body armor is to provide a garment that could be worn continuously and protect against most threats. An FBI Uniform Crime Report analysis of the type of armament most used or most available for assaults on law enforcement personnel reveal that the greatest number of fatalities result from handguns in .38 Special or less energy capacity (.22, .25, .32 and .38 revolvers and automatics). The Law Enforcement Ad-

ministrative Association investigations learned from FBI analyses of types of firearms confiscated during 1971-72 that ninety-four percent of the handguns available were in .38 caliber or less. This meant body armor should be designed to stop .22 caliber 40-grain bullets at 1000 feet per second for armor protection, and the .38 caliber 158-grain bullet at 850 fps for blunt trauma effects. An eight-layer vest weighs less than two pounds, is virtually unnoticeable under a shirt or jacket, and is cool enough to be worn for extended periods of time.

I have conducted tests firing handguns from the diminutive .22 caliber through .357 magnum with 125-grain jacketed hollow-points, to .45 caliber 230-grain metal-jacketed bullets into eight-layer swatches of Kevlar. The units have consistently stopped bullet penetration. I also fired three rounds of .357 magnum into practically the same spot from fifteen feet. Both the second and third rounds pierced the material. Since the possibility of being hit twice in exactly the same spot is remote, the eight-layer vest would appear to be the most comfortable and efficient all-around choice against a handgun assailant.

Defense against high-power center-fire rifles is a completely different situation. Recently, two law enforcement officers confronted a man with a .30 caliber M-1 Garand rifle. Both officers were wearing eight-layer body armor. The man opened fire and both policeman were killed, one

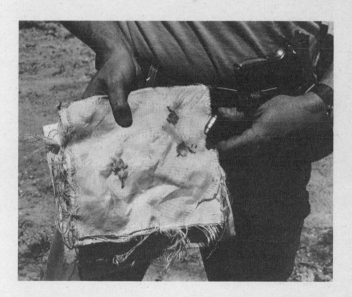

The 168-grain H&G bullets from .45 auto were effectively stopped by Kevlar. Looseness of weave affects protection.

instantly, and the other within moments after the shooting. American vest manufacturers have tested their products using various American high-power rifle ammunition and initially found that fifteen layers minimum of Kevlar were required to prevent penetration. Ongoing tests and the development of new ammunition indicates that additional layers of Kevlar, as well as steel plates and ballistic nylon, are necessary. Most American-made rifle ammunition is designed to mushroom upon impact. Fifteen layers of Kevlar proved quite effective against them. However, new ammunition like the 9mmP with a solid steel core bullet manufactured in Czechoslovakia would require many additional layers of Kevlar to effectively prevent penetration.

Obviously, certain situations require specialized equipment. A businessman traveling in a high-crime area would be well advised to consider an eight-layer Kevlar vest, since the overwhelming odds are that if he's confronted and fired upon by a would-be burglar or kidnapper, the firearm used will be a handgun. He not only is afforded the necessary protection, but can wear it in comfort and secrecy during his journey. The same type of vest would be an excellent choice for a merchant in an American high-crime neighborhood.

The individual seeking protection during an assault on his property or person by a rifle-carrying agressor would be better off looking into a special vest as worn by SWAT teams or certain European special anti-terrorist organi-

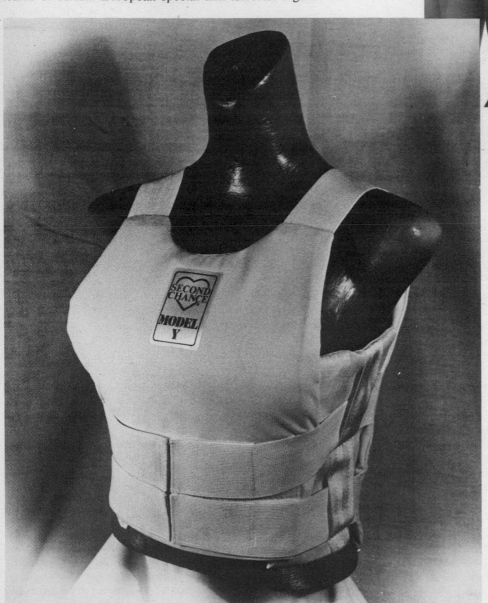

Handgun-wielding assailants are foiled by eight to ten layers of Kevlar (above), which is nearly undetectable underneath uniform shirt.

Women's body armor can be ordered to contour to any woman's dimensions. Shown at left is Model Y from Second Chance Company.

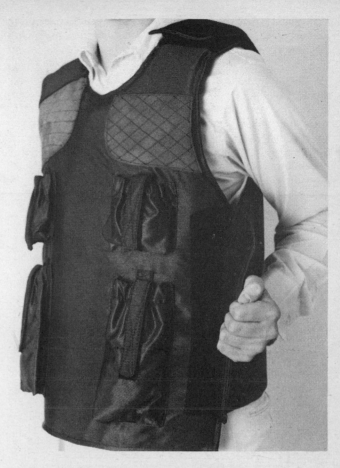

Lightweight, flexible vest from Safariland provides for removable Kevlar armor to be carried in deep pockets.

Police tactical teams may find benefit in pockets. Velcro quick-release fasteners. This also is Safariland's.

zations. One of the finest such specialized vests is the K-30 FLEX Vest manufactured by North American Ordnance. It has the ability to withstand hits from unique ammunition like the aforementioned 9mmP as well as other full-metal jacketed, steel core ammunition.

The K-30 FLEX Vest utilizes four one-eighth-inch thick, three-inch-wide by fifteen-inch-long steel plates. Each is bent to give the wearer flexibility and necessary protection. The plates are attached to a nylon hinge to give each plate independent flexibility. Other 1½-inch plates are used to cover vital organs in an overlapping configuration. Kevlar and ballistic nylon are also included in this vest to protect against fragments entering the gaps between the plates. Weighing approximately 17½ pounds, it's certainly not too heavy for a life-threatening situation. It is not recommended, nor is it intended, to be worn as a regular undergarment.

The availability of body armor to the American public has become publicized on a large scale only within the past two years. Many American manufacturers could not keep up with law enforcement demands and some had the specious argument that if they sold their vests to the public, some may fall into the hands of criminals. This is virtually the same argument the anti-gun faction of this country has voiced at every election period. If there's anyone of sound

mind who does not believe there is a critical need for the right of self-protection in this country, he is indeed viewing the world through rose-colored glasses.

Fortunately, there are reputable manufacturers who do cater to the public and offer several types of body armor. Prices range from approximately $140 for the eight-layer Kevlar vests to about $330 for the new K-30-FLEX Vest in lightweight mode by North American Ordnance.

Body armor is not a one hundred percent guarantee against injury from gunshot wounds. The type of situation should dictate the type of vest or jacket that should be used. The citizen living or working in an environment of high crime would probably be better off wearing an eight-layer Kevlar vest. The person attempting to defend himself during civil unrest or war would be better off with one of the specialized SWAT-type steel and Kevlar jackets. Although these vests have weaknesses such as loss of effectiveness due to water, their inability to prevent penetration from a sharp-pointed instrument like an ice pick, or from Teflon-coated ammunition, they do offer the highest degree of protection yet devised. It would be wise for all individuals interested in obtaining a body armor vest to write to several manufacturers for complete information, specifications, and prices. They are listed in Survival Sources at the end of this book.

Chapter 3

SAFE SHELTER & INDEPENDENT ENERGY

Don't Reinvent The Wheel, Say These Experts, Who Detail Basics In This Overview

By Don & Barbie Stephens

CRISIS SURVIVAL without proper preparation is a crap shoot. A great majority of people refuse to face the possibility of life-threatening situations and when they do occur, depend on little more than dumb luck and animal instincts to get them through. All too often these folks earn a page seven writeup in the newspaper by falling victim to muggers, an unexpected blizzard or other harsh realities of man or nature. Likewise, in the event of more general emergency, these "ostriches," being most vulnerable, are forced to endure the greatest suffering.

However, there are those of us who do not elect to deal with life so passively and readers of this volume no doubt fit that category. We recognize that a bit of foresight and planning does much to tilt the odds in our favor. Individuals who act in advance on this knowledge are the most likely survivors of any crisis with minimal hardship.

But even among those who have made the commitment to prepare, there is wide variation in the soundness, approach and degree of such preparations. Some "purists" limit themselves to mastering skills which utilize only found natural materials unmodified by modern tools. We would encourage a knowledge of such primitive survival methods as a most useful backup, should a person be somehow forced to suddenly function with only Stone Age

technology. However, most of us would not elect this rigorous type of lifestyle and *with proper preparation* are unlikely to find it necessary.

A second element advocates food and water storage alone as being quite sufficient. Loyalty to this approach involves several presumptions: That the only likely crises will be limited to simple temporary shortages of food and water, that those who are prepared will be able and willing to share with those who were caught short and that if supplies do run too low, those without will starve quietly at home while their more frugal neighbors feast next door. Such studies in human nature as the rioting at the Hearst food giveaways would tend to contradict this last assumption. One self-proclaimed survival expert went so far as to suggest that the food storing family go house to house through the neighborhood, persuading their fellow residents to stockpile likewise. We doubt that the neighbors in such a scheme will join in the preparations, but feel confident they will remember where to head when food gets scarce!

A great body of would-be survivors has come to this same conclusion, only to fall victim to what I call the "remoteness myth." They have concluded that they can leave their potentially explosive urban habitat and go out into the backwoods to construct a little retreat cabin so

HOME ENERGY USAGE TODAY AND ALTERNATIVES:

© DON STEPHENS 1983

CLOTHES DRYING - 2%
o AIR, SOLAR

COOKING - 5%
o COMBUSTION, SOLAR

SPACE COOLING - 5%
o BETTER DESIGN
o CONSERVATION

WATER HEATING - 13%
o COMBUSTION
o SOLAR

LIGHTING & APPLIANCES - 10%
o HOME POWER
o CONSERVATION

SPACE HEATING - 65%
o BETTER DESIGN & CONSTRUCTION
o CONSERVATION
o SOLAR
o COMBUSTION (WOOD, COAL, GAS, ETC.)

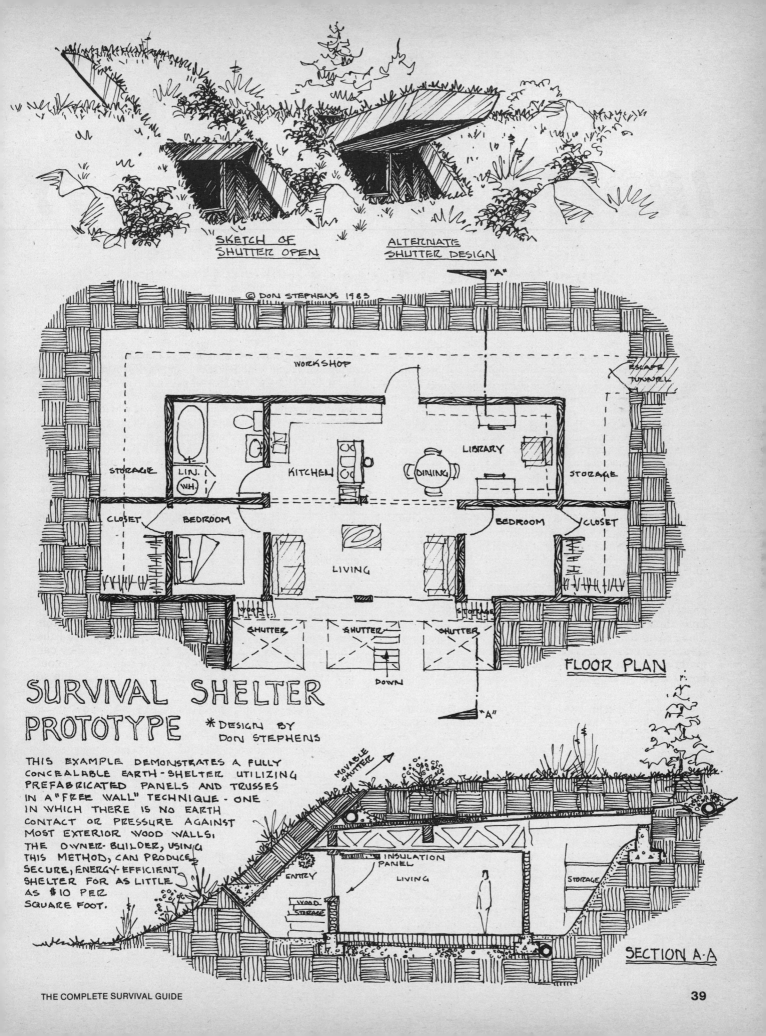

SKETCH OF
SHUTTER OPEN

ALTERNATE
SHUTTER DESIGN

© DON STEPHENS 1983

"A"

WORKSHOP

ESCAPE
TUNNEL

STORAGE

LIN.

KITCHEN

LIBRARY

STORAGE

WH.

DINING

CLOSET

BEDROOM

BEDROOM

CLOSET

STORAGE

LIVING

STORAGE

SHUTTER

SHUTTER

SHUTTER

FLOOR PLAN

DOWN

"A"

SURVIVAL SHELTER
PROTOTYPE *DESIGN BY DON STEPHENS

THIS EXAMPLE DEMONSTRATES A FULLY
CONCEALABLE EARTH-SHELTER UTILIZING
PREFABRICATED PANELS AND TRUSSES
IN A "FREE WALL" TECHNIQUE - ONE
IN WHICH THERE IS NO EARTH
CONTACT OR PRESSURE AGAINST
MOST EXTERIOR WOOD WALLS,
THE OWNER-BUILDER, USING
THIS METHOD, CAN PRODUCE
SECURE, ENERGY-EFFICIENT
SHELTER FOR AS LITTLE
AS $10 PER
SQUARE FOOT.

MOVABLE SHUTTER

INSULATION PANEL

ENTRY

LIVING

STORAGE

WOOD STORAGE

SECTION A-A

All of the corrugated sheet steel and fasteners to enclose an earth-covered space 24 feet in diameter by 80 feet long fits into small area on back of flatbed.

remote no one else will ever find it. These seekers of Shangri-la then spend years in disappointment poring over maps and exploring one possibility after another. But none will do because if they and their rural realtors can find them, so can others — including the walking refugees of crises. So they either continue searching year after year, give up the task as hopeless and decide to live wildly for the here and now, or compromise by purchasing a vacation cabin at Big Bear and hope they never have to use it.

The fourth variation which jumps to mind is that of the "Bullets and Bayonets Survivalists" who have given the media so much gratuitous titilation. These militant Walter Mittys with their battle rifles and camouflage fatigues have decided if you can't get away from hungry, desperate people, you can at least fight them off. But, in the process, they appear to have lost all sight of their original objective while redoubling their efforts. The undue emphasis on para-military hardware may be a great vehicle for fantasies and the writers who feed on them, but is an ill-advised emphasis for those truly seeking to come through a crisis alive and in good health. Living by the gun is hazardous because even in small firefights both sides are likely to incur casualties. And no matter how heavily the little survival squad is armed, someone else who has even more firepower and less scruples may be attracted by the sounds of battle. Realistically, when the chips are down, avoidance is almost always preferable to armed confrontation.

Having evolved through all the above steps, Barbie and I now advocate avoidance through design; with proper planning such a tactic is very possible. Over the years we have prepared many retreat homes for clients which are completely undetectable to passersby.

Shelter design can be the pivotal factor in effective survival strategy in many other ways as well. As this chapter proceeds we will share ways in which the carefully conceived dwelling provides comfortable accommodation for its occupants and their activities, offers commodious and organized storage for a diversity of provisions, and serves as an effective barrier against external hazards, while conserving energy and making minimal maintenance demands on its owners.

Tactics for independently meeting energy needs deserve similar attention in advance. Most people make do during brief power outages with candles or flashlights, snack foods that require no cooking and blankets or sleeping bags for warmth. But any major general crisis is likely to force interruption of conventional energy delivery systems mea-

sured not in hours or days but in weeks, months or even years! It is relatively simple *now* to prepare for such possibilities with dependable, independent and renewable fuel and power sources. Doing so later when the technological roof has caved in could be quite a different story altogether.

Because both shelter and energy are so crucial to the well-rounded survival plan and because there is such a synergistic relationship between shelter designed to conserve energy and energy sources which maximize the safety and comfort of shelter, they are brought together in this chapter. Full development of just these two interrelated topics alone could fill a book (or several), but here is an overview and a place to start off on the right foot, at least.

SHELTER PLANNING

Proper design and construction of a survival-oriented dwelling is a several-step process. Attempts to jump ahead without properly laying the groundwork will almost always lead to grief on down the line. Building a home that may one day be called upon to not only provide comfort, but to actually save the very lives of its occupants is a crucial undertaking; one which deserves thoughtful attention from start to finish. A great aid in this process is to have all information pertinent to the project gathered in one place, perhaps in a file folder or notebook. That way there's less chance of something crucial being lost or overlooked. The logical first step in this planning process is what architects refer to as "establishing a program." This technique defines the task at hand, weeding out deadwood while making certain no important need is neglected. Before proceeding it might be well to have pencil and paper in hand. It also helps to organize the program in outline form, as follows:

PART ONE: CONCERNS

View of the Future — Over the years we have encountered a surprising number of otherwise intelligent individuals who undertook major and often inappropriate survival preparations based on only vaguely defined concerns. Since the kind of hazards anticipated determine which responses would be suitable and because views of the future and its risks vary greatly, no one stock shelter design will meet everyone's needs. So list those crises, changes or sequences of events which *you personally* feel could most plausibly leave you threatened. Only you can know which possibilities you find credible enough to justify significant action.

As a place to start, our clients over the years have expressed apprehension about monetary collapse after hyperinflation, imposition of emergency powers leading to homegrown dictatorship, Communist takeover, skyrocketing crime rates and breakdown of the systems of production and distribution due to energy shortfall or labor revolt on a national scale. Nuclear war or accident, pandemics, massive earth changes and worldwide weather modifications leading to generalized famine are also often shared concerns. Make your own list, including any of these which worry you, too, and adding others that you believe deserve consideraton.

Probabilities — Next expand on the list by assigning your personal probabilities to each scenario from those which you feel represent a primary threat to marginal possibilities only deserving preparation if the outlay of energy or capital is minute.

Specific Hazards — Looking back over your list, determine just how each of these general upheavals would *directly* affect you and those you care most about. You

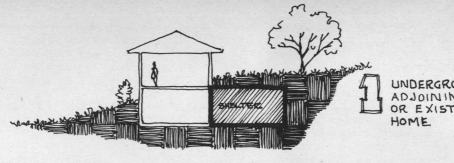

1 UNDERGROUND ADJOINING NEW OR EXISTING HOME

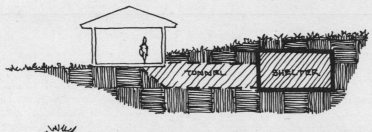

2 UNDERGROUND ELSEWHERE ON PROPERTY—WITH OR WITHOUT CONNECTING TUNNEL

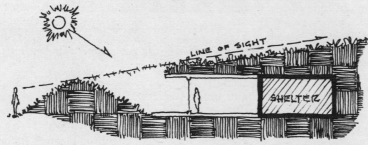

3 UNDERGROUND BEHIND VISUALLY SCREENED BUT EXPOSED FULL-TIME UNDERGROUND HOME

4 UNDERGROUND, SHUTTERED AND VISUALLY SCREENED BUT VISIBLE

5 FULLY BELOW GRADE WITH CAMOUFLAGED SHUTTER OVER DOOR AND WINDOWS— ESCAPE TUNNEL BEHIND (OPTIONAL)

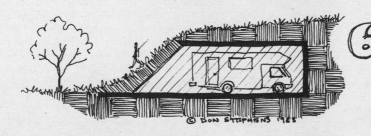

6 RECREATION VEHICLE IN UNDERGROUND BUNKER

© DON STEPHENS 1983

SHELTER PLACEMENT OPTIONS

won't save the world from crises, but you can insulate your family from their most-severe consequences. After each of the concerns on your list, add appropriate notes like "food shortages," "contaminated water," "looting," "restrictions on travel," etc.

Other External Factors — Lest they be overlooked now is the time to jot down other elements from which the dwelling should provide protection: weather (summer heat, winter cold, lightning, hurricanes, tornadoes, heavy snows, flooding, smog and/or destructive weathering), wild fires, vandalism, theft, noise, overly curious neighbors, trespassers, tax collectors and other animals, etc.

PART TWO: NEEDS

Protection — When humankind first abandoned life in the open for caves and improvised dwellings, the primary stimulus was the need for protection; protection from weather, wild animals and the blazing sun. Today's would-be survivor likewise expects protection in the secure shelter, but looking back to Part One we can see that some new elements of concern such as vandalism, noise, radioactive fallout and bacterial warfare may also demand consideration. Integrating here all the externals against which shelter need be provided will help assure that none is inadvertently overlooked in the design process.

Space and Activities — In the most-primitive dwellings only a single space was enclosed and the implements for all indoor activities were brought to that space. As home design evolved, separate areas were established for various functions. List the functions that are to be accommodated in your survival structure and the space allotment for each.

At this point a question is raised: One survival home approach recommends a space for every function. We have found in dealing with our clients that this leads to very large and expensive homes, often so far beyond capital and energy available that the task proves overwhelming. On the other hand, a more Oriental tactic of bringing the tools for every task to one or two spacious multipurpose areas generally proves far more manageable. As you proceed with program establishment, this choice of strategies should be kept in mind.

Storage — Unless you wish to gamble on the primitive survival way of improvising from whatever is at hand, space for stockpiling sizable amounts of tools, materials, goods and provisions will be an essential consideration. Just how much volume you require will depend on the kinds and durations of crises you anticipate and how efficiently your storage space is arranged. There are commercial storage systems which nearly eliminate aisle waste with movable shelving units, but you will have to weigh the tradeoffs between the cost of such systems and building larger storage areas which can be packed with a bit less precision.

To determine the volume of storage you need, make a list of all that you want to have on hand with approximate quantities and volume required for each item or category. Then estimate the accessing volume required to get at that which is stored. Add a contingency figure to allow for those last-minute items and there you have it. We have found that we can comfortably meet our lifetime storage needs in about six thousand cubic feet. Clients with less desire to live simply or grow and fabricate goods as needed have elected to fill three times that much space, or more. Others with less-pessimistic perspectives or even more willingness to improvise and make do, have crammed all they feel is essential into a couple of steamer trunks!

Appliances, Utilities, Tools and Conveniences — Se-

PV panel and two rotated batteries meet basic electric needs of one remote family. Used for eight high-intensity, task oriented lights, car stereo, radio, clock (12-volt).

lections in this category will greatly influence both space and utility (electrical?) requirements and in turn be influenced by lifestyle, willingness to simplify or "rough it" and anticipated length of occupancy of the survival structure. It will also depend on whether the dwelling is only an emergency retreat for times of major crisis, a vacation cabin, or a fulltime here-and-now home, too. More on that in Part Four.

Aesthetics — Too often beauty is neglected in the design of essential shelter and yet this is a crucial consideration in the maintenance of good spirits during a time of isolation and possible stress. While the exterior of such a dwelling may need to be simple, understated, camouflaged or even buried for safety, there is no reason why the interior cannot reflect color, texture, light, design and other tools of delight and familiarity. Why live in a stark dungeon when, with a little imagination and extra effort, you can enjoy the psychological rewards of a subterranean palace?

PART THREE: LIMITATIONS AND RESOURCES

Budget — Given unlimited funds, most of us could dream up grand retreats to rival those of the villains in James Bond movies. But few of us have such resources, so it's necessary to work from what is available. Also, we have day-to-day expenses here and now which must be met. It is our experience that those who budget a disproportionately high percentage of either capital or time to meeting tomorrow's hazards are setting themselves up for failure today.

A safe shelter should be thought of as a kind of life assurance policy and the percentage of your resources delegated to it should be determined by what you can realistically afford, how great you view the probability of needing it and how soon. We have worked successfully with clients who could only put a few dollars a month into preparations but felt certain those would be needed in the next few years, and others who could put hundreds of thousands into the process but only gave a five percent chance that it would ever be required. As one of this latter group said, "I may not think it very likely, but I can afford such a retreat and if I do end up needing it, I'll need it one hundred percent!"

In any case, you must have some place to start. So discuss the question with any others involved and decide on an initial capital budget, and if necessary, a regular schedule of saving to make it possible. Also establish a timetable for various levels of completion of your safe shelter based on that budget, your view of the urgency of the situations to be prepared against and your time availability.

This raises one other point on budget: People's situations differ widely with regard to time vs. money. Some work so ceaselessly at their regular employment, at such high rates of compensation, that they can hardly afford the time to be deeply involved with actual physical preparation of a safe dwelling. A $500 per hour attorney with more clients than time to see them would be hard-pressed to justify doing $5 per hour ditchdigging unless it were for reasons of secrecy. On the other hand, for those with minimal income and time on their hands, a great deal of hard cash outlay can be avoided by doing-it-yourself; with added benefits in privacy and personal understanding of how things go together, should repairs be needed at a later date.

Skills and Willingness to Learn — Here, too, an honest inventory is in order. Just how many of the skills needed to put a house together do you already have? What are your aptitudes and interests in this area? Are you willing and able to invest time learning to strengthen your weak areas?

Distance — Particularly when we work with clients from California or the Eastern states, this can become a difficult factor as they often want a safe shelter hundreds of miles from where they presently live. Unless one can set aside large blocks of time to work at the site, commuting many hours each way often proves overwhelming. Flying a private plane can help, as can having most of the work subcontracted with a qualified overseer. But in many cases it is better to compromise remoteness to some degree, choosing instead more secure design in a sparsely populated area closer to home.

Accessibility — This likewise can be crucial. If your dream site is up a goat trail or across a swamp where cement trucks and pickups loaded with lumber cannot go, your dream may soon prove to be a nightmare instead. And what do you gain? An access route that is a nearly impossible barrier to construction may prove only one more minor inconvenience to the starving hordes already forced to travel on foot.

Equipment, Materials and Energy Resources — That which you have on hand or is provided by your site you won't have to purchase. This can help with the budget and

Like those developed in Europe during WWII, this truck is powered by wood combustion gas generated on board, at rate of over two thousand miles per cord.

influence design of your structure. Likewise, it is important to take into account what skills, equipment and materials are readily available in your chosen areas; it wouldn't do to design a precast plank concrete roof and then find out that the nearest precasting yard is many hundreds of miles away and there is locally no equipment heavy enough to lift the units into place.

Legal Factors — This red tape catchall includes building codes, permits, inspections, zoning ordinances, rights-of-way, easements, taxes, etc., which could either influence or preclude some design options.

PART FOUR: OPTIONS AND DECISION POINTS

Location — As with any real estate undertaking, proper location is pivotal. If you are planning to simply remodel where you now are, turn back to Part One and consider whether or not your current location is uniquely more vulnerable to your concerns than other possibilities. For example, if one of your special worries is fallout from nuclear accidents and you live five miles downwind from a major reactor facility, moving might be a crucial first step. With proper design most high-risk sites can be improved, but why start out with an unnecessary handicap?

If you plan relocation, either within your present region or to an entirely different part of the country, care in making this decision is critical and can hardly be done with too much care. If you are not already intimately familiar with the area under consideration, moving to a temporary location there, hiring a survival-oriented consultant to help you evaluate it, or both are possibilities worthy of deepest consideration. Proper selection at this step can determine the cost, methods and viability of construction and the livability of the result. It is a shame that this most important step is so often executed quickly, after inadequate research from afar utilizing maps which cannot possibly provide enough essential information. If you do plan to bring in professional assistance for the design of your retreat, the time to do so most effectively is *before* committing to land!

Fulltime Home or Second Dwelling — This is one of the paramount decisions to be made and one for which there are few pat answers. Among the drawbacks of separating home and retreat are the division of energy and resources, the vulnerability of whichever domicile is unoccupied at any given time, the hours devoted to travel between dwellings and your chance of being stuck at your vulnerable home when an unexpected emergency prevents reaching your haven.

On the other side of the issue, combining the two can also mean risky compromises. Because it is difficult to maintain an everyday lifestyle without a visible house and at least occasional visitors, the potential for full-structure security through concealment is minimal. In many cases it means having all your eggs in one basket in a more-populated or otherwise-vulnerable location, chosen primarily for convenience to work, shopping, schools and other services rather than safety during crisis. And unlike with the divided approach, your haven cannot double as a holiday and weekend escape from the rat race.

Positioning — This is an extension of the line of consideration started above and can probably be described most easily by the illustration on page 41. The first thing that will strike you about the options shown is that they are all *underground*. We have concluded after years of experience that this is almost always the way to go. If you want to protect yourself and your survival supplies at point of crisis and agree that avoidance is the preferred way, the invisibility possible through earthcovered construction is ideal.

This gravity-fed composting tank odorlessly decomposed family's solid body waste and kitchen organic waste without water. The produce, arriving at the clean-out after two to three years, is soil free of odor, bacteria.

With a bit of know-how a comfortable, dry, well-ventilated earth-sheltered retreat home can also be so invisible that it can be literally walked over without discovery.

But invisibility in the visual spectrum is only the beginning. Earth also helps block infrared, radar, and other means of detection. It lends protection against blast and radiation. It shields the structure from wildfires, windstorms, lightning, tornadoes, hurricanes and even earthquakes. Vandals cannot vandalize and burglars cannot steal what they can't find. (Even tax collectors may be likewise deterred!)

The same blanket of soil blocks noise and summer heat while retaining warmth during the winter. With proper waterproofing, rain and snow present no difficulty and destructive weathering of building surfaces is negligible underground. Hence we see it not as a question of whether or not to go under, but just where and how deep.

Placement options 1, 2 and 3 are ways one can accommodate an earth-shielded shelter adjacent to a more "public," fulltime domicile without the compromises usually associated with this approach. In this way friends and other visitors can be welcomed to the exposed portion of the home without breech of secrecy, yet family members can

enjoy the convenience of the secured portion for additional living and storage space.

Option 4 provides concealment from a distance for remote shelters and option 5 is even more secure. The last approach is for those who prefer the convenience of a factory-built dwelling, be it pickup camper, motorhome, camper trailer, fifth wheel or mobile home combined with the protection afforded by earth-sheltering upon arrival at the pre-established survival site.

Secrecy — As we have pointed out above, an underground survival facility can be invisible to outsiders and provide a great deal of passive protection as a result. But it is vulnerable to discovery when being entered or left and during construction. The former can be addressed by exercising care at these crucial times. We have even arranged for camouflaged periscopes to be installed in some cases, so those inside could verify they had no unwanted audience before "popping the hatch."

There are several ways to handle the construction process. If you are building on a remote site in an area without building codes or permit requirements and can do the construction yourself, no one will need to know. If you are in a more regulated region or need help with construction, it will be necessary to choose tactics.

If you elect to ignore the codes and just do it, there are several things to consider. Can you find help who won't spill the beans? Will neighbors be able to see what's going on and spread the word? Do you want to conceal land ownership with a trust or other legalistic maneuvers? Can you haul in all the supplies yourself without arousing curiosity? (In some areas suppliers of concrete and other building materials work hand-in-hand with the building department and inform them of any non-permit construction sites to which they deliver!) Do you plan to connect to public utilities? (Some won't service non-code structures.)

There are ways around these barriers but they take careful planning. For example, you can get a permit for some other use — silage pit, root cellar, storage shed, etc., and then remodel after final approval to your real intended purpose.

Other Protective Measures — Other passive defenses may also deserve consideration. Earth-sheltering works best in combination with camouflage and illusion to conceal entrances, windows, skylights, vents, chimneys and other surface penetrations. When hiding a survival shelter, the deception is only as effective as its weakest part.

If nuclear war and its deadly fallout are a part of your concerns, ways of countering these with additional hardening and shielding deserve special attention. We advise significantly exceeding government-recommended minimums on both shielding thicknesses and shelter stay. If your home is earth-protected, such extension will present minimal hardship and should return long term health benefits.

Other effective security features can be tailored to specific circumstance and built into shelter or around the site. These can best be developed with the aid of an experienced consultant on a very individual basis.

Utilities — Proper shelter planning necessarily includes careful consideration of water supply, waste disposal and ventilation. If gravity-fed water from an underground source is at hand, this is almost always the best answer. If not, on-site well water with pumping manually or by homegrown electricity will do. If neither of these options is available, surface water from a stream, lake or rain catchment may be diverted into a storage cistern with proper filtration and treatment to assure a safe supply. In instances where water is being obtained through public mains and might be interrupted, a several-thousand-gallon holding vessel on the incoming line with one-way valves will address emergency needs.

Independent waste disposal also is important. In addition to septic systems which consume a good deal of perhaps-precious water, waterless composting toilets deserve consideration.

Ventilation design is crucial in tightly constructed dwellings, particularly those expected to provide fallout protection. Without such planning, toxic gases such as carbon monoxide, formaldehyde and even radon may accumulate with potentially deadly consequences.

Energy Needs — It is important to define the range of energy needs based on your particular scenarios and their anticipated duration. Consider space heating and cooling, air movement, water pumping and heating, cooking, food preservation, lighting, electricity for electronics, tools and appliances, portable power and transportation. The pie diagram shows on page 38 where your residential energy dollar goes today and alternatives available independently through a mix of energy sources.

For the short term it is possible to make do with candles,

kerosene lamps, white gas stoves, portable generators and such. But these require fuel storage with careful attention to amounts, durability, handling methods and safety. Clearly there are practical limits on how long one can depend on such storage-based systems.

Long-term needs suggest renewable sources and each of the several options should be evaluated on the basis of availability, efficiency, safety, economy, visibility, equipment life, reliability and ease of maintenance and repair. In most cases a mix of several energy sources and fuels will provide the best service.

Wood is a promising possibility in many parts of the country. It can heat spaces and water, cook and preserve food, generate steam for power and cleaning, and be fermented to produce fuel alcohol. It can also be burned and the gases recovered to power stationary engines and vehicles. Wood is renewable and enough for basic needs can be produced in a relatively small area with proper species and good woodlot management. Larger sites should produce enough fallen and dead wood so no major trees need be cut. Full-scale logging operations during a long-term period of crisis would be a clue to nearby habitation, so gathering must be done with finesse. Woodsmoke, too, is a giveaway, so burning should be done in stoves of non-smoking design (such as those fitted with catalytic combustors), using dry, seasoned wood (during periods of high risk, burn only at night).

Heat from the sun is a second renewable source. With proper collection devices and techniques, solar infrared radiation will warm air and spaces, cook and dry food, promote growing (in greenhouses, cold frames, etc.) during cold weather, create convective air flows for ventilation and heat water. Unfortunately, the potential for glare in many solar devices compromises secrecy, so most should only be used during low-risk periods.

As the diagram shows, certain needs can be best met only by electricity, so many survivors want some homegrown power as part of their energy mix. Sources which in our experience have the most promise are wind, microhydro and solar photovoltaic, not necessarily in that order. Each has its strengths and drawbacks.

Wind power was *the* independent source for rural America before REA, proven over many years. Some of those same time-tested designs as well as Space Age models are available today. But wind has its problems: A limited number of sites have suitable wind. Many prove unsatisfactory only after lengthy and expensive testing. Wind generators need regular maintenance and repair to prevent sometimes-violent self-destruction and many folks find it unnerving to climb a tall tower to provide these devices. Independent maintenance also suggests having many parts and/or even spare units on hand.

Finally, for the survival shelter, the visibility of a tower higher than surrounding trees is a major compromise of secrecy. One could put the unit in a concealable trench with a cable and counterweight lifting system only raising it during low-risk periods, but between that limitation and the erratic nature of wind it could hardly be considered a reliable fulltime retreat power source.

I have worked with a number of clients over the years who installed microhydro systems to tap into the fall of water in an available stream. If water flows are adequate, this is a more-predictable, on-going source of power. Once in place it tends to require far less maintenance and no aerial work. But it may mean getting into near freezing water from time to time to unplug an intake or break up a log jam. Once in place, such a system can be quite invisible and unheard over normal stream noises, but concealed installation can be a major chore and rather costly. I have watched hydro system expenses for some retreats climb to $30,000 and more and require months of backbreaking work installing flues and underground service lines.

In most areas many bureaucrats divide jurisdiction over such applications and this can mean years of battling red tape with accompanying delays, expense, exposure and, sometimes finally, irreversible rejection. The alternative of putting in the system clandestinely means becoming a sort of criminal and worrying about discovery, particularly if you must have others help with the process.

The other factors that must be considered are the hidden cost and compromise of security involved is being on a hydro stream. A parcel with water flow suitable for a hydro site is likely to cost at least twice as much as otherwise comparable nearby land without surface water. This difference needs to be included to calculate the true cost of the system. Also, in times of upheaval, desperate refugees can be expected to travel along watercourses in their wanderings because of the availability to water and food they represent. This means greater risk of discovery if your haven adjoins a major stream or river.

A more promising alternative is photovoltaics (PV for short). PV is the direct conversion of light energy into electricity as it passes through specially treated wafers of semiconducting materials such as silicon. The first practical "solar cells," hand fabricated for use on early orbital satellites, were very expensive — over $500 per peak watt. But mass-production techniques make panels of such cells available off-the-shelf from several manufacturers today for under $10 a watt. New processes now under development suggest 1990 prices per watt as low as 50¢!

Even today's figure compares favorably with microhydro and offers other benefits as well. Modern panels are expected to produce for over forty years with maintenance limited to occasionally dusting their glass coverplates. They are legal to use with no special permits and hook-up is as basic as attaching jumper cables. Because they are modular, they can be handily moved about or tucked safely into storage when not in use. A beginning system can be as simple as one panel, a storage battery, a diode, one or more low-voltage devices to be operated and the connecting wire.

Additional panels and batteries can be linked into the system as funds permit without waste or duplication. Try hanging a second wind generator on the tower sometime and you'll appreciate this ease of expansion. Likewise, if you decide to move, unhook the panels, pack them carefully in the trunk and you're off; it's a bit harder to yank out a hydro turbine and several hundred feet of pipeline that way!

Drawbacks of PVs are few. They *are* fragile and could easily be broken or stolen if left untended. They must be properly oriented in full sun for maximum production and can be visible from distance if carelessly placed, due to geometric shape and glare. Although they can be visually shielded with a little planning, it would probably be wise to put them in storage and live off batteries and short-term backup systems during highest periods of risk.

For those inclined to innovation or with special resources or interests, other power-generating possibilities exist. Steam is a time-tested energy source which could be attached to a turbine and powered by wood, coal, home-distilled alcohol or even animal waste methane, but steam means water consumption, boiler scale, high fuel demands, the need for noise-dampening and the hazards of explo-

sion. Internal combustion generators can use products produced on-site including wood gas, vegetable oils, alcohol and methane. Even hot air engines and thermopile units powered by solar, wood or other renewable heat sources are possible. Just be certain before jumping into one of these more exotic approaches that you have the aptitude, interest and long-term commitment to complete and maintain what you begin.

The other tactic to remember in developing an independent energy plan is conservation. Wherever energy can be saved or eliminated, the cost of the system and the effort involved in assuring a fuel supply can be reduced. Insulation is better than a larger heating unit; natural illumination and more reflective surfaces can save a lot in lighting demands.

Transportation and Portable Power — During times of highest risk, travel of any kind would be unwise; wandering around on the surface is not a sound avoidance tactic. But during lulls or recovery periods travel may have its purposes. Most outings will be for short distances and on foot, but if your strategy includes greater mobility or hauling power, the same fuels listed above can be generated on-site to suit properly modified tractors, trucks, and all-terrain vehicles. Also, these can be fitted out with DC motors and storage batteries charged with PVs or other generating systems. With any of these possibilities, power takeoff for remote tool operation would be a valuable added feature.

Professional Consultation — Asked whether outside assistance in shelter design and energy planning is advisable, we would almost always have to say yes. Having worked with clients on these topics for almost twenty years, our own approaches are still evolving and becoming more sophisticated. It would be the rare person starting out who would not devote great energy to "reinventing the wheel; and still fall far short of state-of-the-art survival planning. Time and again we have seen even a few hours of consultation save the client thousands of dollars and months of backtracking on ill-conceived tactics and designs.

On the other hand, we would have to caution that this field has its better and its less-capable proponents, so buyer beware! Unfortunately, there are those willing and eager to separate the neophyte survivor and his money, who simply don't have insights to justify their fee scales. And some give information which is downright dangerous!

Reading is probably the best place to start. After studying a number of survival authors as they appear in print, you should be able to separate the good from the bad and pick up many useful tips along the way.

If we have been able to convey here the importance and potential of thoughtful shelter and energy design to successful survival planning, our goal has been met. As indicated at the beginning of the chapter, the topic is too crucial to be fully explored in these few pages, but it's a place to start. The rest is up to you.

Remember, any given survivor's best choices will vary due to individual physical limitations, skills and needs, budget, site conditions, concerns and timetable. It is always best to start simply and then expand as time and funds allow. But start now — it could well mean the difference between death and living comfortably when crisis hits and systems go awry. The real survivor is the one who can look back on each challenge and say, "but for the preparations I had the foresight to make, this adventure *could have been* a survival situation!"

An electric tractor like this can be charged by the residential power system and has 12-volt DC and 110-volt AC takeoffs to provide portable power wherever it may be needed to operate tools remotely. It's a labor saver.

Chapter 4
SURVIVAL SCHOOLING

For Those Who Don't Know How To Get Started Or Lack The Discipline To Learn On Their Own, This School Could Be A Lifesaver!

Camouflage-clad Bill Ungerman addresses class studying survival basics in the field at one of the group's Southern California locations. Heavy scrub in background is where much of hands-on schooling is conducted.

AS EXPERTS will attest, survival preparedness requires sacrifice and work. There's reading to be done, checklists to be prepared, gear to be accumulated, money spent, and serious thought given to the topics presented in this book and others. Those who make survival preparedness a way of life will reap rewards if their planning is tested, which is why they sacrifice today.

But it's not easy and often it's not fun. If you're just brushing up against the survivalist movement, you'll find there are many strata — industries providing goods and services for a surprisingly large number of diverse people. Getting started in survival preparation is confusing when you're presented a chaotic marketplace of goods and services, each of which is "all you need." Which way to turn?

Who do you believe? Who can you trust for good advice?

Enter big Bill Ungerman. As honcho of California Survival Training Center in Westminster, it's his business to help you get started — or become expert. "Our symbol, a winged-hand clutching a dagger surrounded by twin circles, sums up what the center is about," says Ungerman, a Sequoia-sized blond who looks even more so in his Woodland-pattern camouflage clothing. "This international symbol dates to French martial heraldry and symbolizes perseverance in the face of adversity; optimism in the wake of calamity; faith in your country and her principles; self-reliance; and a tenacity for survival through a will for preparedness."

Who better, then, to tell of survival schools than Bill

Donald L. Poss (left), former USAF noncommissioned officer with Vietnam service, goes over rudiments of map and compass with Joe Alli Kalua of Ranger Sales. Poss is police officer when not teaching with CSTC.

Ungerman? What follows is what he says of the need for formal instruction. — *Mark Thiffault*

MANY PEOPLE in the community regard survivalists as having a "Doomsday" or "Bunker Mentality." Used derisively, this peer pressure has turned many prospective survivalists away from preparedness steps that make sense in today's politco-economic climate. As many an ostrich has fatally discovered, burying the head does not make the threat disappear.

Look at just five possible scenarios in which survival preparation could keep you alive. Nuclear war, for instance, used to be unthinkable, but now it's being considered in a tactical battlefield role. There are "doomies" or "doomsters" out there who tell you life as we know it won't survive a nuclear holocaust. Rubbish! The prepared *will* survive — or at least have a fighting chance. An examination of current Soviet nuclear policy will lead one to conclude that the Russians contemplate nuclear war as being primarily designed to attack those targets which will cripple the U.S.'s ability to counterstrike. Estimates are that fully eighty to eighty-five percent of the U.S. population will survive the first strikes.

Natural disasters — earthquakes, tornadoes, floods and fires — affect areas of the globe every year. Any massive disruption of the delicate socio-ecological balance in our cities will throw the populace into panic. Same with major strikes: Remember the panic, confusion and killing over gasoline shortages? What will happen if no food is getting into the cities because of major service disruptions? You say that the government will mobilize the National Guard and take care of it? Maybe — and then on a small or localized scale only. If anything like the 1981 Polish crisis ever occurs here, chaos will result. Remember, most cities carry only a three-day supply of food on store shelves. If no food is delivered after that time, expect trouble.

Americans realize the vulnerability of the U.S. dollar to global economic developments. What happens if there's an economic calamity? Spiraling inflation, definite budgets, falling dollar values — it takes little imagination to conceive the potential problems. Remember New York City in the 1977 blackout? Total chaos and anarchy, and New York has 30,000 policemen!

Major terrorist activity is another sort of extremism which could conceivably bring the economy to a standstill. Suppose radicals gain control of the Persian oil fields and deny this country the millions of barrels it consumes daily?

You ask about the military or the police — what will they be doing in the aforementioned situations? If you really think they'll continue to protect and serve, you have more faith than I. I believe they'll return to their homes to defend their own families. At that point, everything will depend on you — which is why I founded the California Survival Training Center: to prepare the layman so he'll have a future.

CSTC is a leading weapons and survival training institution in the United States, with eighteen instructors capable of starting the novice or improving the expert. The courses we offer fall into five general categories: Survival guidance and orientation; firearms training; unarmed self-defense; law enforcement; and special-purpose classes.

We offer four separate survival courses, the first of which is Survival Orientation. This introductory course is ten hours and introduces subjects such as collapse economics, food preparation and storage, survival group formation, field expedient shelters, and sanitation. Our Basic Survival Course is a two-day, one-night course that covers map and compass, archery, other survival weapons, bartering, first aid, and living off the land. The Intermediate Survival Course is also a two-day, one-night course held on weekends. It expands on the basic course to include self-defense, a shotgun assault course, leadership in adversity, camouflage target identification and range estimation, defense of the retreat, weapons and tactics, and more. The Advanced Course, another two-day, one-night adventure, reinforces the former instruction and incorporates military skills applicable to a survival environment.

While our offices are based in Westminster, our facilities include rifle and pistol ranges in Irvine and Long Beach, 1500 acres of bug-infested, thickly overgrown riverbottom that you'd swear was Vietnam revisited, a martial arts training academy in Upland, another range in Corona, and the rugged interior of Catalina Island, twenty-six miles off the Southern California coast. All are within 1½ hours of downtown Los Angeles.

Ungerman closes eyes to demonstrate how to keep your shotgun low and on target in low-light conditions. Extend free hand in front of you at waist height.

Virtually every survivalist has his own thoughts on exactly what's required in the way of equipment and food, depending on the severity of the disruption. But most experts recommend examination of checklists prepared by others as a starting point. You obviously don't need preparations as extensive for an expected disruption of a few days to a week that's caused, say, by a storm you know is coming. If you're preparing a "life after Doomsday" scenario, you would need to stock away much more than that listed on the Immediate Survival Equipment list which follows. Use this as a guide to the items that, at the onset of any permanent crisis, will enable you to move your family or survival group to your preselected retreat. Store this gear in military-style footlockers or other containers that can be readily transported. Keep an inventory of equipment contained within each container rotating perishables to retain freshness.

IMMEDIATE SURVIVAL EQUIPMENT

( ) Survival books
( ) Knapsack, rucksacks with military-style Alice gear
( ) Sleeping bag — one for each individual
( ) Tent(s) to accommodate all persons

( ) Thermal blanket — one per person ("Space blankets")
( ) Insulated underwear for each person
( ) Stove and fuel
( ) Hunting knife — one for each person
( ) Folding knife
( ) One belt canteen and belt per person
( ) Eating and cooking utensils
( ) Fire starting equipment — waterproof matches or metal match
( ) Small belt ax — one for each adult
( ) Folding "army-type" shovel — one for each two adults
( ) Folding saw
( ) Large ax — one per family
( ) Two wood-splitting wedges
( ) Water purification tablets or filter
( ) One set of binoculars, 7x50mm for night use
( ) Two military compasses
( ) One Heavy-duty flashlight for each person plus one spare (Kel Lite)
( ) Nylon rope — one hundred feet of military rappelling line — in coils
( ) Heavy-duty pulley
( ) Heavy-duty first aid kit
( ) Snakebite kit

Now bring up muzzle of weapon until it touches your hand and that's a guide of where to keep point of aim. This reduces tendency to shoot high — and ineffectively.

( ) Insect repellent
( ) Tool kit
( ) Metal drinking cups, nonreflective, collapsible
( ) Signal mirror and whistle for each person
( ) Fifteen-day food supply for each person, freeze-dried or C-rations
( ) Soap
( ) Waterproofing materials
( ) Candles
( ) Collapsible two-gallon water container — one for each two people
( ) Fishing kit
( ) Ground cloths, 6x8-feet, plus grommets — two for each two people
( ) Hat — one for each person
( ) Outdoor clothing and boots for each person
( ) Weapons and ammunition, gun cleaning equipment
( ) Road maps and topographic maps
( ) Spare batteries and bulbs for flashlight
( ) Portable AM radio and batteries
( ) Mosquito netting
( ) Knife sharpener or stone
( ) Silver and gold coins for bartering
( ) Sunglasses

Compared to the Master Survival Checklist reproduced elsewhere in this chapter, the Immediate List is almost a weekender pack!

While survival instruction is the cornerstone of CSTC, we offer an extensive bill of firearms fare. The student can, at low cost, learn "Firearms: Safety and Self-Protection," "Basic Firearms Training," "Mini Firearms Training," "Shooter's Course," "Introduction to the Shotgun," "Basic Rifle Course," "Shotgun Assault Course," "Military Assault Course," "Intermediate Pistolcraft," "Combat Handgun Course," "Combat Assault Rifle," "Survival Guns and Gear," "Gas and Guns Course," "Laser-Sighted Weapons," and even a "Permits and Licensing Course" to enable you to cut the voluminous red tape associated with a concealed weapons permit.

We recommend functional and reliable weapons like the Colt Model 1911A1 .45 ACP or Heckler & Koch P9S or P7. If you insist on a revolver, make it a .357 magnum or larger.

From the muzzle out to twenty-five yards, there's no deadlier hand-held weapon than a shotgun in trained hands. It's the first weapon a police officer relies upon to extricate himself from a tight situation. The immense psychological impact of that enormous bore and its roar give you an edge in times of mortal peril. In reputation, appearance and actuality, this is a gun with which you can really "talk to a crowd."

The pump and the self-loader or autoloader are the only two real choices available to the serious defense-minded user. The shorter receiver of a double barrel gun may have some particular special-purpose applications, but in general use the magazine capacity, speed of operation and the single sighting plane make the semiautomatic and pumps the natural choices.

The pump is the best choice whenever the "click-clack" of the shucking action is counted upon to inspire a certain puckering of various posterior muscles in the adversary.

Bill Ungerman shows Suzy Carville how recoil can assist in rechambering of fresh round when using pump shotgun. Suzy positions herself, closes action.

After shot, upward motion of recoil establishes a shooting rhythm that increases rate of fire. Bill moves in concert with Suzy to show correct method.

Basic rifle marksmanship is one of the courses that CSTC offers, and Ungerman here gives personal tips to student Bob Covell. M14 is part of $80,000 inventory.

But that's where the advantage of the pump ends. Let's lay to rest forever any myth of unreliability in the semiautomatic action. An autoloader will shuck 'em out with the best of the pumps. In the prone position, the auto has a distinct advantage. And don't forget that you can switch to rifled slugs to convert the shotgun into an acceptable offensive weapon. It's your choice.

Our courses stress safe operation of firearms, basics anyone involved with survival preparedness should follow. Guns can be dear friends when needed, but they are forever unforgiving of mistakes and accidents.

We work with students assuming the home defense situation will be in low light — in a dark house, for example. To ensure the shooter aims low, we practice raising the barrel from the hip until it touches the palm of the outstretched left hand, for the right-handed shooter. This keeps the muzzle pointed about waist high. We also work, if using the pump shotguns, on letting the gun's recoil assist in rechambering a fresh shotshell. Working the slide in concert with the rearward thrust of the recoil establishes a smooth rhythm which enables a faster rate of fire. In a survival situation, this could make the difference between life and second place.

Marksmanship basics with a handgun include point of aim corrections. Rifle courses are more detailed and we train students in the use of offhand, kneeling, sitting and prone positions. We use iron sights and scopes, and train in long-range shooting — how to hit silhouette targets out to four hundred meters. We use the H&K 91 and 93, M1A and BM59s, among others chambered for the .308 Win. cartridge and .223 Remington, which correspond to the 7.62mm and 5.56x25mm NATO rounds. We feel men will do better to consider a survival rifle chambered for the 7.62mm round, since it gives longer range, more penetration and is readily available as surplus. The M1 Garand is a fine rifle, too. It's reliable, available in many configurations and lives up to its reputation as the ultimate assault rifle. Women do well with the 5.6mm round, normally used in the AR15 or military M16. Everyone uses the laser-sighted shotguns and pistols, too.

Whichever rifle is used, there are eight keys to accuracy: A steady hold for the right-handed shooter depends on the left arm and hand, the butt of the rifle placed securely in the pocket of the right shoulder, grip of the right hand, placement of the right elbow, spot weld of cheek to stock, proper breathing, relaxation, and trigger control. We cover these topics in detail so the shooter can benefit from future practice. There is no substitute for shooting to improve accuracy and retain familiarity with firearms' function, but practicing poor shooting techniques does more harm than good.

California Survival Training Center also offers courses on home burglary and small business protection, use of special weapons like the Taser stun gun, use of laser-sighted weapons, tear gas, and other weapons in our $80,000 inventory. We teach martial arts methods, escape and evasion, land navigation, and even rapelling and parachuting. We give courses as needed on security operations for large firms, powers of arrest and handcuffing for police, and National Rifle Association certified courses. We haven't encountered a request we couldn't meet!

WHILE FIREARMS are integral to Bill Ungerman's preparedness programs, Ray Dorr focuses instead on agriculture and cottage industry skills that will ensure survival, even in a new world scenario.

Dorr and his wife, Virginia, own and operate the Adobe Fort Company in Colorado Springs, Colorado, a firm that conducts learning seminars several times each year. Ray has impressive credentials: explorer, expedition leader into deserts and mountains of Mexico, author, wilderness travel instructor at the University of Colorado, emergency medical technician, mountain rescue team leader and, mountain man. Virginia Dorr, raised on a remote ranch in

Phillip C. Snyder, former Marine captain/U.S. Customs agent/FBI agent/Hijacking Assault Team member, helps Carolyn Kirkwood with sight alignment on pistol course.

Combat shotgun course available to police officers and carefully screened citizens, is conducted in jungle-like setting in Norco, California. Shooters walk jungle lanes, alert for hostiles, booby traps, mines, as instructor scores performance. No one has completed the course without being killed at least three times!

the Colorado Rockies that had no electricity or modern conveniences, knows firsthand the problems and needs of women and infants in wilderness situations. She's also a writer, lecturer, and expedition team member into Mexico.

Ray's common-sense approach to survival preparation is this: "In perilous times, if you prepare for the worst and hope for the best, the worst will come as no surprise and everything better will be a bonus."

Following is what Ray Dorr says about self-reliance and preparedness planning:

THE OUTDOORSMAN, teacher, history buff or anyone contemplating the possibility of living in the wilderness or under primitive conditions can benefit from Adobe Fort. Adobe Fort teaches many of the skills necessary for survival on the Western frontier during the mountain man and pioneer eras. Mountain men were called the greatest survivalists in our country's history, and the pioneers brought west skills and trades necessary to create new communities.

Twice a year Adobe Fort conducts four-day frontier skills institutes at Bent's Old Fort National Historic Site, a National Park Service facility situated in cattle ranchland on the high plains of Colorado, eight miles east of La Junta. Bent's Fort was built in the 1830s as headquarters for a

huge trapping and Indian trading empire. It was the largest privately owned fort ever built in the United States and was often called "the adobe castle on the plains." It has been restored as nearly as possible to its original state, including chickens scratching in passageways and herds of horses and buffalo in the meadow between the fort and a tree-shaded river nearby. Trade blankets, tallow candles, twists of tobacco and other old-time items are for sale in the trade room. Park rangers often dress in fringed buckskins and beaded moccasins.

In keeping with the Pioneer atmosphere, Adobe Fort's eight-member staff, most of whom are mountain men and women with college degrees, wear buckskins or period Mexican clothing at the institutes. Most staff members have been professionals for years in the subjects each teaches. Classes are kept small so each participant can learn-by-doing. Everyone who wishes, can saddle a horse, load and shoot a muzzleloading rifle, start fires with flint and steel or spin yarn on a spinning wheel.

Subjects taught at the institute are: blacksmithing and horseshoeing, operating a spinning wheel, where and how to set up a primitive camp, identifying edible wild plants, wilderness survival, frontier camping and cooking, pioneer farming methods, and emergency medical self-help.

You can learn mountain man skills; flint and steel fire starting; muzzleloading rifles, horses — how to saddle, pack, harness; trapping; skinning and cleaning game; In-

Ray Dorr of Adobe Fort downplays role firearms play in survival situation, stresses preparedness now by acquisition of skills to make you indispensible later.

dian method leather tanning; and making buckskin clothes.

Normally, camping is not allowed at Bent's Old Fort. However, during the institutes, participants and their spouses are allowed only to camp in either of two primitive, undeveloped areas. Because of insurance restrictions, children are not allowed at the institutes or in either campsite. One campsite is for recreational vehicles and modern tests, the other — a living history mountain man camp — is for men and women who have pre-1840-style Indian tipis, white canvas tents, or who choose to sleep under a canvas tarp. Two blankets and a piece of white canvas for shelter is an authentic mountain man camp. No modern lanterns or stoves are allowed in the living history camp and all cooking is done over campfires. Ice chests are allowed if kept out of sight. Wood is available in the campsites and water is available at the fort. All participants furnish their own shelter, food and camp gear. Motels, restaurants and a KOA campground are located in La Junta for those not wishing to camp on site.

The institute offers the chance to live the role of a mountain man or woman while learning nearly forgotten frontier skills. The participants elect their camp officers, as did the pioneers. They are encouraged to bring their own musical instruments to play at council campfires after dark. Many find to their surprise that sleeping, cooking and living on the ground in a cottonwood grove is an enjoyable experience.

On the last evening of the institute, Adobe Fort hosts a free barbecue in the main courtyard of Bent's Old Fort.

Cost for the four-day institute is $295 for one person and $495 for two people. Registration is limited to forty.

With your new skills mastered, you have the ability to establish new businesses, which will be indispensable to others. The person who owns a general store, blacksmith shop or a spinning shop today could be in a secure position tomorrow. The person who owns the supplies and tools for all three could have the means for a family empire.

These three businesses are vital to every pioneer community. The blacksmith shop was usually the first and busiest business in a pioneer community. A blacksmith was kept busy making and repairing tools, weapons and wagons. Adobe Fort sells a complete blacksmith shop, including anvil, forge, blower, leg vise, wall-mounted blacksmith drill, two hammers, two tongs and an instruction book.

The general store owner was in the center of the commercial structure of a pioneer town. Starting with an inventory that was often more valuable than gold, he was in the position to be a trader, banker, real estate broker and to be politically influential. We provide tools, seeds, blankets, traps, fishing supplies, sewing items, knives, rope and other vital supplies in quantities to suit the owner.

The third industry vital to a community is the spinning shop. Colonial and pioneer spinners enjoyed security because they were able to make precious yarn from various raw materials for clothes and blankets. In the spinning shop, we sell an Ashford traditional spinning wheel, carding paddle and instruction booklet on spinning are featured.

We also teach such topics as log and adobe construction, trapping, edible wild plants, selecting campsites, and camp security. You can prepare for these and other pioneer skills at little expense — or pay dearly later!

Another company that anticipates survival with some modern conveniences is the Survival Center in Ravenna, Ohio. The center, a 240-acre facility located thirty-five miles southeast of Cleveland, is virtually self-sufficient and a reliable source for survival preparedness.

The center regularly holds workshops on organic gardening, home food dehydration, Indian-style survival, solar equipment, food storage, beekeeping, holistic health care, bread baking, dairy goat husbandry, primitive construction, and more. The center brings in acknowledged experts to provide instruction.

The Survival Center manufactures and/or markets an extensive line of self-reliance products and foods, and has been featured in many publications and on television.

MASTER SURVIVAL LIST
(Prepared by California Survival Training Center)

Literature
( ) Wilderness cookbook
( ) First aid book (American Red Cross)
( ) Assorted survival books and personal reading material
Writing Implements
( ) Note pads
( ) Pencils
( ) Paper
( ) Pens (refills and ink)
( ) Paper scissors
Transportation
( ) 4-wheel drive vehicle
( ) Bicycles
( ) Off-road motorcycles
Fire Starting and Lighting Equipment
( ) Wood and paper matches
( ) Metal match fire starter
( ) Magnifying glass
( ) Disposable butane cigarette lighters
( ) Strikers and flints
( ) Lanterns (white gas and kerosene)
( ) Candles and candle lanterns

Virginia Dorr was ranch-raised and imparts her firsthand learning to students at Adobe Fort seminars. Learning survival skills is main thrust of their programs, conducted in Colorado.

( ) Rechargeable flashlight with solar recharger plus spare bulbs
( ) Road flares

Communication
( ) Walkie-talkies (military PRC-6 type)
( ) Base NCS (PRC-10 type)
( ) Scanner radio (police, fire, aircraft)
( ) Signal mirror(s)
( ) Short-wave set to monitor worldwide conditions

Optical Equipment
( ) Binoculars
( ) Spotting scope
( ) GI compasses

Special Protective Equipment
( ) Radiation detection unit
( ) Fire extinguisher(s)
( ) Gas masks and replacement filter canisters

Medical Supplies
( ) Medical kit
( ) First aid kit
( ) Prescription and non-prescription drugs
( ) Inflatable splints
( ) Snakebite kits
( ) Insect repellent

Camping Gear and Clothing
( ) Thermal blankets ("Space blankets")
( ) Sleeping bags (five pounds or better)
( ) Cold weather clothing
( ) Heavy work socks (wool)
( ) Thermal underwear
( ) Work boots
( ) Work clothing
( ) Hats for all seasons and conditions
( ) Tents
( ) Ground cloths
( ) Rain gear
( ) Gloves
( ) Treadle sewing machine

Supplies, Tools and Hardware
( ) Sewing supplies
( ) Two-man saw
( ) Log wedges
( ) Chain saw
( ) Splitting mauls
( ) Hand tools
( ) Carpenter supplies

Food
( ) Six-month supply of canned goods (military C rations)
( ) Two-year supply of dehydrated and freeze-dried food
( ) Nitrogen-packed whole grains
( ) Powdered milk
( ) Jerky
( ) Vitamins
( ) Vegetable seeds

Hunting and Fishing Equipment
( ) Hunting knife for each individual
( ) Game calls
( ) Traps
( ) Salt blocks to lure game
( ) One large folding knife
( ) Deer musk scent
( ) .22 caliber rifle and five thousand rounds of hollow-point ammunition
( ) 12-gauge shotgun with 2 barrels and two thousand shells loaded with #6 shot
( ) Gun parts and cleaning kits
( ) Fishing accessories and supplies

Defensive Equipment
( ) Handgun and five thousand rounds of ammunition
( ) M1A assault rifle and five thousand rounds of military ball ammunition
( ) 5.56mm rifle and five thousand rounds of 55-grain ammunition
( ) Riot gun with magazine extension and two thousand shells loaded with #4 buckshot
( ) Extra parts and cleaning kits for all weapons
( ) Extra magazines for weapons where applicable
( ) Fighting knife
( ) Bulletproof vest
( ) U.S. Marine Corps issue Vietnam steel-insole combat boots (jungle boots)
( ) Camouflage clothing and camouflage face gear
( ) U.S. Marine Corps pistol belt
( ) Canteen
( ) Assorted ammunition
( ) Load-bearing equipment (Alice gear)
( ) Military helmet
( ) Winter combat clothing

Money and Valuables
( ) Gold
( ) Pre-1964 U.S. silver coins
( ) Cigarettes used for barter
( ) Liquor used for barter
( ) Jewelry used for barter

Chapter 5

THE ARMORY FOR AFTER DOOMSDAY

While It's Difficult To Predict Possible Conditions With Certainty, Here Are Some Thoughts And Suggestions

By Dean A. Grennell

It's all very well to have a gun and supply of ammo, but you'll want to be able to pack it securely, ready for speedy access and that means a good holster, such as this Bianchi Auto-Draw for the .45 auto.

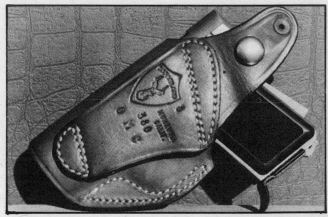

You may not wish to make it widely known that you have a gun — for reasons discussed here — and a small holster such as this Model 8 Safariland for the AMT .380 Back Up is admirably concealable.

PROBABLY THE most thoughtful and plausible exploration into post-chaos lifestyles is the novel, *Alas, Babylon!*, written by Pat Frank shortly before 1959. In that particular narrative, some unfortunate misunderstandings triggered a thermonuclear exchange between the USA and the USSR. The story concerns a small group of people in upstate Florida and how they managed to cope with the ensuing difficulties.

As many may recall, there were some tense times going past in that era and there was a great deal of attention focused upon provisions against the grim day of reckoning. Some of the more-concerned souls constructed fallout shelters and stocked them with iron rations, first-aid supplies and the like against time of dire need.

In the discussion at hand, we are concerned with the comparative merits of various types of weaponry. At the same time, we are mindful of the complexities set upon such ordnance by the contemporary law of the land and sub-paragraphs of the constituent states and local jurisdictions. That's by way of saying if you choose to reside in Morton Grove, Illinois, where handguns are banned, you may have to modify some of the discussion to suit personal exigencies, as but one example.

If we are to contemplate the possibility of rough times with an eye toward weathering them successfully, one of the foremost considerations is the length of the interlude over which there is a manifest need to be self-sufficient before some hope can be harbored for the return of the *status quo*. It could be a few days, weeks, months, or years and there is no hi-fi crystal ball to shed a clue.

A few facts can be culled out and regarded as basic considerations. Most if not all artifacts of a high-tech culture will be discontinued from further manufacture when the black day dawns. A few — by no means all! — examples might include the usual 115-volt AC power supply which we take so blissfully for granted most of the time; drinking water; fuel for internal-combustion engines; drugs and medicines, with special emphasis upon insulin and those materials that must be refrigerated (no more electricity, remember?); gunpowder, either black or smokeless; primers for cartridge reloading; cartridges and shotgun shells; shot and wad columns for reloading shotshells; firearms; telescopic sights; matches, flints and lighter fluid; cartridge cases; bullets; alloys suitable for the home casting of bullets; coffee; tobacco; toothpicks; bathroom tissue...

Many of those items are discussed elsewhere in the work at hand. Here, we're concerned with what to use for shooting and how to keep it operational for as long as possible. It is painful to advise you that there is no single all-purpose answer, but there are several possibilities, varying as to intrinsic merit, and that's what we'll be discussing.

Under such loosely envisioned conditions, there are several considerations that seem worth weighing. For one thing, you're going to have to assume the presence of hostile personnel in the reasonably adjacent area and for another, you must remain mindful that possession of a workable gun will brand you as a target of choice opportunity for the hostile types. Thus, if you let off a round from a .300 Winchester magnum rifle, any person within a radius of a half mile or so can be expected to take keen interest toward taking over its ownership.

The advantage of quiet artillery should be painfully obvious. At the same time, possession of effectively silenced ordnance will be awkward over that indeterminate interlude of normalcy before doomsday erupts. Silencers are legal to possess, so long as you pay the $200 transfer tax and take care of the red tape and paperwork. Silencers

have little or no value on revolvers because a lot of high-pressure gas and noise escape from the gap between the cylinder and the rear of the barrel before it gets to the silencer up front. Guns that drive bullets faster than the speed of sound — roughly 1100 feet per second (fps) — cannot be silenced effectively because the supersonic projectile emits a whip-like crack in moving through the air.

A type of gun well worth considering for use within its specialized capabilities is the air gun, either rifle or pistol. You can write off the versions powered by carbon dioxide because the cartridges of compressed gas will not be available after the Day. The pneumatic varieties, powered by pumping a hand lever, offer inexhaustible supplies of free propellant, via modest quantities of elbow grease. The

There aren't many of the old .38 autos — such as this Pocket Model of 1903 — left around, but the .38 Auto round (above, right), is what it takes and the .38 Super or .38 Auto +P, as here marked, will blow up one of the old guns, if fired. Both cartridges are identical in size, hence the problem.

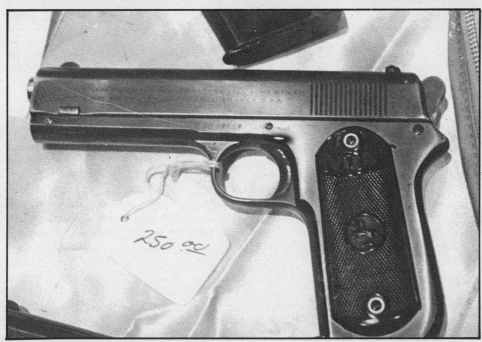

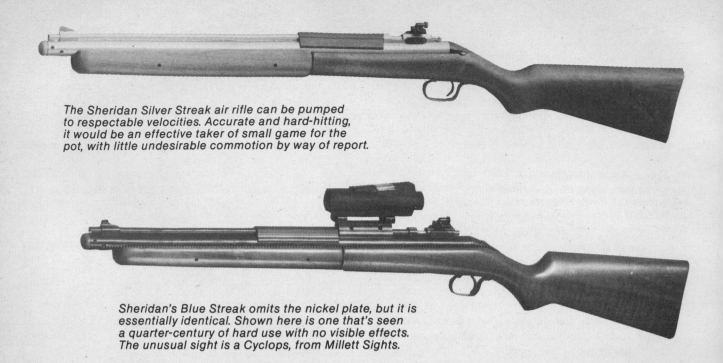

The Sheridan Silver Streak air rifle can be pumped to respectable velocities. Accurate and hard-hitting, it would be an effective taker of small game for the pot, with little undesirable commotion by way of report.

Sheridan's Blue Streak omits the nickel plate, but it is essentially identical. Shown here is one that's seen a quarter-century of hard use with no visible effects. The unusual sight is a Cyclops, from Millett Sights.

pellets are small and inexpensive to purchase and lay-by against the time of future sharp need. Typically, they are put up in packs of five hundred pellets and such a pack takes little more space than a deck of playing cards. Enough pellets for several thousand shots would not take up much space and could be carried without undue difficulties.

The logical choice among the several varieties available would be the Sheridan Blue Streak or Silver Streak air rifles and the Sheridan Model H pneumatic pistol, all of which handle the 5mm or caliber .20 diameter of pellet. Sheridan makes two types of pellets, the original cylindrical version and the skirted Diabolo type. The latter is best suited for target practice and the cylindrical pellet is much better for survival use. The Model H pistol has the obvious

advantage of offering compact and concealable advantages, meanwhile handling the same basic pellet as the substantially more powerful rifles.

Of the two rifles, the blued gunmetal of the Blue Streak has the obvious edge of lowered visibility although the nickel-plated Silver Streak is more resistant to corrosion and the hazards of foul weather. All of the pneumatic Sheridans discussed here are variable in power, depending upon the number of strokes you pump into the reservoir. The Model H pistol can be given about eight pumps, or ten for the rifles. That should be regarded as the practical maximum. Ten pumps on the rifle will drive the cylindrical pellet through an inch of soft pine with steam to spare. As a rough rule of thumb, penetration of a nominal one-inch

Shown beneath the box at left are the two types of 5mm (caliber .20) pellets available for use in the Sheridan. Pinch-waisted type at right is more for target work, while the straight-sided pellet is ideal for small game. Each box of 500 is about the size of a pack of king size cigarettes and not unduly heavy. A standard-size Zippo lighter is shown for scale and is, in itself, a handy thing to have, along with flints and fuel.

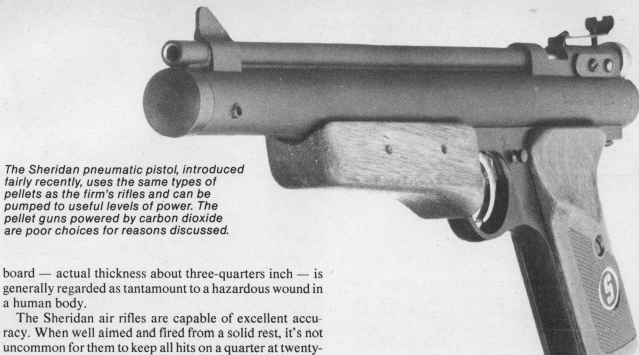

The Sheridan pneumatic pistol, introduced fairly recently, uses the same types of pellets as the firm's rifles and can be pumped to useful levels of power. The pellet guns powered by carbon dioxide are poor choices for reasons discussed.

board — actual thickness about three-quarters inch — is generally regarded as tantamount to a hazardous wound in a human body.

The Sheridan air rifles are capable of excellent accuracy. When well aimed and fired from a solid rest, it's not uncommon for them to keep all hits on a quarter at twenty-five yards or better. That's entirely ample for head shots on rabbits or squirrels and similar small game targets of opportunity. The primary employment for the air rifle or pistol in this discussion is as a taker of small game for the pot, effective yet diffidently unobtrusive as to report. There are many other makes and models of air guns, more or less suitable for the discussed purposes. Most of them cost more, perhaps several times as much. Few if any are as powerful, although some exceed the Sheridan in sheer accuracy.

With no exceptions observed to date, the Sheridan pneumatic system retains its pumped-up pressure over a long span of time. You can pump up the reservoir without opening the bolt to cock the striker that releases the stored air when the trigger is pulled, storing the gun without pellet for safety purposes, if desired.

The next step up from the air gun is the rimfire pistol, revolver or rifle, usually handling the .22 rimfire cartridges such as the .22 short, long or long rifle. There is also the .22 magnum or .22 WMRF — two terms for the same cartridge — for which various handguns and rifles are chambered. At the lower end of the rimfire scale, we have the CB caps, either in short or long cases. The CB caps are quite diffident as to power and report. In the longer rifle barrels,

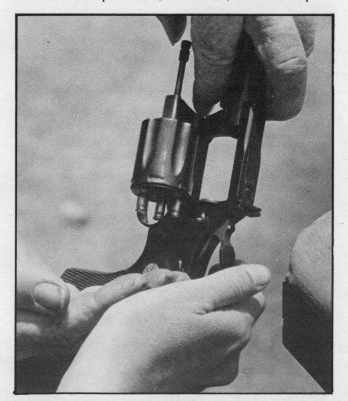

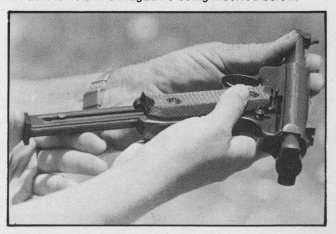

Basic differences between revolvers, left, and auto pistols can be seen here. A revolver carries its cartridges in chambers in its cylinder while ammo for auto is held in a magazine being inserted below.

These are the familiar fifty-round cardboard boxes in which .22 rimfire ammo may be supplied, in a typical assortment of types from Federal Cartridge.

The .22 WMRF packs somewhat more punch than even the hottest .22 long rifle loads and can be had in solid or hollow point bullet loads, as these CCIs.

they make hardly more noise than a typical air gun, thus offering what almost amounts to a silenced system that remains entirely legal through the present. The CB load with the long case is generally preferred because extensive firing of CB loads in the short case will leave a stubborn ring of firing residue in the chamber around the case mouth, posing difficulty in chambering a longer cartridge such as the .22 long rifle unless removed by patient cleaning.

The .22 short, long and long rifle cartridges are available in variations such as standard-velocity, high-velocity, solid-bullet and hollow-point bullet loadings. The S-V loads are quieter, the H-V loads more powerful. The solids give better and deeper penetration, while the hollow points have the edge in expansion and stopping power.

A third rimfire category is the ultra- or hyper-velocity loads in .22 long rifle, as exemplified by the CCI Stinger or Remington's Yellow Jacket and Viper loads. Not all guns nominally chambered for the .22 long rifle will perform

well with these hotter loads. If you have any doubt, ask the maker of the gun in question.

In general, the .22 rimfire guns should be regarded as the next rung up the ladder from the air guns. Their primary use would be in bagging meat for the pot. Their use against armed and hostile human adversaries should be considered only in last-ditch circumstances. The .22 rimfire cartridges really have an impressive mortality rate, but demise tends to occur about three days after the shooting, via peritonitis and similar complications. Their stopping capability against a berserk opponent is marginal at best, unless the shooter possesses skills of the highest order.

A more recent packaging trend is represented by these plastic boxes holding one hundred rounds of .22 rimfire cartridges. It is not a bad idea to put a couple rubber bands around each such box, as they tend to break apart and spill cartridges every which-way if dropped on a hard surface.

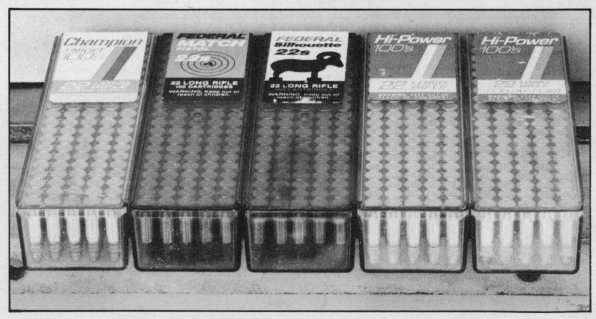

CCI terms their Stinger load the world's fastest, and they seem to have every right to make that claim. The cautionary notice on label bears noting.

long or long rifle, in S-V or H-V loadings. While some revolvers have six-shot cylinders, others hold up to nine rounds, thus approaching the capacities of auto pistols which typically offer ten or eleven shots per loading.

In terms of specific brands, the Sturm, Ruger & Co. .22 Standard Auto and its successor, the Mk II, are well worth considering. They are priced favorably and have excellent reputations for reliability and accuracy. At a somewhat higher cost, much the same can be said of the High Standard .22 auto pistols. They tend to be larger and heavier than the Ruger, costing up to four times as much, but they are fine guns in all other respects.

In .22 rimfire revolvers, the Harrington & Richardson

In handguns, the autoloader has several advantages over the revolver. There is no need to worry about losing the ejected empty case, since you can't reload it anyway. If spare magazines are available, they can be carried fully charged for a rapid return to firing capability. Autos tend to be more compact and concealable than revolvers of comparable barrel length.

The auto pistol does, however, demand a certain minimum power in the cartridge in order to function reliably. Most revolvers will perform quite reliably with .22 short,

Winchester's #X25AXP load in .25 ACP is the only cartridge for such tiny pistols capable of expanding to any useful extent, meanwhile penetrating well.

While most revolvers are limited to six shots per loading, the Harrington & Richardson has up to nine chambers in its cylinder, providing half-again the number of rounds available.

Colt's Vest Pocket Model .25 auto was made from 1908 to 1946. Serial numbers above 141,000 have a magazine disconnector that breaks contact between trigger and sear when the six-shot magazine is out.

Bauer .25 auto, here in chrome, with pearl stocks, is similar in size and design to the Colt above.

Colt's Service Ace is their only .22 auto still in production and it is the exact size of .45 ACP Model 1911.

Norton Model TP-70 is about the same size, but features double-action trigger; it is chambered for the .22 long rifle cartridge.

Capacious, compact, reliable, accurate and inexpensive, Ruger's .22 auto pistols, here in Mark II version, is one of the best possible choices in .22 rimfire chambering.

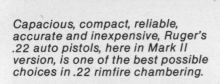

From left, CCI's Mini-Cap in long case, a small bullet atop light charge for soft reports; CCI Stinger with much more power; Federal #514 Power-Flite; Remington Yellow Jacket and Winchester's Xpediter, the last now discontinued. These are but a few examples of the broad versatility the .22 offers.

Here a 1.5X scope with long eye relief has been mounted on a .22 Ruger bull-barrel target model auto to provide remarkable accuracy when fired from a steady rest.

(H&R) offers the nine-shot cylinder capacity and a reasonable choice in overall size. Both Colt and Smith & Wesson offer various models in suitable sizes. Ruger also has a single-action revolver that's available with a swappable auxiliary cylinder so as to handle both the .22 long rifle or the .22 WMRF cartridges. Single-action revolvers must have the hammer cocked manually in order to fire each shot, whereas double-action designs can be cocked manually or fired via a longer pull of the trigger to force the hammer back and drop it by means of internal linkage.

In .22 rifles, the shopper has a choice so broad it is bewildering. One of the more likely possibilities is the little ten-shot auto carbine by Ruger. Extra-capacity magazines are available for that as accessories. There are many other possibilities, including one which resembles a sort of teeny-bopper Lewis gun. With a drum magazine the size of a pie plate atop the receiver, it holds a grand total of 177 rounds when fully charged. Various makers have offered break-open combination guns with a rifle barrel superposed over a shotgun barrel and a selector lever to provide a choice of which load will fire when the trigger is pulled.

In the final analysis, an outside counselor can no more select the ideal gun for you than an equally ideal spouse. Suggestions can be offered, but you have to interview the prospects and make the final choice. Happily, the field of firearms offers less complications if the choice doesn't work out to complete satisfaction. You can always trade it back in on something else that looks likely and then see how you fare with that.

It's hardly a bit too soon to point out that one does not just buy a gun against future time of dire need, stash it in the

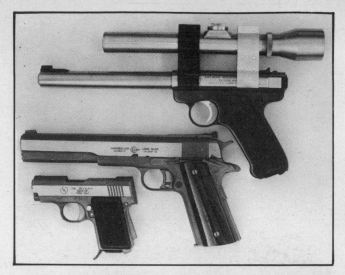

Above, Stainless 8" bull barrel on .22 Mk-II Ruger with Weaver 2X pistol scope is incredibly accurate. AMT's long-slide .45 ACP Hardballer and .380 ACP Back Up also shown. Left, earmuffs, shooting glasses and a .22 LR single-shot such as this T/C Contender make an easy introduction for beginner.

corner of the closet and consider the matter attended to. That would be rather like buying a piano on the off chance that you might experience a yen to render Chabrier's "Espana Rhapsody" some evening for a close circle of friends and amiable passersby. If you've never taken a music lesson in your life, the project might not come off as well as planned.

In the same throbbing vein, if you buy a gun on the theory that it might extend your longevity someday, it behooves you to become well acquainted with it. For but one consideration, few if any rimfire guns will handle any and all makes and types of ammunition equally well. They all have some amount of prejudice in such things and the only way to find out the best load is to try several to see which performs best.

Once you settle upon the preferred loads, plan to lay in a fairly lavish supply of them. Ammo in .22 rimfire is put up in plastic boxes holding one hundred rounds, or in fifty-round packs, five hundred to the carton. It doesn't represent a lot of bulk or weight. By any reasonable envisioning of post-Day conditions, there would be some things that represent the choicest sort of trade goods: Flashlight bulbs

Iver Johnson Model TP-22 is a compact double-action auto holding seven rounds, also available as Model TP25 for .25 ACP ammo.

Colt's .22 LR Diamondback, here has 6" barrel, is nearly an exact replica of their .357 mag Python.

Original Standard Model Ruger .22 did not have the bolt hold-open that was added in the Mark-II version.

Likewise in stainless steel, AMT's .22 LR Back Up is a counterpart of their .380 ACP model of same gun.

and batteries, bottles of pain-relief tablets, lighter flints and cans of fuel, vitamin tablets, writing materials, antiseptics...the list goes on, but high among these good things you'll find that a few boxes of rimfire ammunition could be bartered for all manner of useful and badly needed items, provided you had some to spare. That's to say there's hardly any such thing as too much rimfire ammo, comes the Day. Given reasonable protection against the elements, its storage life verges toward eternity. It would be well to pick up a good supply now and put it away before the hoarders get it.

Standard Model of Ruger's 10/22 is a handy little autoloading rifle and extra-capacity magazines can be had to use with it.

Ruger's Mark I Target Model in .22 LR has a 6⅞" tapered barrel.

Here with factory iron sights, the Bull-Barrel Target Model of the Ruger .22 auto is highly capable.

Speedloaders, such as this one by Safariland, offer capability of saving useful time in refilling revolvers.

Standard .25 ACP cartridge, left, carries the usual round nose, full metal jacketed bullet while round at right has the plated lead bullet with a steel ball embedded in its tip, as supplied by Winchester. The latter is capable of a useful amount of expansion.

Moving in logical sequence, we come to the handguns and rifles that handle center-fire ammunition. The field is bounded largely by the .25 ACP (Automatic Colt Pistol) pistol cartridge on the lower end and the .460 Weatherby magnum at the other extreme. The latter is regarded as a logical choice for elephant and the smaller species of dinosaur.

The center-fire cartridges are characterized by the fact that the fired cases are more or less amenable to being reloaded by replacement of the spent primer, the burnt powder and the departed prior projectile. The simplicity of the reloading operation pivots upon whether the case has a Boxer-type primer or a Berdan-type primer. Boxer-primed cases, as customarily made and sold in the USA, are readily reloadable. Berdan-primed cases, in common use over much of the rest of the world, can be reloaded, but under the handicap of heavy complications.

Again, the handguns offer a choice between autoloaders, revolvers, single-shots and a few renegade sub-species. Rifles are available in break-open single-shots, bolt-action single-shots and repeaters, autoloaders, lever-actions, pump-actions and multi-barrel designs; possibly others as well.

The typical small pocket auto pistol is chambered for such cartridges as the .22 long rifle, .25 ACP, .32 ACP

From left, FMJ and JHP pairs in .25 ACP, .32 ACP and .380 ACP; lone round of .30 Luger with two 9mm Lugers; FMJ and JHP .38 Colt Super with a round, far right, of the .38 ACP loaded to lower pressures.

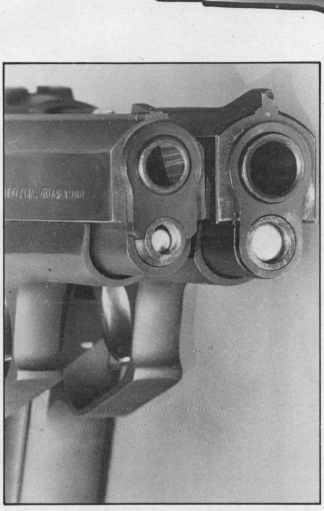

Smith & Wesson's Model 39, in 9mm Luger/Parabellum, can be carried with hammer down on a chambered round, firing first shot via double-action trigger pull and shifting to single-action for subsequent shots.

The difference in bore diameter between the 9mm, left, and .45 ACP is illustrated graphically in this view of a pair of Llama Omni autoloaders.

tured by Colt. For what it is, it's an excellent effort, well-made, reliable and capable of better accuracy than many might expect. By far the most effective ammunition currently available in .25 ACP is the load put up by Winchester with the small steel ball in the nose of the copper-plated lead bullet; manufacturer's index number X25AXP. When fired into a clay-base ballistic test medium, the Winchester load will expand to nearly caliber .45 diameter, producing a wound channel up to .75-inch at the maximum, to a depth of about three inches. It is nothing in front of which the prudent person might care to stand.

A few .32 ACP auto pistols remain in production to the present. The pertinent question is why? There are no .32 autos nearly as compact as the .25 versions and the same

Unlike S&W M39 above, H&K's Model VP70Z fires every shot by a full double-action pull of trigger.

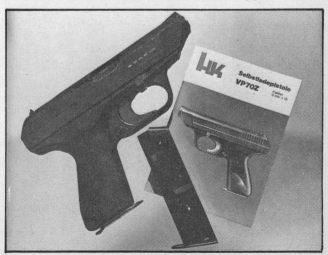

and .380 ACP. All of these have nearby limitations as to all-out stopping power, but their compact contours may enable their effective employment as deterrents against aggression. That's to say you might have one handy at a time of sharp and urgent need where a larger and more effective arm might not be readily available. Hardly anyone would relish the prospect of being perforated with one of the little cartridges and they can constitute a useful bargaining factor. Grimly jocose tone notwithstanding, do not interpret this as license to become careless with the little pistols, since even the humble .25 ACP has incurred an awesome total of funeral expense in its lengthening career.

The smallest, least expensive and most readily available of the .25 ACP autos is the Wilkinson Diane, slightly smaller than the pre-WWII Browning design as manufac-

A .451 Detonics magnum load, left, is slightly longer than .45 ACP, center, and has heavier construction about the head to handle higher pressures, thereby offering capability of substantially higher velocities.

Center-fire cartridges come in a broad range of sizes. From left, the tiny .25 ACP; Winchester's .458 Win mag; the even larger .460 Weatherby mag, and an empty case for the elderly .600 Nitro Express.

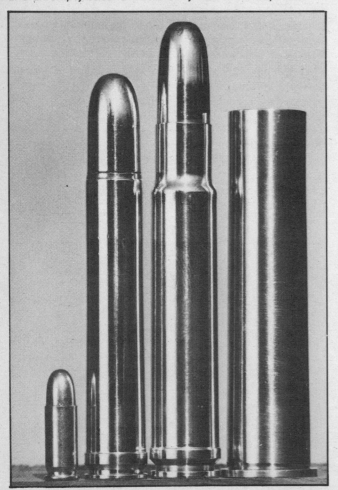

Llama's 9mmP Omni features a staggered-column magazine that holds thirteen cartridges. Same model in .45 ACP has a single-column, seven-shot capacity.

guns that handle the .32 usually are also available in .380 ACP, as well. The latter is not a world-beater against all comers, but it is ever so much more effective than the .32 ACP. The charity required to commend the .32 ACP cartridge is entirely out of reach. Its choice is defendable only if nothing else is available. Many better cartridges are available for which we should be suitably grateful.

Some authorities pinpoint the .380 ACP cartridge as the bedrock minimum capable of useful employment against a determined and hostile aggressor. The topic is open to debate and quite a lot of debate and assorted langrel has been expended, with hardly any end in sight as yet.

One self-appointed Grand Guru of survival weaponry, speaking *ex cathedra,* has denounced the 9mm Luger or Parabellum cartridge as entirely useless and ineffectual for defensive or offensive use. Performance-wise, the 9mmP lies considerably upstream of the .380 ACP, suggesting that, when shopping for gurus, you lay down your greenies and make your judicious choice.

Up to the .380 ACP, pocket-size pistols can function via full-blowback designs. As you move on to the 9mmP, the designs must incorporate a temporary full lock-up or delayed blowback, although some of the carbines and assault pistols in 9mmP continue to use the full-blowback approach, with the aid of vastly heavier bolts and stronger recoil springs.

Some of the acrid acrimony dripped upon the 9mmP cartridge and its stopping capabilities may be due to its performance with the traditional round-nosed, full metal jack-

The .451 Detonics magnum can be handled in a good, strong Model 1911A1-type gun by installing the kit of barrel and springs. Not currently available as a factory load, it has about twice the punch of .45 ACP.

The .38 S&W Special, left, with .38 S&W, .38 Short Colt and .38 Long Colt. The .38 S&W is larger in case diameter and is not interchangeable with the other three cartridges shown here, confusing many.

ployed military pistol cartridge in the world, which should suggest something. It is, likewise, the most popular for use in submachine guns. Winchester, for example, offers four different factory loads for the 9mmP, with muzzle energies ranging from 341 to 387 foot-pounds of energy (fpe), as measured in a four-inch barrel.

It's a moot point whether the .38 Colt Super or .45 ACP cartridge rates the next mention. If we are to go by the maximum power listings in the Winchester ammunition charts, the .38 Super shows a maximum of 475 fpe, while the top

et (FMJ) bullet as employed for military use. The conventions of modern warfare sanction only nonexpanding bullets for use in small arms. Compliance with this rule is conditioned partially by the bleakly philosophical consideration that a wounded foeman is strategically preferable to a dead foeman. The former ties up a lot of critical facilities while the latter needs but brief attention from the burial detail.

In the present state of the art, there are a number of bullets and variants of loaded ammo for the 9mmP that are capable of effective upset and expansion at the velocity of typical guns and loads. Not all such bullets/loads will function reliably through all guns chambered for the 9mmP cartridge, but that remains the responsibility of the buyer/user to establish and work around.

The gritty consideration remains: If the .380 ACP rates as marginally capable in the eyes of some authorities, the considerably more capable 9mmP merits consideration on its manifest merits. The 9mmP is the most broadly em-

The Walther Model P5, in popular 9mmP caliber, is a double-to-single-action design adapted from the Walther P-'38 military autoloader of WWII.

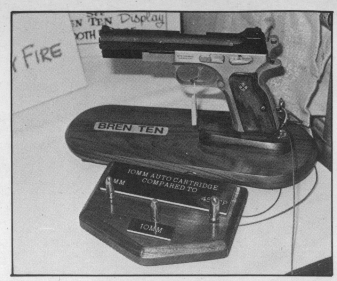

The Bren Ten auto, above, handles a new cartridge with a bullet about .40-inch in diameter. Left, the 14-shot Browning Model BDA 380 is about the same size as the Star Model PD in .45 ACP, but the size of their cartridges vary considerably, as shown.

rating for the .45 ACP is but 411 fpe. As a further enticement, in the Colt Government Model or Commander, the magazine for the .38 Super holds nine rounds as compared to seven in .45 ACP; with the option of carrying an additional round in the chamber in either instance.

In terms of overall popularity, there is no question whatsoever. The .45 ACP has been this country's primary military pistol cartridge for over seventy years and through several wars. The .38 Super has seen considerable use in Mexico, but has never gotten the recognition here that some feel it deserves. As with the 9mmP, its usual load carries an FMJ bullet, typically of 130 grains as compared to about 124 for the 9mmP. While loads for the .38 Super are available with expanding bullets, they do not function

reliably in all guns, participarly if soft lead is exposed at the bullet tip. Assuming the load does function — as it sometimes does — the expanding bullet makes the .38 Super an awesomely capable performer.

There are, at the present time, a few cartridges for auto pistols falling between the .38 Super and .45 ACP. One is called the Bren Ten, nominally ten millimeters in bullet diameter or about caliber .40, designed for use in an auto of the same name. The Bren Ten is said to be nearing production, but has not as yet made it, so it is difficult to provide pertinent comment on its capability.

Another entry — and rather an interesting one — is the .41 Avenger cartridge, fired from a conversion kit that can be installed in the Colt Government Model or Commander pistols originally chambered for the .45 ACP. The cartridge is not presently available as a loaded factory round, but it is easy and simple to make up, given facilities for cartridge reloading; a "wildcat" round, in the usual designa-

Large revolver cartridges, from left: .38-40 WCF; .44-40 WCF; .41 Rem mag; .44 Rem mag/lead; .44 Rem mag/JHP; .45 Colt/JHP and .45 Colt/lead. Not shown is .44 Special, same diameter as .44 mag, but slightly shorter in case.

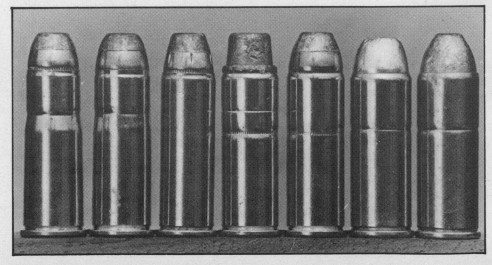

Thompson/Center's single-shot Contender features interchangeable barrels in lengths of ten or fourteen inches in a broad variety of calibers from .22 LR up through .44 magnum. These are for the wildcat 7mm T/CU shown between the two guns.

tion. The conversion kits and loading dies are available from SSK Industries, Route 1, Della Drive, Bloomingdale, OH 43910.

The .41 Avenger cartridge is formed by running an empty .45 ACP case into the full-length resizing die of its set of reloading dies to size down the neck to hold bullets of .410-inch diameter, the same size used in the .41 magnum revolver cartridge. The 170-grain jacketed hollow cavity (JHC) bullet by Speer feeds and functions remarkably well. Driven by 10.6 grains of Hercules Blue Dot powder it averages 1120 fps in the five-inch barrel for a delivery of 474 fpe, putting it about neck-and-neck with the hottest factory load for the .38 Super. Expansion capabilities of

the Sierra bullet, however, put it far ahead of the 130-grain FMJ bullet used in the .38 Super load.

The .45 ACP, not surprisingly, has been the beneficiary of a lot of intent attention along the lines of improving its accuracy, reliability and terminal performance. One of the most effective factory loads currently available in .45 ACP is the 200-grain jacketed hollow point (JHP) version from CCI, rated at 1025 fps and 466 fpe. Since a small increase in bullet diameter provides a considerably greater frontal area, the paper figures are deceptive in this instance. The bullet in the CCI load is the same as available from Speer as a component for reloading and it has been termed, not entirely without justification, "the flying ash

The caliber .32 cartridge family includes, from left: .32 ACP; .32 S&W; .32 Short Colt; .32 Long Colt; .32 S&W Long; and .32-20 Winchester Center-Fire (WCF).

Sterling Model 400 Mark II DA has a capacity of seven rounds in .32 or .380 ACP; one of the few surviving .32 autos.

Detonics .45 is a compact but efficient auto, now also available in .38 Colt Super, 9mmP or .451 Detonics mag.

The venerable M1911A1 Colt Government Model, here with target sights and fancy stocks of Hawaiian koa wood, is a great favorite, capable of infinite modifications.

Star Model PD, in .45 ACP, is a compact, accurate, reliable and efficient choice for that cartridge.

Browning Model BDA 380 is made by Beretta in Italy, imported by Browning.

The .45 Detonics, here seen from the right side with slide locked back, is made with exotic stainless steel alloys in a highly modified adaptation of the basic Colt M1911 design, with a special spring system to reduce the felt recoil.

This is the Colt Python Hunter in .357 magnum, with a 2X Leupold scope, a modification of Colt's basic Python design engineered to obtain maximum accuracy and power from the .357 magnum.

Although nearly always used in auto pistols, there are at least two revolvers that handle the 9mmP cartridge, one by Sturm, Ruger & Co., the other the Model 547 S&W, here between a Llama Omni and the Astra Model A-80 double-action auto.

tray." Fired into clay ballistic test medium, the Speer bullet expands to about the size of a half-dollar at velocities down around 750 fps and does so with proportionally greater vigor when driven faster.

There are, have been and probably will be auto pistol cartridges more capable than the .45 ACP, but none have won a major share of the market to date. As examples, we have the 9mm and .45 Winchester magnums, brought forth for the Wildey pistol. The cartridges exist, but the Wildey has yet to appear in the displays of gun dealers.

The .44 Auto Mag came upon the scene some years back, accompanied later on by the same cartridge necked down to accept bullets of .357-inch and .410-inch diameters. All were notably powerful cartridges, but the guns were rather bulky and cumbersome, likewise expensive; factors that may have curtailed their potential popularity.

Moving on to the other basic handgun design, the revolver, there is a comparable gamut of cartridges, ranging in capability from the .22 rimfires up through the .44 magnum, with several noteworthy examples along the way. In overall dimensions, they range from the Lilliputian Freedom Arms in .22 LR or .22 WMRF to the somewhat Brobdingnagian examples such as the recently introduced Ruger Blackhawk in .357 Remington Maximum, with its 10½-inch barrel: by no means the largest of all revolvers, but ample as an example.

General comments, as made on the .22 rimfire autos, fairly well apply to revolvers for the same cartridge and the basic traits of each were noted earlier. While there are

Ruger's Speed-Six double-action revolver, here in .38 Special, is also made in .357 magnum, has fixed sights in choice of blue or stainless steel; compact and capable.

smaller center-fire cartridges for revolvers, the .38 Special is about the smallest that sees common use. Many writers have reviled the cartridge as woefully deficient in stopping power and there is considerable justification for that in the example of the 158-grain, round-nose lead bullet when driven to about 755 fps for 200 fpe.

As with the .45 ACP, however, a lot of effort has been lavished upon elevating the capability of the .38 Special and an encouraging amount of success has been achieved. A current chart of ammunition performance, appearing on

Winchester's 9mm and .45 Winchester magnum cartridges were designed to go in the Wildey gas-operated auto pistol that has yet to make it into appreciable production or availability.

page 278 of the #37 *Gun Digest*, lists a CCI +P load with the 140-grain Speer JHP bullet at 1275 fps for 504 fpe and a Norma +P load with the 110-grain JHP bullet at 1542 fps for 580 fpe. You may have trouble finding the Norma load on your dealer's shelves, but the CCI version should be obtainable with little difficulty.

The .357 magnum cartridge appeared in 1935, the .44 magnum in 1956 and the .41 magnum in 1964. All were efforts — and generally successful ones — to obtain superior performance in revolvers. The .357 and .44 magnums were created by lengthening the cases of the .38 Special and .44 Special slightly, so as to prevent use of the new cartridges in guns incapable of withstanding the higher pressures. The .41 magnum was a new cartridge in its own right, larger in case diameter and quite incompatible with the earlier and largely obsolescent .41 Long Colt round.

Winchester offers three different loads at present for the .45 ACP: from left, a 185-grain jacketed semi-wadcutter for target; a 185-grain Silvertip JHP; and the 230-grain JHP round nose hardball.

Down the half-century or so of its career to date, the .357 magnum has been severely handicapped by the fact that it's confined to the front-to-back dimensions of its parent .38 Special cartridge. The actions of revolvers provide just so much space for the cylinder, and hardly any more at all. Thus, while the .357 case is .135-inch longer than the .38 Special, the cartridge overall length (col) must be held to a rigid minimum of about 1.6 inches to keep the bullet tips from protruding beyond the front of the cylinder.

The .44 and .41 magnums have suffered from the same problem, although to lesser extents because of their larger diameters. The governing consideration is that revolver designs, and particularly the basic frames or receivers, have changed hardly at all in dimensions since early in the

New and impressive, Ruger's Blackhawk single-action in caliber .357 Remington Maximum with 10½-inch barrel; a bulky bruiser!

From left, the .38 Special, .357 magnum and the new .357 Remington Maximum cartridge for the Ruger Blackhawk and Thompson/Center Contender. As the R-Max has increased space available for both bullet and powder, it can deliver much greater performance.

present century. Late in 1982 Ruger and Remington collaborated in bringing forth the .357 Remington Maximum cartridge, for which Ruger designed their special version of the Blackhawk single-action (SA) revolver.

While retaining the basic head dimensions of the earlier .38 Special and .357 magnum cases, the R-Max case is about 1.600 inches in length, compared to 1.290 inches for the .357 magnum. Of much greater importance, however, is the fact that the cylinder of the R-Max Blackhawk will accept rounds up to about 1.985 inches in length. In other words, the R-Max is .310-inch greater in case length but .385-inch longer is permissible col, with an additional gain of .075-inch in which the bullet nose can protrude without risk of hanging up cylinder rotation.

The dimensions may sound trifling, but they make a considerable difference in performance. In terms of actual delivered performance, as fired out of revolvers with barrels of six or eight inches in length, it proves difficult to obtain much over 700 fpe with the .357 magnum cartridge. In the 10½-inch Ruger Blackhawk, Remington rates the R-Max at 1825 fps with a 158-grain bullet for 1169 fpe. That puts it quite close to performance levels obtainable with the .44 magnum, with less apparent recoil and a usefully flattened trajectory.

That's all very well, but the long-tubed Ruger Black-

The four-inch barrel is a popular length in revolvers. Here are four fairly typical Smith & Wessons handling the .357 magnum, .45 ACP or Auto Rim, .44 Special and .38 Special cartridges.

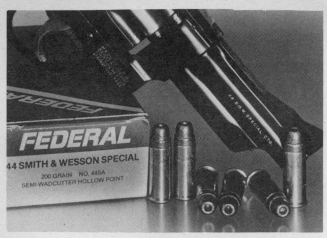

For many years, factory loads in .44 Special were available only with a round nose lead bullet of about 246 grains. Federal recently added this #44SA load with a 200-grain hollow point lead bullet.

hawk is a notably lengthy handful of revolver, hardly suited for desperate employment at close quarters. More, its single-action design requires the hammer to be cocked manually for the firing of each shot. While a few gifted souls, by means of dedicated practice, have achieved the ability to crank off shots in roaring staccato with SAA revolvers, the design poses obvious problems for the typical user. Whether or not a double-action (DA) revolver will be designed and introduced for the .357 Remington Maximum cartridge is anyone's hopeful guess for the moment.

In the meantime, Thompson/Center Arms is producing barrels for the R-Max in lengths of ten and fourteen inches for use on their Contender single-shot pistol. In that sturdy vehicle the R-Max does not have to stay within a minimum col and it can handle bullets at least as large as the 220-grain jacketed soft point (JSP) bullet made by Speer for caliber .35 rifle cartridges. Out of the Contender, the R-Max performance gets downright cataclysmic. True, it sacrifices the fast follow-up shot(s) of the revolver or auto pistol, but for one shot it can be quite decisive.

Such engrossing matters notwithstanding, the survival-oriented buyer probably would find greater interest in the .357, .41 or .44 magnums for the present. The .38 Special is at its best for use in compact, snubnosed revolvers and

Smith & Wesson's L-frame series is a slightly beefier version of their mediumweight K-frame in .357 magnum with integral underbarrel rib.

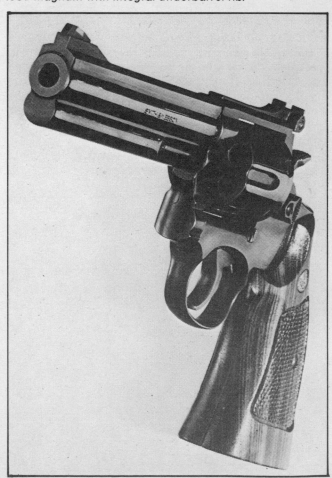

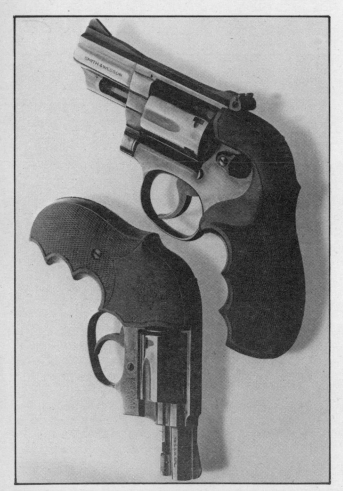

Bianchi's "Lightning" grips are made of rubber with steel reinforcement for small revolvers such as the S&W M19 (top) and M36 Chiefs Special. The design shields the hammer spur to avoid hangups in drawing if the revolvers are carried in a pocket.

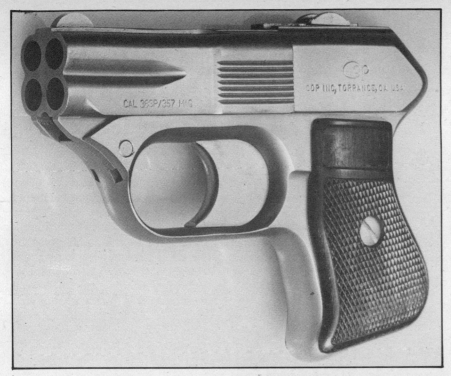

A novel repeating pistol is this Cop, for "compact offduty pistol," with four barrels in .38SP/.357MAG, each fired in turn by a rotating striker and double-action trigger.

SSK Industries, Bloomingdale, OH 43910 offers a conversion kit and loading dies for firing their .41 Avenger cartridge in M1911A1 Colt autos. Marking on installed barrel as seen in ejection port of slide is shown at right. The .41 Avenger (see photo below) is made by necking down the .45 ACP cartridge case. The .41 Avenger uses the magazine normally used in M1911 for .45 ACP.

Left, the .41 Avenger; .45 ACP and .451 Detonics magnum. The Avenger is necked down to take the .410-inch bullets customarily used in the .41 mag revolvers.

some of the .357 designs are not a great deal larger.

One interesting if slightly unlikely offshoot is the revolver for the 9mmP, as presently offered by Ruger or by Smith & Wesson. Once the cartridges are in the chambers, there is no feeding problem of the sort that may plague the shooter of an auto pistol, making all of the expanding-bullet loads eminently usable in a revolver such as the Smith & Wesson Model 547. With the three-inch heavy barrel and round-butt frame, the Model 547 is both usefully compact and impressively capable. An ingenious design of the extractor enables it to eject the rimless 9mmP cases after firing with total reliability.

The .357 magnum revolver is a good compromise in terms of controllability for the average shooter coupled with its ability to handle the milder .38 Special loads. The ammunition is lighter and less bulky for storage or carrying and a variety of factory loads are available in assorted types of bullets ranging in weight from 110 to 158 grains. Several excellent revolvers are available for this cartridge,

Gun right and below is the same with interchangeable barrels in .41 magnum, having started life as a M28 S&W in .357 magnum. It's a conversion done by Leon Smith, Box 773, Redding, CA 96001 on the N-frame S&W, offering nearly any choice of caliber, length.

Big and burly but beautiful: Ruger's stainless steel Redhawk in .44 magnum.

The plus-pressure or +P loads, such as one here at left, develop about 22,400 pounds compared to 18,900 for standard load. The +P should only be used in guns designed to handle the added pressure.

An outstanding example in compact capability in S&W's Model 36 Chiefs Special in caliber .38 Special. Its cylinder is chambered for five shots. It can be had with barrels of two inches, as here, or in three-inch length.

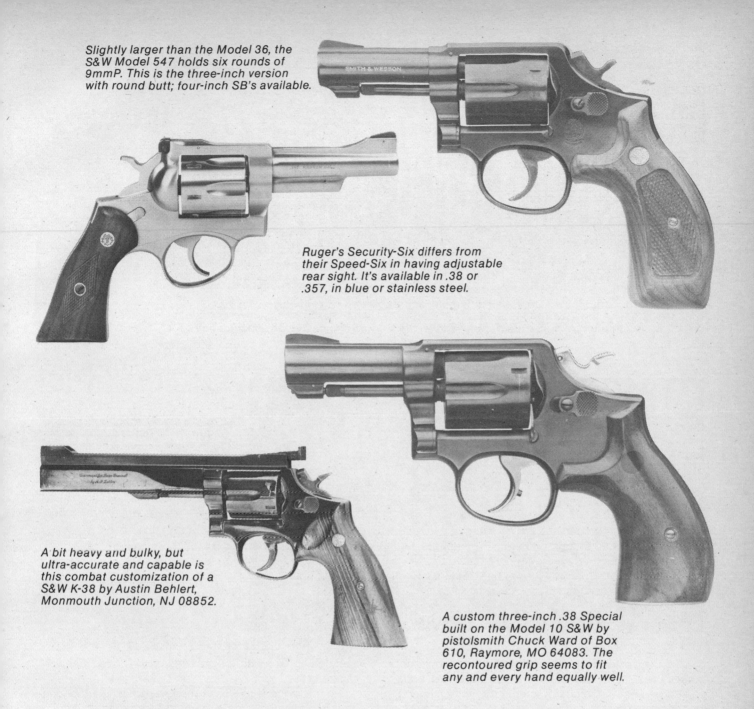

Slightly larger than the Model 36, the S&W Model 547 holds six rounds of 9mmP. This is the three-inch version with round butt; four-inch SB's available.

Ruger's Security-Six differs from their Speed-Six in having adjustable rear sight. It's available in .38 or .357, in blue or stainless steel.

A bit heavy and bulky, but ultra-accurate and capable is this combat customization of a S&W K-38 by Austin Behlert, Monmouth Junction, NJ 08852.

A custom three-inch .38 Special built on the Model 10 S&W by pistolsmith Chuck Ward of Box 610, Raymore, MO 64083. The recontoured grip seems to fit any and every hand equally well.

Military ammo usually carries a headstamp giving only the maker and year of manufacture such as the one at right: Western Cartridge Co./1941.

including such examples as the S&W Model 19. Colt Python, Ruger's Security-Six and Speed-Six or the Dan Wesson Arms Model 14-2.

A feature of possibly special interest of the Model 14-2 DWA is its ability to substitute barrels of various lengths, from two up to eight inches or more, quickly and simply. For good measure, the grips can also be changed by loosening the single holding screw. using the tool provided with the gun. Front sights are available with rear inserts in red, yellow or white, likewise readily replaceable to make the DWA outstanding in terms of versatility. DWA also offers a .44 magnum revolver with the same assortment of barrels and stocks — barrels in lengths of four, six, eight and ten inches — and may bring forth a .41 magnum version of the present .44 design.

A fairly large number of .44 magnum revolvers are said

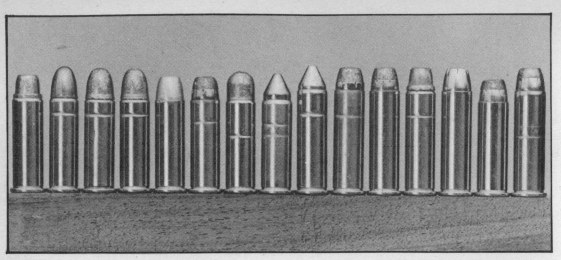

The first eight cartridges above are all different loadings offered by Winchester in .38 Special, with six .357 magnum loads and one more .38 Special. Great popularity of these two cartridges gets a lot of attention from manufacturers, resulting in a broad choice of load specifications.

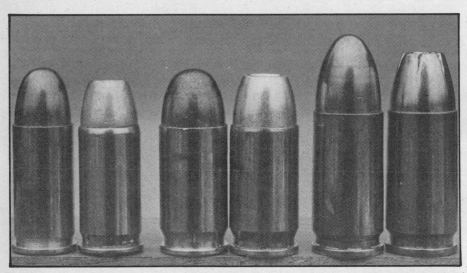

The round nose FMJ bullets tend to feed quite well, but are deficient in stopping capabilities. Hollow point bullets such as these in Winchester loads for .32 ACP, .380 ACP and 9mmP usually feed with little or no problems, meanwhile expanding well.

to have been sold only to be returned for refund or trade on something smaller, with only a few, or perhaps just a single round fired out of the box of ammunition purchased with the revolver. That is by way of noting it's rather more revolver than many prospective shooters feel they need. The recoil and report of the .44 magnum are — to understate somewhat — substantial. Highly publicized by a couple of Clint Eastwood films a few years back, the Model 29 S&W revolver was in such demand that it was difficult to find for sale and usually premium-priced well above the maker's suggested retail figure. It can be stated with assurance that the .44 magnum is not the ideal revolver for every shooter.

The .41 magnum, on the other hand, comes close to the ultimate compromise between the .357 and .44 magnums. The .41 magnum is at its best when using judiciously prepared reloaded ammunition, since the available factory loads leave something to be desired. The dimensional difference between the .41 and .44 magnum is small but noteworthy by the fact that in the same frame the .41 will deliver a much larger number of rounds without getting

battered out of condition in the manner of all too many .44 magnum revolvers.

To this point we've been discussing handguns as contrasted to shoulder guns or — to use the more familiar terms — shotguns and rifles. Long guns, as they are also termed, are not as convenient to carry, nor as quick to bring into use, but they offer certain points of superiority over handguns amply sufficient to merit serious consideration.

That's by way of saying that none of the three basic types of firearms has a clearcut advantage over either of the other two. Ideally speaking, it is preferable to have one or more of each at your disposal, each selected from among the available makes and models with the shrewdest possible comparison of performance capabilities. We've devoted some amount of space to handguns. Let's look at the advantages of rifles and shotguns.

The shotgun discharges a quantity of small spherical projectiles called shot pellets. These are fired through a smoothbore barrel (one without rifling). Upon leaving the muzzle the pellets commence to spread in directions perpendicular to the line of fire or axis of the bore. As the dis-

Shot Sizes

•	•	•
No. 12	No. 11	No. 10
.05	.06	.07
2459	1422	895
•	•	•
No. 9	No. 8	No. 7½
.08	.09	.095
605	422	359
●	●	●
No. 7	No. 6	No. 5
.10	.11	.12
307	231	172
●	●	●
No. 4	No. 3	No. 2
.13	.14	.15
135	108	90
●	●	●
Air Rifle	BB	No. 4 Buck
.175	.18	.24
55	50	340 (lb.)
●	●	●
No. 3 Buck	No. 1 Buck	No. 0 Buck
.25	.30	.32
299 (lb.)	152 (lb.)	144 (lb.)
	●	●
	No. 00 Buck	No. 000 Buck
	.34	.36
	128 (lb.)	112 (lb.)

Taracorp Industries, producers of Lawrence Brand shot, supplied the chart of shot sizes at left. From Nos. 12 to 2, each whole number increases pellet diameter by .01-inch. Weight through BB size is given in pellets per ounce, above that per pound.

tance increases, the diameter of the circle of pellet distribution enlarges in approximate proportion. In typical examples, at forty yards most of the pellets will be fairly uniformly distributed across a circle about thirty inches in diameter.

The virtue of that should be obvious. From the forty-yard distance, even if the aim is off by fifteen inches, there's still a good chance of scoring one or more hits. Each time the trigger is pulled to fire, the shotgun puts out a cone of effect rather than a single point.

Shotgun pellets come in many different sizes, as shown on the accompanying chart, ranging up to respectable diameter and weight. It is purely a matter of compromise and trade-off. You can fire a load of #9 shot, for example, and launch a thick cloud of tiny pellets. In that example, no single pellet carries a large amount of energy and atmospheric resistance reduces their velocity quite rapidly. In the larger sizes of buckshot loadings there may be as few as nine pellets, capable of holding a lot more velocity and energy over a much longer distance, but they do not deliver

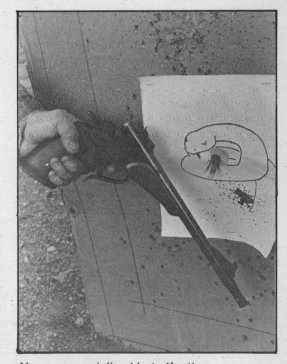

Above, a specialized but effective handgun is the Thompson/Center Contender with shot barrel. Test pattern was from six feet. Left, although not reloadable, the CCI Blazer load in .357 magnum is exceptionally powerful in delivery.

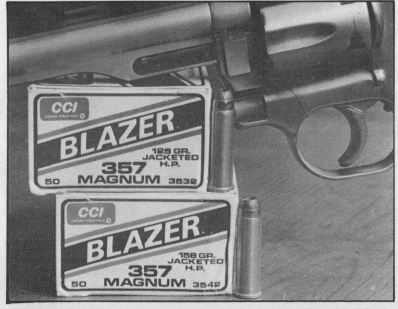

A scope sight on a shotgun? Yes, it's quite practical with Weaver's mount for Remington's Model 870 (here) or 1100, when firing slug loads such as the hollow point by Remington, below.

General Julian S. Hatcher has termed its close-in wound effect as a "bloody rat hole," and the description cannot be faulted. At such distances the size of the shot pellets makes little or no difference. At distances considerably greater than that the shotgun remains a most decisive resolver of differences in opinion and conflicts of interest. It is difficult to set a precise limit for the overall effectiveness of the

"Night Guide," from Bullshooter's Supply, Box 13446, Tucson, AZ 85732, fastens to ribless shotgun barrels and has a small switch on the bottom. When pushed forward, it energizes a tiny LED unit for night aiming.

the close-spaced density of a load with the smaller pellets.

Likewise available for use in shotguns is the slug load, firing a single projectile and putting the picture back to that of handguns and rifles. These deliver an impressively potent punch — at moderate range — but to one point only. Slug loads enable a shotgun to do things that most rifles do considerably better.

At close range — say within fifteen feet or so — the shotgun is one of the most awesomely effective weapons that can be carried, held and fired by a single person. Major

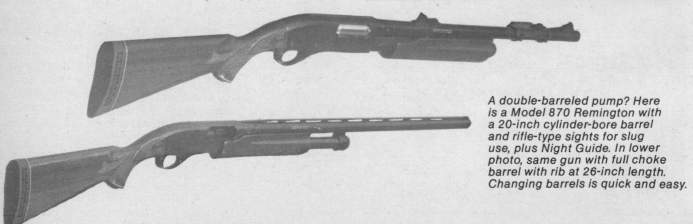

A double-barreled pump? Here is a Model 870 Remington with a 20-inch cylinder-bore barrel and rifle-type sights for slug use, plus Night Guide. In lower photo, same gun with full choke barrel with rib at 26-inch length. Changing barrels is quick and easy.

Remington's Model 1100 LT-20 Limited is a 20-gauge auto proportioned for youth and small adults. In shotguns, a correct fit is of great importance. Below, the spreading pattern of the shotgun from a distance of 25 yards.

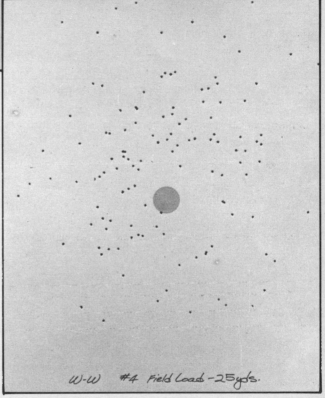

W-W #4 Field Load -25yds.

shotgun, but mindful of several interlocking factors such as diameter of bore, size and diameter of pellets and the like, the limit could be expected to fall within sixty to one hundred yards. Even the slug loads cannot be delivered with satisfactory accuracy much beyond the latter distance, although they are still quite hazardous to encounter at that range.

Shotguns are to be had in several variations. At the most basic level, there is the break-open single-shot. There have been and may still be a few shotguns built around the bolt-action system so successful in rifles. Two distinct types of double-barrel shotguns remain in production: the over/under and side-by-side, with the terms in obvious reference to the positioning of the two barrels.

Repeating shotguns, as opposed to the singles and doubles, fire three or more rounds without need to reload. Examples of these include the pump-action, sometimes called the slide-action, together with the autoloaders or automatic or self-loading shotguns.

The pump shotgun — as we'll call it for this discussion — is actuated manually. After firing, a grasping area on the forend is pulled rearward to eject the spent shell or hull

RIG 2 and RIG 3, from RIG Products, 87 Coney Island Dr., Sparks, NV 89431, are excellent for applying protective coating of lube, or for removing it.

and, upon being pushed back forward, a fresh shell is moved from the magazine into the chamber.

The auto shotgun utilizes the force of recoil or diverted powder gas to perform the same operations. A disconnector system prevents the auto shotgun from firing more than a single round at each pull of the trigger. After firing, you allow the trigger to move forward, then pull it again for the next shot.

A practiced shooter, accustomed to the use of the pump shotgun, can fire it as rapidly and with as good effect as the auto; perhaps even a trifle faster. The shooter of lesser attainment may do better with the auto, although the self-loader still needs to be aimed, the same as any other gun. Incorrectly aimed, any shotgun is rampantly capable of missing the intended target, as uncountable hordes of trap and skeet shooters can profanely attest.

If the quality of the ammunition is more or less dubious — a by-no-means-impossible state of affairs — the pump shotgun is usefully more capable of reliable operation than is the autoloader. If the shell fires at all, it's a fairly simple matter to work the action of a pump and put a fresh load in

The common sizes of shotshells: From left, standard and magnum 10-gauge; magnum and standard 12-gauge; 16-gauge; magnum and standard 20-gauge; 28-gauge; magnum and standard .410-bore. Most makers color the 20-gauge loads yellow for positive identification.

A 122-grain "Spelunker" bullet in .38 size from S&S Precision Bullets, Box 1133, San Juan Capistrano, CA 92693. Above, before and after firing. Below, cavity cast of .38 Special Spelunker in Duxseal.

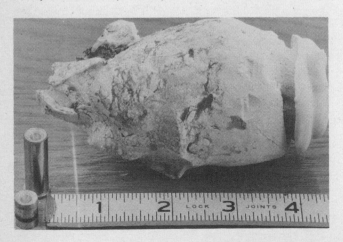

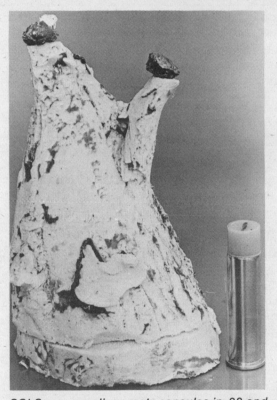

CCI-Speer supplies empty capsules in .38 and .44 size for making up shot loads. This is the cast of a cavity in stiff clay left by three #1 buck pellets from Taracorp, flattened slightly and loaded in capsule of a .357 magnum cartridge.

the chamber. In the same conditions, an auto shotgun may encounter a stoppage or jam and the tactical disadvantage of that in a trying situation is clearly apparent.

Shotguns come in several sizes, of which the 12-gauge is overwhelmingly the most popular. The bore diameter of the 12-gauge is about .729-inch and twelve pure lead balls of that diameter weigh one pound, hence the designation. Twenty lead balls the diameter of a 20-gauge shotgun bore weigh one pound, and so on. Hence, the smaller the gauge number, the larger the bore diameter. An exception to the system is the .410-bore shotgun with its bore diameter of

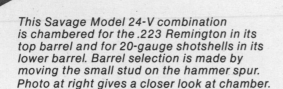

This Savage Model 24-V combination is chambered for the .223 Remington in its top barrel and for 20-gauge shotshells in its lower barrel. Barrel selection is made by moving the small stud on the hammer spur. Photo at right gives a closer look at chamber.

.410-inch, which would be about a 67-gauge in the usual method of designating such things.

The largest shotgun bore in use today is the 10-gauge and they are not at all common. Besides it and the 12-gauge, we have the 16-, 20- and 28-gauges, plus the .410-bore mentioned earlier. The standard length for the 10-gauge shell is 2⅞ inches and there is a magnum version measuring 3½ inches in length. The 12, 20 and .410 are also available in standard and magnum shell lengths, the latter three inches and the standard 2¾ inches for the 12 and 20, 2½ inches for the .410 bore.

It should be emphasized that magnum shotshells should be fired only in guns specifically chambered for their use and marked accordingly on the side of the barrel. Many such shotguns are chambered for exclusive use of the standard-length shell and firing of a magnum shell in such guns is quite apt to blow up the barrel; an extremely hazardous occurrence.

Another potential hazard that needs noting is that the pump shotgun — or at least *some* pump shotguns — will fire if the trigger is held back as the shell is fed into the chamber. Such designs enable a rapid rate of fire, which is fine, but the dangers of firing inadvertently are obvious, if the state of affairs is not known and understood. Some pump designs will not fire as the action is closed and the only prudent way to find out, one way or the other, is to make certain there are no shells in the magazine, then work the action with the trigger pressed rearward, making certain to keep the muzzle pointed in a safe direction.

Since the walls of a shotgun barrel are comparatively thin, such guns are quite vulnerable to any blockage or foreign material in the bore, if fired. A bit of mud or snow inside the muzzle can cause serious damage to the barrel, and perhaps to the shooter or bystanders.

Laws of this country forbid the use of shotguns with barrels of less than eighteen inches in length, or rifles with barrels less than sixteen inches long. Barrels shorter than that require special documentation and paperwork from the government. The minimum overall length for rifles or shotguns is 26½ inches.

The usual shotgun barrel length ranges from twenty to thirty-six inches, with twenty-six or twenty-eight inches the usual length. If the bore is of uniform diameter from chamber to muzzle the shotgun barrel is termed **cylinder bore.** Most shotgun barrels have some varying amount of constriction at the muzzle to redirect the shot charge into tighter patterns, thus increasing their effective range somewhat. The mild constriction is termed **improved cylinder, modified** or **full choke,** and the designation stamped in the barrel may appear as *CYL, IMP, MOD,* or *FULL.* Some shotgun barrels have an adjustable collet device at the muzzle to permit changing the choke as desired and others have screw-in choke tubes that can be changed to produce the desired degree of pattern tightness.

Most pump and auto shotguns are sold with a "plug" in the magazine to restrict its capacity to two shells, thus providing a three-shot capability; this is in line with federal laws governing the hunting of migratory waterfowl. Typically such designs have an actual magazine capacity of four or perhaps five rounds, with the option of carrying an extra shell in the chamber. The plug can be removed to provide increased magazine capacity, but that modification may not be legal in some jurisdictions during normal times. If you remove the magazine plug, or have it removed by a gunsmith, it is well to make certain you are not in violation of local law in so doing.

Some manufacturers offer combination guns of the break-open action design in which rifle barrel is superposed

Here's a GI carbine that has been fitted with a scope mount from Ranch Products, Box 14, Malinta, OH 43535 and a Bushnell Centurion scope with the 2.5X Booster lens up front, vastly improving its groups.

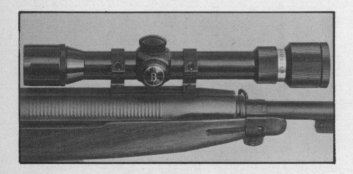

Above, a closer look at the Bushnell sight and its ingenious mount. Below, a pair of "banana clips" for the GI carbine taped together for quick changes.

Caliber .30 GI carbine is almost the exact size of a cigarette butt and some rate it as not a lot deadlier, but use of soft point or hollow point bullet — in load at right — improves its effect slightly.

above a shotgun barrel with some manner of selector device to enable firing of either barrel. In theory at least, this provides the best of both worlds: the spreading pattern of the shotgun or the long-range accuracy of the rifle. In actual practice it is rather rare to find that the rifle barrel is capable of accuracy approaching that of a good conventional rifle, and the potential performance of the shotgun barrel may not be quite up to the best of the scattergun breed. That's by way of noting it is a compromise and, as with most such, some amount of charitable allowance must be made. If you are willing to make such concessions the combination gun may be found to have useful merits, but don't expect miracles of them or you may be disappointed.

A further variant of repeating shotgun design is the lever-action, rather more commonly encountered in rifles

and so seldom seen in shotguns of modern times as to justify mention solely for the sake of completeness.

The field of rifles worthy of the survivalist's consideration is approximately as broad and bewildering as that of the handgun. Rifles with comparatively short barrels — sixteen to twenty inches — usually are termed carbines. Few rifles have barrels much longer than twenty-six inches. All other conditions equal, the longer barrel usually delivers a higher velocity in rifles, although that is not necessarily true in shotguns. Depending somewhat upon the characteristics of the loaded shotshell, an extremely long shotgun barrel may deliver less velocity as the powder charge burns out, due to friction of the charge and wad within the barrel. A similar effect prevails in .22 rimfire rifles since the ammunition for those usually carries a powder charge designed to give top performance in lengths from sixteen to twenty inches.

Typical action designs for rifles include the break-open single-shot, the bolt-action, the pump, the autoloader and the lever-action. Of these the high-quality bolt-action usually is capable of the finest accuracy, at some slight sacrifice in rate of fire. Some of the rimfire autoloaders have magazine capacities that can only be termed prodigious: up to as many as 177 cartridges at a single loading, with the

Two pistols in 9mmP derived from the Sterling submachine gun in use throughout the British Commonwealth and other places. These fire but one shot per pull of the trigger, not full-auto. The shortened magazine holds ten rounds.

butt, with a caliber .30 (.308-inch) bullet of about 110 grains at velocities around 2000 fps, usually somewhat less than that. It is a gas-operated autoloader, usually fitted with a box-type magazine holding fifteen cartridges. It's fairly common practice to tape two magazines end-to-end so as to provide fast access to a second hopperful. Auxiliary magazines of larger capacity have been offered and, if used, their reliability needs to be verified in a thoughtful and careful manner. It should be noted that the same applies to extra-capacity magazines for autoloading pistols. Not all such devices function with the stolid reliability one might wistfully envision.

The GI carbine is quite widely distributed. A vast number were sold by the government and a great many more have been manufactured and sold by commercial firms. You can obtain assorted accessories such as folding stocks or stocks with pistol-type foregrips in the casual image of the Thompson submachine gun, and many other variants. At the bottom line you're still working with the same little cartridge of rather modest power, which needs everything going for it that can possibly be supplied. Even then its adequacy can and has been debated. The load with the round-nosed, full metal jacket bullet is painfully marginal in stopping power.

At the next step upward in cartridge power we find the 5.56mm NATO round, often termed the .223 Remington currently used by the armed forces of many countries, including this one. Its typical performance is on the order of up to 3200 fps for a 55-grain bullet and, given a projectile capable of expansion upon impact, its effectiveness is entirely creditable. A number of autoloading rifles are offered for the 5.56mm as well as other designs such as the bolt-action or break-open single-shot. Its accuracy in a quality bolt-action rifle is often outstanding; an observation that can hardly be made on the .30 GI carbine round with much pretense of a straight face.

The lever-action carbine, as exemplified by the Model

option to slam on a fully loaded spare drum and keep up the good work. The precise practicality of such an approach can be debated, and has been. In other examples, some manufacturers offer fifty-shot magazines for use with the Ruger Model 10/22, in place of the ten-shot magazine furnished by the manufacturer.

Moving up — slightly — to the field of center-fire cartridges, we come to the fairly familiar GI carbine that saw wide if sometimes frustrating use in WWII. It fires a small cartridge, approximately the size and shape of a cigarette

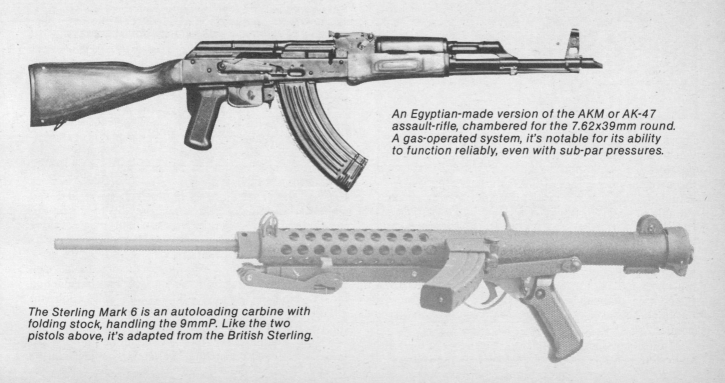

An Egyptian-made version of the AKM or AK-47 assault-rifle, chambered for the 7.62x39mm round. A gas-operated system, it's notable for its ability to function reliably, even with sub-par pressures.

The Sterling Mark 6 is an autoloading carbine with folding stock, handling the 9mmP. Like the two pistols above, it's adapted from the British Sterling.

Wilkinson Arms' "Linda" 9mmP pistol fires from a closed bolt with outstanding accuracy, holds thirty-one rounds in its magazine and can be fitted with a scope, such as this one by Bushnell.

From Interdynamics, a pair of assault pistols: KG-99 at left, firing from a closed bolt. Front grip is an optional accessory and may require registration as a short-rifle. The KG-9 at right fires from an open bolt, making any pretense of accuracy quite hopeless.

Trying the KG-9 on silhouettes, even at this short range, proved discouraging. It made little difference if sights were used. Jolt of the bolt slamming forward threw muzzle every which-way. Shooter below shows favored way to hold the magazine. If thumb is wrapped to the rear, it's apt to release magazine.

Below left, from left, the 5.56mm NATO aka .223 Remington; 7.62mm NATO or .308 Winchester and the .30/06 Springfield. At right, Remington's novel Accelerator .30/06 load carrying caliber .22 bullet is shown with standard round. The Accelerator is capable of extremely high velocity, good accuracy.

Ruger Model 77 Varmint
Model in .22-250 or .25/06.

Ruger Standard Carbine,
in .44 Remington magnum.

Remington Model 788, in .222 Remington,
with Weaver T-6 scope; a real tackdriver!

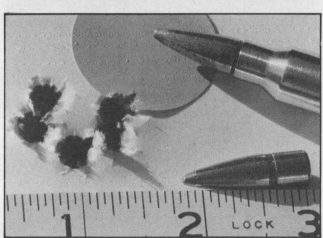

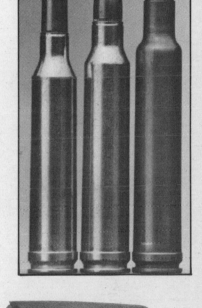

Left, a Winchester
Model 70 in .300 Win
mag, with scope by
Carl Zeiss. Left
below, a group from
the Model 70 at 100
yards. Right, from
left, 7mm Rem mag,
.300 Win mag and
.300 Weatherby mag.

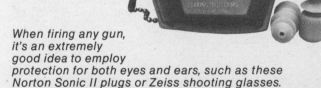

When firing any gun,
it's an extremely
good idea to employ
protection for both eyes and ears, such as these
Norton Sonic II plugs or Zeiss shooting glasses.

94 Winchester in caliber .30-30 Winchester Center-Fire
(WCF) is a moderately formidable affair, so long as cartridges remain in its tubular magazine, but it is painfully
slow and cumbersome when the time comes to replenish
the supply. It should be emphasized that tubular magazines
require cartridges loaded with bullets having flat tips to
bypass the severe hazard of setting off a chain explosion
when a pointed bullet tip is driven against the primer of the
cartridge ahead of it. Although regarded as small cheese in
the company of rifle cartridges, the .30-30 WCF usually
delivers power, accuracy and "reach" excelling that of the
legendary .44 magnum in handguns, which may provide
useful perspective and food for thought.

Two photos above are purely for illustration and no firing was done! Circled area in photo at left indicates the highway sign and view at right is through the scope showing ease of aim.

Powder for reloading is sold in small cans such as the one at right. Primers are sold in "decks" of 100/cartons of 1000. Consult a loading manual or handbook to determine proper type of primer or powder to use.

Center-fire cases, such as these in 9mmP, can be reloaded many times at an attractive saving in cost. Much the same applies to shotshell hulls, as below.

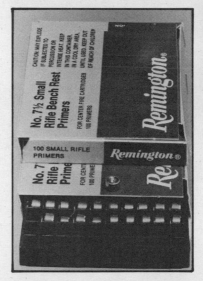

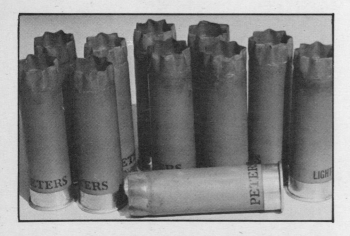

ticularly as to overall length. For that reason the .308 Winchester is the cartridge most apt to be encountered as the shopper's attention shifts to larger sizes. Its major virtue is that it's capable of getting through hard targets that can be expected to resist smaller cartridges such as the .223 Remington round. If that seems relevant, you might package up sixty rounds or so of each cartridge and heft the two containers meditatively, contemplating the prospect of packing rifle, ammunition and a lot of other vital gear over difficult terrain. It could help you arrive at a sound decision.

It should be noted that suitable protection for eyes and ears should be used in the routine firing of any firearm, including handguns. It may not always be possible or prac-

Widely used by the armed forces during the first half of this century, the .30/06 Springfield cartridge remains undeniably capable, but in latter years it has been superseded to a considerable extent by the 7.62mm NATO round, commonly termed the .308 Winchester. The latter, operating at somewhat higher peak pressures, can drive bullets of any given weight to about the same velocities as the .30/06 and has the useful virtue of being somewhat less bulky, par-

Lyman "Orange Crusher" reloading press, C-clamped to a small stand. Right, using C-H Junior Champ and RCBS Uniflow rotary powder measure.

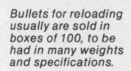

Bullets for reloading usually are sold in boxes of 100, to be had in many weights and specifications.

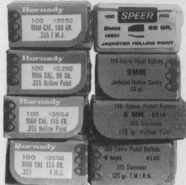

Above, RCBS "Green Machine" is a progressive loader, here for .38 Special, capable of producing reloads in quantity at a highly respectable rate. Right, an overall view of the stand at top of page, carrying the C-H Junior Champ loading press.

Speer's 200-grain JHP for the .45 ACP, also known as the "Flying Ashtray," expands as at left, even at moderate velocities, 859 fps from Detonics, here.

Compact, lightweight and competent, this three-station turret press by Lee Precision costs well under $100, all fitted and ready to put to work.

Three Lawrence Brand #1 buck in each of the Speer shot capsules turned this Ruger Security-Six into a Security-Eighteen. This group was fired at 7 yards.

Two fired bullets from a .45 ACP: FMJ at right is almost capable of being fired again, while the soft point at right made greater amount of fuss on impact.

ticable to rummage about for shooting glasses or earmuffs at a time of dire emergency, but there is no excuse to neglect such sensible precautions when engaged in test firing or practice. The report of firearms is critically damaging to hearing sensitivity and, in firing, there is the ever-present danger that small particles of powder residue or bullet shavings can be driven rearward at high velocities.

The same chart previously quoted from *Gun Digest* lists typical retail prices for handgun ammunition and provides compelling persuasion for the benefits of being able to reload center-fire ammunition. It is not possible — or at least it's enormously impractical — to reload rimfire cartridges such as the .22 long rifle. The most expensive item that goes to make up a center-fire cartridge is its brass case and, after firing, that remains virtually as good as new, capable of being reloaded and fired many additional times at a gratifying saving in cost.

At the same time, the tactical advantages, from the viewpoint of the survivalist, in being able to resurrect fired cartridge cases are almost painfully obvious. A few decks of primers, a can or three of powder and a supply of bullets are all you need, in addition to the basic press or loading kit. While some reloading presses are manifestly unsuited

THE COMPLETE SURVIVAL GUIDE

Considered by many to be the best cast bullet for .45 ACP, these are from #68 mould out of Hensley & Gibbs, Box 10, Murphy, OR 97533; weigh 190 grains.

Reloading the 9mmP is a bit of a challenge, since many of the loads call for enough powder to fill the case level-full, calling for care in seating the bullet.

Here's a four-cavity Hensley & Gibbs mould for their #264, an excellent performer in 9mm or, if sized to .358-inch, in .38 Spl.

to backpacking and the like, others are lighter, more compact and some will even fit comfortably in a pocket of generous size.

It is likewise possible and practical to make your own bullets, usually by means of melting a suitable alloy of lead, antimony and tin to pour into moulds made for the purpose; casting, as it's termed. Such cast bullets must be sized and lubricated before being reloaded or, at the very least, must be lubricated lest they foul the bore of the gun atrociously.

The making of bullets and the reloading of ammunition — for shotguns as well as rifles or pistols — is an undertaking too complex to make any reasonable pretext of adequate coverage in the space available. The publisher of the book at hand, however, has several other titles that deal with the topics in comprehensive detail, including *ABC's Of Reloading, Metallic Cartridge Reloading,* and *Reloading For Shotgunners.* It is suggested that the interested reader refer to these or similar works for the full particulars of that absorbing and rewarding activity.

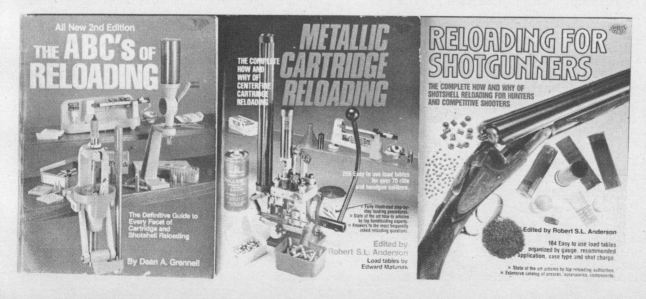

WHICH HANDGUN FOR YOU?

Consider Accuracy, Range, Signaling Value And Your Choices Are Made Easier

By Claud S. Hamilton

NOPE. This is not another of those exhortations to get you to drop everything and go hole up in a woods cabin 'til the "coming upheaval" has blown over. No, it's just that something happened to me a while back that got me to thinking. It wasn't very serious, as it turned out, but it could have been.

Last summer while on a flying trip out West, I had an afternoon free and a surprise invitation from my good host to photograph unusual rock formations in the mountains near Colorado Springs. My host knew of my special interest in unusual geological examples. He couldn't take time off to go with me, but insisted I take his '73 Buick station wagon and provided an excellent sketch map to get me to the spot.

I was delighted to fill in the time and readily accepted. In no time, it seemed, I was well out of town and climbing fast. The road soon lost its paving and became a one-track trail...it was only marginally worthy of that name by the time I found the rocks. They were well worth the trip. I got my pictures then paused briefly to think of the reactions of the first white men when they saw these mountains.

Enough daydreaming. I packed my gear, loaded it and headed for the motel — or rather, I tried to. The Buick wouldn't start. It wasn't the battery, it just wouldn't turn over. That wagon was far too big to push and I'd managed to stop on the one piece of level trail in miles.

For 'bout half an hour I tried everything within my limited mechanical ability. I tried to rock the starter loose, but it didn't seem to be caught, anyway. I found an old screwdriver and tried to bypass the starter, but that failed, too. The one other thing I found in the wagon was an old 1917 Army Smith & Wesson .45 revolver and eighteen cartridges.

Here I was, only a few miles from civilization, but very

Value of handgun in survival situations depends primarily upon its value in getting small game for food. Martha Penso uses stump for support.

hard mountain miles, with no food or water and no means of communication. Luckily, at that time of year weather was no problem. Walking out would not have been easy for a youngster, but for an arthritic old typewriter pounder like me? Forget it!

My first thought was for water, but that didn't worry me much. I've never seen it hard to find in mountains like these. Then I began to wonder seriously what animals I might be able to kill with the old revolver.

That's as far as it got, for to my eternal delight a forest

Off Ransom Rest at 100 yards, .41 mag shot well, but is harder to shoot accurately due to big recoil.

Old .45 Colt Government model proved unsuitable for hunting out to 100 yards due to excessive bullet drop.

This is the Python .357 revolver author tested as a survival arm. Results of his tests are in text.

ranger pulled up behind the Buick and asked if I was having any trouble. Bless those rangers! He had me out of there in no time. Three hours later I was savoring a Tanqueray martini in the motel lounge and pondering "what might have been..." It was a brief but memorable experience, and I don't think I shall ever let myself be caught like that again.

That's what started me thinking about handguns and survival. I'm no handgun hunter. When I hunt or when I think there is a danger — I might accidentally find myself between a sow bear and her cub — I take a rifle along. For me, anything any handgun can do in the woods a rifle can do better. When I take a handgun on a trip it's because I'm concerned about trouble with humans.

How, I began to wonder, would a handgun be most useful in a survival situation? Obviously to put small game in the pot, but I think there's more. Some places we travel there are still dangerous animals like bear, and there's always the possibility of encountering the rare rabid beast. These can be vicious and dangerous. Finally, there's the matter of signaling to attract the attention of searchers.

Talking to friends who frequently carry a handgun on trips for the same reason I do, I reached the conclusion that not many have considered the survival potential of the guns they carry. Here are their favorites: Model 10 .38 Special S&W Revolver, four-inch; Model 39 9mm S&W Pistol; Colt Python .357 magnum, six-inch; Model 57 .41 magnum S&W Revolver, four-inch; Model 29 .44 magnum S&W Revolver, 6½-inch; and Government Model Colt .45 Auto Colt Pistol.

I managed to borrow the lot and with a friend, Martha Penso, I took them out to the range to see what we could discover. On the way we talked over what we were after and decided on three main points: How could each gun group at, say, one hundred yards? Was each practical for use at such a range? How did they compare for use as signaling guns at different distances?

First we set up the Ransom Rest on the upper bench range on one of the heavy, firmly anchored tables. Our target consisted of large sheets of plain poster paper mounted on wide rifle target frames. On these I drew a heavy, black Magic Marker line horizontally to serve as a series of aiming points. As we tested each gun we moved the point of aim from left to right along the line. This way the groups were recorded and we measured the amount of "holdover" needed in inches as well. Results are in the accompanying chart.

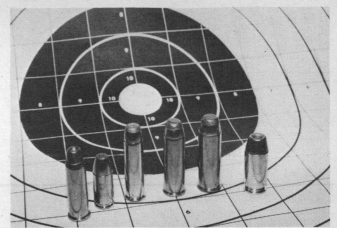
Cartridges tested were (from left): .38 Special lead hollow point, 9mm JHP, .357 magnum JHP, .41 magnum JSP, .44 magnum JSP, and .45 ACP 185-gr JHP.

This turned out to be a revealing shoot. It convinced me that the .38 Special and the .45 Colt Government Model are not for game at one hundred yards — holdover is just too great and neither gun has adjustable sights. The remaining handguns do have sights which can be "zeroed" for this long range because of their smaller holdover.

Considering the species of small game likely to be available brought us to other conclusions. Consider the size of the vulnerable areas offered by such game: If the gun cannot group within that space off the Ransom Rest, it's foolish to

Surprisingly small groups were shot by the author and companion at 100-yard range with Model 39 Smith & Wesson in 9mm. It scored groups of 6½ inches.

Gun	Ammunition	Average Group (inches)	Holdover (inches)
S&W Model 10 .38 Special	Winchester-Western 158-grain lead HP +P)	6	19
S&W Model 39 9mm Pistol	Federal 115-grain JHP	6½	14
Colt Python .357 magnum	CCI/Speer 140-grain JHP	5	7
S&W Model 57 .41 magnum	Remington-Peters 210-grain JHP	7	9
S&W Model 29 .44 magnum	Remington-Peters 240-grain JSP	7½	8½
Colt Gov't Model .45 ACP	Remington-Peters 185-grain JHP	9½	22

Equipped with a walkie-talkie, Martha listens to sounds of handguns in the distance to rate their relative abilities to aid searchers in the woods.

With the .45 Government Colt, you'd have to hold over this twenty-two inches at 100 yards to score a kill. Such accuracy isn't impossible — but dang remarkable!

expect you can kill except by pure, dumb luck. Here are the vulnerable areas in inches we calculated for the common small game one might encounter: squirrel, three-by-one; pigeon, four-by-two; rabbit, six-by-four; pheasant, seven-by-four; turkey, nine-by-six; and deer, twelve-by-twelve. You can argue about these estimates all day, but I think they come reasonably close — close enough to convince me that nothing smaller than turkey ought to be attempted at one-hundred-yard ranges, and then only with the .41 and .44 magnums. You could possibly use the .357 magnum out to perhaps sixty to seventy-five yards. My gut feeling is that the .357 magnum as factory loaded today is marginal in killing power on game such as deer. (Time was when the .357 had hair on its chest. I have today some old commercial ammunition dating from before the Korean War that cobs a 158-grain lead semi-wadcuter out of a six-inch Smith Model 27 at 1550 feet per second [fps]!)

This logically brings up the question of ammunition. Game, pound for pound, takes a bit more killing than man, and you usually get that penetration in modern handgun loads by using soft points rather than hollow points. Something to keep in mind in trip planning.

I'm speaking of handguns equipped only with metal sights, not scoped hunters' guns. Over the years of this century, handgun iron sights have gone through a period of evolution from thin front blades and corresponding rear notches to today's broad one-tenth-inch blades. This was

A view of the 100-yard target (left) used to collect groups and measure the holdover needed for each gun.

96

done to meet the requirements of defensive handgun shooters who needed to be able to pick up the sights quickly and recover them again quickly for repeat shots.

Unfortunately for the man in a survival situation, the result has been that it becomes very hard to hold these broad front sights accurately enough to hit a small game target at long ranges. For a person of normal conformation holding a gun at arm's length on a rest, the front sight may cover six to eight inches at one hundred yards! The way I deal with this is to use the left edge of the front blade as though it were a vertical crosshair and center the target on that. It helps, but it also moves the center of impact of my hits to the right by an amount I have to discover for each gun I shoot. For those having adjustable sights this is easy to compensate. For the iron-sight service guns you just have to learn Kentucky windage.

Of course, if the nature of the cover and stalking possibilities make it obvious that you'll have to depend on seventy-five and one-hundred-yard shots, and if ammunition is available, I'd go ahead and zero my gun in for, say, seventy-five yards. Usually the quantity of handgun ammunition carried on a trip is pretty small.

As far as dangerous game is concerned, for me that puts the emphasis on fast gun handling, which means a gun that

I am used to and can use well. If I live to be a hundred I shall never forget one rabid fox I came upon on a hunting trip. We ended up beating the little fellow to death with rifle butts. Were I to face that situation again with a handgun, I'd opt for the Colt Python in .357 magnum. For me, it combines the needed power and accuracy with the ease of handling I need for fast, effective shooting.

The matter of signaling is a new one for me, and I'd never given it much thought. We decided that Martha would backtrack from the range, radio in hand, and make a record of the relative strengths of the reports of the various guns as I shot them. We wanted to see at what point they would catch the attention of searchers. We did this on two different days to see differences wind variations might make.

Signaling value seems a direct function of power. The guns ranked uniformly for each station: the .38 Special and the 9mm, the .357 magnum and .45 ACP, and finally the .41 and .44 magnums in increasing order of "strength of signal." As one might logically expect, on quiet, windless days the signal value was best. Almost any wind, even from the shooter toward the searcher, managed to distort the signal to some extent. What we learned is shown in the accompanying chart.

HANDGUN SIGNAL VALUE

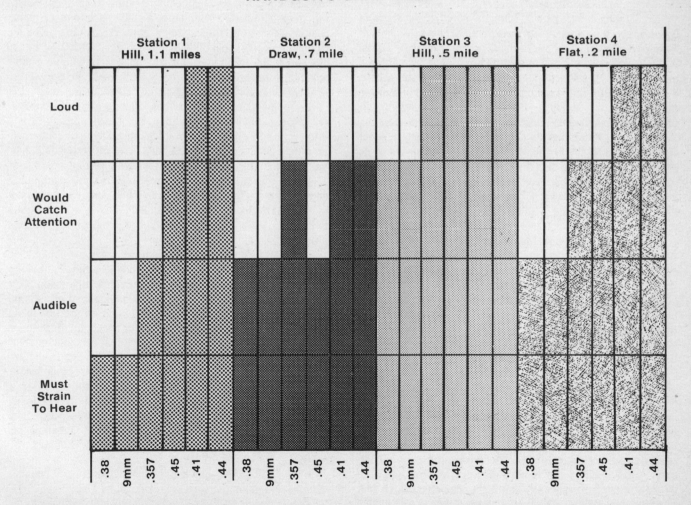

SHOTGUN OR HANDGUN FOR HOME DEFENSE

Research Led Author — And Others — To Conclude Shotgun Is Best

By Gerald FitzGerald

AN EVER-INCREASING number of law-abiding Americans are buying firearms for personal and home defense. Many have never bought or considered buying a firearm before. But their concerns over rising crime rates or possible disintegration of law enforcement in a survival situation prompt them to seek self-protection. They aren't interested in offensive armament — only in preserving what they've had the foresight to stockpile.

But what firearm is best? This section will look at factors involved with selection of a defensive firearm. Many will have personal opinions about the type firearm "best" suited for the purpose outlined, and most will vote for a handgun as the "best" personal and home weapon. Until recently so did I — a preference based on thirty-five years of hunting and competitive shooting. But during a discussion at our club range with a police officer friend, I began re-evaluating my ideas on handguns as home defense firearms. After careful research, experiments and conversations with three police chiefs, an assistant district attorney, several deputy sheriffs and patrolmen, I now feel the shotgun to be superior to a handgun for use in the home. This is particularly true of those persons who lack skill and/or experience with handguns.

To begin my research I talked with twenty-two owners of large gun shops. I sought to establish a trend in the type of guns sold to the first-time buyer. I was interested only in those novices, and anyone who said the gun was for home/personal protection. Those chats confirmed what I suspected: About ninety-seven percent of such purchases are handguns.

Here are the results of my informal poll. The most frequently sold handgun is the inexpensive model — not the "Saturday Night Specials" — well-made but plainer models like those with adjustable rear sights or stainless steel finishes. The selection of a moderately priced gun is understandable — the buyer doesn't intend to use it frequently for plinking or target shooting, and probably hopes he or she won't have to use it at all! One box of ammo is bought with the gun. (This is not enough for practice to gain skill, experience and familiarity with the firearm. And with little or frequently no firearms handling experience, the buyer has little chance in a defensive situation. Many people feel that merely pointing a gun at an intruder has the psychological effect of setting him in hasty retreat. According to my police sources, this is a dangerous misconception. Remember the intruder is usually a pro, and the defender isn't!)

The most frequently bought calibers are .25, .32, and .38 in that order. One gun shop owner/friend said he sells about four cases of .25 ammo a year. Since a .25 is all but useless for competitive shooting — can you imagine bowling over a metallic ram with a .25? — it can only be assumed these cartridges are purchased for home defense. In the opinion of most of those experienced with firearms, a .25 and a .32 are inadequate against a determined assailant. A .38 is marginal, as the U.S. Army learned during the Philippine Insurrection of 1898 to 1901.

Since few .25 and .32 caliber guns are made in revolvers, most sales of these calibers are autoloaders. Here I interject a personal opinion: I definitely favor a revolver to an auto because the "wheel guns" are more reliable. On hunts, and in particular when after dangerous game, I carry a Ruger Super Blackhawk in .44 Remington magnum caliber as a backup gun. I have taken several deer and one black bear with this single-action Ruger. Never has it failed to function even under some highly adverse weather conditions.

To bring this point closer to home, here are two more reasons for the revolver: I use .38 and .45 caliber autos for competitive shooting. Even with methodically assembled handloads and careful routine cleaning, these guns jam. They are not "El Cheapos," either, but high-quality guns. A few weeks ago I was present at our local gun club range for an area police department qualification course. The officers were using .45 autos. I witnessed no less than thirteen alibis due to: failure to feed, failure to extract, or failure to eject. After one officer experienced his third alibi in a row, I commented to him that he would be up the local tributary without a paddle should that happen during a shootout. He assured me it would not happen since he would not be packing an auto, but his .357 magnum revolver!

My gun shop owner/friend told me he always tries to steer a would-be auto buyer from that to a revolver.

If after the foregoing comments you still feel you must

have an autoloader, then please buy a high-quality one. Like my military range instructor used to shout at us, "Take care of them rifles, boys! They just might save your life someday!" Enough said.

The event that started me thinking along the lines of a shotgun for residence protection was the final phase of the police qualifications course I've mentioned. Over my years of hunting I've used a scattergun for ducks, geese, pheasants, doves, quail, etc., but I considered the shotgun only as a bird gun, or for trap and skeet. I've seen many short-barreled shotguns in squad cars and seen them "used" in the Dirty Harry type movies. I was not very impressed. However, when the officer-in-charge brought out the Remington Model 870 in 12-gauge with its twenty-inch barrel sporting rifle-type sights, it got my immediate undivided attention. It looked...imposing. When he cycled the slide, that sound jogged my memory.

Many years ago, while I was in the United States Air Force, another officer and myself accidentally triggered a silent alarm in a security area. We were both cleared to be and supposed to be there. But the two Air Police who shortly arrived didn't know that. Suddenly we found ourselves gazing at the behemoth muzzle of a 12-gauge riot gun! To say the least, that was a very thought-provoking experience. I don't think I blinked more than twice during the time it took our superior officer to arrive and clear up the situation. The other AP pointed a .45 at us — it did not have the "I-better-not-sneeze" effect that damned 12-gauge had! The

Point-blank firing with a load of #4 shot tore 4½-inch hole in file folder and target. This would easily have penetrated a sheetrock wall, another concern.

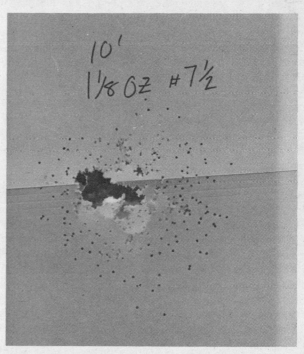

Pattern at ten feet from 1⅛ ounces of #7½ shot is 7½ inches. Hole at 9 o'clock was caused by the wad.

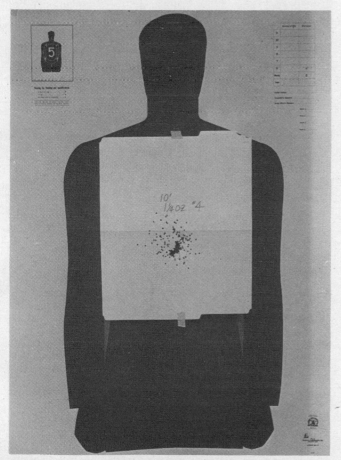

Legal-sized file folders taped to black silhouette target made results of shotgun testing easy, even from 25 yards.

.45 would poke only one hole in me, but the scattergun would provide multiple holes!

I told the officer about that event. He laughed and said when he'd had to enter a bar brawl, his methodical operation of the shotgun's slide got everyone's attention post haste!

The next step in my self-appointed project to determine if I was correct in believing a shotgun is superior for home defense was to make a list of questions. I wrote these questions assuming the defender had little or no experience with firearms.

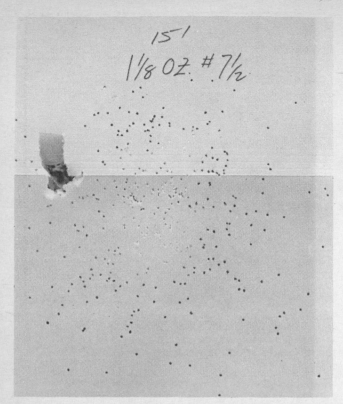

At fifteen feet, the same 1⅛-ounce load of #7½ shot has enlarged to a nine-inch circle. Wad made large hole shown.

Question One: Which is less complex and poses the least problems in learning to handle: autoloader, revolver or shotgun? This question immediately posed a problem. I would have to find people who were neophytes with firearms and who would be willing to become "guinea pigs." After a few days of talking to people with whom I work, I found three women and three men. I was surprised at the number of men who didn't know much about shooting sports.

The next step was to give my "subjects" what I consider bare minimum instruction, since that seems to be what most first-time gun buyers have. To teach proper loading and unloading, I seated bullets without powder or primers in a .45 auto and a Ruger Security-Six in .357 magnum. For the shotgun, I used a Remington Model 870 Wingmaster and dummy shells. Each type gun was equally simple for my pupils to master in loading and unloading safely. The only problem — if it is a problem — was the ladies had difficulty loading the auto's magazine after the fourth or fifth round, due to the stiff follower spring.

Question Two: Can a novice hit what he's shooting at with any degree of consistency? After a session of dry firing and a lecture on proper sight picture, we went out to the range. For this part I borrowed a .32 auto and used .38 Special loads in the .357 Ruger. From my gun shop owner/friend, I got a twenty-inch barrel for my 870 Wingmaster. The loads for the shotgun were 2¾-inch shells with #0 shot (this was an error I will explain later). Knowing only one box of ammo is usually bought with a new gun, and that this box will likely never be used up, I allotted only six shots for each gun "to get the feel of it." Those shots were fired from twenty-five yards at twenty-five-yard, slow-fire

pistol targets. The shooters used a combat hold.

Of the seventy-two shots fired (each of the six students fired six shots from the two handguns) only fourteen were on the target! My proteges were surprised. "I thought it was easier than this" was the general consensus. I wasn't surprised.

Question Three: Can my "trainees" hit a silhouette target at close range under stress? Keep in mind that personal defense is always a traumatic experience.

We moved to fifteen feet from the standard law enforcement silhouette. The .32 was put in a drawer and under a towel on a card table I'd brought. There was one round in the magazine and the chamber was empty. The idea of the card table and drawer was to simulate an in-home situation.

Each person, in turn, stood five or six feet from the card table. On my shout "Go!" they were to get the gun, load it

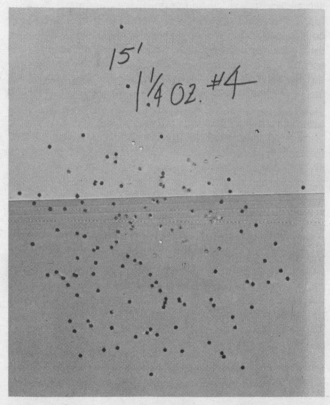

A shotshell with #4 fired at fifteen feet patterns at just over eight inches — less density than with #7½ load.

then fire the single round at the silhouette. To add stress, I yelled continuously until the shot was fired.

The results? Disaster! The ladies had difficulty operating the slide to chamber the round, and one completely ejected it. One man dropped the gun. All eventually got their rounds fired and of the six shots, only two would likely have been stoppers. One gal's shot struck the silhouette far below the belt — which would have surely discouraged a rapist, if not ended his career!

Next, the .32 was loaded with five rounds, including one in the chamber. This went much better.

The entire experiment was then repeated with the revolver. While there weren't many more stopping hits, the firing time was much less.

I had each member of my team fire one shell from the shotgun into the backstop to get an idea of the recoil. The M-870 was leaned against the table and on command, each person in turn ran to it, chambered, and fired one shell. As you would suspect, the stopping hits were much more frequent.

After the session, I know six people — seven, including myself — who are convinced a shotgun is a more-effective gun for home defense than a handgun.

I mentioned earlier, use of #0 buckshot was an error. This is due to excessive penetration. That concern lead me to the following experiments.

Number 0 buck has a diameter of .32-inch or .32 caliber. In a 12-gauge 2¾-inch shell, there are twelve #0 pellets — roughly the same thing as twelve .32 caliber bullets turned loose at once. I fired five rounds of #0 buck over my Oehler chronograph. Average velocity was 1178 feet per second (fps). A .32 caliber pistol has a velocity of only 680 fps. The point? Excessive penetration. This you MUST be concerned about where Americans live in apartments, townhouses, condos and duplex-type housing. Most walls are made of sheetrock — not too difficult to put your fist through it. Guess what a bullet will do to such a wall? Even in a private home you must be concerned that a stray pellet or bullet will go into another room and injure the innocent.

That in mind, I conducted experiments to test the amount of penetration from various calibers and shot sizes. Results are shown in the table.

Since most people buying guns for home defense are not handloaders, I used only factory loads in the tests. And since factory ballistics tend to be a bit optimistic, I chronographed all loads using the Oehler M-33 chronograph with the Sky Screens set at five feet, the start screen ten feet from the muzzle. Two shots from each gun were fired into the sheetrock from a distance of fifteen feet to roughly approximate a room size. Five additional squares were placed at three-inch intervals behind the target sheet. The total of six sheetrock squares would be three room walls. The table shows the number of sheets penetrated.

Shot Size	Diameter (inches)	Approximate # of Pellets Per Ounce
12	.05	2385
9	.08	585
8	.09	410
7½	.09½	350
6	.11	225
5	.12	170
4	.13	135
2	.15	90
BB	.18	50
Buck		**Per Pound**
4	.24	340
3	.25	300
1	.30	175
0	.32	145
00	.33	130
000	.36	100

NOTE: The gauges are not given since the approximate number of pellets per ounce would be the same.

APPROXIMATE PELLET SPREAD FROM DIFFERENT CHOKES

Choke	10 Yards	20 Yards	30 Yards	40 Yards
Full	10"	20"	30"	45"
Mod.	15"	25"	35"	50"
Cyl.	20"	40"	60"	

NOTE: These are only approximate patterns. I have tested guns marked Modified that threw patterns tighter than guns marked Full at the same ranges.

Caliber	Bullet Weight (grains)	Velocity (fps)	Penetration, Sheetrock	Penetration, 2x4s
.22 Short	29 Lead	987	1, Lodged in 2	Neither
.22 Long	29 Lead	1213	2, Lodged in 2	Neither
.22 LR	40 Lead	1233	2, Lodged in 2	Neither
.25 Auto	50 FMJ	779	4, Lodged in 5	1, entered 2
.32 Auto	88 Lead	635	4, Lodged in 5	1, entered 2
.38 S&W	146 Lead	681	5, Dented 5	1, entered 2
.38 Spl	158 Lead	788	6	Both
.357 mag	158 Lead	1343	6	Both, heavy
.41 mag	210 Lead	1286	6, Keyholed in 5-6	Both, splintered!
.44 mag	240 HP	1367	6, Big holes in 3-6	Both, splintered!
.45 ACP	230 MC	798	6	1, entered 2
.45 Colt	250 Lead	953	6	1, almost 2

Shotgun loads not chronographed due to difficulty in shooting over screens. Penetration tests shown only for sheetrock. All testing was done with a 12-gauge Remington Model 870 with 18½-inch improved cylinder.

Most walls are constructed with two-by-four studs on a sixteen-inch center. It's unlikely a bullet would strike a stud, thus slowing or stopping it before it could enter the adjoining room. It is even more unlikely that the bullet would strike a stud in the next room's opposite wall. However, I butted two two-by-fours together and fired one shot from each gun in the two-inch width. The chart indicates if one or both studs were penetrated.

After evaluating the results of the tests run, in particular the penetration tests, I am convinced a shotgun is the better choice for residence protection. That conclusion is also the consensus of those law enforcement officers with whom I talked and all but four gun shop owners.

To summarize from the data gathered: A novice cannot be sure of hitting a target with a handgun. Accuracy declines further if the defender is under stress, as would be the case if confronted by an intruder. Also, these tests show a real danger to persons or property in adjoining rooms when using even the more mild-mannered handguns. The danger to others is increased if the defender fires a series of shots. Bullets could leave the premises entirely; in such event, the person firing is putting himself in serious legal jeopardy.

I feel handguns have an important role in hunting, protection and the shooting sports. But in communities that have legislated against private ownership of handguns — Morton Grove, Illinois, for example — the best alternative for personal-home protection is a shotgun. Don't use a high-powered rifle within the home! Compared to a .30/06, the handguns in my penetration tests are mere BB guns.

The penetration tests chart shows the use of any size of buckshot is not advisable because wall penetration is too great. The same applies to BB shot. I feel that shot from #6 to #9 is best — anything larger than 6s is simply not needed.

My own choice is #7½, based on the tests. A charge of #7½ is more than adequate to halt the most determined thug. Also, this shot size will not go through two sheets of sheetrock, the equivalent of one wall.

Gun selection depends on judgment. My opinions are based on experience and my data.

Gauge and barrel length: For the type of hunting I do, I see no need for anything but a 12-gauge. That, however, is personal preference. As to barrel length, law enforcement agencies use the so-called riot guns, which are simply shotguns with 18-, 18½- or 20-inch barrels and have an improved-cylinder choke. A representative list of these guns is: Remington Model 1100 (auto) with a 22-inch barrel; Remington Model 870 with an 18½- or 20-inch barrel with or without rifle sights (I prefer the rifle sights so the gun can also be used for hunting); Winchester's Model 1200 Defender and Riot Gun (pumps) with 18-inch barrels; Smith & Wesson's Model 1000 slug gun with a 22-inch barrel; Ithaca's Model 37 in Military and Police versions; and Mossberg's 500 series riot guns in 18½- and 20-inch barrel lengths. All of these guns are 12 gauge. It would be wise to check local laws as to minimum barrel lengths.

Winchester, Remington, S&W, Ithaca and Mossberg all sell extra barrels for the models I've listed. These come in about any configuration you want: plain, ventilated rib; full, modified, improved-cylinder chokes; and in different lengths. The point here is that the gun can be used for several purposes simply by adding another barrel. It takes only about a minute to change barrels on my Remington

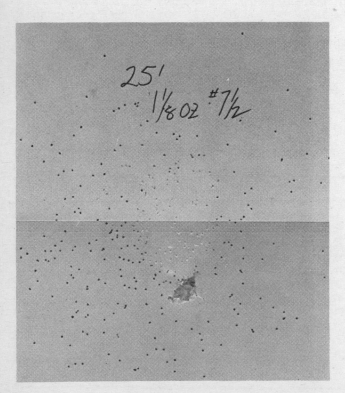

From 25 feet, #7½ load would ventilate 13½-inch width of intruder, without penetrating wall into another room.

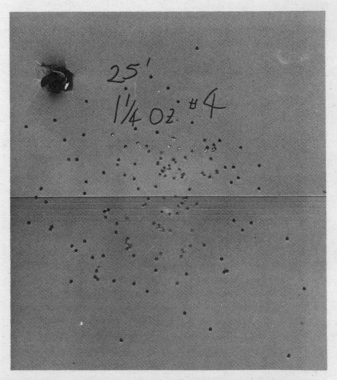

The #4 shot pattern didn't expand more at 25 feet than at 15 feet — still less than nine inches. Note wad.

Author's opinion is a shotgun with short barrel of improved cylinder bore, like the Remington Model 870 shown here, is ideal for home defense due to ease of handling and larger patterns, at shorter distances. What is your opinion?

870 and the process is simple. If I were buying a shotgun only for home defense, I would choose the eighteen- to twenty-inch barrel.

Under no circumstances should you use rifled slugs for home protection! These behemoth missiles will go through a house!

One final consideration: Should the gun be left loaded? Each person will have to decide that for himself, but I offer the following thoughts. If the gun is a slide-action (pump), the magazine can be left loaded. The loud *click-clack* of the action being cycled has a sobering effect on most intruders, as Bill Ungerman notes in Chapter 7 on Survival Schools. He instantly thinks, "SHOTGUN!" and can imagine all those pellets penetrating his hide.

I consider a pump relatively safe with a loaded magazine. But if you have kids about, and if pump's magazine is loaded, the action should be left closed, and the hammer cocked with the gun on "safe." In this configuration, the gun cannot be cycled unless: (1) safety is moved to FIRE; (2) the trigger pulled; and (3) the slide then cycled. Or you can depress the action bar lock and then cycle the action.

Most kids would have a tough time figuring this sequence out.

Much safer is to unload your shotgun in the morning when you arise, reloading the magazine just before retiring. With shells stored away from the gun, kids would be safe. If intruders come in the daylight, however...

Most autoloaders do not have an action bar lock. To load the chamber, all that is needed is to pull back and release the bolt. Again, if you have kids, consider this: I "borrowed" a few neighbor kids, with the permission and in the presence of their parents, to determine if they could operate an auto bolt. Most kids from about 6 up, depending on the size of the child, CAN operate an autoloader's bolt!

All that's needed to fire double-barrels and single-barrels is to simply move the safety to FIRE.

If you have children, the best possible deterrent to an accident is education. Teach them guns ARE NOT TOYS!

I hope you never have to put to use the data given here.

IS AN ADAPTER THE ANSWER?

Get Several Guns From The Same Hardware By Using Small — Not Perfect — Adapters

By William E. Haynes

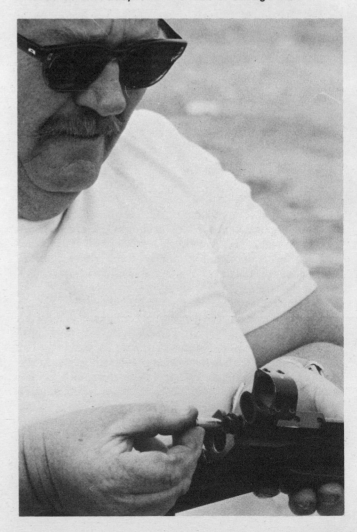

The shortage of .30/06 brass made the .308/7.62mm NATO adapter particularly desirable to author. At left is shown the 7.62 round wearing the collar that makes it usable in .30/06 rifle. Compare the shoulder height with .30/06 round at right. Below: Author's son-in-law, Kirk, slips .32 ACP cartridge into .30-30 Win. adapter in the tube of Savage M24-V.

YOU'RE OUT on a meat-getter trek with your .30 caliber rifle. There's no big game stirring, but up pops a cottontail that would look mighty toothsome in the stew pot. But your .30 caliber rifle would blow half of him into the next county, so your stomach rumbles your bad luck. How nice it would've been to chamber a smaller and less-destructive .22 long rifle in your .308 or .30/06!

To fire the inexpensive .22 caliber bullets in .223 rifle you'll need this adapter (center) and rimfire plug that slips into adapter after the .22 round.

tive marksmanship training aid for the M-16 family of weapons. Familiarity is a key to hunter success — why shouldn't you benefit from this proven approach, with the side-benefit of lower-cost ammo and a dual-purpose firearm? As with other calibers in this test, you have the advantage of a round suited for use in a sidearm, just like the smart men of the Old West who used and carried a cartridge compatible to both handgun and saddlegun.

The .22 LR and .223 marriage has other pluses: They share the same bore diameter. Unlike the .22 LR in a handgun, you have the advantage of a longer barrel and the added sighting plane of such a barrel. The aid of the shoulder stock is another plus for improved accuracy.

Because the .223 is a center-fire cartridge and .22 LR a rimfire, you need a plug that seats into the adapter after the round is loaded into it. This plug has an offset protrusion to hold the cartridge in the adapter by the aid of an O-ring. The advantage of the O-ring is that you can carry the load adapter in pocket or pouch without the .22 round falling out. The loaded adapter is only a single-shot device — one

You can, by use of adapters. They're not perfect, but what is? The idea of sub-calibers or low-level cartridges isn't new, dating to 1869. The military used sub-calibers in both large and small arms, the former for training purposes. And combination guns like rifles with shotgun tubes above have been made and favorably used for decades.

An adaptor could save problems in terrain populated by hostile forces. A .308 or .30/06 report carries much farther than does the .30 caliber M-1 carbine or .32 ACP ammunition. The latter duo are lighter in weight and take up less room in pockets or retreat, too. Save your heavier ammunition for game of appropriate size.

Adapters are available for calibers other than the .30 caliber I tested, supplied by manufacturer Harry Owen. (Owen sells more than forty for rifles and pistols, plus cartridge adapters to convert shotguns to rifles. There are also more than twenty adapters designed specifically for the Thompson/Center Contender single-shot pistol.)

One caliber currently in favor among survivalists is the .223 (5.56mm NATO) cartridge. Several companies now manufacture firearms for this cartridge. It can be an effective weapon for both survival or defense, but due to the round's extremely high velocity, it certainly isn't an ideal small game round. If you haven't tried the .223 on small game, you're in for a surprise: All that will remain of a rabbit is hair, teeth, and eyeballs!

The logical choice is the .22 LR round with a suitable adapter, deadly on game in the rabbit-squirrel class. It's also a good way to kill fowl on the ground — head shots to minimize meat spoilage.

Even the military has seen the advantage of the .22 LR for training purposes and found it an inexpensive and effec-

Make your selected weapons perform with different cartridges. At left is the .30 carbine round with .30/06 adapter. Right is .32 ACP round, .30-30 adapter.

Kirk's group with .30 cal. bullet in .30-30 insert for Savage M24-V were disappointing, measuring five inches at 25 yards. Good enough for bagging lunch.

Another look at Kirk loading the .32 ACP bullet into the adapter, pulled out for photo purposes (above). It is inserted flush with breech (below) and when action is snapped closed, is ready to fire. Slow reloading speed is one of the trade-offs you make.

A shocked author learned the .32 ACP in the .30-30 Marlin with adapter was honey of a shooter. It clocked 1003 fps with Federal bullets in 5-shot groups.

of the trade-offs you must accept — and must be hand-ejected before feeding in a fresh round.

Some may want a couple of these adapters loaded and ready in a pocket. Inserting the adapter takes time too, but it wasn't designed as a rapid-fire device. With practice, three to five shots per minute are possible.

Accuracy was highly satisfactory in tests out to fifty yards with a new Ruger Mini-14 (which was fussy about the brand of cartridges it liked best for accuracy.) The best group shot with the Mini came from a box of CCI Green Label match ammo. Winchester Super-Match along with a couple of other CCI offerings couldn't compare. This could work out differently in your Mini or AR-15. The photo of the target proves the combination adequate for your small-game needs. The point of impact with the .22 LR compared favorably with the .223 and won't require sight adjustment in most cases. Velocity was nearly 900

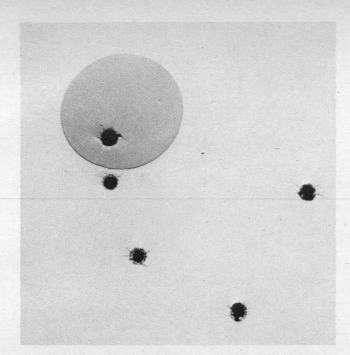

The .30 carbine shot through .30/06 Enfield fitted with appropriate adapter shows at 50 yards you'll group tightly, if you can excuse the one flyer.

Author felt groups fired through Marlin M336 using .30 carbine ammo with .30-30 Winchester adapter could be tightened less than this 1½ inches at 25 yards. Below: Another 50-yard group with Marlin housing .30-30 adapter. There are 100 combinations for weapon.

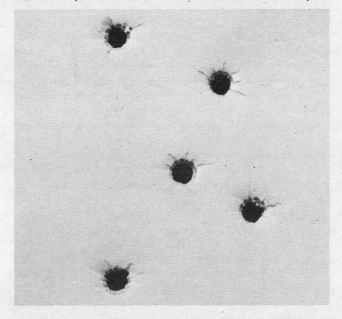

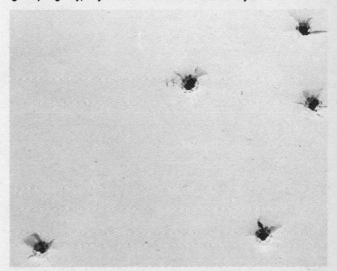

Author's surprising group with .32 ACP in .30/06 Enfield at 50 yards. See text for reasons why.

feet per second (fps), generating 81 foot-pounds of energy (fpe) — more than enough to dispatch small game.

Harry Owen offers an adapter for use in the .308 and .30/06 chamber. You can get a long-barreled or cartridge-length adapter for this. Because the effective barrel length is something like three-quarters-inch long, the test targets weren't great — but at least made the conversion possible. With practice and the proper brand of cartridge, five-inch groups are possible. For use in a bolt-action .30 caliber rifle, the six-inch tube would be too much for rabbits.

As a training aid, the short adapter soon alerts you to bad shooting habits, as there's little noise or recoil in an eight-pound rifle. It's fun to use and lets you know if you're "bucking" the shot.

Happily, the adapter fed from the magazine of both my Springfield and Enfield. It wasn't quite as happy in the M-1 Garand, but chambered well when hand-fed. Like the .22/.223 combo, hand-ejection was required in the semi-auto.

I really looked forward to checking out the .30 carbine/ .30/06 adapter. I've never been really impressed with the carbine round as a rifle cartridge, but it's hell on wheels in a revolver and a tremendous game and defensive cartridge with something like the 110-grain Sierra bullet. Harry Owen supplied five inserts for this combination so I could try to magazine feed them from my Enfield and Springfield. Like the .22/.223 combo, the carbine bullet is compatible with the bore diameter of the .30/06 or .308/ 7.62mm NATO round.

I was also interested in chronograph readings and GUN WORLD'S Dean Grennell, author of an accompanying story, volunteered to shoot the Federal cartridges with full metal jackets. The .30 caliber carbine loads were of 110 grains and very similar to the Government loads.

After the speed tests it was decided to shoot at twenty-five- and fifty-yard groups, the thought being that most

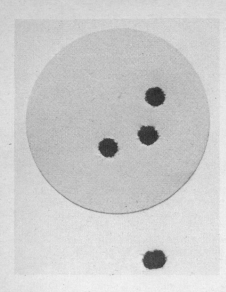
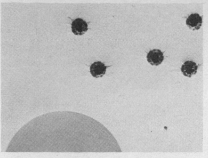
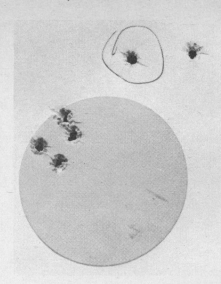

From left: Five-shot group from .30-30 Marlin M336 at 25 yards to check accuracy before using inserts. Above: 173-grain cast lead bullets in .30/06 through Springfield '03A3 at 25 yards — tight but together. Right: Four tight with one flyer from .22 ammo in .223 Mini-14. The circled hole is from other group.

small game is taken between those ranges. Hot match shooter and benchrest types might not be impressed with the result, but for our purposes the combo did well — perhaps even a little better than expected with the short, 110-grain bullet. Also bear in mind the groups were shot with standard military iron sights.

Harry Owen urged me to try the adapter for a .32 ACP/ .30/06 combination. He claimed it would outperform the .30 carbine round and made less noise to boot. I like a big-bore handgun — I love the recoil and the blast — so I've had nothing to do with the .32 caliber line and was never interested in the .32 ACP cartridge. I've always considered the .32 ACP to be something a woman would carry in her purse and hope that, if she had to use it to for self-defense, there'd be a clergyman of the proper faith around to say a good word or two over her body.

So, with tongue in cheek and a box of .32 ACP in hand, Dean and I proceeded to have at it. Harry Owen knew what he was talking about. Again the brand was Federal and the bullet a 71-grain full-jacketed bullet. They did make less noise and grouped better than the more-powerful .30 carbine fodder. What a shock!

Unless you need the carbine round for other reasons, the .32 ACP sure would be the ticket for a light survival round in a .30 caliber rifle. I'll continue to count on the carbine load for my needs as it fits into my inventory better and works well, but if you're looking for a good small-game cartridge that's considerably quieter than the standard .30 caliber round, consider the little .32 ACP.

Tests showed the average velocity of the .30 carbine round to be 1913 fps with 894 fpe at fifteen feet. The little .32 ACP averaged out at 965 fps and a respectable 147 fpe, which compares to a .38 wadcutter in fpe — not all that bad.

Both the .30 carbine/.30/06 and .32 ACP/.30/06 being center-fire cartridges, the adapters are just one-piece units. They're a little faster and easier to load than the .22 caliber variety. Because there's no firing pin/plug, the cartridge falls out of the adapter; thus, you must load the unit just before chambering.

For the .32 ACP target I selected my old Remington-made Model 1917 Enfield. Despite a lack of windage adjustment on the Enfield, I like the peep sight better.

Using small spotters on a plain paper background, I felt I could hold a tighter group than with the '03 Springfield. I also felt the extra two inches of barrel might be of value.

Despite the added barrel length, average speed through the chronograph showed little variation from the Springfield. I was pleased to shoot a triangular group with the longest side measuring 1 5/8 inches (center to center), with the remaining two shots within the triangle and touching. As mentioned, the report was light with recoil almost non-existent. Although I like the bark and bite of the standard '06 round, I found the test interesting and fun. Grouping as well as the .32 ACP did, I think I'll tote that adapter in the field from now on just to panic jackrabbits! The .32 ACP might be considered costly for plinking, though.

For the .30 carbine/.30/06 shoot, I also selected the Enfield. I felt this was best as I wanted a comparison between the two calibers. I had great expectations after the performance of the smaller pistol cartridge. Although I wasn't disappointed with the carbine round, I was shocked to find the group opening up — a third-shot flier spoiled an otherwise satisfactory group and could've cost me lunch in a small game hunt. In a larger target, it could've been a damaging hit. The four hits in the group had a maximum center-to-center spread of slightly less than three inches at twenty-five yards, with the flier measuring six inches at the extreme. Recognizing the speed and accuracy of this round in the .30/06 tube, this combination could be considered dangerous to larger game. With a ball bullet or, better still, a soft- or hollow-point, it'd be deadly on a man-size target at reasonable range.

In the brute force department, the .30 carbine load was faster. With the heavier bullet it was harder-hitting as well. This was as expected. In the Ruger or Thompson/Center Contender, it can be hand-loaded up to a real boomer. This heavier load would be safe in a .30/06 or .308 rifle and afford even higher velocity, energy and destructive force.

While at the range and concentrating on the twenty-five-yard study, I also wanted to try the .30-30 Winchester adapter with the carbine and .32 ACP load. Many folks swear by their .30-30s and the lever guns made by both Winchester and Marlin have a long history of dependability. Being lightweight and compact, they're a possible choice for a survival tool.

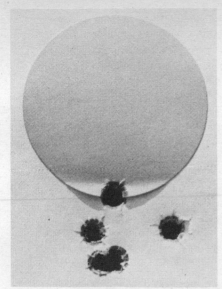

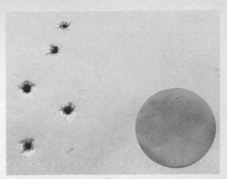

Pleasing results (left) of .308 round through '06 adapter in '03A3 at 25 yards. Above: Kirk's group with same rifle during Arizona session.

Kirk couldn't much improve the .32 groups fired through .30-30 Win. adapter at 25 yards. Still, these are within kill radius for game.

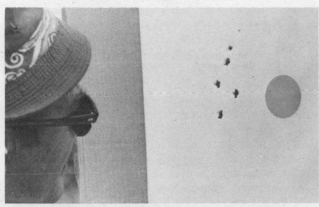

Kirk examines his tight 100-yard group shot using 7.62mm ammo within .30/06 Enfield. Darn accurate!

For this work I selected a Marlin Model 336 carbine with an old and proven Tasco 4X32 scope. Simmer down, Winchester owners — the Marlin was selected because I had it in the rack. It also gave me a comparison with previous targets using the standard .30-30 round.

Loading into the open side of the Marlin was no problem — perhaps the Winchester would be even easier. If careful, I could load the adapter with cartridge into the loading gate without the cartridge falling out. It fed nicely in the normal fashion. I chose to load through the ejection port while shooting on the target.

Starting with the .32 ACP, velocity from the shorter Marlin barrel, as opposed to the Enfield, averaged about 40 fps faster. Perhaps this can be attributed to less drag or perhaps the Microgroove barrel of the Marlin. (Average velocity was 1003 fps with the same 71-grain Federal batch. Energy increased from 147 to 159 fpe.) The five-shot group sure looks different: almost a perfect vertical line! My shooting ability might be the cause of this, but even so, the group measures only 1½ inches and I feel additional groups could be brought even closer. I guess impressive is the best way to describe the group and the possibilities of this small pistol cartridge in .30 caliber arms.

Shooting with the .30 carbine round in the .30-30 adapter started on a bad note: With the first shot, the adapter split about one-half inch from the forward end to the rear.

Enfield's group with .32 ACP at 25 yards (below left) is compared with .32 ACP through Marlin M336 .30-30. At right is .30 carbine through .30/06 Enfield.

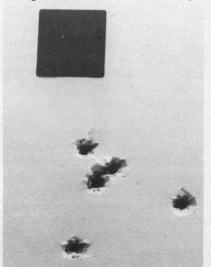

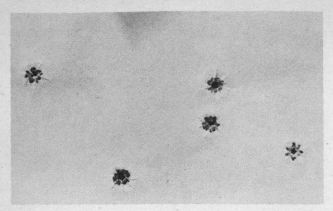

Shooting the match grade .30/06 Springfield fitted with .32 ACP at 25 yards proved author's conclusions.

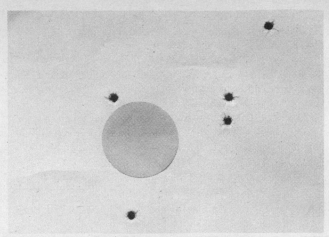

Still another group with the venerable weapon at 25 yards led to the inescapable truth about groups.

Considerable effort was needed to extract the adapter and fired case. This isn't necessarily the fault of the adapter. They're made to close tolerances for what should be a standard chamber. The problem is the .30-30 head spaces on the rim of the case; thus, .30-30 chambers tend to be a little sloppy. While brass will fire form to the chamber without splits, the less-flexible steel of the inserts won't conform as well.

Close comparison of the .30 carbine and .30-30 cartridge will also tell a story. The difference in case size isn't great. It leaves little metal in some areas of the adapter to ward off the higher chamber pressures of the .30 carbine round. After a quick touchup with a fine, small file, I was again able to chamber the insert and resume shooting with no further problems.

Five-shot groups at both twenty-five and fifty yards were satisfactory. As with the .32 ACP, an increase of about 40 fps was indicated in the .30-30 Marlin barrel. At twenty-five yards the group held together with a maximum spread of slightly less than 2½ inches. Again the .32 ACP seemed to be a tighter shooter. I think most will agree that is still good enough for the survivalist as a small-game getter and even in a defense situation.

With generally good results on paper at twenty-five yards, the target was moved out to the fifty-yard line. At this range the added velocity and heavier bullet of the .30 carbine began to show its worth. Although the groups opened up slightly, they still stayed in an area good enough for hitting what you wanted. In both the .30/06 and the .30-30 the results were nearly identical. The lower velocity of the .32 ACP showed up as drop from the point of aim to a larger degree than the .30 carbine. A little "Kentucky windage" would be necessary to compensate for about three inches of drop — a problem on rabbit-class game, but no real sweat on larger targets.

I didn't push my luck by moving the target out to one hundred yards — I didn't consider it necessary. These adapters are intended to supplement your existing weapon as described earlier. A little off-hand plinking out to one hundred yards did prove you could hit at least a man-sized target. That was good enough for me. A hit was possible if I absolutely had no other choice. But that's why I carry 168-grain hollow-point boat-tail rounds for the .30/06!

Elsewhere in this chapter you'll find discussions of firearms for the survivalist. But because of the possibilities of this Savage Model 24-V with the adapters available, I had to try it. I've always been fond of this type of gun, dating to my childhood with a .22 LR over a .410 bore. I was able to borrow a 24-V in .30-30 over 20-gauge. I'd have preferred to have the top tube in .30/06, but one can't have everything! The beauty of this lightweight and simple weapon is the possibility of converting it into over one hundred possible combinations. The shot barrel can even be converted into a rifle and because of the break-open design, will accept a full-length insert. So it's easy to see a wide variety of calibers can be used even in a double-rifle mode.

The shooting session for the Model 24-V was held in north-central Arizona's Verde Valley. This time I had my hefty son-in-law do the shooting from a portable shooting bench. Again the plan was to shoot the .30 carbine and .32 ACP rounds in a .30-30 adapter. Both of the adapters worked well in the Savage, chambering smoothly with no extraction problems.

Unhappily, the Savage groups weren't up to those shot with the Marlin. The trigger pull was stiff and a bit on the rough side, which might have influenced the groups. Also, no scope was used.

Again the .32 ACP proved to be capable of producing the smaller groups. The 71-grain bullet seems to thrive on the longer rifle barrel. Perhaps a really hot pistol shooter could match the groups shot from the rifles used, but I'd have to see it to believe it. The .32 ACP and .30 carbine groups averaged four and five inches, respectively: good enough to get your lunch, but a little less than we'd hoped for from the 24-V.

So long as we were on the range I took advantage of having a different shooter to try a few groups from my favorite '03 Springfield. Additional groups were shot with the .30 and .32 cartridges. I've always considered my son-in-law, Kirk, to be a better bench shooter than I. Perhaps he was having a bad day — our targets were very close and no better than the groups shot in California with my Enfield. Perhaps it's just a situation of the cartridge/rifle combination limitations. We were happy to see good performance in the Springfield. It proves to me the idea of a small-game or light-load feature from a high-powered rifle is workable.

There was one more trick in my bag: to see how the .308/.30/06 insert would work. This small insert is just big enough to make up the difference in a .30/06 chamber so the .308/7.62mm NATO cartridge will function. With surplus .30/06 cartridges almost non-existent and brass becoming hard to find, the thought of using the more-available .308 might appeal to some.

GI Lake City 7.62mm ammo was used in one of my '03A3 Springfields. The twenty-five-yard groups were a waste of good ammo. The groups were less than 1¼ inches, so we moved the target frame to one hundred yards and tried again. Considering the sights of the '03A3 with just a two-inch spot, it was interesting getting a good sight picture. Excuses aside, the one-hundred-yard groups were

more than satisfactory. A heart/lung shot on a deer would be no problem. Kirk was able to hold a tighter group at one hundred yards by close to two inches, so I was glad to have the help.

ADAPTER ANALYSIS

Although this wasn't written as a product report, it's only fair to the prospective user to draw a few conclusions. For the most part, the use of the adapters was fun and a learning experience.

Some of us learn the hard way, so perhaps one problem I had was my own fault. Harry Owen warned that it was unwise to change rifles and thus chambers, especially with the .30 carbine/.30/06 adapter. I ignored the warning and it became necessary to remove one of the jammed adapters the hard way. They will stick in the chamber and are very hard to get out if you don't follow this advice. If you are going to change rifles with any given adapter, proceed with caution and don't get it stuck. I'm happy to say there was no damage to the match-grade '03A3 Springfield because of this error.

As mentioned, the .30 carbine/.30-30 adapter split. Again no damage was done and Harry is working on that problem. The .30-30 adapters for the Savage, and especially for the Thompson/Center pistol, are made just a little bit tougher and will stand up better than the ones for the rifle. Factors are different with the Savage and T/C which make this possible. Even at that, the crack caused no real problems and no chamber damage.

A lot of rounds were fired through the .22/.223 adapter. In spite of this, I was unhappy to have that adapter fail due to indenting of the plug/firing pin. To protect the firing pin of the rifle, the plug is made of a softer steel. After about fifty rounds the hammering of the firing pin indented the plug such that it would no longer set off the cartridge. I'm not sure you can call this a fault in design, but should be a consideration if you plan to use it a lot. Get a spare or two.

On the plus side is the relatively low cost of the adapters and insert barrels. The adapters sell for less than $20, while the inserts range from $25 up, depending on size and length. A $3 catalog is a good investment and refundable with the first order. You will be amazed at the number of adapters and inserts available.

A couple of other possibilities for sub-caliber and reduced loads might be considered as a part of your survival bag. Remington makes a round called the Accelerator which was found to be very accurate in the .30-30 loading tested. The velocity is extreme on this sub-caliber load, running out the barrel in excess of 3000 fps. It's a hard-hitting round that could do great damage against large game.

Another consideration is loading with cast lead bullets. In a favorite loading for .30/06, I drive a 173-grain bullet at about 1783 fps. At that speed with a bullet of that weight, the foot-pound figure comes to about 1222 fpe. A similar load could be put together for .308. Because of the shape and relative hardness of the bullet used, it doesn't deform to any great degree. Because of this it's a good meat-saver load on even small game. Because of the energy created by this round, it's still effective against large game and man-sized targets.

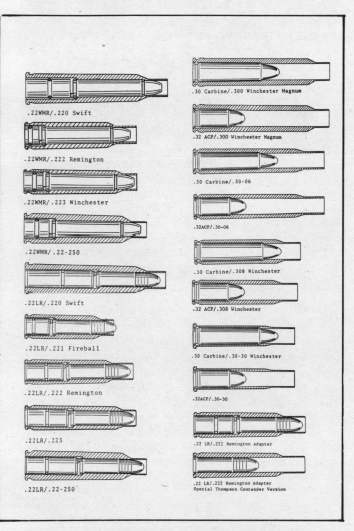

The adapters sold by Harry Owen are partially listed here. You can acquire other caliber configurations, also. Author found some problems with extracting the adapters, which means you the purchaser should always check fit carefully before slamming the bolt home with shell inserted. Any problems encountered were solved by Owen, whose advice proved sound in test firings.

BLACK POWDER

Consider Black Powder Guns For The Survival Retreat And Your Worries Are Few

By C.R. Learn

To load the black powder shotgun, first ram home powder, then the wad column, then an overshot card, making sure they are rammed down tightly against powder. Developing a consistency in loading can help your ultimate accuracy.

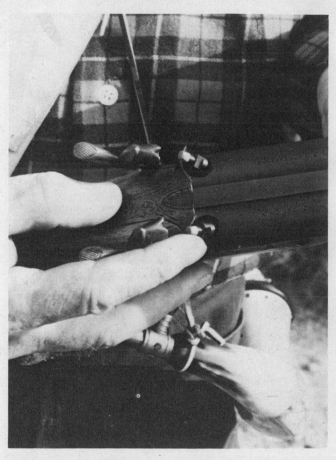

When both barrels have been loaded with powder and the protective card, one can put shot in one barrel and a round ball in the other, if desired. All of this should be done before the percussion cap is placed on nipple.

THERE ARE many weapons you can choose to put in your retreat for protection and food production. Sometimes overlooked are the modern versions of black powder rifles, pistols and shotguns. They worked in the Seventeenth and Eighteenth centuries and today are even better.

There are many advantages to black powder. You can use the same powder and lead stock in many calibers of rifles, muskets and the ever-popular shotguns, depending on the task at hand. You can stock powder and lead in small areas for indefinite periods.

The choice of rifles can be confusing, but all you really need to do is figure out the caliber you need. Two units that will work well are the .45 caliber Kentucky rifle and matching-caliber pistol, both in single shot, made by Connecticut Valley Arms. These units are available in finished form or as inexpensive kits, practically finished except for minor inletting of metal to wood — you can save up to one hundred dollars and have fun finishing them, too.

The .45 will down big game for the food bin, but isn't too heavy for small game. It is accurate — or more accurate than the shooter — and has classic lines that are appealing

This particular gun has double triggers and you can fire either the ball or the shot charge by selection of the proper trigger. Home defense is another use for the gun.

as well as functional. The Kentucky rifle put out by CVA and others puts a .45 caliber round ball weighing in at 125 grains in a good tight group for accuracy that will down a deer with ease. You can also buy and use a conical bullet that looks like a modern projectile, but some rifles won't shoot them accurately because of rifling. The only way to find out is to try the 300-grain conicals, which are far heavier than many modern rifles put out.

The black powder shooting system is very simple. You need powder for propellant and you can buy this in two basic granulations: The one recommended for this rifle and

for shotguns is FFg — a medium granule neither too fine nor too coarse. With this one powder you can arm and fire your rifle, pistol and shotgun — consider the savings in storage! Stocking powder is simple since you need only one type. It is highly flammable, however, even more so than modern smokeless powder, so be certain your storage area is safe.

The bullets or balls as they are termed, can be cast from any type of lead. Stockpile soft, pure lead such as plumber's lead or "pigs" from accessory suppliers, although you also can melt down wheel weights and other types

Such game as deer and even elk is plentiful in many areas of this country today. By stalking within sure range of these species, it is possible to take them with replica black powder firearms, but firearms' range is quite short.

THE COMPLETE SURVIVAL GUIDE

Animals as big as moose were taken with black powder arms in the days of the pioneers. If modern day replicas of muzzleloaders are used properly, same game is available.

when necessary. When you're interested in surviving, you will overlook a purist's picky points!

You will need a supply of percussion caps for detonating the FFg powder. The #11 fits all three of these units, another plus. The cap fits over the nipple of the rifle, pistol or shotgun. When the hammer falls upon trigger pull, the cap acts as a primer to fire the powder in the barrel. The ball roars on its way.

There is another system for black powder guns: flintlock ignition. This uses a hammer and flint to ignite fine powder in a pan on the side of the rifle. The powder ignites by sparks from the flint striking steel when it falls. This "flash in the pan" ignites your coarser powder in the barrel, which fires the load.

This system works, but you should consider its drawbacks before you buy a flintlock. When the flash from flint and pan ignites, you have a tendency to flinch and pull off target. Firing a percussion-style (smokepole) is similar to shooting a modern rifle and there is no super flash on ignition.

The round ball will work in your .45 caliber pistol as well as in the rifle. You will need some patches, which are pieces of cloth used to seal around the back surface of the ball to prevent gases from escaping upon ignition. This

projects the ball outward. You can buy patches ready-cut or cut them from any material except synthetics, which melt on contact with open flame. The best is Irish linen, but you can use tightly woven cotton materials, pillow ticking, light canvas — almost any material that will fit the ball and go down the barrel.

That's all you need to fire the rifle and pistol. Naturally you will have to check the proper loads by test firing to determine which works best for your rifle, following data tables or maker's instructions. The pistol will take the same powder and ball, but less powder, of course.

You'll need a method of carrying powder, percussion caps and patch-cutting knife among all the other materials needed for firing and feeding these rifles and pistols. You can make all of them yourself from leather or fabrics. The powder can be carried in the traditional powder horn, made from a cow horn, or in a metal flask designed for that purpose. You need only one bag.

To fire the rifle or pistol you go through the similar procedure used for firing any powder weapon. First, be certain the barrel is cool — a spark may set off the powder as you pour it into the barrel. Pour a measured amount of powder into the barrel of the rifle. Tap the side of the barrel to be certain it's fully seated at the rear of the barrel. Place a

A single-shot black powder pistol such as this can shoot FFg powder, but the finer granualated FFFg is better. If you load as shown, be sure no sparks are left in barrel from a previous shot or entire powder horn could ignite.

A pistol can be chosen to fire the same size ball as a black powder rifle. Ball is rammed down on the powder and care must be taken to be sure it is seated tightly.

patch over the end of the barrel. Put the round ball on the patch, start it down the bore with a starter rod, and after it is in the barrel ram it home with your ramrod.

When you're ready to fire, cock the hammer, place a cap on the nipple, aim and shoot. You'll find there is little or no recoil with these black powder guns — or at least not what you'd expect when you fire a .45 bullet. You will be en-

veloped by a vision-obscuring fog of heavy smoke after firing, one of the drawbacks to black powder shooting.

To load and shoot a conical slug, proceed as in the ball method. But after pouring in the powder, start the conical, its base lubricated with grease, into the barrel. Use no patch: The conical seals as it is forced into the rifling of the barrel and you need no patch. Before you rely on the conical bullet, however, test it to be certain your rifle will fire it accurately.

You don't fire conicals from some pistols. They won't work, so stay with the round ball for those single-shot powder-burners that won't shoot them accurately.

If there's a second disadvantage to shooting any black powder gun, it's cleaning them. They aren't hard to clean, but you use hot water and swab the bore with lots of cleaning patches until they emerge clean. Now take an oiled patch and swab the barrel inside and out to keep rust from forming. This cleaning is done outside, since there is a strong odor when you clean these rifles.

With the percussion cap placed on the nipple, pistol is ready to fire. It will handle small game with ease and matching rifle will drop deer if range is right.

Ramrod is carried in thimbles beneath the barrel of the rifle so that it is always available. Note the pistol in Learn's belt. Keep primer off nipple until you need it for safety. (Below) Use of Kentucky windage may be required to bring fixed rifle sights to bear on target.

The black powder shotgun is something of a sleeper. You can get almost the same ranges with them as with shotshell eaters. You can down the same birds and use the same shot sizes as with modern shotguns. You can't use steel shot, which will ruin the barrel. These old-style shotguns can be made from kits like the rifle and pistol, or you can buy them ready-made.

A good choice for the pellet shooter would be one of Dixie Gun Works' 12-gauge double-barrel kits. The big 12-gauge is one of the most popular sizes. If you feel it isn't big enough, Dixie also offers a 10-gauge.

If you left the hammers off the sides of the double-barrel Dixie shotgun, you couldn't tell it from the modern doubles. It has two triggers, as do many modern guns, which means two quick shots. If there's a disadvantage to the black powder shotgun, it's that it's offered with cylinder bore — there's no choke to the barrels, as have modern guns. This is because you load them from the end of the barrel instead of from the breech.

You will use the same FFg powder that you used for the rifle and pistol, and you can shoot a 1¼-ounce load of shot from these tubes. Make a measure for that amount of shot and use the same measure for the powder. Like volumes make things simple.

The firing sequence starts when you drop the measured powder down a clean, dry barrel. Put a slip of over-powder nitro card of about three-hundredths-inch thickness over the powder to seal the powder. Measure out and drop the same measure of shot ranging from the very fine #9 to 00 buck. Ram home an overshot card and you're ready to fire the shotgun after you place the cap on the nipple. You can cap both nipples and shoot in rapid succession or as a side-by-side single shot.

You can use copper-plated shot or the regular lead spheres in various sizes. If you feel you need a really hefty slug to get a deer, bear or other game down, you can also load a .690-inch-diameter ball down the barrel and turn the shotgun into a close-range, large-caliber rifle. This .690-inch ball weighs in at 470 grains — over one ounce — and if what it hits gets up, I don't want to be around!

You might load the right barrel with a slug and the left barrel with birdshot to have a game-getter of a choice. The big ball is patched like a rifle ball. You just need a larger patch.

These three weapons can give you years of service. They are basic, with a minimum of parts and low probability of malfunction. You can mould balls over a fire if you need to, pouring the molten lead into a mould for casting to your selected sizes. These can be purchased and last for many moons. You can stock any type of lead and you need no cartridges for reloading, no scales, no presses or any of the other items needed for the cartridge-style rifle, pistol or shotgun.

If there's any disadvantage to these single-shot units, its just that — they are single shot and your rate of fire depends on your reloading capabilities. You therefore must get closer, say, within one hundred yards, to get a clean shot — as you likely won't get a second! This forces you to become a better hunter and these weapons will do that for you or you go hungry.

A second disadvantage is that the powder must be kept dry, only common sense. Your storage should be away

The fodder for feeding 12-gauge muzzleloading shotgun includes any of the modern wads at rear, FFg powder, a cannister of powder, overshot wads of cardboard, shot of your choice or a .690-inch round ball for larger game.

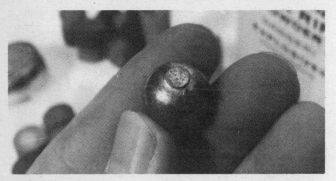

The ball that can be used in the 12-gauge shotgun has been cast in a mould. For best accuracy it would prove wise to remove the casting projection from the side.

If firing a rifle and you feel you may want to reload in a hurry, this reloading block wil hold patched balls. The conical round is shown for sake of size comparison.

Primers for black powder firearms come in round cans, but care should be taken, as they are highly explosive. Those shown are No. 11 size for rifle, pistol, shotgun ignition.

There are more antelope in this country today than at the turn of the century. They are curious and can be drawn in close for a shot by waving a rag from cover.

The bobcat is a predator that will attack chickens, small animals if hungry. There are instances when this feline has been eaten and reports are that meat is delicious.

from heat or flames. Carry just what you need in your powder horn and replenish as needed from main supply. Store all caps in another place so they don't destroy your ammunition dump if they detonate and ignite the powder.

Black powder weapons worked for our forefathers and will work for the survivalist. Practice now and you will find they are reliable and accurate. Fine tune the sights and

Rabbits constitute an easy target for a black powder shotgun if one should be in need of food in the wilderness.

Using a black powder rifle, the obvious placement of the ball or bullet for sure kill would be just behind shoulder.

powder load for accuracy out to one hundred yards. They will shoot farther and with practice you may learn to place bullets where you want them farther out. The sights are a simple blade front and notch rear for the rifle and pistol — no adjustments to worry about. You merely hold on target, high or low for various ranges. If the wind is blowing, allow for it by educated guessing, which is where we got the term "Kentucky windage" in the first place.

Choosing black powder for your rifle, pistol and shotgun can be a good decision. You need only the basics and the moulds will cast many bullets. You have only one type of powder, one size of cap and you can use old clothing for the patch material if you need to. Levi's make good patch material, anyway. You need no elaborate reloading tools, no factory bullets or cartridge cases as you will with modern rifles.

About the only bad thing that could happen when you are in the field would be to get your powder supply damp. Heed the old motto and "Keep your powder dry" and you'll have a battery of weapons that will keep food in the pot and protect you and yours from predators, whatever they may be.

Chapter 6
A SURVIVALIST'S PRIMER ON ARCHERY

Learn The Types Of Tackle Available, See What You Can Afford, And Practice!

By C.R. Learn

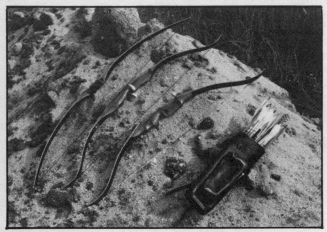

Three bow styles are shown here. From left: Bingham longbow, Howatt Hunter recurve, and Bingham takedown.

Eccentrics on Bear Alaskan compound are adjustable for different draw weights. Compounds are tops in popularity.

MAN SURVIVED and fought his battles for centuries with the same stick and string that you can use today. Archery isn't new — you might say it is the first step above and beyond the throwing spear; a projected missile, or arrow as it is called today.

If you plan to include a bow and some arrows in your survival system, you should know you just can't pick up the stick and string and go out to fill the game bag. It takes practice and you need to learn how to handle the weapon the same as you do any other type of hunting gear. First, let's take a look at the propelling system, the bow.

There are many types of bows on the market today. These range from the simplest, a longbow, to the more complex units we call compound bows. In between are the midrange, so far as age is concerned, recurve bows. Each type has something going for it or it wouldn't be around.

Let's look at the oldest and perhaps one of the more rugged systems: the longbow. In the past it was a stave of long, hard, tough wood, usually yew, osage orange or similar types of hardwood. These staves or long sticks were carved from one unit, occasionally from two sections mated at the handle, but they were called self bows because they were basically made from one unit of wood.

Three top-selling compounds are (from left): Bear Alaskan, Martin Cougar, and camouflaged Indian Archery's Stalker. Wheels and cables permit shooting heavy draw weights.

The old longbows were temperamental. In hot weather they became weaker, and stiffer in cold weather. The old bows can still be found today, but are basically collector's items.

The modern longbow looks similar to its older brother, but is made of maple and fiberglass laminates. It is impervious to weather and has better cast for the arrow. It is one of the most rugged and dependable bows on the market. You can spend from under a hundred dollars for a unit you

Photo by Charles L. Cadieux

Deer is a primary target for bowhunter today and it's an elusive one. You must learn hunting techniques, also.

Photo by Tennessee Tourist Development

If you'll be relying on archery skills in primitive country as in Smokey Mountains time to practice is now!

sand and finish out yourself, or several hundred for the more exotic models.

Shooting the longbow employs what's traditionally called the instinctive method — no sights. You just look at the target and put the arrow into it, whether game or paper. Some bowmen can't shoot instinctively, but with practice most folks can get the hang of it. There is a slight amount of recoil to the left arm (of the right-handed bowman) when you shoot the longbow. It is minor, but you will notice it in comparison to the other bows on the market today.

The longbow is rugged, almost impossible to get out of alignment with simple care, and will last for many years. It may not be so fast in the speed department as the other units, but from the survivalist's perspective, it is dependable. It was used in the battles of Europe until replaced by gunpowder weapons. Many hunters today use the longbow. Modern chemistry developed fiberglass and bows today are made with this material.

When the Crusaders went to the Middle East, they found archers using bows with recurved limbs. They usually were made of sinew, bone and hardwoods. They were fast, smoother-shooting than a longbow and could be shot from horseback because of their shorter length.

The recurve is alive and well today. Now hardwood makes up the handle section, called the riser, and the upper and lower limbs are laminated from maple strips for the core and fiberglass front and back. This gives it good cast, stability and more speed than the longbow. It also is more pleasant to shoot since it has minimized recoil to the shooting arm by the amount of "deflex" put into the riser. Deflex is the angle from the arm and the curve or reflex they put on

the upper and lower limbs.

These bows are also an excellent choice for the basic survival unit. They are faster, almost as rugged as a longbow, and you can mount sights on them to allow for better accuracy if you have problems with the instinctive style of shooting. They come in two basic styles of manufacture: the single bow is made of many laminates in one unit and the modern take-down style allows you more versatility than the single-unit bows by interchangeability of limbs.

The recurve bow can develop a twisted limb, in which the limb actually goes out of alignment from bad string bracing when putting on the string, or from falling on hard ground. It can happen to any bow, but the recurve has been plagued with this problem since it was developed.

The three-piece take-down bow is an excellent choice for your survival unit. You have a single riser or handle section and the upper and lower limbs are fastened to this riser by many different methods, depending on the manufacturer. The take-down has the properties of a recurve for

An advantage of archery tackle over firearm is you can take small game for pot without destroying much meat.

Bracket-tipped compound (above) may weigh a bit more, but it's nearly impossible to damage the eccentrics. Below: A sampling of the broadheads available to bow and arrow shooters today. At top is a fishing point.

The Kolpin modular insert-style broadhead uses blades that are replaced when dulled. Arrows kill by bleeding.

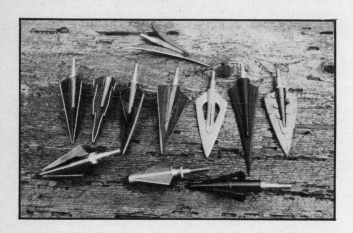

speed and ruggedness, but its main advantage over the single-unit recurve is that you can purchase several sets of limbs for the riser section. You can have one set of matched limbs at thirty-five pounds for small game and practice, and a set of sixty or more pounds for bigger game or for protection from animals such as bear, if you have any around your area. You can stock two or more sets of limbs with the one riser and you have a variety of bows from which to pick. It's a good choice and you can buy them from several sources at moderate prices.

The newest bow design in the archery field is the compound. This unit came on the market in the 1960s and has become the most popular hunting and target bow sold today. It combines a regular riser and in some cases partially working limbs with an elliptical wheel on the limb tips that allows an archer to draw and shoot a heavier bow than he might be able with the longbow or recurve.

There are many models on the market and prices range from under one-hundred dollars to six-hundred dollars.

There are two basic styles of compound: the more-adjustable units have four or in some cases six wheels and the pulleys wind around eccentrics on the limb tips to adjust for draw and weight. The more-popular units are those with two wheels and a cable system along with the string. They are simpler in construction and may not be as adjustable, but are better for the survival system.

The compound comes with a draw length, usually with a two-inch adjustment, and a weight-range adjustment of about fifteen pounds. This gives you the advantage of several weights for the job to be done. The biggest disadvantage to the compound from the survival standpoint is the gear you need to keep it shooting. Some units might require as many as four Allen wrenches to make the adjustments for its different systems. Even the simplest, other than a few on the market which allow no adjustments, require an Allen wrench to make the weight adjustment. If you lose the wrench you might find it a problem to change the bowstring if it breaks or is cut.

There are other units on the market that go beyond the compound, too. These would include the Dynabow systems which have a more or less conventional upper limb and a weird action system on the base limb. It is fast, deadly and a good unit, but any damage to the lower limb system and you are out of business. You should consider all units for your survival needs, but the basic system is the simplest system.

Which bow would be best for survival systems? That is a loaded question and one you will have to decide according to budget, ability to handle the units, and where and how long you plan to store them. The longbow is rugged but slow. But when not using the longbow or recurve, you can take the string off and they will be ready, unaffected by storage. The recurve is faster and almost as rugged as the longbow. You can add sights that would be helpful for most people and the recurve is dependable. I feel the last choice

Exactly what type of game that will remain after a disaster is unclear, but Indians once thought buffalo innumerable...

Archer skilled in use of tackle can take big caribou. Legendary Fred Bear is at left with Dall sheep.

for a survivalist would be the compound, due to its cables, strings, wheels and many adjustments needed to keep functioning. Most archers leave the compound under tension when not in use and limbs have been known to collapse after time. No one bow is perfect. If you have doubts, store several bows.

All bows require a string on which to place the arrow when you shoot. Regardless of the unit, buy several strings of the proper length, shoot them and set them up for the correct bow. Tape them to the riser of that bow. A backup string back in camp isn't much good if you cut your bowstring when out for meat. Tape a spare to the bow and keep it there against the day it is needed.

One bow on the market, made by Indian Archery, has a good gimmick: A four-wheel compound, it is marketed with a two-wheel unit that uses no string. The cable that is used for the propelling system is continued and used as the string to shoot the arrow. This is good in that the cable will probably outlast the bow, but it does make arrow speed slower and it's rougher to shoot. It can be found in some shops and isn't a bad idea for survival.

The choice of bow is the most important decision to make when selecting your survival archery tackle. But you also need the projectile, in this case an arrow. There are three basic types on the market today and all are good. The oldest and still going strong is the wood shaft. They are made from Port Orford cedar found in Oregon and are least expensive of the arrow materials on the market. You can order them by the dozen or the thousand and they perform very well.

Wooden arrows, like others, will break, but they have the advantage of low price, can be recovered and shot many times, and you will find that you will take shots that you wouldn't otherwise take with a more expensive material. Match them to the bow you buy. They can be purchased as bare shafts that you dip, nock and fletch to make your own colors and styles. And you just can't beat the cost! They will warp if stored improperly, but you can place them in a tube or other sealed container to keep moisture from them. Don't stack canned goods on top of them when laying flat or you will find arrows so crooked you can shoot around corners!

The next step up from cedar shafts is fiberglass arrows.

These actually fall into two categories: regular fiberglass shafts or those with graphite woven into the system for lighter arrows. Either is a good choice, and graphite is a bit more expensive. Fiberglass is either straight or broken. It is tougher than cedar arrows and costs a bit more, too. You need inserts for the nock on one end and the head of your choice on the other. With the cedars you merely turn the end of the shaft with a tapering tool. The tips on the fiberglass arrows are usually applied with epoxy cement.

The third arrow material is aluminum. It ranges in price from close to fiberglass to as much as four to five dollars *each*. It is impervious to weather and if you slightly bend one on a rock, you can straighten it. It will shatter if you hit a rock head-on, but no arrow will take that punishment. One end of the aluminum is swaged for a nock and the other is fitted with an insert after the arrow is cut to length.

You can buy ready-made arrows in any of the materials mentioned or you can buy the shafts and necessary tools and make them up yourself. Fletching is of two main types, the traditional turkey feather and newer plastics that are injection-moulded in shapes similar to real feathers. Feathers are faster if speed is important and they can be waterproofed with silicone sprays or simple hair sprays. Plastic is impervious to weather and works well if you shoot from a rest on the side of the bow window, not straight from the shelf.

You have now selected a bow and arrows. What sort of tip is best for that arrow? It depends on the job you want it to do. To take birds or small game, cedar arrows with tips on which you've fitted empty pistol brass (.38 revolver brass fits perfectly) are fine.

When you go for bigger game — deer, elk, bear or varmints like coyotes that might be bothering the camp — you need a cutting edge. The arrow propelled by any bow kills by bleeding, not by blasting through as a bullet does. To cause that bleeding you will use a steel tip termed a broadhead. These range from a simple but excellent two-blade to as many as six cutting edges and they come in many shapes and variations.

The older-style broadheads are the two-bladed ones that you sharpen with a stone to a razor edge. They can be used many times until lost or damaged by missing the deer and hitting a rock. They're excellent since they have longer life than other types of broadheads, called three-bladed, four-bladed and two-bladed heads with inserts. These latter, however, obtain better bleeding from the game animal.

The newer broadheads on the market use inserts that allow you to get a razor edge by merely inserting preshaped blades into a base unit. They are sharp, they do work and some are more rugged than others. The big advantage is that they are really sharp. The big disadvantage is they are more or less a one-shot unit. If you miss, or even sometimes after you hit the game, the inserts will come off, fall out or be damaged beyond use. If you buy this type of head, and there are many on the market, you should also stock up on replacement blades for that unit. They don't cost much and in many cases you can use the base unit for small game as well as large game.

You now have a bow, arrows with tips and are ready to head for the hills. How are you going to carry the arrows? Again you have two basic choices: a small unit that fits on the bow called a bow quiver, or a bigger back quiver. The small bow quiver carries about eight arrows, while a back quiver can carry up to two dozen. The bow quiver is light, fast to work with, safe for the hunter and is always with the bow — a good choice for short runs. Many bowhunters prefer the back quiver since they like to take shots at small game and will lose arrows this way. One method is to use the bow quiver for big game. Cull out slightly damaged arrows and use them in the back quiver for small game such as rabbits and birds.

What can you shoot and hope to kill with a simple weapon like the bow and arrow? Anything, and that is no exaggeration! Archers not using poisoned arrows have killed elephants and rhinos, grizzly bear, polar bear and countless game animals such as deer or elk. You also can shoot small game and not blow them apart as you might with a rifle. You can shoot birds on the wing or on the ground if it comes to a choice of being a good sport or eating tonight. And you can do something else with the stick and string you can't do with powder-burning weapons: You can fish with it!

There have been times when you see big fish just resting on the bottom of a pool and you can't get them to take any bait or lure. Now you can bag them by rigging up your bow with a reel (several types available, including regular fishing reel), some line and a barbed head on a heavy arrow (usually solid fiberglass or aluminum). The arrow will penetrate the water and, if you allow for the refraction of light in the water, you will put the point through the fish and reel him in for the dinner table. If you can see them you can hit them, once you get the hang of it. Try that with a shotgun or rifle and see how far you get! (Since carp are the bowfisherman's mainstay, see Chapter 11 for tips on smoking the bony fish.)

The bow and arrow is a versatile weapon and an excellent choice for survival in any time. You can protect yourself from any kind of predator, no one hears it when you shoot, it is very deadly after you learn to handle it. You can

As there will be situations in which standing shot is impossible, it's smart to practice with bow and your matched arrows in a variety of shooting positions.

Author initiates drawing sequence by taking arrow from back quiver. Advantage of this type of quiver is large arrow capacity.

Field-pointed arrow is next nocked on string and pulled to full draw, as seen at right. The bow used in this case is Bear Alaskan. It shoots an arrow capable of penetrating thick hides of elephants!

To fire PSE's crossbow, you first set front sight pins for expected shooting ranges (left). Rear sight is vertical bar with peep and notch. Prod is cocked by standing on crossarm at front of stock and pulling up string with both hands. This bow draws 125 pounds, but cocks easily.

Above left: Firing crossbow is like shooting long arm, with which more people are familiar. The stock is put into shoulder, cheek on stock, sighted, switched off of safe, then trigger pulled. Keep fingers below string height or ouch! Left: Closeup of PSE unit and bolts it fires. The bolts or quarrels are 21 inches long and weigh 500 grains. Above: Linda Vittor hefts substantial weight of unit. She was able to hit cardboard box within three shots.

Zebco fishing system uses closed-face spinning reel and 90-pound line. Rod attaches directly to takedown riser.

do more to fill the larder than with any other weapon. Big game, small game, birds, fish — if it swims, walks or flies, you can get it!

Since the bow and arrow is such a great system, why doesn't everyone have one, or two or three? The biggest problem with archery is that you must learn how to shoot with the stick and string. It isn't like picking up a shotgun or rifle. You need to learn different systems and how to handle the bow to hit with an arrow. If you plan to place an archery system in your survival shelter, get some instruction and learn how to use it. You don't need to be an expert — you merely want to hit what you aim at, to get something to eat. You must also learn to hunt, since most archery kills today are at around thirty yards or closer.

If you feel the work or time needed to master the bow and arrow might be prohibitive, you have an alternate system that some say isn't archery and isn't rifle — the crossbow. This is a marriage of the bow, now called a prod, and a stock similar to what you have on a rifle. There are many types and models on the market and they all shoot an arrow, now called a bolt or quarrel, into a target or animal perhaps easier than trying to master the bow and arrow.

The traditional crossbow has a prod of various draw weights on the end of a stock. This prod weight can vary from fifty to over two hundred pounds. The modern hunting crossbow will run about 90 to 150 pounds pull or draw weight. This is compared to sixty pounds for the bow and arrow hunter. You have a trigger system that releases the string of the prod. The string is drawn back until cocked and will remain in this position until you pull the trigger. Some units have a safety on the trigger — an excellent idea.

The bolt usually is about twelve inches long but can be shorter or longer, depending on the unit. To cock the crossbow you pull the string up to the trigger unit while bending over, your feet standing on a bar. After cocking the crossbow, fit a bolt onto the string or into the channel, bring the unit to your shoulder as you would a rifle, and sight in on your target. When your target is in your sights, release the safety and pull the trigger. If you have done your homework and set the prod, bolt and sights properly, you can hit

It will take a few shots to develop correct aiming point, since light refracting off water alters position of quarry (above). The fiberglass shaft, attached to heavy line at the nock and fitted with barbed fish point, makes a mighty splash in quiet waters generally sought out by spawning carp that will be bowfisherman's primary quarry.

Upon contact with fish, barbs spring from fish point and you jerk struggling supper on the bank. If you need to, you can use reel handle to help crank 'em in.

Another crossbow with different design is from Provisions Unlimited, Oakland, Maine. This is Balista II Survival Tool with fiberglass broadhead arrows. Cable is nylon.

your target. You can dispatch the same game with the crossbow that you can with the bow and arrow: big game, small game, birds and fish, too. If you are lucky you'll find any bolts that miss. Those that connect usually will pass completely through your game and become lost somewhere on the other side.

Crossbows are much easier to learn to handle and come with two basic systems. The traditional style found on most crossbows marketed today has a channel in which the bolt rides. The string propels it down the channel toward the target. With this crossbow you can shoot bolts of any length and in a pinch even a rock, if you are careful.

The newest gimmick to hit the crossbow field is the compound crossbow. This combines the compound principle of the hand-held bows with the stock of the crossbow system. It has no channel and you must shoot bolts of twenty-one-inch length or longer. Don't try shooting rocks with this one.

The sights on a crossbow can vary from merely aiming over the tip of the bolt to more exotic pins set for different yardages, simple notched sights, or optics like scope sights. All work, once you find out how it works with each unit.

The advantage of the crossbow over the normal archery tackle is that with a few shots almost anyone familiar with long arms can be on target. To prove this, a new compound crossbow made by Precision Shooting Equipment, Incorporated, of Tucson, was handed to a young lady and after three shots she could hit a cardboard box the size of a deer's vital area at twenty yards. She had never fired a crossbow and did nothing but listen to instructions.

The addition of archery equipment to your survival system would be of great advantage. If you need silence, you have it. If you need killing power, you have it. If you need to keep the pot full, you can do it with fur, feather or fin. Look into the different types of archery tackle on the market today. Make the choice you feel is best for your system and pocketbook. You can stock a lot or just a few items that you feel will be useful.

Practice with your bow until you can hit your target. It isn't hard, but you will find it different from any sport or hunting method you have tried before. If you have problems with the hand units, go for the crossbow system. Any-

Carp are bony, but sure beat nothing if you're hungry! Zebco Fishgetter outfit screws into threaded hole that's designed for stabilizer bar. It's something to consider...

one can shoot it and they have gadgets that help you cock the bow, if you need them.

Regardless of which system you pick, the stock and string method of hunting for survival and combat has been proven for centuries. It has just become more sophisticated. In fact, you can make the bow from a bent stick, attach any line for a string and use reeds or straight sticks if you have nothing else. After all, that's the way the whole system started!

Chapter 7

FISHING TO STAY ALIVE

Rid Yourself Of Sportsman's Notions And Learn How To Get Fish On The Bank!

By Bob Zwirz

Waters of Jackson Hole, Wyoming, receive less fishing pressure than rivers closer to populated areas, so taking fish may be easier for backwoods residents.

Planned survival may well include stocking a private aircraft with fishing gear to enable survival if you crash in the wilderness — and survive *that!* In a total war scenario where we head for the back-of-beyond, you'll require far more than a compact rod and reel and a few effective lures. Such an all-out undertaking would demand knowledge of how to fish successfully while utilizing the tools of nature — plus great imagination and well-primed brain power as a basis for believing you're up to the job at hand.

My advice on planned survival will be relatively brief, just as the fishing equipment will be kept compact and to a minimum, and is based on my better than twenty years of flying over Central and South American jungles and across northern and sub-Arctic regions of the U.S. and Canada.

I don't carry a tackle box! Instead, I long ago found a chemically treated canvas roll-pack nineteen inches long. This carries a hollow tubular fiberglass rod that collapses

LIVING OFF the land and waters has been regulated for years, largely due to escalating populations and resultant pressure on populations of wild birds, game or fish. In a time where such man-made controls are eliminated by lack of game wardens, individuals will seek out and take possession of fish and game, unmindful of "ownership" of forests or waterways. Hunger is a powerful motivator, and this chapter is designed to prepare you to catch fish — and survive.

Most of this information will apply to freshwater angling, for inland is where most people envision facing the grass-roots question of survival.

I feel there are two distinct levels of survival: planned survival and, for want of a better description, reactionary — as if war catches us unprepared and wilderness areas are the ultimate hope of the fittest.

Author's survival roll holds two compact rod and reel combos, each spooled with monofilament; selection of proven lures; hooks; weights; and extra mono spools.

Giant lake trout, muskies, northern pike and salt water species respond to spoons author packs in canvas roll.

to eighteen inches. A closed-face spinning reel spooled with twelve-pound-test monofilament is the mainstay for versatility. I also pack four extra spools carrying 8-, 10-, 15- and 17-pound-test mono. The rod and reel combination allows me to cast or jig lures of varying weights and sizes, or hooks with baits provided by nature, with or without sinker or split-shot weights. Natural baits are of course far more abundant in spring through fall than during winter.

Though you'll find an assortment of spinning lures capable of solving most fishing requirements, there will be times when a hook and natural bait will out-produce all the fishing hardware on a tackle dealer's shelves. Study the geographical area you are flying over or going into, and match artificial lures to native fish food. You'll also learn what natural baits exist and where they're commonly found.

The most common natural bait will be worms. Three

Gros Ventre River in Wyoming has healthy population of fish. Fish trapping methods author discusses can be used to good effect in many spots.

In sportsman situation, angling with open-face spinning rod and light lures provides top action — but enough fish?

types that prove great are: small redworms (one to three inches long), any size of so-called garden worms, and nightcrawlers, all of which are found in organic debris. Among the litter of still waters seek out leeches — these critters are long-lived, even on the hook. Never forget crayfish — they work dead or alive. Depending on where you live, crayfish may be known as crawdads, craws or crawfish. Ponds or streams are favorite haunts of this fine bait, which you can eat boiled or even raw.

Insects of great variety can be handy baits. A basic list would surely include catalpa worms, grasshoppers, hellgrammites, caddis worms, the lowly cockroach, crickets, bee or wasp larvae, meal worms and freshwater nymphal life. There are dozens more critters that can be used once you put your imagination to the task: Seven or eight types of freshwater minnows can be used dead or alive, even cut into bait sections; frogs and salamanders are excellent — assuming you haven't eaten the frogs you managed to catch — and tadpoles work just fine, too.

Once you become adept at procuring a fair selection of the above-mentioned natural baits, you'll be well along the

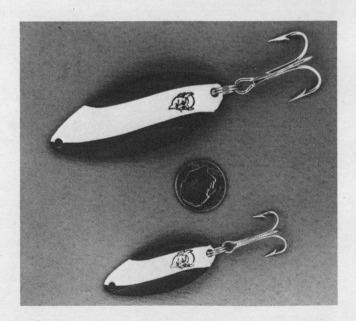

Few spoons have caught more fresh and salt water fish than time-tested Eppinger Dardevles. A must for you!

path to guaranteed fishing success. Add your selection of artificial lures to your arsenal of angler's magic and you should have no trouble procuring fish, eels or turtles.

In an accompanying photo I show both a compact spinning rod and reel and bait-casting rig, plus an assortment of lures. Common sense coupled with trial and error will show you the size of lure most suited to the size and species of fish present in the waters you are to fish. There will be a spoon, spinner, small plug or weighted fly that will do the job properly in 'most every situation I've encountered over the years. And remember, you have the powerful backup of those natural baits.

If you don't mind just a little more bulk and weight in that canvas survival roll, consider the plastic jars of preserved baits. You have readily available such items as minnows, salmon eggs, carp and catfish; although you may find catalpa worms and a few other odd offerings worth more than their weight in gold to those who must survive.

There is much more to consider when we're challenged by the prospect of living off the land indefinitely. You must alter your attitude from sportsman — in fact, you must fast develop the outlook, cunning and base instincts of a skilled and heartless poacher. Either that or you perish.

If you're facing an extended period on your own, with no sporting goods store handy, you'll be glad you stocked up on hooks, weights, line, etc. Hooks, as are these pre-snelled #8s, are virtually weightless and take up little space in survival roll, tackle box or in retreat.

Photo: Wyoming Travel Commission

You'd be smart to begin scouting fishing grounds well in advance of your need, and you'll have fun doing it.

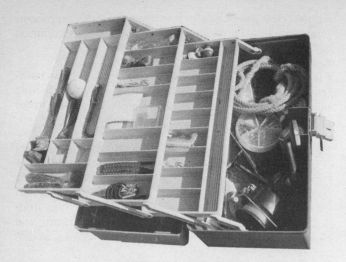

Author found tackle box, like one above, too bulky and cumbersome for many back country trips. Still, for retreat it's a possibility.

Veteran angler Jay Ingliss has, through many days on the waters, acquired skills useful in survival scene.

In a survival scenario, the equipment I've discussed is the bare minimum. Be sensible and prepare such gear now, against the day it's needed. Hopefully it won't be, but what cheap insurance!

Let me surprise you: If you're to survive over a lengthy period and are limited to the total, all-inclusive equipment you can take with you, you'll be packing little more than in the planned survival situation. But you'll take with you *learning and practical knowledge,* because you began your study *now!* Thus, you'll be ready to practice the arts of poaching and living and equipping yourself off the land. One day you may lose or break a fishing rod, break a reel or run out of line. Your prized lures may snag and be lost deep among unapproachable rocks in a fast-running river.

I advise stockpiling a large supply of hooks in varying sizes and extra-large-capacity spools of monofilament, most of this line in pound-tests that will guarantee no lost fish or frayed knots. Sportsmanship be damned!

Before specifically addressing poaching fish and related

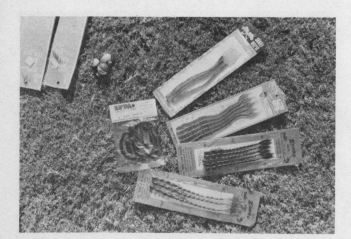

Plastic worms of varying colors and even in assorted flavors have proved effective in bringing to net many species of large fish.

If you have room in your survival roll or tackle box, slip in some salmon eggs or other bait you know works. A supply of swivels is useful for your drop lines, too.

Stream or river bottoms are rich in aquatic insects and nymphal life. Angler here picks off fish-getters caught on screen positioned downstream as he kicked rocks.

Bobbers have long been used to signal a fish's interest in your bait. You can employ them to tell you status of trot lines, or, where security precautions prevent such arrangements, when using conventional tackle which is moved when you leave. You can use hands to other purposes while keeping an eye on your bobber.

Photo: Oregon Dept. of Transportation

In many instances, a boat is a virtual requirement to get into position to reach fish, especially larger members of species. You could improvise a raft with anchor, or?

edibles, let's talk woods lore required to create equipment. Learn to recognize and use the following. All are common to North America.

Switch Cane — The stems of this native American bamboo can be cut and used as a simple but adequate fishing pole for small- and medium-sized fish. You can also make a blow-gun.

Basswood — With patience it's possible to use the fibers of this tree for fish strings, and even for making up a fish net (seine net). In a stream a net will trap trout and other species as you kick the water and rocks to panic fish into your basswood net. You can also make bowstrings from this fiber. Coupled with handmade arrows with a barb, you can take a toll of carp or salmon when in shallows, as discussed in **Chapter 6**.

Red Mulberry — Again, a great wood for making a bow. The carp of the world will never know the difference.

Photo: Manitoba Government Travel

Fast-flowing rivers as found in Canada's Manitoba Province present unique challenges to survivalist. A fish-holding pool or resting location must be determined.

A selection of the author's favorite jigs, some feathered and some flashers. Darting motion created by jigging technique has fooled salt and fresh water behemoths.

While stringing it could be a problem in whitewater stretch, a gill net will take fish here, even migratory species like Atlantic salmon. Not sporting, but it works!

White Ash — Natural forks, sharpened, provide you with a strong spear for fishing the shallows, spearing frogs, flipping and spearing turtles. Great for barbed arrows — same use.

PawPaw — The inner bark is coarse but extremely strong. Many an old-time fisherman used this to string his catches.

Buckeye — Of unusual interest, here's a natural for small streams, backwaters and ponds. A mash made of the highly narcotic seeds of this tree was used by Indians and poachers. Dumped into pools and slow streams, it stupefies fish,

Lazy Mistik Creek in Manitoba provides ideal setting for fish traps outlined by author. Baited traps will be easy to check in deeper water. Shallows can hold rock traps.

An enjoyable day spent fishing with children can have positive, far-reaching consequences. Youths develop the ability to help with food-gathering task, freeing adults.

making them float to the surface where they can easily be seized.

If you were "poor" in hooks and line but "rich" in dynamite or lime, I'm certain you would use your "wealth" in spring holes, deep holes that hold natural food, and fishing waters in general. "Shooting" a hole certainly does work!

Traps, whether fashioned of rocks, sticks, sticks and nets or from chicken wire produce excellent catches. If I were to use this type of arrangement, or even a manufactured chicken-wire fish trap, I'd look to slow-moving waters where I could walk in the water flow without worrying about being upended by the current. You have to bait or chum wire traps before you can look to cash in on edible fish.

All traps must be designed either as a single fish pen or capable of holding multiple fish. Each must utilize a "V" opening through which your fish will travel on a downstream approach. This brand of trap does not require baiting since natural fish movement will cause your quarry to move into your rigged area. In the case of a wire trap, bait does the trick for fish, crayfish and even freshwater eels. Here we're not talking of a small fish trap for taking minnows as bait, but a trap big enough to allow entry of the size of fish we'd crave to eat.

Just the type of trout stream for a rock fish trap. Once built, noisily jog over two- to three-hundred feet of flow, panicking fish downstream into your waiting "stockade."

These two anglers are searching for action in weedy lake near Hollywood, Florida. The area will hold big fish population, and could be candidate for dynamite.

We're interested today in "sporting" fish and for the most part turn up our noses at "trash fish." We may not be so lucky in the future. Adjust attitude accordingly.

I've never doubted the degree of success experienced by those poachers who will set a snag line and know how to both rig and work it for such species as suckers, shad, white perch, walleye or even salmon. Usually #2 treble hooks do the trick; these I'll tie on short monofilament droppers spaced at three- or four-inch intervals. The main snag line calls for either thirty- or forty-pound-test monofilament. Rigged with rubber tubing and an end weight, the snag line is cast out so it sinks across the avenue through which these migratory school fish are passing. Every ten or fifteen seconds you yank hard on the line so as to foul-hook any fish in reach of the snag-hooks. Continue until you've retrieved the length of line, then cast and repeat the process.

Never sell a trotline short. They're old as sin and well proven. In big lakes they've been used for sturgeon, trash fish and Lord knows what: I do know they take catfish fairly well, as I've seen them in use. For the purposes we're discussing here, I'd think a one-hundred-foot line would suffice for average streams and rivers, for in truth just about seventy-five or eighty feet of your line will be used for the all-important hooks.

To make up your trotline, start about twelve feet from the end by tying in sixteen-inch dropper lines about twenty

The ability to read water and understand fish behavior enables you to take dinner from any stream — even the Murray River in Australia's Alps in Kosciusko National Park. Study insect life present before you head into unfamiliar territory and you'll seldom go without fish.

While natural disaster could alter riverbeds, you must proceed with preparations as if this won't happen. You learn prime fishing spots now, then use them later.

inches apart. Your hooks should match the size of the fish you expect to be present, and as an average choice you won't be far wrong if you use #4 hooks. Use the best bait you can come up with, be it worms, cut fish or small bits of scrap meat. Each dropper and hook should be weighted simply to keep your offering down in the water within sight of moving fish that will be drawn to the scent.

One end of your rig is tied low along the far side, the other end in the same manner, where you can check it with some ease at least once or twice a day. Done correctly you have spanned the water with baited hooks.

With experience you can learn to keep this type of rig on the bottom, mid-depth or close to the surface. Species present will dictate the positioning that is best. These silent anglers are deadly when you practice the magic of proper placement.

Today, it's much more sporting to fool hefty rainbow with artificial fly than to create rock trap on the Illinois River in Oregon. If the need arises...

This imitation of common bait fish will take 'most all species that feed on minnows. In this case, it's a good-sized trout. Know your quarry before you seek him!

Zwirz poses with four trophy lakers taken in far north on rod and reel, and for a long time held record for largest lake trout taken on fly rod and cast streamer fly. However, he could have jigged for trout with large spoon.

Whether you're working a catfish stream, a trout or walleye river, the degree of success lies in how well you've learned to "read the water." The same is true when seeking muskellunge, big trout, or the lunker-size channel cats that can tax one-hundred-pound-test lines and stout droppers. The same is true of a single set-line as it is of our multi-hooked trotline setup.

Gill nets, not unknown in our greedy world of commercial fishing, are capable of trapping all manner of fish. The size of the openings dictate the size of fish caught, and of course the length of your gill net controls the area of water you will block. A salmon river blocked by a well-strung gill net is not about to see many salmon make it past the deadly barrier. And such nets work on most moving fish where there's a fair flow of water. Enough said!

There's yet another item that is and can be used for claiming better than your share of fish, even large fish: the snare. I've been known to make one up from vines not uncommon to the shores of tropical rivers, such as located in Paraguay and northern Argentina. With such a rig I've found myself wrestling forty- to sixty-pound tropical catfish, and on one occasion a python I'd been dared to snare.

Photo: Redwood Empire Association

From the same impoundments you can take black bass, catfish, crappie, shad, striped bass, sturgeon and all species of so-called "trash fish." Stink baits are super on the bottom hugging suckers and cats, which might taste damn good when you're hungry! Remember to match your tackle to the size of the fish!

During the hours of darkness, many species move into shallows to feed. At this time they are easily reached by fisherman, such as these salt water striper anglers. This is where your knowledge of fish habits helps!

Who needs a rod and reel to fish? This Wisconsin catfish could not avoid an expert thrust with barbed version of a "fishing pitchfork." Sporting, no — but effective, yes!

Chunk of bloody deer meat tied to weighted hook on 150 feet of 50-pound mono was irresistible to large South American catfish taken from Rio Parana near Argentina.

Photo: Wisconsin Natural Resources Dept.

In the hands of a patient individual, a commercially made snare is quite a gadget.

I'll not talk here of fish poisons since I'd believe it unlikely that anyone in a grass-roots survival situation would have any such supply on hand. A fishing spear, or even a spear and torch I can imagine — a fifty-five-gallon drum of Ratenone, no.

If you are into the survival game there is little sense in my telling you that all manner of little items, such as safety pins, bent and sharpened nails, plus carved wooden forks of various shapes have long been used by primitive man in order to use bait — or snag fish. Imagination and a steel will to survive breed their own ingenious devices.

Keep in mind that the farther you wander away from the beaten track, the less of man that chunk of geography has seen over the years. Thus, the fish and game are less apt to easily spook, or pass up your lure, whether cast or jigged. It is still a fact that survival is never easy — but it is within human grasp.

Photo: Nebraska Games & Parks Commission

These Nebraska carp didn't elude this "elite troop" who fast learned use of simple gig spears. While the fish is extremely bony, it can be smoked to rid oily flavor and dry flesh, as discussed later in this book.

Chapter 8

SURVIVAL KNIVES

What Constitutes The Best Blade? This Expert Feels Bigger Is Better!

By Roger J. Combs

Most hunters would not venture afield without at least one knife for emergency or convenience use. Whitetail deer hunting in Alberta, Canada, may be cold and snowy and a warming fire is welcome. Rifle is Remington Model Seven.

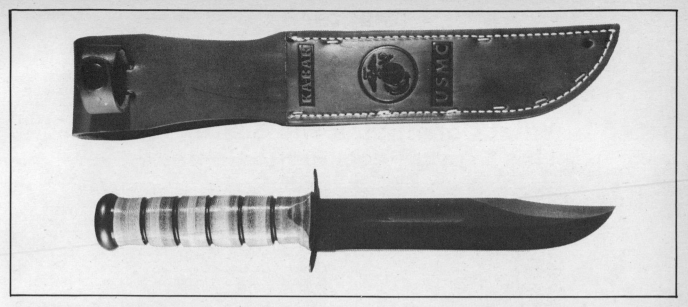

Perhaps the most famous survival knife of the 20th Century is the U.S. Marine Corps fighting and utility knife, first issued in WWII. Ka-Bar still offers a modern version, complete with imprinted USMC sheath.

IF YOU HAD but one tool suitable for any survival situation, you would be wise to choose a knife. Primitive man chipped stone and flint blades — our first tools — and later attached these primitive blades to wooden shafts to create arrows, spears and digging tools. Materials used today for these tools have been improved, but the basic employment of knife blades hasn't changed much — a blade is still our most-basic survival tool.

What's a survival knife? Reduced to basic function, any knife is a survival knife, even if it's only a tiny pocket knife. But considerable field research indicates "big is better." In preplanned situations, a longer, heavier blade — the large, fixed-blade sheath knife — seems capable of doing more jobs of a survival nature.

The type, shape, size and design of a knife or other bladed tool to be selected depends on the job to be performed. Selection is a personal matter and there seem as

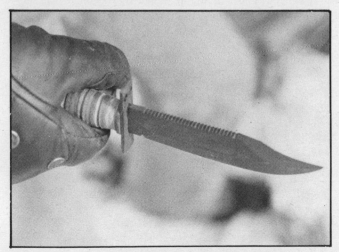

Camillus Cutlery's Pilot Survival knife measures 9½ inches; 5-inch carbon steel blade, leather handle.

many answers to the selection question as manufacturers can produce. Perhaps some basic information can help narrow the choice.

A sheath knife or folder? There are advantages and disadvantages to each. Generally a folder, even a big one, is smaller and more compact to carry. The folded length of the knife is only as long as the handle; perhaps five or six inches. When carried in a leather belt pouch, the folding blade knife is less obtrusive, light in weight and unlikely to interfere with hiking, riding a horse or in a vehicle, fishing, climbing or whatever, as might a folder carried in a pocket. Some argue that these virtues make the folder more likely to be carried in the first place and thus be available for emergency work: A knife is good only if it's at hand when the need arises.

The survival folding knife should be big, with some sort of blade-locking mechanism to hold the blade open when in use. Some small pocket knives also have a locking system. For heavy use the blade must be locked open so that no accidental closure occurs in use. Bad things happen to fingers in such cases!

Locking mechanisms and designs are as varied as the makers can invent. The most common lever location is the rear lock, near the back bolster. But some makers favor the forward lock; others use a side, slide-lock mechanism. There are side push-button locks, hidden bolster locks, toggle locks and sliders. The important thing is that the blade must lock solidly open, with absolutely no play either side-to-side or up-and-down when open. If even the slightest play is felt between blade and handle when open, it probably will worsen with age and should be rejected as a candidate for survival. Work the blade and lock several times to get the feel of the action before you lay out any money for the folder.

Upon closing the blade, observe fit of the folded blade inside the liner or side scales. The blade shouldn't droop out and the blade tip should be completely enclosed inside the liner. The back square of the blade should not protrude

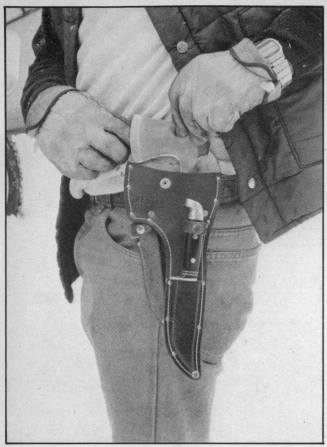

Western's ax knife combination features 4½-inch blade knife with 11-inch ax carried in single leather sheath. Both found use during five-day Oregon elk hunt in snow.

too far out of the liner, either, where it can catch on its sheath or unwary fingers. The blade pivot pin should be massive enough to offer strength and a solid feel during movement and use. While no knife should be routinely used as a pry bar, there may be times in any survival situation when it must be so and overall construction must be heavy enough to withstand rough use and abuse when unavoidable.

A big folder has a couple of disadvantages: One is that in a wet or cold environment, it may not always be easy to open the blade. There may be situations when two hands are not available and most folders require two hands to open the blade. Also, there are legal situations where locking folders are banned, such as aboard commercial airline flights and, unfortunately, in some local communities. The locking-blade knife user should be aware of these potential problems.

No matter what material is used for the blade and liners, any metal is subject to corrosion. These days, most folding knife blades are made of stainless steel. Some years ago stainless steel had a poor reputation for edge-holding properties — the ability to stay sharp. This problem has been overcome by the metallurgical industry and stainless knife blades will take and hold an edge as well as the tool steels of old. The survival knife, folding or fixed-blade, should be made of stainless steel. The knife user should understand, however, that there is really no such thing as a completely stainless, totally non-corrosive steel that can be used as a

blade. Any metal will eventually give in to the right — or wrong — substances.

The folding knife must be kept as clean and dry as possible. A blade folded into its liner coated with water, blood, citrus juice, acids or some other corrosive substance will soon corrode enough to lose its keen edge. Rust on the locking and folding mechanism may render the knife useless just when it's needed most. Sand and dirt left down inside the liners will soon grind off the blade edge. Clean and lub-

Skachet from Charter Arms is another combination tool used as ax, knife, skinner, pry or hammer. Head is carried in pouch, handle attached at site.

ricate all moving parts along with the blade. A cotton-tipped swab or even a tiny stick or toothbrush will do the job when nothing else is available.

The amount of extra care needed for the folder will rule out the design for some knife users. Many prefer the standard, fixed-blade sheath knife as a survival tool. As with the folder, most modern sheath knives are built of a stainless steel; steels called 154CM and the 440 series are the most popular and durable. Those alloys are produced with maximum edge-holding and corrosion-resistance properties in mind. The sheath knife is generally longer and bulkier to carry, but has the advantage of being available for use as soon as it's drawn from the sheath.

Blade lengths of up to ten inches are produced, but there seems to be a practical limit. Most of today's factory-made hunting knives tend to feature blades of four to five inches in length. For most survival use, a blade length of four to seven inches seems the most practical compromise.

For maximum strength, the full tang is preferred. A full tang means the blade and handle portion of the knife are of one piece of steel. The tang may be drilled with rivets or bolts through it and the handle material, along with a strong epoxy substance binding handle slabs to the tang. Some tang designs are hollowed out for lightness and balance, depending on the length of the blade. Some designs call for a tubular or hollowed-out handle with a screw cap on the butt to store additional survival items such as matches, fish hooks, medicines, etc. Of necessity, these are more massive, but the items carried may save a life.

The steel stock from which the blade is ground should be somewhere between three-sixteenths and one-quarter inch thick. The planned survival situation knife would be too flexible for heavy work if formed from one-eighth-inch

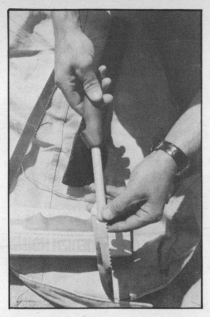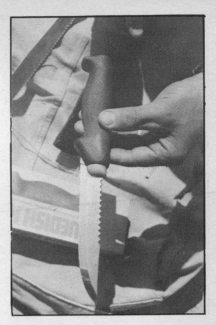

The Swedish Kombin knife features five quickly changed blades: a 4½-inch general purpose blade as shown, an 11-inch saw blade, 5-inch filleting blade, a butcher blade and 4-inch skinner. All interchange as shown and a scabbard is included for safely transporting blades, ready for any situation.

steel. While prying, digging or other abuse is not recommended, it may be unavoidable and the blade should be tough enough to withstand such action.

Blade shapes are limited only by the manufacturer's imagination and knowledge of the marketplace. The two most popular are the skinning blade — with an upswept-tip profile — and the drop point or hunting blade. Many will argue in favor of the typical boot knife blade shape; a double-edge design offered by most makers and popular with survivalists. A serrated or saw edge back has found favor with many outdoor people who rely on a knife for everyday use in the wilderness. There are several such designs on the market which the buyer may consider.

Handles, whether on folders or sheath knives, should be rugged and durable. One of the most durable materials is known as Micarta, a man-made product which seems impervious to most foreign substances. Micarta may be found in several colors from white to black, in wood-grain, impregnated with patterns and textures. Water, blood, oil, acids, heat, cold or light do not affect Micarta. It is a practical, tough handle material for the survival knife. Resin-impregnated woods have also been used for knives of the type under discussion and are as tough as the Micartas.

Natural horn, wood, ivory and antlers are beautiful to look at and feel, but are not the kind of handle you should consider for a survival knife as they may eventually crack

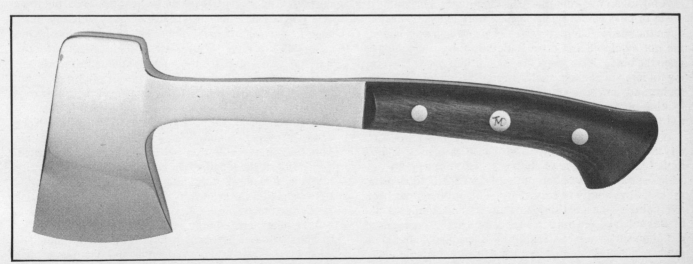

Ted Dowell is a custom knifemaker who produces beautiful as well as functional one-piece trail axes for the survivalist.

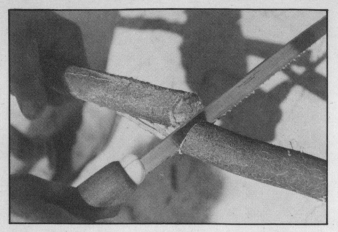

With saw blade locked into polypropylene handle, Kombin easily cuts through small branches for firewood, ax handles, litters, splints, other uses.

or chip with use. On the other hand, dense wood from tropical areas of Africa, Asia, Central or South America has been used successfully for tough knife handles for years with little or no deterioration.

Whatever the handle material selected, it should offer a firm, non-slip grip for the user. A soft plastic or rubberized material will be favored by many, offering a good hold when wet or cold.

A brass, aluminum or steel butt cap is another option to be considered. Yes, there are times when a spike must be pounded, a nut cracked, ice broken, glass smashed. A metal end cap will serve well for such emergencies.

Finger grooves on the handle are another option a potential survivalist may want. Many folders and some sheath knives are offered with finger grooves in the handle. Along the same lines are the questions of a finger guard or hilt. Some folding knives and most large sheath knives are built with some sort of hilt to prevent a wet hand from slipping down over the handle onto the sharpened blade. For heavy use, a finger-guard design would seem essential.

Folder or sheath knife, large or small, whatever the steel and the handle material, every knife or ax must be kept sharp to be properly and safely used. Knife sharpening is an art which some find easy, some difficult, some never seem to master. But it must be done.

Such saw blades are not intended to cut down big trees, left, but will do in emergency situation. Below: Kershaw also offers interchangeable blade set. The Blade Trader is primarily a kitchen tool but includes handle with carving blade, wood or bone saw, bread knife, frozen food blade, boning blade and a deep cook's blade.

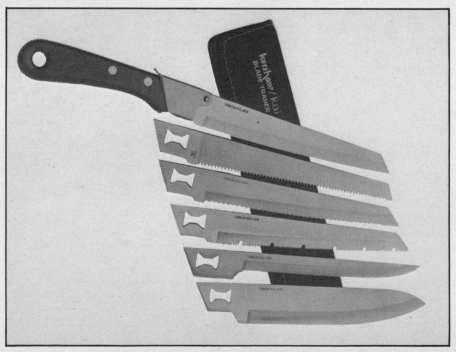

The sharper the blade edge, the easier and safer it is to use. A dull edge can get you into trouble; catching, slipping, causing undue force to be used. A sharp blade will cut when and where it is intended. No blade will remain sharp indefinitely with use, but each kind of blade steel will dull differently, depending upon what is being cut. As a rule, the harder steels — that is, those which have been tempered and heat-treated to a higher level of hardness — will maintain an edge longer, but will be more difficult to sharpen. Softer tempered blades will need honing more often, but the user will find the task easier and faster.

There are all kinds of products available with which to sharpen knives and axes. Perhaps the most common is the so-called oil stone, Carborundum, found on the shop bench. This is a manmade substance, of fine to medium grit. Plenty of special honing oil is applied to the surface of the stone as the knife edge is sharpened. The oil is supposed to carry off the excess grit and tiny steel particles so that they

clean for each sharpening session. Some field stones are intended to be used with water, or saliva in situations where nothing else is available. Another common device carried into the field in a backpack or with the knife sheath is a steel rod impregnated with a grit abrasive; others use diamond dust or ceramic bonded to the rod for touch-ups during long skinning or cutting jobs. A circular hand stone of 240-grit abrasive or coarser is generally recommended for sharpening an ax blade. Some prefer to use a fine file for axes and hatchets.

No matter what kind of sharpener you use, the important and most difficult thing to remember is to keep each stroke of the blade to the surface at the same angle. Change the angle slightly at each stroke and the edge will become rounded, reducing sharpness. Some people find this easy to do, others can't do it at all. Plenty of practice seems to be the answer.

The best place to practice is in the comfort of your own

Imperial Frontier's P-IV folder is attractive, large enough to do a job but small enough for daily carry. Blade measures 3¾ inches, knife is five inches closed; handle insert is natural American birch.

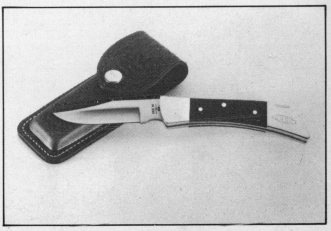

Case is a well known American knife producer; their model 2159L folder will perform most survival tasks.

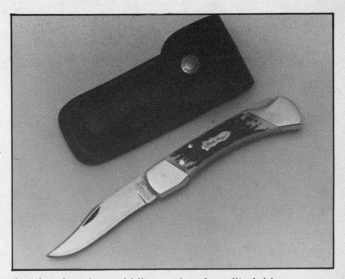

Another American old-line make of quality folders is Schrade Cutlery. The LB8 Grizzly folder is five inches long closed with 3½-inch blade, rear lock, solid brass bolster and liners, Staglon handle.

do not re-dig into the blade metal, not simply to lubricate the stone.

Honing oil is specific. It is not the same as household machine oil as used on firearms or the garage door. Honing oil is formulated to hold in suspension the undesirable tiny particles which the sharpening process produces. It is generally thinner than most lubricants, although in an emergency any oil is better than none.

Some of the best sharpening stones found anywhere are the Arkansas natural stones, sold under various brand names. The stones are mined of novaculite, a hard, fine-grained rock. The novaculite is quarried and cut into different shapes, grades and sizes, to be sold as pocket-size field sharpening stones up to large bench stones a foot or more long. The most common is called the soft Arkansas. With practice, the soft Arkansas stone will put as keen an edge on any blade as the user desires.

Other stones, such as those made from ceramics, are used with nothing on them at all. They are simply kept kitchen or workshop. An oil stone eight, ten or twelve inches long is the easiest to use when sharpening kitchen knives or the larger survival blades. An hour spent on all the household knives will pay dividends at home as well as in the field. Wood or metal box-like stone holders that can be C-clamped to the work surface will hold the stone firmly down while applying pressure with the knife. Several brands of holders are for sale, but the handyman can make his own out of scrap wood. They don't have to be fancy, but they have to fit the stone. In the workshop, the holder may be permanently affixed to the bench.

The first step is to apply plenty of honing oil to the stone. The honing oil allows the stone to produce the maximum abrasion by keeping the surface pores open; regular oil is likely to clog those pores and should not be used except in an emergency. Most authorities recommend an angle between blade and stone of about twenty degrees, although that varies with the type of edge desired. A close look at the knife with the edge on the stone as it was factory sharpened will show the angle at which it should be held. As mentioned, the important thing is to keep the same angle for each stroke of the knife, both sides of the blade.

Chuck Stapel's drilled out handle model has 4-inch 440C blade. Gerber's survival knife also of 440C steel, 4¾-inch blade, non-slip coated handle.

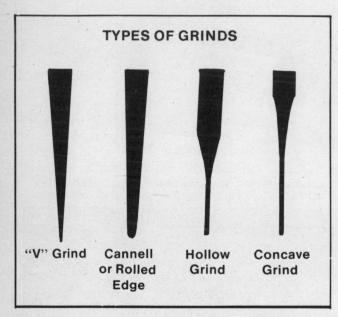

TYPES OF GRINDS

"V" Grind   **Cannell or Rolled Edge**   **Hollow Grind**   **Concave Grind**

Most knives carry the V or hollow grind, above. No knife will work without a good edge. Correct sharpening is a task which must be practiced to be done well. Basics are contained in text.

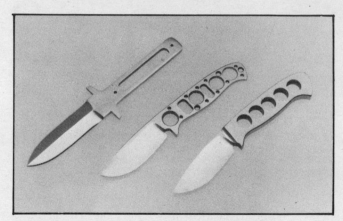

California custom knifemaker Chuck Stapel is experimenting with all-steel, lightened handles and glass beading finish for his survival knives. All are constructed from 440C stainless steel; Micarta handles are easily added when requested.

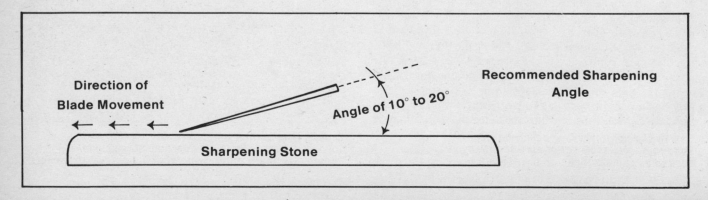

Direction of Blade Movement

Angle of 10° to 20°

Recommended Sharpening Angle

Sharpening Stone

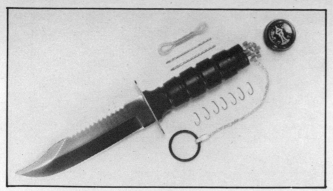

Pete Klika's Lifeknife survival model is complete with compass, matches, hooks, wire saw, needles, etc.

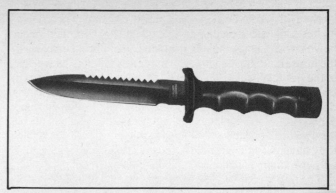

Gutmann's Explorer Wilderness survival model is another knife with hollow handle, threaded cap.

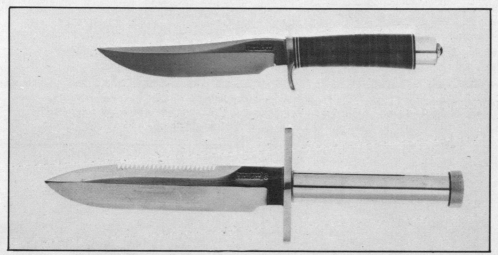

Legendary Randall survival knife with saw tooth blade top, hollow threaded cap handle.

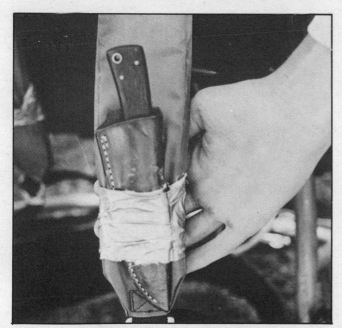

This backpacker has taped his custom Tinker knife to pack's shoulder strap where it is always available for instant use on or off the trail.

Bianchi Gunleather, better known for high-quality holsters, offers large hollow-handle survival knife. Sheath has sharpening stone pouch, tie-down grommets.

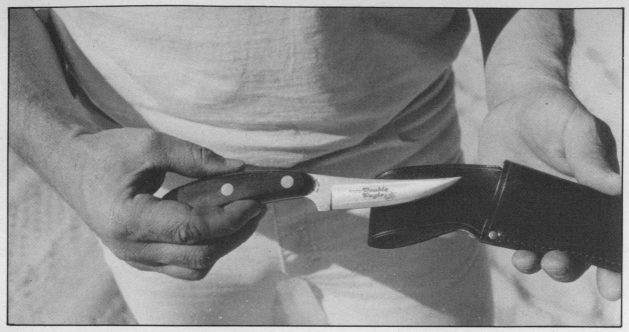

Frontier Double Eagle Utility Hunter is a medium size versatile sheath knife preferred by any hunters, campers. Stainless steel blade measures 3⅝ inches; leather belt sheath is included.

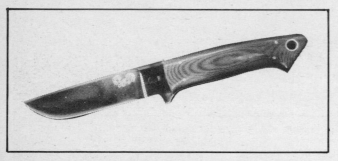

Most of the knives custom maker Glen Hornby makes feature exotic, expensive handles. Hunter, above, utilizes tough linen Micarta for rugged work. Kershaw's Camp & Field knife at right, is made from Japanese Kai stainless steel, 4 inches long, 8¼ inches overall, ideal size and shape for field survival.

Maintaining a firm pressure on the oiled stone, push the blade across the surface as if trying to cut a thin slice from the top of the stone. Change sides and repeat, one side, one stroke. Alternate sides, maintaining pressure and angle across the stone. When the oil begins to darken, indicating it's loading up with grit, wipe it clean and apply new honing oil. Keep stroking until the desired edge is achieved. The blade may be tested by carefully feeling the edge with fingertips. Use extreme care for this job. Once the edge seems sharp enough, one trick is to test evenness by dragging the blade lightly across the thumbnail. Any irregularities will be felt as snags. But again, be careful.

Slicing off strips of newspaper with the knife is a nice trick for demonstration purposes, but it plays hell with the edge. Paper will dull a knife faster than just about anything else. Better to try the knife out on a fresh tomato or piece of salami.

Several manufacturers realize the difficulty of maintain-

ing the exact blade angle when sharpening and offer a clamp or jig designed to hold the blade off the stone correctly. The blade is clamped into the little device and honing is carried out as outlined above.

Shaving the hair off the forearm is another demonstration often seen with a razor-sharp knife. It can be done, but most heavy-duty survival knives should not be honed to such a fine edge. Razor sharpness is too fine an edge for heavy cutting or skinning jobs. A V-grind or hollow-grind edge is the most practical for the uses under discussion.

A sharpening steel or rod will put a different kind of edge on a blade than the stone. The main advantage is that the steel, ceramic or diamond-impregnated rod is easily carried along to the field and will be put to use in any emergency situation when the knife is in action.

Some of the larger sheath knives have built-in pockets for a small stone or rod. A few minutes with a few strips of industrial tape will substitute if the sheath isn't so equip-

Honing steel, above, works well for quick edge touch ups but sharpening job requires Arkansas stone and oil, right.

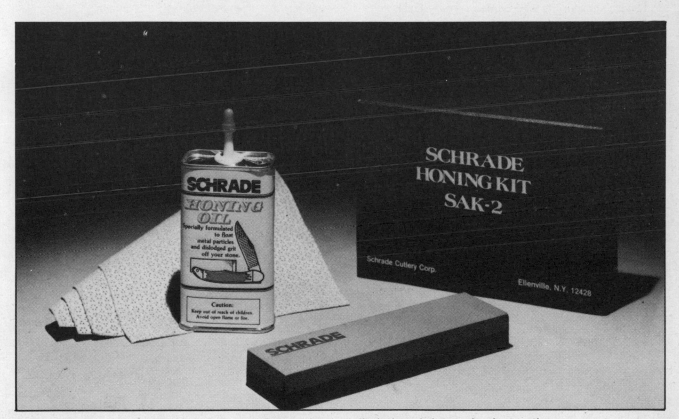

Schrade Cutlery's honing kit includes special stone, honing oil, cloth and sharpening instructions.

ped. It should be standard equipment for any survivalist.

The steel is designed to align the edge in a straight line; the stone will put a microscopic toothed edge on it. The almost-gone corner butcher always used a large steel for his knives used for carving your favorite cutlet. Experienced hunters will carry a medium-grit steel with them and leave the oil or water stone back at camp. Some brands of steel will have a wedge-shaped edge or a chisel point, intended to be used for opening the pelvis of a deer. It is bet-

ter to use a steel for this purpose than hammering on the back of a knife blade.

No discussion of edged tools would be complete without some mention of axes and hatchets. Many sizes, shapes and weights are available. For splitting firewood or cutting down trees, they can't be beat. A number of knifemakers also produce small trail axes, intended to be carried on the belt in a leather sheath. And some sheaths are constructed so as to carry both a knife and small ax in one neat package.

E-Z Sharp sharpening kit includes clamp to hold knife at desirable angle, coarse, medium and fine abrasives.

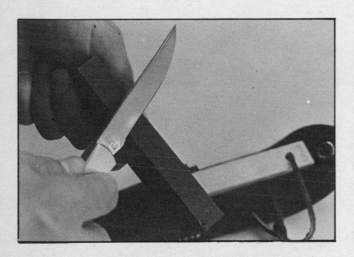

Field Sharpening kit from Gerber, above, includes coarse and medium grit oil-impregnated whetstone and five-inch steel carried in leather pouch. Small ceramic rod, oil stone, below, are handy in backpack or pocket to bring back blade edge.

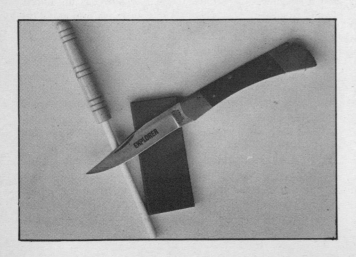

Gerber also offers 8-inch sharpening steel, above, which pivots out of leather sheath. Below, Brass Rat steel rod telescopes out of handle.

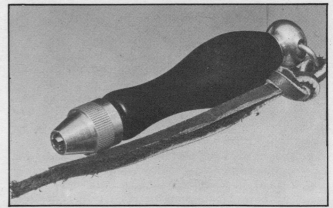

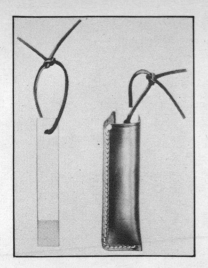

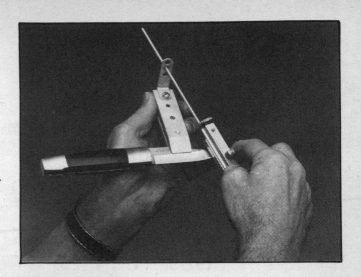

Five-inch Gerber steel, left, fashioned with chisel point for prying, splitting, as well as edge dressing. Loray knife sharpener, right, features angle guide to insure correct, consistent blade edge honing.

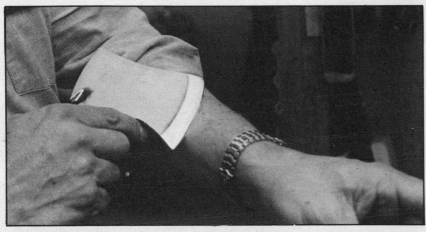

New Mexico's Joseph Cordova, left, proves that with practice, even his survival ax can be honed sharp enough to shave arm hair.

Most wilderness hunting, fishing or backpacking camps will, where permitted, have a campfire for cooking and warmth. It seems to be man's nature to want to sit by a fire, no matter the season. To have a fire, you must have firewood and it usually has to be split or cut. Even a small, lightweight trail ax is capable of splitting a surprising amount of firewood with considerable ease. In a pinch, a heavy knife blade will split kindling, but an ax or hatchet will make the job easier.

A couple of outfits are selling a sort of combination ax and knife head for which the user is to cut his own handle from a stick when the need arises. They work well and will perform all kinds of tasks essential for survival and comfort in the field. Carried in the backpack or on a belt, they don't weigh much or take up a lot of room.

Another category that fits into this chapter is small saws for trimming, cutting, field dressing and other like chores. Some custom knifemakers will produce a small saw blade, often folding, that may be carried in the backpack or on the belt. There are a couple of outfits that offer changeable-blade saws, locking into the knife handle. Some flexible ring saws will fold down small enough to fit into the hollow survival knife handle. Larger hardware stores, specialty shops, outfitters and some mail-order companies have ring saws and trimming saws listed. When hunting from a stand, the little saws can be used to trim away unwanted small branches for a clear view or shot; a popular item with bowhunters. Given enough time and sweat, the survivalist can cut through most heavy limbs with a hatchet, ax or heavy knife blade, but the small saw will make quicker and easier work of the task. It's another item to make life in the field that much simpler.

As mentioned, any sort of blade may become a survival blade. But if we're looking for the best, bigger is better. A heavy, thick blade with a serrated saw edge on the back will handle all but the heavier jobs in an emergency situation. If but one knife is all you have, a hollow handle with a threaded cap for small emergency items is ideal. The leather sheath should be heavy enough to handle rough usage and a pocket for a small sharpening stone is an added benefit. Carry along a small trail ax and saw, and you'll be ready for almost any situation.

A good custom or factory-produced knife is still one of the best bargains around, even without an emergency. One may find a tough, well-designed knife for under $25 at the hardware or sporting goods counter. Generally, you may expect to pay $30 to $50 for one of the big hunting knives of well-known name. Special survival designs will probably be a few bucks more. Prices from custom knifemakers will run upwards from $80 and you may pay considerably more if you specify a special design or feature. Most custom makers will quote you six or more months delivery time; the factory-produced knife is on display and available as soon as you have the money.

Remember, when you need it and don't have it, it's too late to go out to buy it.

Chapter 9

EARTHQUAKE: PREPARE & SURVIVE

How To Prepare For, Live Through, And Recover From Nature's Shaker

EVERY YEAR, movement of the earth destroys life and property all over the globe. The Guatemala quake of 1976 killed an estimated 23,000. The Tangshan quake of the same year killed a quarter of a million! Had the San Francisco quake of 1906 occurred today, when the city's population numbers five million instead of a half-million, between three and ten thousand people would be killed. In 1906, about seven hundred people died.

Virtually every state in the U.S. is affected by earthquakes and massive destruction has occurred in Alaska, California, Hawaii, Missouri, Montana, Nevada, South Carolina, Utah, Washington, and Wyoming. Quakes will continue to shake us, but we can take steps to keep from being rattled!

What causes earthquakes? Science tells us that earthquakes result from continental drift. The earth's crust is divided into what are called horizontal plates, immense slabs of rock floating on a viscous layer of molten rock. In such areas as the middle Atlantic the continents are drifting apart. Magma escapes to the surface through the tear in the crust. The result is a Mid-Atlantic Ridge of volcanoes, lava flows and towering underwater mountains that equal America's Rocky Mountains.

On the West Coast, continents are moving horizontally to one another, creating a fracture or fault line, the most

At 6:01 a.m. on February 9, 1971, the Los Angeles basin was rocked by the infamous Sylmar quake that produced destruction seen at left. Many injuries were reported.

Rescue workers dig through rubble, assisted by American Red Cross, in search for victims of Sylmar shaker.

famous being the San Andreas Fault. Earthquakes are frequent and range from mild to extremely destructive, as was the San Fernando or Sylmar quake of 1971.

Along the coast of Japan, another type of continental drift occurs. The horizontal plates are forced together and this action of "butting heads" forces one of the horizontal plates atop the other. The result is a complex fracture and folding zone, with gigantic rock folds, deep ocean trenches, many earthquakes and plenty of volcanic activity.

PREPARING FOR AN EARTHQUAKE

While you can do nothing to prevent an earthquake, and science has yet to perfect a technique for predicting one, there are steps you take to improve your chances of surviving through an earthquake. Much of what follows has been prepared by James M. Gere and Haresh C. Shah, professors of Civil Engineering at Stanford University in California. They are co-directors of The John A. Blume Earthquake Engineering Center at Stanford and will send a free copy of *Earthquakes, How To Protect Your Life And Property,* and the Earthquake Society's *Earthquake Emergency Guide For Your Family's Safety* if you send a stamped, business-size, self-addressed envelope to The John A. Blume Earthquake Engineering Center, Department of Civil Engineering, Stanford University, Stanford, CA 94305.

Let's start with your structure, since most loss of life results from the partial or total collapse of buildings. The shaking ground causes little damage — it's the effect on manmade structures that's destructive. Flying glass from broken windows and toppling bookcases or china cabinets cause injuries, too.

If you're building a new home in earthquake country, your competent architect will suggest appropriate structural design. To survive a quake the foundation must stay on the ground and the building atop the foundation. Metal strapping to reinforce all joints is recommended by Gere and Shah. If your wooden-framed building isn't bolted to the foundation with half-inch expansion bolts — and many buildings erected prior to 1950 weren't — this can be cheaply and relatively easily done. If your exterior is stucco, as are most California dwellings, they can be strengthened with plywood sheeting before the sheetrock or gypsum is attached to walls. (For existing structures, you could add a layer of plywood at least one-fourth-inch thick topped with another layer of sheetrock, or remove the present sheetrock to expose wall framing to which the plywood is securely nailed.

Masonry facades may be lovely, but also can be deadly. They should be strongly reinforced, especially taller ones, or eliminated from your planning. And solid brick homes built around wooden framing may not survive an earthquake. While timber framing will "give" as nature's forces act on it, brick will crack and collapse.

Mobile homes on nonreinforced foundations are subject to displacement by even mild tremors, say the experts. The

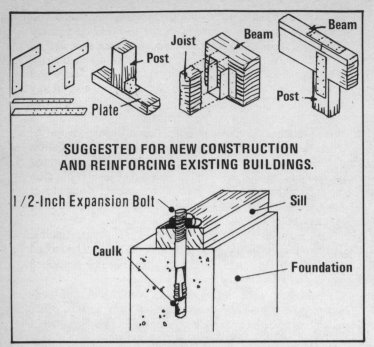

SUGGESTED FOR NEW CONSTRUCTION AND REINFORCING EXISTING BUILDINGS.

1/2-Inch Expansion Bolt

Caulk

Sill

Foundation

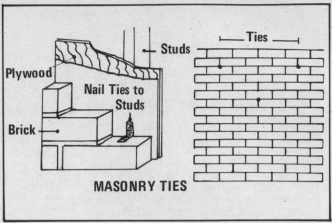

MASONRY TIES

If you can't bear to remove masonry facades, you can strengthen them by attaching ties to studs, as shown here. Of course, it's stronger still if you have attached a sheet of plywood before any masonry.

The Earthquake Society says that a building's ability to survive an earthquake depends on its being fastened together: foundations must stay on the ground, the substructure on the foundation, floor on the substructure, walls on the floor and roof on the walls. Reinforcing helps.

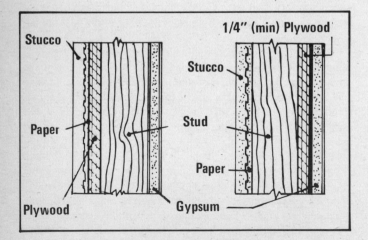

1/4" (min) Plywood

Stucco

Paper

Plywood

Stucco

Stud

Paper

Gypsum

Stucco walls are not terribly strong, but can be made stronger by addition of a layer of plywood a minimum of one-fourth-inch thick. If building your structure, you can add a layer of plywood atop the tar paper before stucco exterior is applied. Alternative is to add a layer to interior, either atop the gypsum or by removing sheetrock layer and attaching directly to studs. This requires another layer of sheetrock atop the plywood.

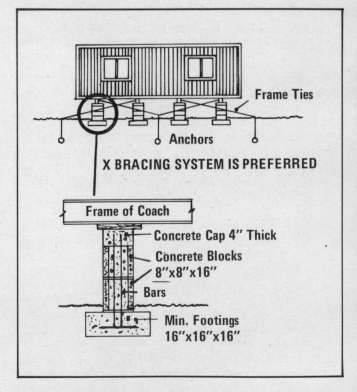

Frame Ties

Anchors

X BRACING SYSTEM IS PREFERRED

Frame of Coach

Concrete Cap 4" Thick

Concrete Blocks 8"x8"x16"

Bars

Min. Footings 16"x16"x16"

Cross-bracing system favored for mobile homes is shown here, including the piers on which it should rest. This is best guarantee against jostling.

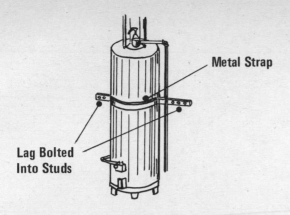

Metal Strap

Lag Bolted Into Studs

Your water heater represents up to forty or fifty gallons of precious water, and to keep the heater in place you should strap it securely to studs.

foundation should consist of an in-ground footing measuring at least sixteen cubic inches, topped by two standard-sized concrete blocks (eight inches high by eight inches wide by sixteen inches long), topped with a four-inch-thick concrete cap on which rests the mobile home frame. Running from the cap through the blocks and into your footing should be reinforcing bars of steel. Complete the quake-ready foundation by tying the frame together with cross-braces anchored securely in the ground.

Now tour your home looking for trouble spots. Run a

metal strap or two around your water heater and bolt it into wall studs. It could otherwise topple and spill up to forty precious gallons of water, to be discussed later. Run a strap around your furnace to immobilize it and eliminate the risk of a severed natural gas line (more on this later). Have you tall bookcases, china cabinets, refrigerators and heavy pieces of furniture? If so, fasten them to wall studs with hooks, angle brackets or braided wire.

Falling objects cause most trouble during an earthquake. Remove them from high shelves and the installation of child-proof latches on cupboard doors will keep canned goods and jars inside — and not on top of you. What's on the wall above your bed — a heavy painting? Keep closet doors closed and doors leading outside unobstructed both at home and at work.

Dangerous or flammable liquids — poisons, pesticides, kerosene and gasoline, for example — should not be stored on high shelves, especially if in glass bottles. A locked storage cabinet affixed to a wall is preferable.

Familiarize each family member with the shutoff locations for your water and gas, and keep a crescent or other suitable wrench near each. Know how to turn off your electricity at the fuse box or circuit breaker panel.

You may lose electricity in a quake, so keep a flashlight next to your bed. Store extra batteries in the refrigerator (they last longer).

Have at least one battery-powered radio with spare batteries capable of receiving the Emergency Broadcast System station in your area. Telephone service may be inter-

Darkest areas on map below indicate areas of major seismic activity within Continental U.S., while other shaded areas are periodically affected by quakes. If you live in these areas, take precautions!

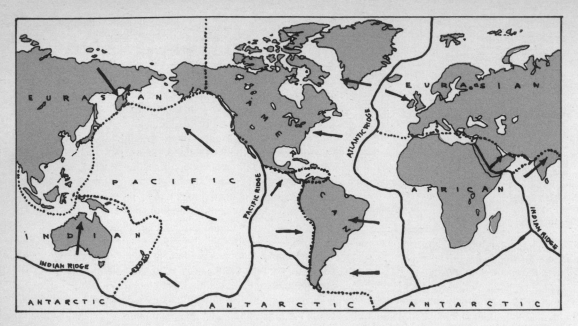

The "why" of earth tremors is explained in above illustration. Solid lines represent midocean ridge system, while dotted and solid lines show the horizontal plates and arrows indicate direction of drift.

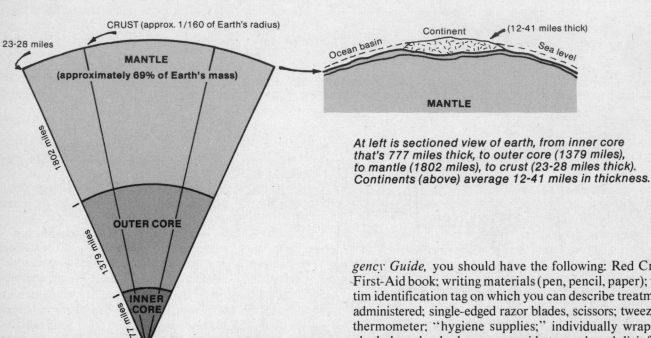

At left is sectioned view of earth, from inner core that's 777 miles thick, to outer core (1379 miles), to mantle (1802 miles), to crust (23-28 miles thick). Continents (above) average 12-41 miles in thickness.

rupted and the radio could be your only information source. Communication with the outside, while perhaps slanted by authorities who don't want citizens aware of the severity of a disaster, is better than total silence.

An appropriately stocked first-aid kit is essential, but you also should know how to use it. Taking first-aid or Cardiopulmonary Resuscitation (CPR) courses now is strongly urged. If family members require special medications like insulin, keep extra quantities on hand. Hospitals may be unreachable or overcrowded.

In your first-aid kit, recommends the *Earthquake Emer-gency Guide,* you should have the following: Red Cross First-Aid book; writing materials (pen, pencil, paper); victim identification tag on which you can describe treatment administered; single-edged razor blades, scissors; tweezers; thermometer; "hygiene supplies;" individually wrapped alcohol swabs; hydrogen peroxide to wash and disinfect; Bacitracin or Neosporin ointment for dressing wounds; one-inch adhesive bandages; various sizes of sterile dressings; tape; instant ice packs for sprains or burns; meat tenderizer for stings or insect bites; motion sickness tablets for nausea; antacid; non-aspirin pain reliever; pair of eyeglasses for each member who wears them; ammonia inhalant; water purification materials (filter, tablets, iodine, or bleach); and any prescription drugs required by family members.

You should consider adding a toothache reliever like Anbesol, cough mixtures, decongestant, anti-diarrhea medicine, ear drops, eye drops, Ipecac to induce vomiting, laxative, nose drops, toothpicks and dental floss. Life can be more comfortble with drinking cups, measuring spoons,

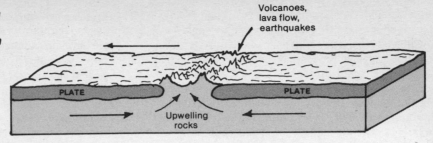

Movement of the earth's horizontal plates away from each other, as in the Mid Atlantic Ridge, leaves open space in crust that is filled by magma from molten mantle below.

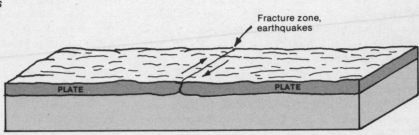

Fracture zones like the San Andreas Fault in California result from the horizontal movement in opposite directions of the continental plates.

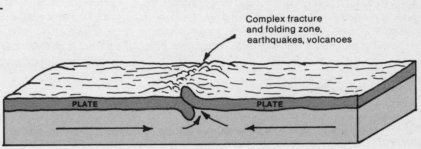

Where two plates are colliding head-to-head, as in the coast of Japan, one plate is thrust atop the other. This leads to major seismic activity like volcanoes and earthquakes.

medicine droppers, splints, tongue depressors, tissues, baby needs, towelettes for washing and drying, salt and pet tranquilizers. Don't forget tools like prybar, shovel, axe, crowbar, wire cutters, pails, tarps, wire, rope and such as may be needed during rescue operations.

Every home should have a fire extinguisher, even if small. Leave garden hose attached to faucets. These can be used to extinguish most household fires, providing you have water pressure

Water and food should be stored for emergency use, and most authorities suggest a week's supply isn't too much. While relief organizations like the American Red Cross or National Guard will mobilize in a disaster, there's no telling when they'll arrive to help you. Therefore, you must be prepared to care for your own family.

The *Earthquake Emergency Guide* suggest you store the following food items that will suffice for a family of four for four days:

Milk: Powdered non-fat dry, two packages; and four fourteen-ounce cans of evaporated milk.

Juices: Six fourteen-ounce cans of tomato, orange or grapefruit. (Larger cans will lose their vitamins if left open)

Fruits: Four fourteen-ounce cans of a variety of fruits, plus two pounds of dried fruit.

Vegetables: Twelve sixteen-ounce cans of a variety of vegetables.

Soups: Eight 10½-ounce cans of a variety of soups, plus four packages of dry soup mix.

Meat & Meat Substitutes: Two jars of peanut butter, two jars of cheese, plus twelve cans of miscellaneous meats like hash, stew, tuna, etc.

Cereal, Crackers & Cookies: Three boxes of each.

Beverages: Four ounces of instant coffee, tea or bullion, two packages of instant cocoa mix, and twenty-four bottles of soft drinks. Forget alcohol — it hastens dehydration.

If you store these separate from daily consumables, rotate foods so they're eaten and replaced with fresh within one year. It may lose taste and vitamins after long periods. Freeze-dried or dehydrated foods last five years or longer. Adjust to your family's peculiarities and special requirements.

Don't forget about your pets. Lay in a week's supply of food for them, since you'll likely be remaining in or near your home or taking the pets with you to an evacuation headquarters, if you opt for the plan discussed later. Animals require water, too, and this will vary depending on the weather and size of the pet.

Your family's water supply may be interrupted following an earthquake, so you should store water. (For information on purification and storage, see Chapter 17.) As stated, well-rinsed plastic gallon milk jugs work well if tightly sealed, or you can obtain poly tubs suitable for storage. But you have other water sources available: Your water heater, which has not crashed and spilled because you've strapped it to a wall, holds usually forty gallons of potable water. Ice cubes will melt without refrigeration. Your toilet holding tank, providing it isn't contaminated by chemicals or dyes, can provide a couple of gallons each. Don't use the toilet until you're sure the sewage system is operating and tht water service has been restored. If possible, fill your bathtub with water. You may need it if water pressure fails later. Don't, however, drain your waterbed. It isn't potable.

While this section deals with preparation, it's appropriate here to mention that under no circumstances should you eat or drink anything from open containers if there's broken glass in the vicinity. You can strain liquids through a cloth to eliminate shards.

You'll need some type of cooking arrangement for the food you've stockpiled. While a campfire certainly works, it's less convenient than indoors under shelter — providing your home isn't rendered unsafe. Therefore, common camping supplies like a camp stove and lantern with suitable fuel are nice to have handy. Your barbeque grill with charcoal can be pressed into service — have lighter fluid and matches on hand. If your home is unsafe, your camping tent with sleeping bags and the like may keep you hale and hearty.

"Plan as if you are taking a three-day camping trip," suggests *Earthquake Emergency Guide,* which also advises you to take along a rope, shovel, soap, matches, light sticks, cooking utensils and extra clothes.

Now we come to perhaps the single most important step in preparing for an earthquake: Preparing a plan of what you'll do in the event there is a temblor. The plan will include the preparedness steps already discussed, plus evacuation procedures, select three sites where you'll meet family members if separated or if the residential area is evacuated, which neighbors will assist children and pets in your absence, and so forth.

As part of your earthquake preparedness, make a detailed inventory of your possessions. Take photographs of each room and of especially valuable items for insurance purposes. Your valuables should be stored in a metal box or safe deposit box, along with wills, deeds and similar documents.

"You should also select an out-of-town relative or friend as your 'family contact center,' should you not be able to link up in the immediate area," says *Earthquake Emergency Guide.* "See that the person's address and phone number are known by all family members."

The Earthquake Society, which put together the *Earthquake Emergency Guide,* recommends formation of neighborhood cooperatives to prepare for and react to an earth-

Good Friday — March 29, 1964 — was anything but for residents of Anchorage as the area was rocked by powerful earthquake that crumbled buildings like matchsticks in a matter of just minutes. Would you have survived?

While this extinguisher was allegedly recharged just two months before photo was snapped, needle indicates it now should be recharged again. Is there leaky valve? It's not of much good if inoperable. Label on inexpensive extinguisher (right) tells how to operate, fire to fight.

Extinguishers, which should be positioned properly in homes and offices, are designed for specific uses. You must read label and know origin of fire.

quake. The Society recommends a maximum group size of thirty families, with one coordinator per ten families. These coordinators will set up earthquake evacuation headquarters at sites previously determined by the cooperative members. Families participating will have filled out registration forms, listing such information as adult names and business addresses with telephone numbers; names, ages and schools attended by children; pets; names of those authorized to pick up children from school in case parents can't; emergency notification data (who to contact outside immediate area); location of emergency supplies (extra water, water heater, first-aid, food); special skills like first-aid or CPR; map of location of gas, water and electricity shutoffs, with signature block authorizing shutoff "if necessary to do so for the safety of the house and/or the neighborhood;" pertinent medical information; and what special equipment the family could provide.

If there's an earthquake, neighborhood co-op members first shut off gas, water and electricity, (emergency data may appear in the front of your local telephone book), then check on immediate neighbors and render assistance where needed. As soon as possible, check in with the earthquake evacuation headquarters; if they fail to check in within a reasonable period, the coordinator will try to send someone looking for them. Even if members aren't home, he may shut off the utilities.

Members of the family should plan to meet at the headquarters, and use the headquarters as a message center; phones will either be nonoperational or restricted to emergency use. "If your children are alone, and you have not made other arrangements, let them know there will be neighbors at the headquarters," the Society says in its literature.

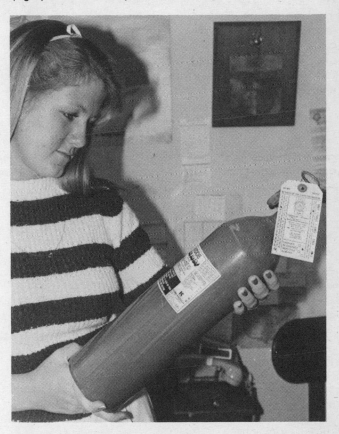

Roxanne Hanson does what few employees would — takes time to read label and become familiar with firefighting and/or evacuation procedures at office building.

If damage to your home is sufficient to warrant evacuation, co-op families bring sleeping bags with them to the evacuation headquarters, which could be a school building since most states mandate earthquake-proof design and therefore should remain standing. Those families who have recreational vehicles will drive them to the headquarters, where they'll be used as first-aid stations, cooking for infants only, emergency sanitary facilities, and as a water source. Pets, which will be more frightened than people,

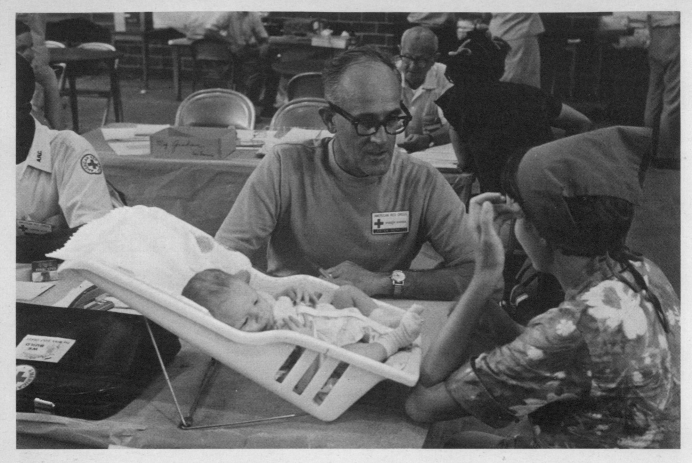

Lester E. Kemnitz, of the American Red Cross, interviews disaster victim at temporary shelter set up in public building. Do your relatives know where you can be found after a disaster? What have you planned?

should be leashed and brought to the headquarters. This is a major difference between the neighborhood co-op headquarters and a Red Cross Survival Station: at the latter, you can't bring your animals.

Earthquake Safety is concerned for youngsters and gives lengthy advice for parents in their booklet, taken from a pamphlet entitled *Coping with Children's Reactions to Earthquakes and Other Disasters* prepared by the San Fernando Valley Child Guidance Clinic (9650 Zelzah Avenue, Northridge, CA 91325). "It's of great importance for the family to remain together," the group says. "Being together with the family provides immediate reassurance to a child. Fears of being abandoned and unprotected are immeditely alleviated. For example, immediately after a disaster parents should not leave the child in a 'safe' place while they themselves go elsewhere to inspect possible damage. They should not leave the child alone in the evacuation center while they go back to the damaged area; mother should not leave her child to go shopping, but should take him along. With no opportunity to experience the fear of being left alone, the child is less likely to develop clinging behavior."

While parents are going to be afraid, adults can mask these fears and have the maturity to cope with the stresses upon them. Parents should promote the idea that "We're all together and nothing has happened to us," and "Don't worry, we will look after you." Such a demonstration of strength will be apparent to the child and reassure him. "However, it will not harm the child to him know that are also afraid," says the pamphlet, prepared with the experience of the Sylmar quake of 1971 to draw upon, "As a matter of fact, it's good to put these feelings into words. This sharing will encourage him to talk about his own feelings or fears. Communication is most helpful in reducing the child's anxiety and, for that matter, the adult's anxiety. The child may then express some fears which are not real and the parents will have an opportunity to explore these fears and reassure the child."

Communication is the key to overcoming fears, and parents are encouraged to explain to the children exactly what's transpired. "A child may express his fears in play or in actions," the clinic claims. "If these are unrealistic, explain and reassure him. You may even have to repeat yourself many times. Don't stop explaining just because you've told him once before."

Stress and shock may be manifested by silence, and such children must be encouraged to share what's happening inside. "His difficulty in expressing himself may be very frustrating to parents," says *Earthquake Emergency Guide.* "It can be helpful to include other members of the

Roger Combs and Dick Nicklin pass the time during an earthquake drill at office in California. If you can't get under desk, an interior doorjam is good shelter.

cut. If the child's needs are not met, the problem will persist for a longer period."

Earthquake Emergency Guide recommends that children be included in the preparation phases, since they can be the most vulnerable to earthquake injuries — or the best prepared against them. "Most children haven't been instructed how to react during an earthquake," the booklet says. "Consequently, if an earthquake hits, they would be the first to panic and become injured. Once trained, however, children can be the best prepared because of their lack of inhibition to dive under a table for safety while an adult waits to see if this is really the 'big one'."

The guide contains two "games" that are particularly effective in preparing a family for an earthquake: a family earthquake drill and an earthquake hazard hunt.

The family earthquake drill can save your life since you may have just one or two seconds in which to react correctly and automatically to prevent injury or death. "By thinking before the earthquake occurs, you can condition yourself and your family to react correctly when the first jolt is felt," the guide says. "This is done by practicing a game called earthquake drill. The first step of the game is to acquaint each member with safe spots in each room of your home. Go throughout each room and try to pick out the

June Carlier could tangle with trophy elk — and would doubtless come out on the losing end! — if mounted head toppled during tremor. Remove such head hazards.

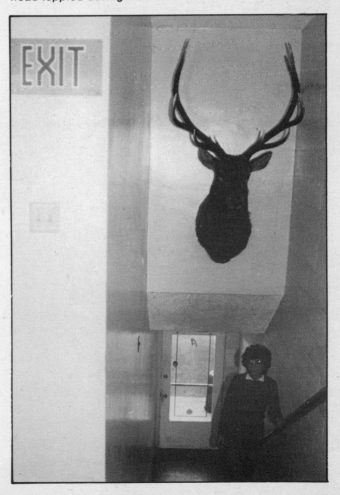

family, neighbors and their children in a talk about reactions to the disaster. Through the sharing of common experiences, fears are further reduced. It's essential that an attempt be made to provide an atmosphere of acceptance where a child will feel free to talk about his fears, be it at home or at school. Adults are often reluctant to encourage the child to talk about fears and anxiety. Also, parents feel helpless in reassuring the child. and may be afraid of actually harming the child by continued discussions. Statements like 'I know you're afraid or 'It's a scary feeling' are helpful and should be used. Being told it's normal and natural to be afraid is also reassuring."

Following the San Fernando Valley disaster of 1971, parents had more to do than simply calming their children's fears, and these fears needn't disrupt their and the family's activities. A child can be included in the activities like checking on damage, cleaning up broken glass or fallen furniture. "It's actually reassuring to see progress being made in bringing the house back to order and the routine of the household resume: meals prepared, dishes washed, beds made, playmates coming over," the Clinic found. "For the parents of a very young child, the task is more difficult. Such a child may need more physical care, more holding; and this makes it harder for parents to attend to the other things that should be done. Unfortunately, there's no short-

Artist John Vitale would be wise to jump beneath his art table, away from extensive glass windows, during and earthquake. This is to avoid flying glass, debris.

Magnitude of destruction in Good Friday quake in Alaska is seen below. Gas and water mains were severed, creating extreme explosive hazard. Any open flame would have been devastating.

safe places. Then reinforce this knowledge by physically placing yourselves in these locations. This is a very important step for your children because it psychologically conditions the child to react. They must learn to react automatically in case you're not beside them at the critical time.

"In the days ahead, practice the earthquake drill. Call out 'Earthquake!' from the living room or kitchen. Each family member should respond by moving to the nearest safe place. Once a month, let a child call a surprise earthquake and follow through with what you've learned. Test each other. Was David's choice the safest? Did Anne realize that the closet door could be sealed shut?"

The second game recommended by the Earthquake Society is called Earthquake Hazard Hunt and should include all family members as participants. "Foresight, imagination and common sense are all that are needed as you go from room to room and imagine what would happen when the earth and house started shaking," the guide instructs. "Look at the floor-to-ceiling bookshelf: How many things are likely to fall? Which items are heavy enough to cause injury? During a moderate shake, objects may topple from shelves and fall in a vertical path. During a violent shake, however, heavy objects may be propelled to fall in a diagonal path. Secure the bookshelves to wall

In the event there's an earthquake, Deborah O'Brien-Kinsey would know what to do. She's working away...

...and doesn't hesitate to hit the floor at the first sway or shake. She's not going to wait for "big" shock!

By seeking safety beneath her thick desktop, Debbie will live to smile another day. Will you, likewise?

studs. Be sure that shelf brackets are fixed to shelves. Remove all heavy objects from shelves above head level of the shortest family member. Where do you sit or sleep? Is there a heavy picture frame or mirror over your head? Remove glass bottles from the medicine cabinet and from around the bathtub. After a damaging earthquake, you may need to draw water into the tub. Don't forget to check your garage. Where do you store weed killers and pesticides? Don't do the detective work alone. Invite all family members to join in. Children are especially perceptive; they're likely to mention several hazards you have missed."

DURING AN EARTHQUAKE

During an earthquake, the ground shakes for just a very short time — it may last up to a minute during an exceptionally strong quake, but hopefully nothing like the endless shaking detailed in Jerry Pournelle's and Larry Niven's end-of-the world scenario in *Lucifer's Hammer*. There's

Tall cabinets could easily tip during a quake to cause injury or block escape routes. Move 'em.

Tons of debris waiting to deposit itself on unwitting office occupant. Heavy stuff should be lowered.

little you can do besides seek shelter and wait for the shaking to subside.

Where's a safe place? If indoors, get under a desk, table or workbench, if possible. Remember, greatest danger is from collapsing ceilings and walls. If you can't get under something solid stand in an interior doorway or in a corner away from windows, chimneys and heavy furniture or appliances like refrigerators that may tip and slide.

In Time Of Emergency, a booklet prepared by the Defense Civil Preparedness Agency of the Office of Civil Defense, advises that you remain where you are, as most injuries are caused when moving into or out of buildings as walls collapse, wires fall, and so on. "If you're in an unreinforced brick building or other hazardous structure, you may feel it is better to take a chance on leaving the building than to stay inside," says Gere's and Shah's booklet, *Earthquakes: How To Protect Your Life and Property.* "Then leave quickly but cautiously, being on the alert for falling bricks, fallen electrical wiring, and other hazards."

But the booklet says, "as a general rule, don't run out of a building. It's better to seek safety where you are, wait until the quake is over and then leave calmly if evacuation is necessary."

Many who work in high-rise buildings may head for the stairs when their building starts swaying, but authorities advise otherwise. "Exits are likely to be jammed and elevators often stop operating. Seek safety where you are. Get under a desk and stay away from the windows. Don't be surprised if the electricity goes out, or if elevator, fire

Connie Royce tests rigidity of metal shelving and finds it's not anchored to studs in back wall. It may spill contents and topple. Take precautions now.

164

and burglar alarms start ringing, or if sprinkler systems go on. Expect to hear noise from breaking glass, cracks in walls, and falling objects," say authors Gere and Shah. "Tell yourself to remain calm and don't do things that upset other people, such as shouting or running around."

If you're outside in a downtown area, step into a doorway to avoid debris falling from above. If you're outdoors, stay away from buildings, trees, power lines and walls.

If you're in a car, pull your car to the side, away from buildings, overpasses and bridges or overhead wires. Stay in the car until the earthquake is over, then proceed carefully, alert for road hazards. Don't try to cross bridges or overpasses that have been damaged. Have a book, some games for the kids and supplies of food and water in the trunk in case you're stranded for hours.

Aftershocks or secondary jolts are common. "After the first motion is felt there may be a temporary decrease in the motion, followed by another shock," Gere and Shah claim. "This phenomenon is merely the arrival of differseismic waves from the same earthquake. Also, aftershocks may occur — these are separate quakes which follow the main shock. Aftershocks may occur several minutes, hours or even days afterwards. Sometimes aftershocks will cause damage or collapse of structures that were already weakened by the main earthquake."

AFTER AN EARTHQUAKE

Hopefully, you've prepared your family and coworkers such that no one has been injured by the quake. If you aren't so fortunate, begin to calmly take stock of the situation and begin treating any injured. Use your first-aid knowledge and first-aid book to render immediate and often lifesaving treatment. Refer to Chapter 15 for immediate first-aid techniques.

Now turn your attention to extinguishing any fires, using hoses or extinguishers. Take the time to dress including sturdy shoes — there will likely be broken glass.

Immediately check your appliances. If you smell or suspect leaking gas, turn off the supply at the main. NEVER bring lighted matches into a home — explosions from accumulated gas could result. Don't use electrical switches or appliances if gas leaks are suspected because sparks can ignite gas from broken lines. Shut off electricity if there's suspected damage to the lines, and check your water supply. If you have leaking pipes, shut off your water at the main — you could save your house from flooding when the water comes back on. Use the phone only to call for help or report medical, fire, or criminal emergencies. Contact friends and relatives when the disaster is resolved.

As a general rule, you'll find it preferable to stay off the streets. You'll likely be busy enough taking care of your own damage without going sightseeing or worrying about other areas. Be sure to avoid coastal areas: Earthquakes may create seismic sea waves, also called tsunamis, which can cause great damage to certain coastal areas. "For instance, the 1964 earthquake in Alaska generated a tsunami that killed eleven people and caused seven million dollars in property damage to Crescent City, California, over 1600 miles away," says Gere and Shah.

Use great caution when moving in and around your home or other buildings, since they may have severe structural damage. When you begin cleaning up, start with

dangerous spills like lye, bleach or gasoline. Set up your transistor radio and monitor the Emergency Broadcast System station serving your area, and move to your Earthquake Evacuation Headquarters site if your neighborhood has developed such a co-op.

When you return to your home, use caution when opening cupboard and closet doors — contents may spill out and hurt you. If possible, use food stored in your freezer first — without electricity it will spoil and you may be on your own for an extended period. Break out your emergency supplies and begin getting back to business — reassuring to children and adults alike. Don't resume use of toilets until you're certain service has been restored.

Don't touch downed power lines or electrical wiring of any kind, and don't touch any object in contact with same. You could receive a fatal shock.

Motorists must be cautious when driving following a quake — this roadway in California was virtually destroyed by Sylmar tremor in 1971. What a mess!

Chapter 10

Hurricane, Tornado, Blizzard, Thunderstorms And Floods
Are Discussed For Your Safety

STORMS — NATURE AT HER WORST

NATURE CAN provide us with incredible beauty — a salmon sunset, a drake wood duck, and some of the scenic vistas peppered throughout this book as just three examples. But this chapter deals with Nature's black side, when her destructive power is manifest.

Nature regularly disrupts — or terminates — the lives of many Americans through hurricanes (called typhoons in other parts of the world), tornadoes, blizzards, thunderstorms, and floods. By understanding the cause of each, then preparing for those relevant to your geographic area, it's hoped you'll survive with minimal inconvenience.

Rippled cirrus clouds herald coming of weather front, although many days and miles ahead of stormy change.

WHAT CAUSES STORMS?

To understand the why of storm formation, you must know the basic factors involved: air masses, wind, and terrain. The atmosphere surrounding the earth isn't uniform. Rather, it's composed of many individual parcels of air, called cells, which are distinct from parcels surrounding them. These cells, which have uniform temperature and humidity levels, are called air masses and may stretch over hundreds or thousands of miles. Formation of air masses is influenced by earth's surface below, and North American

Droplets left after a rain. Storms play such an important role in our lives, yet few really know causes of changing weather, where storms originate.

Heavy cumulus clouds silhouetted against clearing sky indicate the tail of a storm front moving through (left). At right, steely clouds back up against a now-obscured mountain range and begin to unload precipitation. This is orographic precipitation.

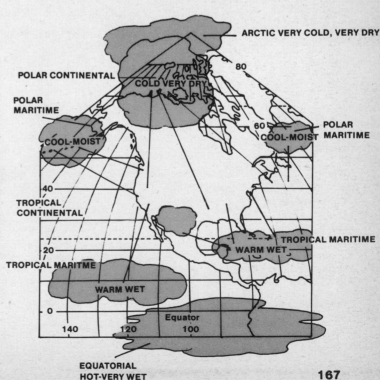

ARCTIC VERY COLD, VERY DRY

POLAR CONTINENTAL
COLD VERY DRY

POLAR MARITIME
COOL-MOIST

POLAR MARITIME
COOL-MOIST

TROPICAL CONTINENTAL

TROPICAL MARITIME
WARM WET

TROPICAL MARITME

WARM WET

Equator

80
60
40
20
0
140   120   100

EQUATORIAL HOT-VERY WET

weather is caused by interaction of air masses from eight general regions. From the ice floes of the Polar cap comes Arctic air, very cold and very dry. The land surface of the frozen North produces Polar Continental air masses, with cold, very dry air. Far northern Pacific and Atlantic water produces Polar Maritime air masses, characterized by cool, moist air. From the Pacific equatorial region near Central America comes warm, moist air called Tropical Maritime. Another source of Tropical Maritime air masses is the Caribbean. When this warm, moist air moves over the arid land of Mexico or the Southwest, it produces air masses that are hot and dry, or Tropical Continental. From the hot, humid equatorial belt comes our last air mass — hot and very wet, called Equatorial.

These hugh air masses, which can cover hundreds of thousands of square miles horizontally, are moved by our planet's wind system. Their speed of movement and the terrain over which they move control, to large extent, what the weather will be. The air mass may be heated through radiation of heat from the land surface, or cooled through conduction — transfer of heat from the air mass to the colder surface below. When air masses with different properties meet — for example, a warm, moist Tropical Maritime air mass moving northward and a very cold, very dry Arctic air mass moving south — the "fronts" or leading edges collide and precipitation is the usual result.

Cyclones form when a Tropical Maritime air mass forces a bulge into a cold air mass. The hot air tends to rise, creating

FORMATION & DEVELOPMENT OF A CYCLONIC STORM

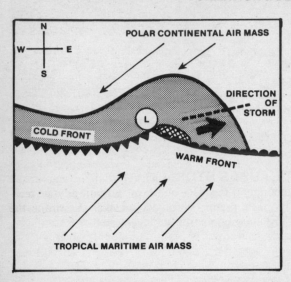
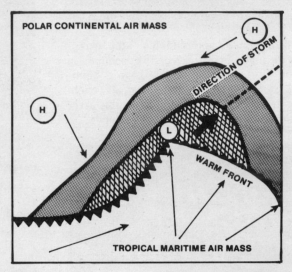
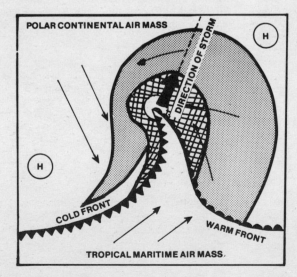
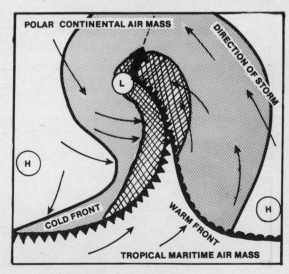

Illustrated above are the four steps in the formation and development of a cyclonic storm. At top left, warm front moving up from equator pushed a bulge into cold air mass moving down from polar region. Shading indicates area of clouds, while crosshatching indicates area of rainfall. In second drawing, the low-pressure cell attracts air from both warm and cold fronts, which acts to swing cold front in behind warm front, like a gate closing. Cloudiness and precipitation increase. In third drawing, cold front continues its swing in behind warm front, and low-pressure cell is trapped between two high-pressure cells. Finally, occluded front is produced and characterized by huge band of clouds, heavy rain. Meteorologists are watching for these.

Two different weather situations over the same area in Southern California. Rain was produced in both storms.

Thickness of cloud layer above distinguishes it from storm at left. More and heavier rainfall this time.

a low-pressure cell. Nature compensates for the imbalance by sending in air from surrounding areas. Some of the air rushing to fill the vacancy created by the rising hot air comes from the cold air mass which, because of its stable density, has created a high-pressure cell. Cold air swings like a gate into the bulge created by the Tropical Maritime air mass, creating the high winds and precipitation common to cyclones.

Frontal systems don't always result in cyclones, but normally cause precipitation. The shape of the edge of the front influences what will result. Examine the accompanying illustrations to understand what happens.

Take the triangular-shaped cold front that's stationary. A warm front approaches, driven by prevailing winds. The warm air is forced up the slope or hypotenuse of the triangle. As it's forced higher into the atmosphere, colder temperatures cause moisture to condense. Normally this is first seen in the form of cirrus clouds, and even cumulus or cumulonimbus clouds which discharge their moisture in form of rain or, in colder conditions, snow. The size, temperature and humidity of the air masses determine the severity of the storm activity.

HURRICANES/TYPHOONS

A hurricane is a special form of cyclone originating near the equator and featuring winds at over seventy-five miles per hour. They are most prevalent north of the equator in summer and south of the equator in winter. (Remember, seasons are reversed south of the equator.) North America's hurricanes form mostly over the mid-Atlantic, then trade winds move them westward toward the Caribbean and Gulf of Mexico, where others are sometimes formed. As the hurricanes move over land, they lose their source of moisture and eventually dissipate — but not before causing immense loss of property and life, and disrupting shipping.

Whereas the cyclone has an occluded center, the hurricane has an opening that's relatively calm, cloudless and rainless which ranges from five to thirty miles in diameter. This is the original low-pressure cell that led to whirling winds sometimes exceeding 120 miles per hour.

Their heads all but torn off, palm trees whip in fury of savage hurricane off Florida's Gold Coast in 1949. Winds up to 125mph, with gusts to 150mph, tore roofs from houses, smashed windows, toppled trees, blew tops off parking meters. Some 5000 fled before the storm.

HURRICANE PREPARATION

Hurricanes don't form overnight and the conditions required to spawn a hurricane are well-known to meteorologists who study satellite pictures which tell what's happening over the ocean. When a hurricane is seen forming, alarm is spread through the media; usually there's plenty of time to implement evacuation plans.

During storm season, whether for hurricanes, tornadoes, blizzards, thunderstorms or floods, you should have the following emergency supplies stockpiled and accessible. Of course, if you've made survival preparedness a way of life, then you'll have these goods already stockpiled (see Chapter 14):

In wake of Hurricane Carmen in 1974, Tom Meachan of American Red Cross disaster team (second from right) tells resident of Abbeville, Louisiana, how to get help. In background are parts of a wrecked mobile home.

Expect limbs to be sheared during gusty windstorms.

It takes lots of power to break off a tree at ground level, but here's example of how it can be done!

Water in plastic jugs or other stoppered containers
Canned or sealed-package foods requiring no refrigeration or heating for cooking
Medicines needed by the family
First-aid kit with book
Blankets or sleeping bags
Flashlights with batteries
Battery-powered radio with batteries
Covered container for emergency toilet
Automobile with full gas tank
Plywood sheeting and plastic/tarps for floods or hurricane protection

If evacuation is required by local authorities, you should promptly follow instructions. Before leaving, shut off your gas, water and electricity. Bring your possessions indoors, or tie them down securely: lawn furniture, tools, garbage cans, barbecues and the like may otherwise blow away. Put plywood sheeting over windows and glass doors to prevent breakage by flying objects. Get your livestock or pets under cover, or evacuate them to high ground if time and circumstances permit.

If you're to be evacuated by rescue authorities, lock and leave your vehicle with windows rolled up in the garage. Lock doors and windows of your residence before departing. Take emergency supplies with you; valuables should be secured as outlined in Chapter 4.

If you're going to drive to an evacuation center, first ensure you know its exact location. These should be regularly broadcast on the radio. You're advised to leave early, before roads become clogged or damaged; you don't want to be marooned by flooded roads, downed trees or fallen power lines.

Watch for the above-mentioned hazards when evacuating along recommended routes. Other hazards you may encounter are undermined or washed-out roads, rock or mudslides, broken sewer and water mains, loose or downed wires and falling objects. If you approach a stream crossing, watch for sudden flooding. If there's water over the roadway, don't attempt to cross if water is deeper than your knees or the middle of the car's wheel. Examine the bridge construction — if there's any damage, don't attempt to cross. And if you do proceed through water at relatively safe levels, keep the car in low gear. Go slowly to avoid flooding the engine. When you're on dry ground again, depress the brake pedal while you accelerate slowly to dry out brake drums, shoes and pads.

Some may stay behind if on high ground. Stay indoors if permitted to remain — flying debris may cause injury.

Don't be misled by a sudden becalming of wind and rain — this is the eye of the hurricane passing over your area, and wind will resume in the opposite direction in a short time. Attempting to flee during this calm spell is dangerous. Monitor your radio and don't emerge until authorities determine it's safe.

Telephone service probably will be interrupted. If not, it should be reserved for emergency use — reporting dangerous conditions or circumstances. Tell your relatives you'll contact them when the situation returns to normal. Don't use sewer or drinking water systems until assured by radio that it's safe to do so; cholera and typhus could result. Your emergency supplies should hold you for a week or more if you're isolated. It is wise to follow instructions of personnel at evacuation shelters.

Photos: Stephen Anderson, American Red Cross

Mr. and Mrs. Cecil Barrett of Grand Island, Nebraska, fled tornado and received shelter, food, from American Red Cross.

THUNDERSTORMS

There are three causes of a thunderstorm, which are termed convectional, orographic or frontal.

Convectional precipitation results when a warm, moist air mass passes over an extremely hot land mass, such as the American Southwest. Heat radiating from the baking soil causes the air to rise. As it rises, moisture within is given off in the form of cloud condensation, and a byproduct of this moisture loss is production of latent heat. This heat forces the air higher still, causing a rapid updraft of air. Clouds form vertically up as high as 75,000 feet as updrafts in excess of one hundred miles per hour push the warm, moist air.

Cloudburst results in virtual ribbon of water from this roof. In desert areas, such rain causes flash floods.

Geography and direction of prevailing winds determine, to some extent, moisture patterns. Winds from the west rise to clear these hills, leading to moisture loss.

The reason Nevada is arid is because the Sierra Nevada Mountains in eastern California squeeze moisture from storms, leaving little to fall on the leeward side.

Moisture in excess of what the ground can absorb often leads to mudslides, shown in two photos above. Earth slippage here is minimal, destroying just a fence.

Size and volume of raindrops is function of type of clouds involved, winds within, and moisture content. It doesn't take much to fill gutters, erode soil.

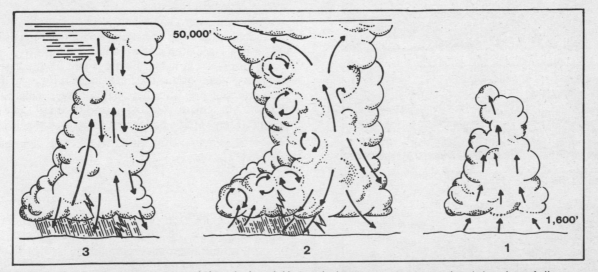

From right to left, three stages of thunderhead. Note wind patterns as storm cloud develops fully.

Excess moisture not produced as clouds condenses into raindrops. These raindrops begin to fall, attracting more moisture and gaining size until forced upward again by the strong air current. This up and down motion of the raindrops continues until a strong downward or oblique air current overcomes the updraft, resulting in a deluge, commonly called a cloudburst.

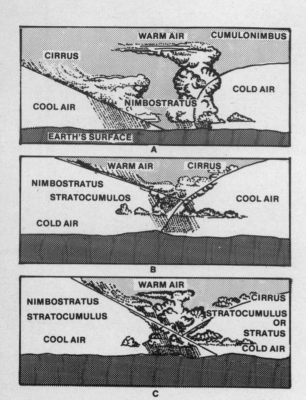

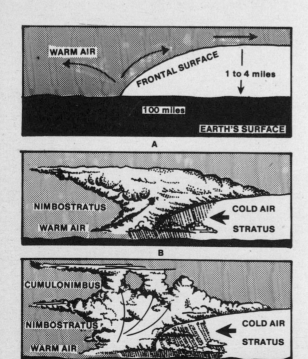

Thunderstorms also result from warm, moist air being forced up and over a mountain range, which is called orographic precipitation. As the air rises to clear the obstacle, it gives up moisture in the form of cloud formation and rain or hail. This is why the western slopes of the Sierra Nevada and Rocky Mountains are lush, while the eastern slopes are dry and harsh — most storm fronts travel from west to east across our continent. The moisture is squeezed out on the western slopes and none is left to water the eastern side.

The third type of thunderstorm results when a warm, moist frontal system meets a cold front. The warm, moist air is forced upward, triggering the sequence discussed above.

FLOODING

Flooding is obviously water in excess of the soil's capacity to absorb it. Flooding results from hurricanes, thunderstorms or cyclonic activity, less frequently from such causes as rupture of a dike or dam. Some types of flooding can be anticipated by following news and weather reports; flash floods, however, can occur with little or no advance warning.

Some areas of the country are affected regularly, and residents of pertinent geographic areas are encouraged to stockpile the emergency supplies listed under hurricanes, if self-reliance isn't your lifestyle.

Floods in conjunction with heavy rain or hurricanes pose peculiar problems. In some cases, attempting to prevent flooding does more harm than good!

If flooding is expected, the homeowner should move furniture and other possessions to the second floor; if you don't have a second story, stacking furniture atop less-valuable items such as a kitchen table may prevent water damage. If your garage is securely fastened to a solid foundation, you may be able to store some items in rafters or attics.

Not only should your utilities be turned off, but your electrical appliances should be unplugged. Do not, however, touch them if you are standing in water or are wet — you could be electrocuted!

If your home has a basement, you may be sorely tempted to sandbag its exterior to prevent flooding. Officials of the Office of Civil Defense warn against the practice, especially if flooding is likely: Seepage will fill the basement and may collect around the basement walls and under the floor, creating pressure that could damage walls or raise the entire basement — causing it to float right out of the ground! They say it's better to let water fill the basement

Opposite page, top: Cedar River flood caused serious loss in seven Washington counties in 1977, just two years after another bad flood. Right: A couple of trees restrain house from floating farther downriver during bad flooding in 1979 in Peoria, Illinois.

Photo: Jim Waring, American Red Cross

or, if you're certain to be flooded, to fill it with fresh water before floodwaters arrive. This equalizes water pressure on the inside and outside of the basement, thus avoiding structural damage to the foundation and the house.

Evacuation procedures have already been detailed and are the same.

Particularly during summer, atmospheric conditions create a danger from flash floods. Thunderstorms dump great quantities of rain in a short time and creeks, gullies, streambeds, ravines, culverts or low-lying ground fill with water. Water roars down the washes, carrying boulders, logs and debris that do bad things to animals and people in its path.

Your protection against flash flooding is to monitor weather forecasts. When flash flood warnings are broadcast, immediately seek high ground. Keep an eye on the weather and do your part by spreading the word to other campers or residents you encounter. Following a flood, use caution when driving — roads are frequently washed out and bridges are unsafe. Watch for the road hazards previously listed.

TORNADOES

If you understand how a cyclone forms, with a low-pressure cell to which air is attracted, then you have the basics of tornado formation. Tornadoes are most prevalent during summer. Very heavy cumulonimbus clouds are close to the ground. An extreme low-pressure column of air forms, sucking into an inward spiral surrounding air at speeds clocked at three hundred miles per hour. Upward velocities can reach two hundred miles per hour as the funnel-shaped cloud forms and begins moving over the land or water (in the latter case, it's called a waterspout). The tornado may be no larger than fifty yards across at ground level, but it is the most violent of all storms. The accompanying photographs prove that.

A tornado watch will be broadcast if tornadoes are expected in or near your area. Keep an eye on the sky to the south and southwest, unless the tornado watch is announced with the approach of a hurricane; then watch the sky to the east. If you spot one, notify authorities, who then will announce a tornado warning. That's the difference between a watch and warning: the latter means a tornado has been sighted and you're advised to take cover to keep from being blown off your feet or injured by flying debris.

Your best protection, according to civil defense authorities, is to seek shelter underground, in a cave, or in a big, steel-framed or reinforced-concrete building. If you have a storm cellar at home, seek refuge there; if not, get into your basement under a heavy workbench or table away from

Tree before and after tornado touched down in Southern California. Below: Half of Xenia, Ohio, was destroyed by terrible tornado in 1974, affecting 27,000 residents.

Photo: Ted Carland, American Red Cross

Opposite page: A severe flood in mid-July 1977 caused severe hardship for residents of 17 Pennsylvania counties. Note power lines, car. Elderly woman (right) searches rubble of Xenia home. In the background is Red Cross emergency canteen, delivering offd to relief and rescue workers.

Photos: Stephen Anderson, American Red Cross

Cars and debris from motel in background litter field in southern section of Grand Island, Nebraska, hard hit by tornado in June 1980. One New York couple searched a week for their car and found it in a nearby lake. Another view of devastation caused by tornado in Nebraska. No wonder it's called nature's fiercest storm!

heavy appliances on the upper floor: You don't want it crashing through the floor and landing on your table — you could be pinned beneath or crushed. If you have no basement or cellar, position yourself beneath heavy furniture in the center of the room, away from windows which should be left open on the side *away* from the approach of the tornado. This reduces damage to the building. Another spot to seek shelter is inside a small room on the ground floor, away from windows and doors. An inner hallway of the ground floor may be a safe office refuge.

You should not, authorities say, remain inside a trailer or mobile home, since these are frequently wrenched from even the solid foundation described in Chapter 9. You could be hurt or killed as the trailer is tossed about.

If you're driving, steer away from the path of the tornado at a ninety-degree angle. If you must quit your vehicle or are trapped in the open as a tornado approaches, seek shelter in a ditch, excavation, culvert or ravine — any depression that protects you from debris flying at ground level over your prone form.

Photo: Jack Shere, American Red Cross

Twenty Kentucky counties were affected when tornadoes displaced 4,592 families in April 1974. This town used to be Bowling Green, but parts are gone forever.

Photo: Rudolph Vetter, American Red Cross

Tornado: One of nature's most destructive forces

SANTA ANA, CA — In March 1977, a tornado twisted westward through five Orange County cities, smashing telephone poles, rooftops and trees, injuring three people in Fullerton and knocking out power to 13,000 homes in that city...

In February 1978, tornadolike winds gusting up to 92 mph destroyed 35 coaches at a Huntington Beach mobile-home park, exploding many of the coaches' walls and up-ending one of the large double-wide units.

In January 1979, tornadolike winds felled trees and brought them crashing down on houses and cars in Costa Mesa. Windows shattered and rooftops were ripped off.

In February 1979, similar winds struck Santa Ana, tearing down signs and strewing debris over a wide area. — *Santa Ana Register*

WINTER STORMS

Snow, sleet, hail — all are different forms of precipitation that started as raindrops. Snowflakes form when moisture condenses into raindrops that pass through atmosphere of sufficiently low temperatures to freeze them into ice crystals. Hail forms when raindrops descending toward land are carried aloft by updrafts where they freeze. The ice now falls through the warmer layer of air, which remelts

Three died and 200 were injured when twister cut ten-mile swath through Jonesboro, Arkansas, in May 1973. Text gives instructions for evacuating or preparing. Right: Fox Glacier on New Zealand's South Island was probably product of severest winter storm and cold.

Rugged mountains, cold peaks — not a place to venture unprepared. Above right: Austrians know about snow!

the outer edge and attracts other moisture to it, thus enlarging in size. Before the precipitation reaches land, however, it is forced upward again by the strong updraft. It continues its up-and-down journey, growing in size, until it has sufficient weight to overcome the updraft. The stronger the updraft, the larger the hail. Hail has been recorded as large as hens' eggs...take cover!

Sleet is the result of rain passing through a band of frigid air en route to land. The infamous ice storms, or glaze, result from raindrops falling on surfaces well below freezing.

A blizzard is the most dangerous of all winter storms, since it combines heavy snow with freezing cold and biting winds. Weather forecasters issue either blizzard warnings or severe blizzard warnings. A blizzard warning means you can expect considerable snow, winds at least thirty-five miles per hour, and temperature of 10F degrees below zero (-23.3C). A severe blizzard warning means you can expect very heavy snow, winds at least forty-five miles per hour, and temperatures of 20F degrees below zero (-28.9C) and lower. (You also may hear a heavy snow warning, which means you can expect more than four inches in twelve hours, or more than six inches in twenty-four hours.)

Even a few hours' preparation can make a big difference when a blizzard is on the way. If you live in a rural area,

Donner Pass is near South Lake Tahoe and blizzard there stranded ill-fated Donner Party in 1800s.

expect that you might be isolated for up to two weeks. You should stockpile heating fuel and use it sparingly when the blizzard hits — you never know how long you'll have to go without resupply. Turn the thermostat down and close off all nonessential rooms. Shades of Leningrad in 1943!

Plan to keep one room heated. Move your camp stove

Opposite page: on lovely sunny day, Franz Josef Glacier in New Zealand makes enjoyable outing. But not when winter returns! Above: Innsbruck, in the Tyrol region of Austria, is incomparably beautiful. People who live and play there also take precautions when heavy weather is expected. You should do the same.

Photo: Icelandic National Tourist Office

Surreal scene is a lagoon at foot of Vatnajokull, largest glacier in Europe, filled with icebergs from moving glacier. Iceland can be bleak, and those unprepared for severe winters would become statistics soon.

and lantern with fuel into this room. Plan to sleep near the heat source, usually a fireplace or stove. Remember that the blower on an electric or oil furnace won't operate with the power out.

You will have stocked up on food and water. At first mention of blizzard, fill your bathtub with water. Move your water supplies into your warm room — ice may ruin your plastic containers. Have your emergency equipment — radio, batteries, flashlights, games for the kids, food and fuel accessible.

When a winter storm hits, you want to avoid going out as much as possible. If you must travel, try to use public transportation. If you must use your own car, observe the following cautions:

- See that it's in good operating condition, fuel tank full, with either snow tires or chains (or both) on the drive axle.

- You should have the following emergency tools and supplies in the vehicle: shovel, ice scraper, tow chain or rope, sand, flashlight, heavy gloves or mittens, over-shoes woolen socks, headgear to cover head and face, canteen with water, a couple of dehydrated meals and heat tabs with cooking utensiles, paperback books, and a space blanket.

- Take a second person with you and ensure someone

THE COMPLETE SURVIVAL GUIDE

Skis are among popular — and often only — means of transportation in Yellowstone National Park during Winter. These skiers are passing the park's upper geyser basin, a remarkable sight even in summer.

knows your proposed route and estimated time of arrival. If you don't show, they can initiate a search along your proposed route.

● Drive only in daylight on major roads. Use your radio to update road conditions. If you get off main roads, you may be stuck and those back roads are generally the last ones to be plowed.

● Drive carefully, as road conditions will be slippery and dangerous. It's better to turn back than risk being stalled, lost or isolated. And if a blizzard hits, seek refuge immediately or you'll be like the cars you've seen on the evening news. being towed out of snowdrifts two days later!

● If your vehicle should stall, the rule is don't panic and do something stupid like abandon the vehicle. Use your warning lights and wait in the car for help. If you run the engine, keep a window open to avoid carbon monoxide poisoning. If there's no house in sight, don't leave the car — you could become confused, disoriented, lost and dead.

● Don't overexert. Cold weather strains your heart and heavy work druing a storm — shoveling snow, pushing stalled cars, etc. — risks heart attack or stroke.

Chapter 11
WILDFIRE PREVENTION

Eliminate The Causes Of Wildfires And Home Fires, And Know What To Do If One Comes!

Forest fire rages through Alaskan tundra, soon to be engaged by native Alaskans seen parachuting into the area in this Bureau of Land Management photo. These men create fire breaks by rolling up tundra in foot-thick strips, as trained in villages during winter.

E VERY YEAR, thousands of lives are claimed, ten thousand square miles of valuable watershed is charred, $200 million in resources is lost. The cause is one of the most frightening and relentless of nature's disasters — wildfire.

Many people feel wildfires don't affect them directly. Without going into the economic impact of fires on the building industry, or how tree losses increase cost of paper for books such as this one, examine the accompanying pictures. Many show flames perilously close to a tract of million-dollar homes near the ocean in Southern California. These were lucky — other homes valued in the millions were destroyed by the raging brushfires.

Wildfires result from lightning in some cases, but most are started by careless people or children playing with matches. Supervision and education are the keys to eliminating these fires. Using machinery without proper spark arrestors starts fires; ensure your vehicles, chain saws and other internal combustion engines are so equipped.

Careless campfires cause many fires. In some cases, the careless camper — country singer Johnny Cash as one notable example — has received a bill for firefighting equipment and personnel used. You can save your money — and natural resources — by practicing safety with campfires. Camp only where permitted, and build fires in fire rings if required. If in primitive country, clear a circle ten feet in diameter around the fire site, and go down to bare ground.

Has to be California (left), where spectators observe with detachment as firefighters battle brushfire beyond. Top: Smoke billows above freeway as major blaze licks parched hills. Tongues of flame (center) can be seen moving down ridgelines toward $1 million homes behind. Bottom: Two bulldozers frantically clear brush ahead of advancing flames, hoping to check fire, end threat.

Orange County (California) firefighters and policemen watch idly as brush adjacent to roadway goes up into flames (above). There was little they could do here but watch, and no structures were threatened on hill.

Dig a small hole in the center and build your campfire in it. Never start a fire near logs, trees or brush. Before leaving the campsite, put out the fire completely by stirring the ashes as you completely saturate them with water. Completely soak the wood, then feel the ashes. Take the extra time to really be sure.

Careless trash burning has caused many forest and brush fires. Never burn outside in dry weather on windy days — burning cinders may be carried by winds to new and unintentional fuel sources. You should have tools and water nearby whenever burning outside, and fires should not be left unsupervised. Of course, keep your fire well away from wooded areas, buildings, dry fields or grass. You should have already procured a permit (where required) and it's best to use a metal container or burn on bare ground around which you've cleared all foliage.

Most national parks, forests or grasslands post fire conditions so motorists realize the fire danger. In some instances smoking is not permitted, even in vehicles. Where smoking is permitted, use the ashtray. While discarding burning materials is punishable by a substantial fine, think of the waste of natural resources that cigarette may cause! And if smoking in the bush, grind out all smokes and matches; ensure they're cold before moving on.

As mentioned, brush and forest fires threaten homes, as do fires of domestic origin. You can prevent home fires by

Wildfires destroy valuable watershed each year, but can be prevented by sound management and safety precautions when afield. This is Mummy Range in National Park, Colorado.

In Spring '83, hundreds of square miles of Australian bushland were scorched and 71 people died. Loss of sheep and cattle was enormous, too, with ranchers and humane officials shooting the badly burned animals. Fires were the result of arsonists. Blazes were pushed by high winds and longest drought on record — four years.

A collection of hand tools could well save your property from burning — if you know where tools are and have developed a firefighting plan, as advocated in text. From left are common pick, mattock, rake, hoe, shovels.

Enormous damage was done to the Kansas plains by grass fires in 1982, and the destructive power of nature is evident in these two photos. How easy to prevent fires, but how hard to fight!

eliminating sources of fires: junk in attics, basements, closets and garages. Rags soaked with oil or turpentine can ignite spontaneously, especially if stored near newspapers. Flammable liquids like gasoline, benzine and naphtha should be stored in tightly sealed containers outside the home; fumes from leaking containers can explode if they reach your furnace or oven pilot light, or if someone lights a match.

Worn or frayed electrical wiring on appliances leads to many home fires. Replace them and save your home. Another electrical problem is overloading sockets by running too many extension cords or appliances from one outlet. Never run an extension cord under a rug, and use irons or heating pads with care. Keep your lampshades away from the incandescent bulbs, and don't carelessly put magazines or newspapers atop radiators or stoves.

Improperly installed woodstoves cause fires, especially if the stovepipe is choked with soot. Check your furnace, stove and chimney and clean soot as needed. Replace rusty stovepipes.

Twice in a half dozen years I have seen homes endangered by cooking oil heated to the ignition point. In one case the flaming pot of oil for french fries was hustled outside, where it unfortunately was spilled on the leg of a sleeping dog. It was a slow battle to heal the dog, while the blackened kitchen ceiling was good as new with a wipe down and new coat of paint. The second oil fire was extinguished by pouring flour on the flames. Baking soda also will smother

THE COMPLETE SURVIVAL GUIDE

When vacationing or camping in rural or wilderness areas, be extra-careful with fires. Follow extinguishing tips found in the text.

flames, but with grease fires, don't use water — it will only spread the fire, since oil and water don't mix.

You should move quickly to keep the fire small. Fire is extinguished by removing its fuel, smothering, or cooling with water or chemicals. You can smother flames with dirt or sand. Buckets with shovels kept close by when burning

Sightseers on accessible roads often interfere with rescue or firefighting efforts of authorities. Unless you have official business, stay away from disaster site.

outdoors is wise. A garden hose connected to a water source can be used for outdoor or indoor fires, providing the indoor fire isn't electrical; if it is, turn off the power and then use water. If you can't get to the circuit breaker panel or fuse box, then don't use water — use an extinguisher suitable for electrical fires. Same with your natural gas: Use water after you cut off the gas. If you can't reach the shutoff valve, smother the flames with sand or earth. In a pinch, a wet blanket can be used to smother flames.

There generally is good warning via the media as a wildfire moves along, although it can move faster than reported. If your structure is threatened, raise the alarm first and then begin fighting the fire. You should have a written firefighting plan and now is the time to implement it. If you have time, remove all vegetation within thirty feet of the house. Close windows and cover them if possible. Move your furnishings away from the windows, as heat may ignite them. Secure your livestock and pets. Some homeowners have saved their dwellings by taking up station with a garden hose on the shingle rooftops. Wind-blown embers can lead to home loss while the main fire is far away.

In brushy country hampered by frequent brushfires — the canyons near Malibu, California, for instance — some homeowners have taken to keeping a goat or two. These herbivores keep brush trimmed down well away from homes, an ingestment that could save your home!

You can also take a free firefighting course from your local Civil Defense agency (see the telephone book), county agricultural extension agent, or by writing to the U.S. Forest Service, U.S. Department of Agriculture, Washington, D.C. 20250.

Chapter 12

SURVIVING A NUCLEAR BLAST

Let's Try To Correct Much Of The Myth & Misinformation Dispensed By The Uninformed

By Duncan Long

IT WOULD be nice to live in a world without war or danger...but we don't. There are two ways to handle the problems of the world. One is to hide from the dangers and let others look out for you (if they will). This works well until a major problem occurs and then you will be dead or a helpless refugee looking for a handout.

The second is to try to look out for yourself and try to be responsible for your own future. All eventualities can't be covered, but many can. If the worst never happens, at least you and your family won't have lived in fear. If the worst happens, your preparations may save the lives of your family or save them from living as beggars. Preparing for the worst is like buying insurance.

History shows that nuclear, chemical, and biological weapons have all been used. Anyone who argues that they are too awful to ever be used has forgotten history. If a country thinks it can survive no other way or can "take over" by the use of these weapons, there is no reason to think that they won't use them. There has never been a type of weapon which wasn't eventually used!

Modern weapons are quickly deployed; you must know what to do and you must not do the wrong thing. The wrong information can get you killed just as surely as no information if you're facing the "unthinkable." Forget the Hollywood fright shows and the political rhetoric for a minute and read with an open mind.

If you're in ground zero when the bombs fly, you are a write-off. That's also the way it is with a regular bomb, a mortar shell, or a rifle bullet through the head...so what's new? Really the only difference is in magnitude; the nuclear bomb will kill more people at a time. Nuclear war would be awful — all wars are.

A lot of misinformation and disinformation have been spread by a lot of groups. Frankly, a lot of the peace/ antinuclear movement is either at the back of the class when it's time to study the facts or they are outright liars. Either way, you should look into the facts yourself.

Check *The Effects of Nuclear War* by the Office of Technology Assessment and *The Effects of Nuclear Weapons* by Glasstone and Dolan. Both should be available in your public library or from the U.S. Government Printing Office in Washington, D.C.

The facts are clear: With the current size of weapons (which, with ever-greater accuracy, are getting smaller and not larger) everything won't be destroyed. Areas not downwind from a warring country would be completely safe. Most of the earth's inhabitants wouldn't even have to take shelter if the U.S. and USSR used all of their weapons in a nuclear war.

There won't be firestorms; modern cities aren't built with enough flammable materials or built densely enough to support one. Nuclear explosions tend to scorch materials and often blow out the initial fires created by their thermal impulse. Fire would be a danger from broken gas mains, leaking gas tanks and the like, but there wouldn't be a firestorm in most areas except in those which are actually

Survey meter (right) shows dangerous radiation level, while low-level geiger (left) registers zero. Newer, smaller meters like DX-1 from RDX Nuclear (center) register zero, but issues warning beeper.

at ground zero. A large nuclear bomb's thermal pulse will ignite fires or char objects up to ten miles away, but it won't create a firestorm.

Radiation-induced mutations will not be a problem. The Radiation Effects Research Foundation (RERF) in Washington, D.C., after studying the Japanese involved in the two nuclear blasts of World War II, has found that there were no genetic defects created by the weapons. Likewise, there will not be permanent sterility produced by large nuclear explosions. Nuclear workers who were accidentally exposed to high levels of radioactivity usually suffer only from temporary sterility. (The temporary sterility is probably the reason that no mutations are created.)

If a fetus is exposed to radiation, it may be deformed. There were several dozen cases of this from the two Japanese populations studied by the RERF. After the nuclear exposure ends, the potential harm to other fetuses is over;

M870 Remington 12-gauge and chemical suit give all kinds of protection in chemical environment. This guy has too much equipment (left) — decontamination would take forever! Below is from Christy and Kearny's Expedient Shelter Handbook. *Their work is a classic.*

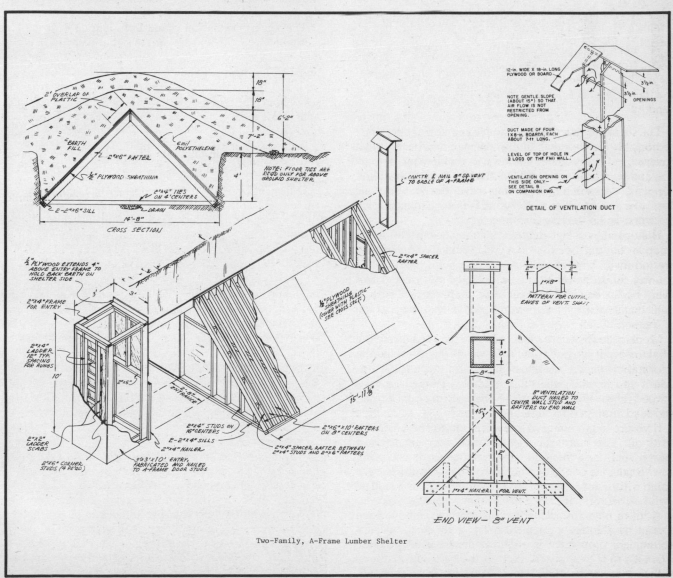

Two-Family, A-Frame Lumber Shelter

there aren't any additional occurrences of deformed children to parents exposed to radiation before the child was conceived. The RERF found that there were no more stillbirths, birth defects, or infant mortality than there would be in any population not exposed to nuclear radiation.

Following exposure to large amounts of radiation, your chances of suffering from leukemia increases by thirty or forty times. That sounds like a lot, but since only two or three people in one-hundred-thousand get leukemia, an increase of forty times would mean that the worst would be one chance in one thousand of your getting leukemia — hardly insurmountable odds.

Likewise, RERF studies found only a one-tenth of one percent increase in a person's chances of getting cancer following exposure to a large amount of radiation.

Life will not be destroyed on the face of the earth in an all-out nuclear war. It would take thousands — possibly millions — as many nuclear weapons as are now stockpiled to do that. Since the current trend is toward smaller warheads, the possibility of the extinction of life because of a nuclear war is just sci-fi stuff.

In a 1975 study, the National Academy of Sciences (NAS) concluded that in an all-out nuclear war, many plants and animals would probably not survive in a heavily contaminated fallout area. However, they also concluded that after several years most plants and animals would be back in the area by "migrating" from non-damaged areas.

The NAS study also concluded that the ozone layer — which might suffer up to seventy percent damage — would regenerate itself within several years' time. (Recent research indicates that they may have been overly pessimistic in their assessment of the damage the ozone might receive.) Granted, you will have to shield your skin and eyes to keep from getting a super sunburn or "snow blindness," but the idea of life being wiped out by ultraviolet radiation let in when the ozone layer is damaged is not founded on up-to-date scientific facts.

Life would not be a picnic after a nuclear war; it *would* be survivable if you knew what to do and had made some preparations beforehand.

Nuclear radiation can't be detected by your senses. That makes it a little hard for most people to deal with. In an age of radio waves, microwave ovens, etc., it isn't unique, however.

When a nuclear weapon goes off, the flash sends out various types of radiation. One of the types is thermal radiation, which can cause burns and start small fires (although the blast wave will probably extinguish most of these fires). Along with these thermal rays, more dangerous radiation is released in the form of gamma rays and neutrons. The amount of radiation diminishes with distance from the bomb. Since the shock wave is great enough to be dangerous inside the ten-mile range, if you aren't sheltered from the thermal radiation and the shock wave, the dangerous dosage you receive in the open won't make much difference. If you're in the open you'll be burned or blown to your death before the radiation has time to affect you. If you're sheltered from those two, the shelter will also cut down on enough of the radiation so that you'll probably have no ill effects.

Material sucked up through the nuclear fireball becomes

Popular bumper sticker says it all — or does it?

radioactive. With ground bursts, considerable radioactive fallout is produced in this manner. Since the fallout that follows the blast in fifteen or more minutes (depending on the weather and distance the bomb was from you) gives off gamma and neutron radiation, you will need protection from this radiation even if you didn't need protection from the initial flash radiation.

The nuclear radiation found in fallout decreases by a factor of ten (divide the amount of radiation by ten), while time increases by a factor of seven (multiply the time by seven). This means, in an area covered with fallout giving off 1000 rems (Roentgen Equivalent Man) per hour, in seven hours the radioactivity would decay to 100 rems per hour and in forty-nine hours, it would decay to 10 rems per hour (provided no new fallout fell into the area). Density shielding is your key to surviving those weeks (months to you pessimists) until the radioactive fallout decays to safe levels.

Different kinds of dense materials will stop different amounts of radiation. The thickness of any material needed to reduce the amount of radiation getting through it to one-half of its original amount is called the shielding material's half-value thickness (HVT). The HVT of steel is .7 inch; of concrete 2.2 inches; and of earth 3.3 inches.

Thus, twenty-two inches of concrete (or thirty-three inches of dirt) in a shelter's walls and ceiling would give ten HVTs. If the outside radiation were 1000 rems per hour (much higher than would be a reasonable amount — unless you're finding shelter in the backyard of the White House!), the amount inside would be equal to one thousand divided by two, ten times. That would give you .97 rem per hour. Since this level of radiation drops off with time, .97 rem would be an amount you could "live with." Provided you aren't directly in the dangerous blast of the initial explosion, surviving through the worst of fallout is possible with some good shielding.

It should be remembered that matter becomes radioactive only by passing upward through the nuclear blast, in which case it is melted by the extreme heat and becomes fallout. Objects or people can become contaminated by having fallout on them, but the fallout can be brushed off and washing will get rid of almost all such contamination. People won't become dangerous because of exposure to radiation provided they carefully clean off their skin, hair, and clothing. Radiation isn't a disease. It isn't contagious, although the contaminated dust of fallout can be tracked about if care isn't taken when entering the fallout shelter.

Some type of shelter can mean your survival. It must be large enough to accommodate you and your family. Ten square feet per person (width in feet multiplied by the length in feet equals the square feet of floor space) is the minimum amount you should go for. The shelter must also have room for water, food and equipment for your stay in the shelter.

There are two basic types of shelters: those outside the home (above or below-ground) and those in the house (usually the basement). The basement shelter is more convenient to enter and the shielding of your house helps reduce the radioactivity in your shelter. On the other hand, a basement shelter could also force you to have to "dig

your way out" when leaving your shelter as your house could quite possibly have burned down above you. There will be no fire fighters out — for long — in the radioactive fallout. Unless you're in the middle of nowhere, don't build a basement shelter (though the main entrance to the shelter could be in the basement).

When picking a spot for your shelter, try to gain maximum shielding from the surrounding area. The only thing that limits the depth you can go into the earth is the water table in your area or the bedrock depth.

In a bind, magazines and books can be used as shielding. They have almost the density-shielding power of earth, provided fallout dust doesn't settle into them. You should also remember that metal tools, water, and food will all provide some shielding. Therefore, whenever possible,

WHAT MIGHT CAUSE A NUCLEAR WAR?

HAVE YOU wondered what major incident might spark a nuclear attack? Planners in the Pentagon and at universities around the globe have spent long years doing just that, and yet they return with nervous anxiety to a minor incident in 1914 that began a domino effect even the world's strongest leaders could not stop.

The incident was the assassination of Archduke Francis Ferdinand of Austria-Hungary in what's now Yugoslavia. The result was World War I (and as an onflow of that conflict, World War II, since the seeds of the latter were sown in the former).

That's what worries planners, strategists and scholars: That any of the hundreds of unpredictable events that occur each year could lead to a confrontation. "You can think of a hundred ways in which nuclear war might start, and it could still start in a thoroughly unpredictable way." That's what Jerome B. Wisener, a former presidential science advisor, former president of Massachusetts Institute of Technology, and an architect of America's air defense system, told David Shribman of the New York Times late in 1982.

Topping the list is a nuclear accident — that somehow a missile is fired by mistake. "There's no way intellectually to say which potential risk of nuclear attack is most likely," said Fred C. Ikle, Reagan Administration undersecretary of defense for policy, in an interview, but he doubts one would come from a technological accident or miscalculation. "We bend every effort, and hopefully the Soviets bend every effort, to make a technological accident as unlikely as possible. For thirty years nuclear weapons have been around, and there never has been an accidental major missile firing. That's an indication of the care that every country that now has nuclear weapons applies to this issue."

What about bogus information? A number of congressmen fear failure in a computer chip, for example, might tell one side it's being attacked and cause a counterstrike. According to a defense specialist, false information has been fed into North American Air Defense computers three times, and nuclear warning systems have been set off "probably dozens of times since 1972."

More worrisome is the possibility a small conflict may escalate into a nuclear confrontation. One scenario focuses on the Middle East and involves Israel, a longstanding American ally and potential nuclear power; Saudi Arabia,

a nation friendly to the West with huge oil reserves; and Iran, a traditional intersection between East and West. "Because we don't have comparable conventional capacity in the area, the temptation might be strong to compensate by relying on tactical nuclear weapons," Marshall D. Shulman, director of the Russian Institute at Columbia University and a Carter administration specialist in Soviet affairs, told Shribman of the Times. "This would breach the firebreak between conventional and nuclear weapons. The concern that seems most to be watched for is the risk of escalation from a local conflict, and particularly if the separation between nuclear and conventional weapons becomes blurred."

Another Middle East scenario envisions Israel about to be overrun and it threatens to use nuclear weapons against the hostile Arabs. Then, says Jeremy J. Stone, director of the Federation of American Scientists and a respected figure among strategic thinkers, the Soviets might threaten to use nuclear force against Israel, or to equip their Arab proxies with nuclear weapons.

More likely, says Stone, is European involvement in any nuclear incident. "Europe is still the tinderbox," he told the Times. "That's where all the weapons are, and that's where the confrontation is."

A common scenario in the Pentagon begins with a bloody uprising in a Soviet satellite like East Germany which prompts West German sympathizers to try to aid their Berlin Walled-off countrymen. If troops from the North Atlantic Treaty Organization (NATO) became involved and find themselves at a disadvantage, the temptation to use nuclear arms might be irresistible. "The number of weapons, the variety and the deployment are such that what begins as a conventional conflict is extremely likely to change over into a nuclear conflict," said George B. Kistiakowski, former head of the explosives division of the Los Alamos Laboratory and science advisor to President Eisenhower. "There is ample reason to worry."

As Duncan Long mentions in the accompanying text, nuclear arms could be employed if one side — presumably the Soviets — perceives a golden opportunity to disarm the U.S. Along these lines, one expert said: "If it looked as if the other side might be thinking of using its nuclear forces, there's incentive to use them first. In a deep political crisis, the existence of these weapons alone would contribute to an intensification of the crisis." — Mark Thiffault

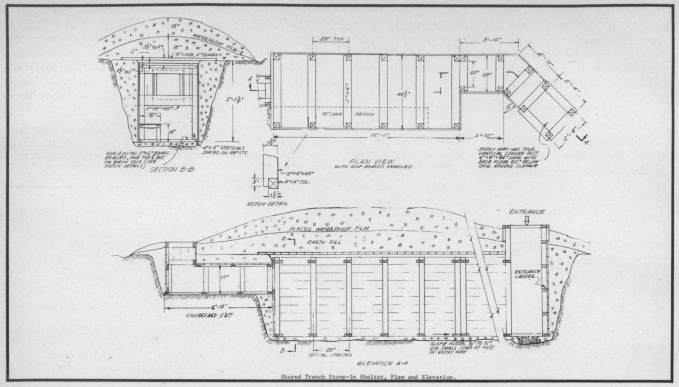

Shored trench stoop-in shelter, plan and elevation, from Christy and Kearny of Oak Ridge National Laboratory. It's just one of a variety of shelter designs you may build, based on evaulation of need, budget.

these should be placed between you and the source of the radiation coming into your shelter.

Be sure fallout cannot seep into the shelter's walls or be washed into the shelter by rain or melted snow. In an area with a lot of rain or poor drainage, a bilge pump might be needed to clear water from your shelter.

Air should be taken in from an area away from any large buildings, bushes, etc., which might catch fire. This will prevent fumes and carbon monoxide from being sucked into the shelter. Ideally, the vent would also be hidden from view so that your shelter can't easily be spotted by passersby.

In cold climates you can use ice or snow to augment a shelter's density shielding. Don't rely solely on these, though, as weather and climatic changes may raise the temperature following a nuclear war. You should have density shielding that won't leave on a warm day! Use snow or ice to enhance your protection. Solid blocks of ice

"Ready for the worst" is how author describes this photo of man with AR-15 in Chemical/Biological/ Radiation suit.

are not quite equal to the shielding of water because water **expands as it freezes. Because of its form, snow is often more** air space than water, so use lots of snow: three or four times as much for the equivalent protection of ice.

Small rooms are more blast-resistant than large rooms, all things being equal. You might consider a modular shelter comprising several small underground rooms interconnected by short tunnels.

When you're thinking about making a shelter, you should also think about defending it. Though the thought that people might try to take over your shelter isn't a pleasant idea, it isn't unrealistic. The best route is to not let anyone know about your shelter. If you think you may need to defend your shelter, probably a short-barreled shotgun is the very best self-defense weapon for a shelter. The Model 870 Remington functions well, even with a little shelter grit in it. With an eighteen-inch barrel, a Choate folding stock and magazine extension, and a box of birdshot shells, you would be able to keep all but shock troops out of your lair. Think about it. It would be ridiculous to spend all your time and money if the first yo-yo with a gun could come along and take over your shelter.

It is possible to create a shelter from simple scrounged materials. The "Expedient Shelters" shown were designed and carefully tested by the Oak Ridge National Laboratory under the direction of Cresson H. Kearny. Blasts of conventional explosives were used in amounts equivalent to the nuclear blasts that could be expected during a war. Not only are these shelters fallout-proof, they're also heat- and blast-proof.

When you first look at these, they look like a joke. In fact, the press — apparently unaware that these designs were carefully tested — often pokes fun at the idea that a person could survive a nuclear blast in an earthen shelter. How can some wooden poles and dirt give you as much protection as a concrete bunker? Fortunately, physics comes to the rescue with a phenomenon called "earth arching." When pressure is put on dirt, the earth particles spread the tension out at right angles and create a supporting arch. All that is necessary is to get the right depth of earth as well as the minimum width to be arched, and to hold the earth in place over the area to be protected. Pressures that would flatten buildings above ground will be uneventful underground in an expedient shelter!

A properly constructed expedient shelter will withstand the overpressure produced by a one-megaton bomb at less that 1½ miles away, or 3½ miles from a super-large, twenty-megaton bomb (much larger than any you would normally expect to be facing).

The expedient shelter might also be adapted to a permanent shelter design. If so, be sure to use treated wood if you are in an area where there is any chance at all of wood rot or termite damage — if the wooden support members are damaged, the shelter will become a death trap. Also, be sure that the earth where you build your shelter is firm enough to not cave in. The way to check this is to dig down eighteen inches and stick your thumb into the undisturbed earth that's been uncovered at the bottom of your test hole. If your thumb goes no more than one inch into this earth, you can dig a shelter in that area. If your thumb sinks in more than an inch, you'll have to go through the tedious process of shoring up the walls to prevent a cave-in. This takes a lot of extra time and building materials, so it's better to locate another spot if possible.

It is also possible to create an above-ground shelter if you can't dig down because of bedrock, water table; or the inability of the earth to pass your thumb test. This, too, takes a lot of extra time and should be avoided if possible.

Don't dig only with a shovel. In most areas a pick should be used to break out chunks of earth. Then use a shovel to throw it out of the hole. A bow saw will be needed for cutting wood. Be sure to wear gloves — blisters could become infected when you have to stay for some time in a shelter.

In addition to the materials shown for a shelter roof, doors, plywood, planks, and metal might all be used in the shelter roof if trees aren't abundant in your area.

Plastic sheets should be used to waterproof the roof of your shelter. Shower curtains, tarps, building materials, etc., could all be employed for this. It is essential that this step be employed or a little rain can quickly ruin your shelter's ability to protect you. Likewise, be sure to cover the plastic with a layer of earth so that the plastic can't be blown away.

Build a narrow passageway leading into your shelter and use an expedient "blast door" if you think you may be close enough to warrant it (within twenty to thirty miles of a prime target). The blast door should be a minimum of two inches thick if made of wood. If a flexible material is placed over it, it will be much more effective. The door should be tied down as the blast wind will be followed by a suction return wind which will pull off an unsecured door.

Following the blast and suction wave there will be at least fifteen minutes' pause before fallout enters your area. This time can be employed to put out fires, repair damage to the outside of your shelter, etc. Be sure, though, that another blast isn't following the first and be ready to dive for cover if a nuclear flash warns you of another blast wave on its way. (Keep your skin covered with light-colored clothing while outside and wear sunglasses if possible to

Diagrams below show construction and use of Kearny Air Pump. As you pull swinging pump frame, flaps close to draw air toward you. When you slack, flaps open as frame swings back away from you. See text.

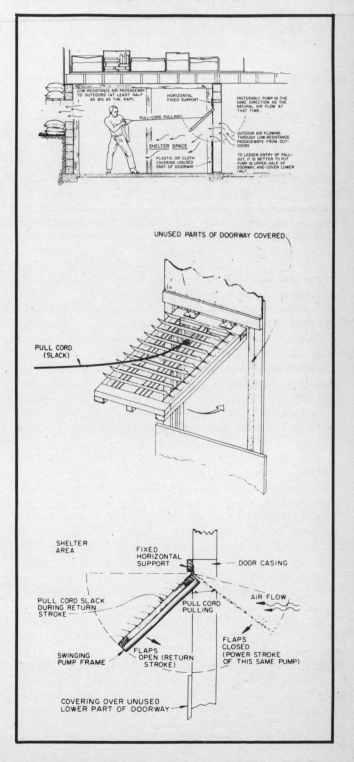

minimize the effects of a flash if one takes you by surprise.)

Fallout will appear as a gray/white ash with larger sand-like particles falling first if you are close to ground zero. Get out of this immediately as it is extremely dangerous during the first few days following the nuclear explosion. If any gets on you, brush it off immediately and be careful not to carry any into your shelter on your clothing or shoes.

If you have a long, narrow entrance leading into your shelter through which you also obtain your air, the fallout will fall near its entrance and you shouldn't need air filters in your shelter. If you have separate air intake vents, an inverted "J" will keep fallout from entering.

Though you only require three cubic feet of air per minute (per person) to breathe in a shelter, you'll need much more to ventilate your shelter so that heat doesn't build up in it. This is of prime importance in all but the very coldest areas. The alternative is being driven from your shelter in several days' time or dying from heat stroke.

There are two solutions, both developed by Kearny. One is the KAP (Kearny Air Pump) and the other is a variation of an old method used by miners. Both work very well and use "people" power rather than electrical. (Full instructions and plans for both are available from Long Survival Publications.)

The shock wave of a nuclear explosion will travel faster through the earth than it will through the air, so the floor and walls of your shelter may suddenly bulge out slightly at the speed of perhaps several hundred miles per hour. Obviously, you don't want to be sitting on a hard floor or leaning against the wall. Though they'll only move perhaps a fraction of an inch, they would be capable of creating injury. The best route is to sit on a cushion or some flexible object away from the wall. Following this, the roof will be pushed downward slightly before earth arching occurs, so keep your head down, too.

The inside of your shelter can be made much more comfortable if you use plastic sheeting to cover the inside walls to prevent your group from becoming caked with mud or dust when they lean against the walls.

Chances are you won't be camped out in a shelter when a nuclear war starts. You could still survive. People survived the Nagasaki blast just one-third-mile from ground zero! Not in a concrete bunker, either. It was a simple wood-framed shelter with earth shielding (even though they didn't know about atomic weapons, they did know what would survive a near miss of a conventional bomb; good design covered the unexpected).

You could do the same thing with an expedient shelter if you had time to construct it. But suppose you didn't expect the blast and you're at work. Now what? If you won't be able to get back to your own shelter before fallout arrives (about fifteen minutes at the least, maybe more time), then you start making plans on surviving where you are. You can go for a long time without food provided you don't have to move around a lot and you have water. So you might be able to sit tight for a couple of weeks until the fallout danger is lessened enough for you to head to your own family shelter or at least forage for food.

Many buildings can offer you protection from fallout. Look for a building which is constructed of concrete and has a deep basement. Get to an inside room without win-

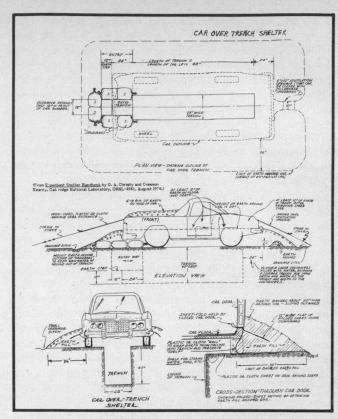

Emergency shelter is shown in this Car-Over-Trench design. It's amazingly simple and most effective.

dows, under a stairwell, or some other area which will offer a lot of shielding from radiation. Keep the dust — possible fallout — from drifting into your area by quickly sweeping it away if it accumulates near you. Heat buildup may be a problem if others are with you or you're confined to a small space, so try to create a "fan" to push air through your shelter. A "bug out" bag of essentials, food concentrates, water containers, tools, etc., in the trunk of your car would greatly improve your survival chances and is worth considering.

If you find yourself outside of any shelter during the actual explosion of a nuclear bomb (which isn't too far-fetched, considering the poor showing the Civil Defense warning system has shown during the last few alerts), some quick actions can greatly improve your survival chances and minimize your injuries. The first thing you'll be aware of is a flash which is brighter than the sun. That can mean only one thing: a nuclear fireball is nearby.

What you do in the next few seconds may mean the difference between life and death. If you are in the open, fall prone instantly and cover exposed areas of your body. If possible, crawl behind some dense object. Do not look at the flash as it will cause blindness (perhaps permanent) and possible burns on your exposed skin.

If you are indoors, get away from windows as the blast following the flash may cause the glass to fly into the room like hundreds of slashing knives. The wave will reach you within two minutes if it is going to be dangerous. After the two minutes are up you can move elsewhere unless there is a second flash (which dictates another two-minute wait).

The flash may cause temporary blindness lasting from a

few seconds up to hours. This is similar to snow blindness. The less you expose your eyes during the flash, the less problem you'll have with this. Closing both eyes the moment a "flash" is detected will help lessen temporary (or prevent permanent) loss of sight.

Small fires may be started following a blast wave. If you'll be staying in the area, put them out before they can spread.

During periods of international tension when war may be a possibility, you can minimize the damage to your person if you are wearing sunglasses, hat, and light-colored clothes when a flash occurs. Likewise, damage to your house can be reduced if you coat the windows with white paint or draw the curtains to keep the thermal rays from a nearby flash from igniting flammable materials in your house.

When gamma radiation from a high-altitude nuclear detonation interacts with the atmosphere below the detonation, EMP (electromagnetic pulse) is created. The electrons generated by this interaction spiral in the earth's magnetic field and send out the pulse of electromagnetic radiation called EMP. EMP is similar to a radio wave and travels at the speed of light. It is much more powerful than a radio wave and becomes as dangerous as a bolt of lightning if it is concentrated by an expanse of metal. During a time of possible nuclear attack, it would be wise to avoid contact with large expanses of metal or long wires to avoid being injured if an EMP wave were collected by the metal.

Several high-altitude nuclear blasts could wipe out much of the communications and other electrical equipment in the whole U.S....so you can be sure such blasts would be used.

Electric motors, relays, transformers and to some extent vacuum tube equipment are relatively immune to EMP if they aren't connected to long runs of wiring or long antennas. Integrated circuits (ICs), microwave equipment, and field effect transistors (FETs) are very sensitive to the effects of EMP. Computers, much of the telephone equipment, and any transistorized equipment connected to AC outlets would probably be damaged. Also, the generators of many major power utilities will probably go off-line until their relays can be reset or replaced.

Most battery-operated equipment would not be damaged. Transistor radios and walkie-talkies with antennas under thirty inches in length won't be damaged, provided they aren't plugged into an AC outlet. If rumors of war are about, it would be wise to unplug AC equipment if it's not in use. Ditto with antennas: disconnect them when the equipment is sitting idle.

Stored equipment can be protected by a "Faraday Box." A Faraday Box is created when a sheet of metal is wrapped around a non-conductive box. The metal coat keeps the EMP from affecting anything inside the box. The shielding metal can be metal foil, metal screen, or any metal container as long as it completely encircles the area being protected, and as long as the shielding metal is physically touching all parts of itself to make an electrical connection. Wood, plastic, cardboard, or other non-conductive materials must be used to keep the object being protected from touching the shielding metal. Once something touches the shield, it may become subject to the EMP charge (depending on the thickness of the shield).

Equipment stored in cardboard boxes can be wrapped in

Log-covered trench shelter requires little materials, lots of sweat. It can be camouflaged to invisibility.

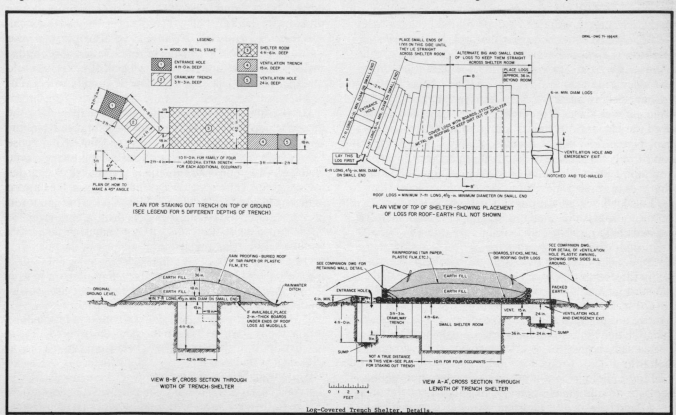

Log-Covered Trench Shelter, Details.

aluminum foil to create a Faraday Box. Just be careful not to tear a hole in the foil while it's stored. Putting the whole works into a second, larger box would protect the foil from abuse. Equipment wrapped in plastic and stored in metal filing cabinets, old metal ammunition boxes, etc., would also be safe from EMP.

A whole shelter can be turned into a Faraday Box. Just line it with screen, aluminum foil, etc., and put metal screen over the air vents, windows, or other openings. Cover the inside of the door and keep it closed as much as possible. Finally, connect all metal shielding by soldering or otherwise connecting it to create one continuous shield of electrically conducting metal. Provided you do not run wires or cables through the shield, it will protect everything inside the shelter from EMP.

A radiation-detection device is a must for outside operations. Since the amounts of fallout will drift somewhat just like snow, it is essential to have a fallout meter in order not to wander into dangerous areas.

Each person in the shelter should keep track of total rem exposure to determine the maximum time they can remain outside the shelter. Remember: The less radiation you are exposed to, the less damage it does to your body. Some radiation-detection devices measure radiation in roentgens. For the human body, rems and roentgens are practically equivalent.

A number of companies offer meters and it is probably a good idea to write to each and see what they have to offer: Victoreen Instrument Division, 10101 Woodland Avenue, Cleveland, OH 44104; Eberline Instrument Corporation, Box 2108, Santa Fe, NM 87501; and Dosimeter Corporation, Box 42377, Cincinnati, OH 45242. Be sure you get a meter designed for large readings as well as small, often called a survey meter. Check the ranges: They should go up to hundreds of rems as well as down to fractions of a rem. Be sure, too, that the meter will read gamma radiation. It is also very convenient to be able to measure alpha and beta radiation, but not essential.

Dosimeters are also very useful. These are small, tube-shaped instruments that tell the total amount of radiation you've been exposed to (if you're wearing the dosimeter) from the time it was last zeroed. If you're traveling in and out of areas with varying amounts of radiation, the dosimeter can take a lot of guesswork out of just how much exposure you've actually received. If you get a dosimeter, you'll also need a charger for it. One charger will charge any number of dosimeters.

Get a lot of spare batteries. There is no telling how long it might be before replacement batteries are available. Batteries should be stored in a cool area (above freezing).

If money permits, consider getting at least one meter, one dosimeter charger, radiation logbook (so everyone can keep track of his total exposure), and a dosimeter for each shelter member.

A meter which picks up lower levels of radiation might also be useful to check members of your group for contamination or to inspect food. One excellent, inexpensive meter is RDX Nuclear, 2003 Canyon Drive, Los Angeles, CA 90068 for $71. Just do not try to use it as a survey meter since it will "lock up" on extremely hot spots and register "0" radiation when you're actually being exposed to an excessive amount of radiation. If this limitation is kept in mind, the RDX meter would be good to have in addition to a survey meter and individual dosimeters.

The M17 and M17A1 masks will keep you from inhaling radioactive dust particles (the masks are described elsewhere in this chapter). Simple dust masks could also be used for this purpose.

Dust masks should be worn outside the shelter (or inside the shelter, if you feel fallout particles might have entered the shelter), as well as gloves. Whenever someone leaves the shelter he must be careful to avoid being exposed to too much radiation. When he re-enters the shelter he must also be careful not to bring radioactive dust back with him. Rubber overshoes (for outside the shelter only) are handy to leave at the door. Plastic bags taped over your feet will also work for short trips outside (just remember they're pretty thin and will sag if you run).

Heavy clothing will protect all covered parts of your skin from alpha and beta particles and will give you some — though very small — geometric protection from fallout particles which are on the clothing rather than being on your skin. Tape around the ankles, wrist, and neck so that the tape seals the edge of the clothing against your skin. This will help keep fallout particles from getting into your clothing.

When returning from a contaminated environment, scrubbing under some type of shower (but not taking a bath sitting in a tub) is most ideal for complete decontamination. If water is unavailable for showering, just wiping off with a clean cloth and shaking out clothing would get rid of much of the fallout contamination you might pick up after being outside your shelter.

Food will be a problem following a nuclear war. Many farming methods depend on large amounts of fuel and energy to operate. That probably won't be available. You'll probably be on your own for some time to produce your own food.

Growing plants outside would be rough, since many pests have a higher resistance to radiation than human beings, mammals and birds. It's highly likely that veritable "plagues" of grasshoppers and other insects will quickly riddle any gardening you may do following an attack. Likewise, the ultraviolet radiation let through by the ozone layer (which will remain depleted for several years following a nuclear war) is detrimental to many food crops. Therefore, you would be wise to consider growing food in some type of improvised greenhouse (clear plastic draped over dead tree limbs or scrap lumber frames, perhaps) in which to plant your "garden." Though it isn't as glamorous as figuring out your weapons stockpile or planning on how to defend your shelter, the ho-hum task of growing food will be just as important.

In addition to regular methods, hydroponics holds much promise for year-round yields and a minimum of worries about insects, since they can be kept out of the growing area with physical barriers. Several excellent books are available on hydroponics. One of the best is *Hydroponic Food Production,* by Dr. Howard M. Resh. It's available from Woodbridge Press, Box 6189, Santa Barbara, CA 93111 for $14.95.

Food that has been exposed to fallout can usually be salvaged for use immediately following a nuclear attack. Care must be exercised, though, because levels of radiation that are safe for your skin can be very harmful to your more-sensitive digestive tract.

Food sealed in airtight containers would be safe to eat. Just carefully wipe off any dust (which might be fallout) with a rag before you open the container so that radioactive dust doesn't fall into the food.

Most fruits and vegetables have built-in fallout-proof containers in the form of their skins. If you carefully rinse or wipe off fruits and vegetables, then peel off their skins and discard the peelings, the fruit or vegetables will be safe to eat.

Most fallout will be on the surface of the ground. Clearing off the top layer (one or two inches) would expose uncontaminated earth for use in gardening. Plants like peanuts or potatoes could be harvested and eaten — even if they'd been exposed to fallout — by first clearing off the surface area before digging them. Try to store all removed topsoil in one area and mark it so it can be avoided.

Storing enough food and food supplements for a year or more is a good idea. This takes the pressure off the neo-farmer (you) to have a bounteous crop the first year. Don't forget to have enough seeds to plant several crops in case one ends in disaster. It would be wise to try your hand at gardening now, before the stakes are high.

Of all food animals, chickens have very high resistance to radiation and are small. They also produce eggs so that you can eat without depleting your "herd" of chickens. Again, if you want to do this for survival, the time to learn how is now, not when the chips are down.

Many "survivalists" seem to think they will be able to go out and hunt for all their needs. The problem with this idea is that if you're in an area that received only a small amount of damage, there will be a lot of other hunters in the area

Remington Model 870 in 12-gauge with cylinder barrel and Choate folding stock is author's "shelter defender."

and the hunting stock will soon be depleted. If you are in an area of enough damage to limit the number of survivors or keep people out of the area, most game animals will be dead. Either way, you need other sources of food. Hunting is not an effective way to support very many people, which is why all civilizations are based on farm food production rather than hunting.

That being said, you may occasionally encounter animals that could be eaten. Would they be safe? The rule of thumb is that any animal that appears sick should be left alone. Radiation lowers an animal's immunity to disease; if it looks sick it may be a walking incubator for bacteria. Even though cooking the meat from such an animal would kill the bacteria in it, the toxins that are making the animal sick would still be active and would make you very sick.

If the animal is well it would be safe to eat. Be sure you aren't killing off any potential breeding stock.

Animals selected to be eaten will probably have been contaminated by fallout. This is not an overwhelming problem, however, if care is taken to avoid the parts of the animal's carcass in which the contamination will be concentrated. The safest course is to eat only muscle meat. Avoid eating any of the animal's organs if possible and especially avoid eating the heart, kidneys, liver, or thyroid glands (located in the animal's neck). Also avoid meat close to the bone and don't use the bones for soup. This applies to birds or fish as well as mammals.

Try to balance your food intake with as much variety as possible. Because plants don't supply complete proteins, it is a good idea to add some type of animal protein or fat to every meal. If this is not possible, effort should be made to mix several types of grains and beans in each meal so that the different proteins available will enable your body to synthesize the proteins it needs. Vitamin/mineral supplements would also aid the health value of a somewhat iffy diet.

The amount of radiation a person can receive without ill effects varies from person to person. Older people and young children cannot tolerate as much as healthy adults without ill effects.

In general, an adult can receive up to 100 rems in a short period of time without any short-term ill effects (his chances for cancer, etc., will be increased slightly). The upper limit of exposure should be 200 rems for an adult during a short period. More than this amount of exposure may necessitate medical help for survival.

If exposure is spread out over a longer period of time rather than a few hours, the body is able to repair itself and more exposure is possible. An adult can be exposed to 150 rems during a week's time without any ill effects, 200 rems over a month, or up to 300 rems over four months. The less exposure the better, but if you can spread out the time of your exposure, you can take a larger exposure without ill effects.

You and everyone in your group should try to keep an accurate as possible account of how much total exposure to radiation you have experienced. A little care will allow work to be done in contaminated areas without risk to the person's health.

Radiation lowers your resistance to disease. It is especially important that all cuts be treated and that rest and medication be taken for even the most minor of ailments.

Chapter 13

CHEMICAL & BIOLOGICAL SURVIVAL

History Shows These Horrible Weapons Have Been Used — And Probably Will Be Again

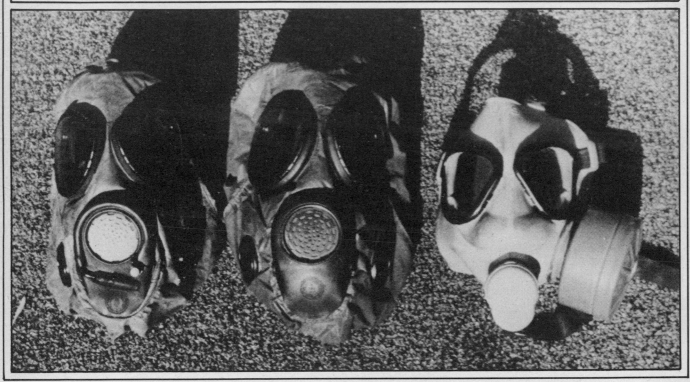

Three of the current U.S. masks available on the surplus market. From left: M17A1, M17 and M9A1. The preferred masks are first two, since spares are hard to find for M9A1 and side-mounted filter makes it unusable for left-handed shooters. Also, no provision has been made for those who need to wear glasses.

By Duncan Long

BECAUSE CHEMICAL weapons are cheap to make and because the U.S. has lost much of its chemical warfare deterrence as its stockpiles of chemical weapons have deteriorated, many experts feel a chemical attack is more likely than a nuclear one. Indeed, chemical weapons have been readily used in Cambodia, Afghanistan, and Laos during the last few years.

Unfortunately, many people think that a mask makes it possible for them to dive into a contaminated area for hours just as a scuba diver dives into the water. This isn't

so. Modern chemical weapons attack the human body through the skin as well as the throat and even with the best of protective suits, you still face a good chance of being adversely affected if you're in a contaminated area for more than a few minutes.

Military surplus masks are the cheapest and most reliable place to start when looking at protective gear. The M17A1 and the M17 are the best with the only difference between the two being the resuscitation/drinking tube controls in the nosepiece of the M17A1. Since it is doubtful that you'd be in a contaminated area long enough to make

Author models complete chemical/biological "breathing" suit which allows heat to escape. Although more comfortable to wear, these suits can be damaged by water. Rifle is Mini-14 with Choate folding stock.

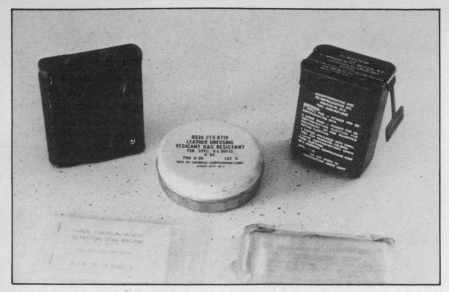

Much chemical decontamination and detection equipment is on the market today, but author advises leaving it alone — it's heat-sensitive and who knows if its age/heat limits have been exceeded? Better to use your own household chemical decontamination brew, he advises. Below: Another batch of decontamination stuff you should avoid to be safe.

use of the extras of the M17A1 (unlike military personnel, you're not trying to hold ground), the M17 would be just as good as an M17A1 and is generally cheaper. (The U.S. Army's new XM-30 mask would be even better, but is not currently available on the surplus market.)

A mask must have the correct filters in it to work. Use the new green-ringed filters. Black is for riot gas only and the yellow, though better than the black, is the outdated all-purpose filter. Just having a green filter isn't enough, though — it must be a working filter. To keep it in working order, it must be sealed in its package or, if placed in the mask, the mask must be kept airtight. When exposed to air, the filter pulls out particles in the air and will — over time — lose its ability to protect you from poison gas. Filters are also sensitive to moisture, so don't let them get wet. If they do, discard them.

In the M17 and M17A1, the filters are hard to change. Use the filters that come with the mask (since they'll probably be shot) for practice. If you aren't sure about the procedure, get a copy of Army training manual TM 3-4240-279-10 Operator's Manual Mask or a commercial book like my *Chemical/Biological Warfare Survival*. On-the-job learning can be hazardous!

Rubber gloves and boots along with the M17 hood for your mask are the next orders of business. Butyl rubber is the best type for resistance to chemical weapons, though any type of rubber will do in a scrape. (The glove/suit and boot/suit can be made safer by using duct tape to seal them; be sure to make the end of the tape a tab so it can be pulled off in a hurry if your suit gets contaminated.)

Any non-porous material gives some protection from chemical weapons. The best are military surplus suits. New suits which breathe are cooler to wear but are sensitive (like mask filters) to moisture and must be kept stored in airtight containers.

No matter what you wear, it won't keep you safe for long if chemical weapons (agents) actually get onto your outfit. Such mateiral — in the form of droplets — will soon soak through your suit or vaporize and enter your suit as lethal fumes. Though such agents can be neutralized, the best bet is to get out of the contaminated area and remove your contaminated suit.

Military surplus decontamination chemicals are not recommended since there is no way of telling if they are still good (the decontaminants are sensitive to high temperatures). The best route is to "mix your own" decontamination brew. A number of common over-the-counter products can be used for decontamination.

Some of the best are soap (alkaline soap is superior to others), detergents (including most dishwashing liquid), sodium hydroxide (lye or caustic soda are the same as sodium hydroxide), sodium carbonate (washing soda, sal soda, and laundry soda are the common names), and any of the chlorine bleaches available. These are best used with hot water — cold will work, but not as well — to neutralize many chemical weapons' contamination on suits or gear. (Obviously, you'll need to take care not to get mask filters wet or use water on the "breathing" quilted military suits which are ruined when they become wet.)

Another group of household chemicals can be used to lift off, but not neutralize, chemical agents. This group is known as the organic solvents and includes gasoline, kerosene, acetone, and alcohol. These chemicals just remove agents. Remember they are poisonous after they have lifted off the agents. Likewise, the fumes given off in the

Do-it-yourself nuclear/biological/ chemical outfit. Since military surplus boots and gloves are not currently available, shown are rain boots and heavy rubber gloves to round out NATO suit. Included also are M17 mask and carrier bag.

decontamination process may be dangerous as well.

If you can't decontaminate equipment with such home-brew chemicals, most of the chemical agents will eventually evaporate off of contaminated items in warm climates in about a week. Letting equipment air out will eventually decontaminate it, but remember it is dangerous while it's airing out. In cold weather, the time needed for equipment decontamination becomes much longer. (Clothespins could be some of your most important survival equipment!)

Avoiding dangerous areas during a chemical attack could improve your survival chances and might even allow you to get along without a mask or other equipment.

Since most chemical agents are heavier than air, going for the "high ground" is usually a safe bet and — for the same reason — low-lying areas can be very dangerous. Take the "high ground" and avoid valleys, river beds, basements, streets with tall buildings on either side, etc.

(A temperature inversion could occur which would operate in a different manner. If the weather suddenly warms up, an agent in a low area may remain near the ground and be pulled uphill as the warm air travels upward while close to the ground.)

As agents vaporize they are carried downwind. Take note of where the wind is blowing and go at right angles to it. Stay upwind from a contaminated area or one in which you suspect chemical agents are being released. Five hundred meters is usually the maximum range that a cloud of agent will travel from its point of release.

Since most chemical releases can be seen when they're first released, it may be possible to keep out of the way of their travel. Several signs to watch for are abnormally appearing clouds of vapor, strangely soft non-explosive shells, non-explosive grenades, or missile warheads with noticeable clouds coming from them. Agent might also be released as sprays by planes or helicopters (a la crop duster).

The rougher the terrain the longer it will remain contaminated. The colder the climate the longer an area will remain contaminated. The first, because the air doesn't travel as quickly through a rough area and the second, because cold air doesn't warm an agent to the evaporation point as quickly as warm. Thus, wooded areas should remain dangerous longer than grassy areas, sand longer than concrete, and a snowy plain longer than its hot summer self.

During very low temperatures (freezing or below) evaporation of agents almost comes to a stop. A contaminated area would be safe to be in, but would become dangerous again when it became warm.

When agents are released, even colorless ones are initially visible as a cloud of mist or fog. They may also clump up during release to form oily clumps on plants or on the ground. Avoid these concentrations as they are very dangerous.

Since you won't always see the actual release of the chemical agent or see globules of it on the ground or plants, you should also watch animals and birds in the area. If they appear sick or are not even about in the area, avoid it. Agents that attack warm-blooded animals will harm you.

Another danger sign is if you see someone else wearing protective gear. If so, remember your appointment at the other side of town and leave with haste.

Despite all you do, you may be exposed to the agent. Though this isn't the most healthful thing that could happen to you, it doesn't necessarily mean you'll be facing the pearly gates shortly. Get out of the contaminated area and clothing and take it easy. Small exposures of chemical agents aren't necessarily fatal, provided you have a small dose and get out of the contamination.

If you have been exposed to an agent, there will probably be little doubt in your mind. Modern weapons will attack the mucous membranes in your nose and throat as well as your nervous system. Among symptoms you'll experience are a running nose or eyes; too much salivation (or not enough — a very dry mouth); nausea or diarrhea (which may be caused by nervousness and aren't always

While survey meter shows dangerous level of radiation, most low-level geiger meters register zero. Use of incorrect type can have fatal consequences for you.

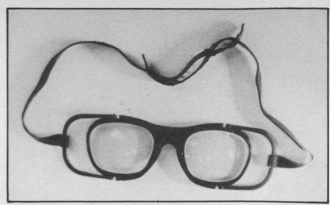

MAG-1 combat glasses are essential if you're to see when wearing M17 or M17A1 masks without breaking the airtight seal. Find maker in Survival Sources.

reliable indications); or disorientation or muscle spasms. If these are happening to you, get out of the area and get a gas mask and other protective gear if they are available.

Unless you know what you've been exposed to and what type of medication to use for an antidote, any cure may be more dangerous than your ailment. Best bet is to let the body take care of itself; if you are caring for someone who has been exposed, try to keep them breathing and keep their airways clear of mucous and vomit.

With a little care, you can avoid chemical weapons altogether. Chemical weapons are not the all-pervasive weapons many people think they are; with a little thought you can survive such an attack.

BIOLOGICAL WARFARE SURVIVAL

Biological weapons are insidious in that they may take weeks before they actually weaken or kill their victims. Because of this "incubation time" from the time a weapon is used until it actually takes effect, the potential for surprise is very great. At the same time, a country can innoculate its population to make it immune. Such a program can take place under the guise of treating a flu epidemic or in a nationwide effort to wipe out measles, etc. Likewise, innoculations are one of the common steps for preparing troops for battle. Adding one more group to the shots wouldn't arouse many suspicions. The argument that no country would use biological warfare because their own people might be affected displays a lack of knowledge about biological warfare.

Biological agents include anything living that can be used to attack men, animals or plants. At one time only known parasites and diseases could be used for warfare, but new genetic engineering techniques promise to create "bugs" that mimic bacteria the human body accepts as being harmless.

Though any living thing might be used for biological warfare, it is generally limited to microorganisms. These organisms are often carried and spread by nonhuman carriers such as insects, birds, small rodents, etc. Such carriers are called vectors. In addition, most biological weapon organisms can be passed on by victims of the original attack, thus making secondary casualties as the "disease" spreads.

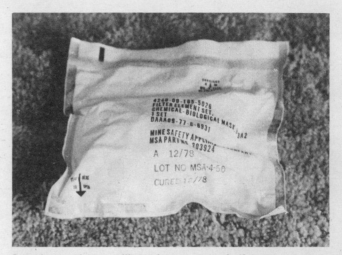

Get plenty of spare filters for your mask, then leave them in protective wrapper because exposure to air will gradually downgrade protective ability.

Protecting yourself from biological agents begins with good hygiene: washing, using disinfectants on minor wounds, and sterlizing equipment all help prevent your picking up any "bug." A second line of defense is to eliminate possible animal vectors (carriers) from your area by killing all rats, mice, or other animals that act abnormally or are out of place in your area. Keep flies, mosquitoes, gnats and other pests out of your area with screens; use repellents and netting when you're outside. If they're available, use insecticides if any insect population seems to be larger than normal.

People in good health are more apt to survive biological attacks. Getting rest, eating properly, and being in good physical shape could save your life.

Biological agents can be delivered in the same way that chemical ones are: unusual bombs, rockets, grenades, shells, or sprays/fogs from planes. If a weapon has more smoke than boom, it may be a chemical or biological weapon.

The best way to deal with an area that seems to be contaminated with biological agents is to move out of the area and/or avoid it altogether. If you can't leave a contaminated area, your first task is to create an area that is

Don't get excited about buying a resuscitation tube. It would be of doubtful use and only on M17A1.

safe to stay in. This will give you a "home base" to rest in and from which to carry out larger decontamination steps.

Wind and sunlight are effective in killing or at least weakening many biological agents. If the humidity is low, many biological agents will be killed within a day's time. Spores aren't killed in this manner, nor are those biological agents riding in vectors, so a few days of sunlight doesn't necessarily make everything hunky-dory.

Hot water with soap or detergent is quite effective in decontamination and can be used to wash off areas or objects that need to be decontaminated. Care must be exercised in dealing with the run-off from such cleaning as the biological agents in the waste water may still be active.

Contaminated articles should not be buried unless there is no other route. Clearly mark such sites so they won't be excavated at a later date. Some buried biological agents can remain dangerous for decades. An extremely hot fire may be used to sterilize and burn contaminated materials.

Steam is useful for decontamination if it is available. Heating articles to 335F (169C) degrees for two to three hours will also decontaminate them.

Sodium hydroxide (caustic soda or lye), formalin (formaldehyde solution), and methyl alcohol (and to some extent other alcohols) are all useful as decontaminants, especially indoors.

Use a thirty-six to forty percent solution of formaldehyde and avoid the fumes created by it (rubber boots, gloves, protective suit, and gas mask would be a good idea) when using it. If you use this indoors, the mask will not give enough protection for more than two to three minutes. You'll need a breathing tube to the outdoors.

Don't dilute the formaldehyde and use one quart per one thousand cubic feet of space to be decontaminated. Inside areas can be well decontaminated if the space is kept closed up for sixteen hours.

A mix of formaldehyde with methanol (five parts to three parts methanol) will also work and decontamination takes places within eight hours in a closed area.

Sodium hypochlorite (household bleach) can be used at full strength for decontamination. Clothing can be soaked in a diluted solution (one-half cup bleach to one gallon [4.5L] of water) for thirty minutes then rinsed in clear water. (This may ruin wool clothing.)

Boiling objects for twenty minutes will decontaminate

them. Leather and rubber can be cleaned in hot water and detergent (or soap) and then dipped into a two percent solution of household bleach.

Unlike chemical contamination, biologically contaminated food can be sterilized and eaten. Food in sealed containers will be safe provided you sterilize the outside of the container before opening it. Contaminated food can be baked for forty minutes or more at 400F (204C) degrees or at 325F (162C) degrees for two hours. Food and water can also be made safe by boiling it (at a complete boil) for twenty or more minutes. Water can also be sterilized with purification tablets as well as ten drops of tincture of iodine or seven drops of household bleach per gallon of water (see Chapter 17).

Antibiotics would be useful for treating victims of biological agents. Unfortunately, these are not available over-the-counter (though some animal antibiotics are and might be used in a pinch). If you contact your doctor and tell him your worries and needs, you might be able to get some potent antibiotics. Do not use any of your stock except in an extreme emergency. Do not even try to get antibiotics if you're not certain about how to use them or if you don't know whether you or members of your family might be allergic to the antibiotics. Your doctor may not be making house calls if you mess up.

Supportive care is probably the best first-aid you'll be able to engage in when treating biological weapons victimes. Good hygiene is essential, keeps pests out of your living area.

It's impossible to cover all the ins and outs of nuclear, chemical, and biological warfare in one chapter of a book. You'd be doing well, therefore, to follow up on your "education" by getting a copy of Kearny's *Nuclear War Survival Skills* available from most survival stores. I've also written several books on surviving during and in the aftermath of a modern nuclear, chemical, and/or biological war. Write and we'll send you a free catalog. The address: Long Survival Publications, Box 163, Wamego, KS 66547.

War is hazardous to all involved. It's always been that way and it always will until the end of this world's woes. A modern war is survivable and the "unthinkable" weapons do not make it impossible to survive if you are prepared and know what to do.

Start preparing now.

Chapter 14

FOOD PRESERVATION AND STORAGE

Learn The Methods For Canning, Smoking, Dehydrating And More In Worlds And Picture

By Grace Calcagno

CANNING PROCEUDRES

CANNING IS defined by Webster's Seventh New Collegiate as "to preserve by sealing in airtight cans or jars." It's a straightforward definition of a straightforward process that, unfortunately, has acquired an air of mystery or remoteness through the years...the idea that *"I can't can! It's too hard!"*

There is no basis for this, says Mrs. Grace Calcagno of Fullerton, California, who's shown in this chapter preserving the yield from her small garden and from good buys at the market. She should know — Mom's been canning off and on for about forty years and our family's enjoyed it all the while. Coming from a large family she learned firsthand about shortages, and when she grew an overabundance of fresh fruits and vegetables, "I couldn't bear the thought of throwing it away. So I started canning. Besides the self-satisfaction that comes from eating foods you've grown or put up, you also know exactly which chemicals went into the fruits and vegetables, your produce is rendered at the peak of flavor, and it's a heckuva lot cheaper than buying it in the food store!"

From the survivalist perspective, there's a larger benefit: staying alive. Our pioneer predecessors routinely preserved food during years of plenty, anticipating correctly that lean years would follow. Then, as now, it made sense to lay by foodstuffs for bad times. What follows is the canning method and equipment used by Grace — er, Mom — in her own words. When you see how easy it is, you'll be wanting to try it! — *Mark Thiffault*

First, rid yourself of notions that canning fruits, meats or vegetables is difficult. It isn't! It does take time and work, but there's really no magic to it. In fact, just following the directions in most excellent cookbooks like my old standby, the *Better Homes and Gardens Cookbook,* you can safely preserve food in airtight glass jars. I've never had the equipment to try canning using tins, but directions are available

A popular and cost-saving way of preserving food is canning. This dozen quart jars cost less than $5.

if you have the stuff. The U.S. Department of Agriculture publications that are good sources for beginner or expert alike all give directions for preserving in tins or glass. The bibliography at the end of this chapter lists some of the better periodicals, books or pamphlets you'll want to buy. They're inexpensive compared to content, and some, like *Joy of Cooking* is extensively cross-indexed for ease in finding just the right information.

You doubtless ran up a warning flag at my use of the word "safely" in the previous paragraph. This is where some of the mystery becomes attached to canning: the idea that, if you don't do it *just right*, you'll be sick — or worse. But the chance of this happening if you follow directions given in the cookbooks or here is nil.

Air, soil, fruits and vegetables, and even meat contain the organisms that cause food to go bad — mold, yeast, and bacteria — or enzymes that affect taste. Of these, most familiar to the layman is *Clostridium botulinum,* com-

An inexpensive canner kettle uses boiling water and is found at many food stores. You should preserve most vegetables and meats with pressure canner.

The water-bath canner suitable for fruits (see text) is fitted with a metal rack that keeps jars up off bottom, to avoid cracking and loss of the contents.

monly known as botulism. A cousin of *C. tetani,* which causes tetanus or lockjaw, it's been claimed that botulism is so deadly that one ounce could kill one hundred million people. That's a grisly hypothesis I don't care to test even on a million-to-one basis!

So how do we ensure we don't become a statistic after ingesting our canned produce? That's part of the reasons for canning. Whether you use a boiling-water bath or pressure canner, you're employing heat to both cook the food and destroy contaminants that could lead to illness or death. Boiling water (212F or 100C degrees) destroys the germs inside the sealed containers when processed for regulated periods of time (except for *C. botulinum,* that is, which can resist boiling temperatures for hours without succumbing). That's why it's recommended by all experts that you cook *any* and *all* home-canned food uncovered a minimum of fifteen minutes in boiling liquid. Stir frequently. The combination of boiling solution and air destroys the botulism spores. *This is the only safe way to go.*

I've been canning for many years and have always used the boiling-water bath according to cookbook directions for everything except meat. Meat always should be processed in a pressure canner, to ensure heat penetrates all the way through the flesh, to destroy any sources of botulism or parasites. Using just the boiling water even for lengthy periods may not render the food completely safe, even with precooking. The combination of pressure and heat is required to be truly safe.

And there's been a change of attitude among many of the cooking experts in recent times. They now advocate the use of a pressure canner for all vegetables except tomatoes. Fruits and tomatoes or pickled vegetables are the only candidates for the boiling-water method, and this view is shared by the U.S. Department of Agriculture. I presume they've gone this route to avoid possible cases of botulism from canners using the boiling-water technique incorrectly. Because any Joe Blow will have access to Government publications, they must take "overkill" precautions to avoid any incidents that could land them in

legal hot water. Used to be if you read the directions and failed to follow them, YOU were the one who paid the price. Nowadays, however, it's always somebody else who's paying with you!

So, to avoid complications, I'm going to stick with the U.S. Department of Agriculture and recommend in the following instructions how to can with both the boiling-water bath and the pressure canner. But first, let's talk about what kind of equipment you need for both.

While boiling jars filled with fruits will destroy bacteria, author prefers sanitation step of washing new jars in hot, soapy water prior to filling.

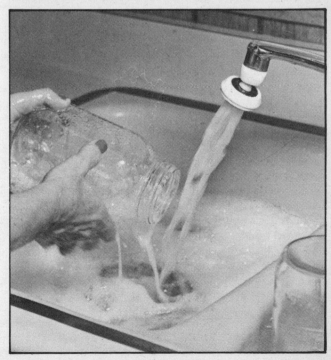

To ensure sterilization, author keeps jars inside boiling kettle until ready for filling. Use appropriate utensils to avoid a painful burn. Same with lids.

EQUIPMENT

You'll need a large kettle or canning vessel for the boiling-water bath. You'll need a rack or some type of metal insert inside the pot to keep glass jars up off the bottom and away from each other, where heat could crack them. The kettle must be deep enough to completely submerge the jars (usually pint [half-liter] or quart [liter], although you can get up to a half-gallon [two-liter] size).

For canning non-acid vegetables and meats, you'll need a pressure canner. Often a pressure cooker with calibrated weight or dial gauge is satisfactory, although special pressure canners are readily available. (If using an older one, ensure that you clean the canner's petcock by running a pipe cleaner through it, or even a string or narrow strip of cloth. This prevents incorrect pressure from building inside the canner, which could burst at worst or at least ruin the food and/or jars. Check your pressure gauge (follow the manufacturer's directions that came with the unit for dial gauges), or see that your weighted gauge is clean. It's common sense that your foods aren't going to process properly if the gauge you're following is awry.

Jars are of two main types: those with sealing compound attached to metal lids, or those with separate rubber rings or gaskets. Self-sealing jars are sealed with metal screw bands, while those with rubber rings use porcelain-lined screw caps or wire bail and glass lid; these last ones aren't so popular today.

Whichever type you have, they should be inspected carefully before canning. Looking first at the metal lids with sealing compound attached: Metal bands free of rust can be reused, but your lids should be used just once — they normally bend when removed, anyway.

Regardless of type, your jars must be perfect to prevent spoilage of food. Discard any jars with cracks, chips or other flaws, and dented or rusty closures should also be trashed. Wash them in hot, soapy water and rinse thoroughly, doing the same with lids and closures. Jars should be placed mouth-down on clean cloth for draining. They don't need sterilization as cooking kills all germs, but I frequently keep my jars in a boiling-water kettle so I have more uncluttered counter space. I also put my self-sealing lids in the water until needed, so they're out of the way. Rubber

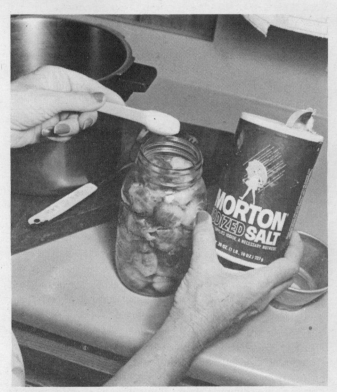

While text tracks all required steps, this photo jumps ahead to filled vegetable jar. Add teaspoon of salt as flavor dictates before canning.

gaskets should be scrubbed and rinsed. They should not be cracked or dry, but don't test them by stretching — even if they don't break, you'll ruin the shape and prevent a vacuum seal when used. USDA recommends these rings not be reused.

CANNINGS FRUITS AND VEGETABLES

When your food has been prepared according to directions provided later in this chapter, you now fill jars using either cold pack, hot pack or raw pack methods (meats). To cold pack fruits and tomatoes, wedge them as tightly as pos-

This boiling-water bath canner is ready to cook six quarts of fruit for times specified in cookbooks. Wipe mouth clean before securing lids or seal may be jeopardized (above). When cooked, place jars out of drafts from windows to avoid cracking jars (below). Author uses kitchen shelf and closes window here.

Two models of pressure canner are shown, both made by National Presto Industries. Steam gauge (below) gives interior pressure, which should be adjusted according to altitude or gauge peculiarities. The eleven-pound model above has adjustable regulator.

sible without crushing to within one-half inch (1.25cm) of the top. Just cover with syrup, juice or boiling water, which allows for expansion during cooking. For the hot pack method, precook food as directed and pack into jars hot. Cover with cooking juice, syrup or boiling water to within one-half inch (1.25cm) of the jar top; for lima beans, peas and corn, pack loosely and allow one inch (2.54cm) of headspace.

If raw packing meat or poultry, don't get the idea that the food is preserved raw. Rather, it is cooked in the jars instead of in another cooking vessel. This is the procedure: Meat is loosely packed into jars to within one inch (2.54cm) of the top. Jars are then placed into a pressure canner and water is poured to within two inches (5cm) of the jar tops. Insert a thermometer into a jar, cover, then cook slowly to 170F (77C) degrees. If you have no thermometer, cover and heat for seventy-five minutes; thus, meat is partially cooked, even though packed raw. Jars then are removed and sealed for further processing, which is the same as for fruits or vegetables.

It's imperative that, after adding syrup, cooking liquid, broth or juice as determined by the food, you wipe the jar lip. A speck of food or seed will break your vacuum seal and lead to spoilage.

If using self-sealing lids: Take one from scalding water with tongs and place it atop the jar, sealing compound against the glass. Screw down the metal band by hand until tight. Air will escape from within the jar during cooking. When removed from your kettle or canner, do not tighten

further; the jar lid will seal on its own during cooling, after which you may remove the metal screw band.

If using rubber gaskets with porcelain-lined lids: Fit a wet rubber gasket atop the neck of the jar before filling. Pack as above, then wipe the jar mouth and rubber ring. Screw cap down firmly, then back off one-quarter turn. After cooking, immediately tighten cap as much as you can to seal.

If you still use jars with glass dome lids, wire bail and rubber sealing rings, you're working harder than you need. Still, you should first install the wet rubber gasket on the jar, fill as above, then wipe the ring. Fit the dome lid on top and push the long wire over the top of the lid until it fits into the groove. When jar is extracted from canner, push the short wire down to complete the seal.

When removed from the canner, put jars out of air drafts that could break the jars. As the self-sealing jars cool, you may hear a metallic ping as jar seals airtight; even if you

Let's walk through canning procedure, starting with smart supermarket shopping (above). Take advantage of reduced prices and save money on the food bill! Below: After rinsing, Bartlett pears are peeled. "Trim away any bad spots or bruises," author says. "Your fruit will look better after it's processed."

Fruits and vegetables which discolor after peeling — apples, pears and potatoes, for example — can be kept looking fresh by soaking peeled chunks or slices in mixture of vinegar, water and salt.

don't hear the distinctive sound, check by tapping the jar top with a spoon or by depressing it with your fingers. If you can push it in or there's no ringing sound when tapped, the jar hasn't yet sealed. When completely cool, check the lids again. If you can depress the lid, then your seal is imperfect and the food will not last; eat at once or discard. Check the lid to see what the problem was. You can now remove the metal band and the jar will remain vacuum-sealed. Note: If removal of the screw band is difficult, cover the top with a hot, damp cloth for a moment or two to loosen it. With porcelain-lined lids or glass domes, the lid stays intact.

These Bartlett pear halves will retain creamy color by soaking in vinegar water. See text for details.

You'll want to rinse the pears thoroughly before canning, to eliminate any vinegar odor or taste.

Get more produce into each jar if you slice pears, rather than leave as halves. Pack slices tightly together for better use of precious jar space (left). Syrup is poured into jars, made by heating mixture of sugar and water according to level of sweetness you desire (below). When the fruit is covered, you'll use a knife to free all trapped air bubbles before wiping rim and sealing.

After cooling for about twelve hours, label the jars with contents, lot number (if more than one batch is canned), and date prepared, then store in your shelter or dark, cool place until needed. Taste and color are optimal up to eighteen months. Canned food stored in a warm place, like near pipes, heating ducts or furnaces, may change color and lose some taste or quality. Dampness leads to corrosion of lids and spoilage.

I've never had any canned food freeze, but I understand

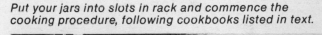

Put your jars into slots in rack and commence the cooking procedure, following cookbooks listed in text.

A sampling of fruits awaiting enjoyment at author's home are shown above left, with veggies at right. Once the jars have cooled and the airtight seal formed, you can remove sealing rings, as for the fruit.

that taste can be influenced — food isn't as good. There is, however, no problem with eating canned food that's been frozen, providing the seal is intact. A problem with freezing is that it could break your jars as the liquid becomes solid. To protect against freezing, wrap jars in newspaper or a blanket if stored in an unheated location.

When you're ready to eat the canned food, examine jars closely. Look for any signs of spoilage — bulging lids, leaks, cracked rubber rings. These mean the seal has been broken and the food must be discarded. See that your animals can't eat it — botulism kills them, too!

If you notice an off odor when opening a jar, do not taste the contents — discard. If liquid spurts from a jar when opened or there are signs of mold, discard contents. But remember that botulism may not be apparent, which is why you must boil in an uncovered pot all canned food, even that to be served cold. Boil for at least ten minutes; spinach and corn require twenty minutes. Begin timing when vegetables begin a rolling boil. If the food foams or smells off, discard.

PRONTO CHICKEN PICKERS

The fastest recorded time for plucking chickens was set in 1976 in Masaryktown, Florida, on October 9, when a team of four women plucked twelve birds totally featherless in 32.9 seconds.

CANNING POULTRY

Poultry has assumed a large role in the American diet due to high beef prices. Chicken leads turkey, goose and ducks in the domestic poultry hit parade and the following, while centered around the clucker, is applicable also to its feathered cousins.

If the bird is alive, select one with a healthy appearance and alert attitude. Bright eyes and wary disposition indicate overall general health. Never cook and eat a bird you suspect is ill.

Soft legs and feet and moist skin are signs of a good bird of any age, and chickens are classified by age and size: *Broilers* are young birds weighing up to 2½ pounds (1.1 kg) *Fryers* weigh between 2½ and 3½ pounds (1 to 1.6 kg); *Roasters* weigh 3½ to 5 pounds (1.6 to 2.3 kg) and are of either sex under 8 months of age; *Capons* are castrated males averaging six to eight pounds (2.7 to 3.6 kg); *Fowl* describes any hen aged over 10 months; and *Stag* or *Cock* describe male birds over 10 months in age.

Younger birds will have a flexible breastbone that yields to pressure, and wingtips that are easy to bend. Poultry with dry skin, broken skin, discoloration (bruising) or hard spots, or with long hairs erupting from the skin may be past their prime. Avoid them.

While ganders and hens (geese) and drakes and hens (ducks) appreciate their glandular differences, they are unisex to us at the retail level. Hen and tom or cock turkeys are so labeled in your retail outlets, with hens commanding higher prices. The breast portion of our seasonal favorite furnishes about forty-six percent edible meat (minus skin and fat), compared to chicken (forty-one percent) and duckling (twenty-two percent).

Chicken has been of increasing importance to American consumer since price of red meat began rising in '70s. It's also easier for you to raise hens than steers!

HOW TO MAKE BROTH

Place bony pieces like chicken backs or necks, or beef tail bones or neck bones into a saucepan and cover with cold water. Simmer until the meat is cooked and tender, then pour off liquid into another container. Skim off fat with a spoon and your broth is ready for addition to canned meats for processing, or for quick consumption. Simple!

PROCESSING POULTRY

The first step after killing the bird is to drain its blood. This valuable food item should be collected and can be used in sauces and gravies, or to make blood sausage or black pudding. Consult a cookbook like the unequaled *Joy Of Cooking* for recipes using the drained blood, which can be refrigerated up to forty-eight hours without concern. Add a little vinegar to prevent clotting. If you have no refrigeration, the blood must be cooked immediately, although many cultures imbibe the fluid without any processing.

After wringing the neck, position the bird head down. Place a catch basin beneath the head, then either remove the head or slit the jugular at the base of the neck on the left side. If beheading a large bird that may be roasted later with neck attached, at this time grab the two tubes leading to the craw and tie them off. They may later retract and force you to remove another portion of the neck to find them again. Tying prevents loss of fluid during cooking, especially an undrawn bird.

Blood drained, now remove the feathers (game birds may need aging before plucking — see Aging Game Birds elsewhere in this chapter). While I've saturated birds in boiling water, this I've learned breaks down the skin's fatty tissue and speeds putrefaction. This could be a problem if you can't freeze the bird or eat it immediately. Dry plucking is preferable and the task is eased by thoroughly chilling the carcass.

Feathers are removed by a short, sharp tug. Save feathers for other uses, and the fine downy layer hugging the carcass is excellent insulation material found in down-filled outerwear today. Remove all pin feathers, using tweezers if you need to. Another method is to trap the quill between your thumb and a knife blade; it pulls out easier.

When heavy plummage is gone, the bird still sports the aforementioned layer of fine, downy hairs and feathers. Remove and save as much as you can, then clean the carcass by singeing over an open flame. Turn the bird continuously near the flame to avoid burning the flesh. Problems with singeing are the smell — awful! — and you can't singe before storage. The bird should be singed just before cooking, as the heat breaks down the fatty tissue in the skin to hasten spoilage.

If you can spare the paraffin, another way of removing the fine body hairs is to mix three-eighths-pound (170g) of paraffin with seven quarts (6.75L) of water. Coat the bird with the mixture and, when the paraffin hardens, pulling it off will remove the coating with the feathers.

If you're going to can the flesh, as it's assumed here that you will be, then the internal organs will be removed after the neck. (If you're going to cook a freshly killed bird, consult a cookbook. You can cook undrawn [entrails intact] or drawn [entrails removed].) First, slide loose skin down the neck toward the base, then cut off or twist off the neck close to the body. Don't sever the tubes leading to the craw — reach inside the cavity at the base of the neck and pull out the usually seed- and sand-filled sac.

Author's method of dressing poultry starts below left as she cleaves off bony bottom of legs to preserve valuable jar space. Next, downward snap of leg breaks thigh socket, seen at limb, is severed from carcass. Third photo from left shows removal of opposite leg and thigh. Far right shows separation of leg, thigh.

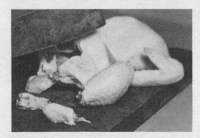 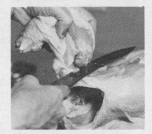 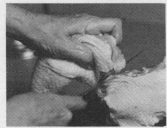 

Almost all store-bought chickens have had oil gland removed from tail, as in below left. Remove entire structure or leave it on, as preferred. Next, ball socket of wing is broken and severed at joint. Breast and back are separated by slicing through center of ribs, as in third and fourth photos from left.

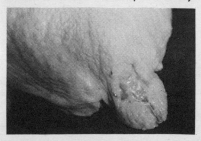   

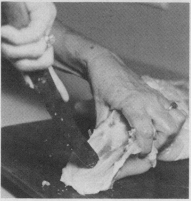
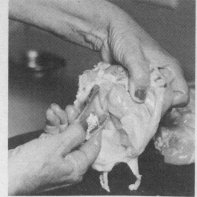

A cleaver separates back into two more-manageable pieces. They're best used for broth.

Author's method of removing breastbone is shown in above photos. Tip of knife cuts through cartilage, and Y-shaped breastbone is pulled free.

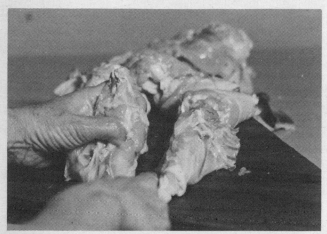

It's now a simple matter to separate fleshy breast into two narrow, thick pieces, which fit into jar much better than if left a single, chunky piece.

Next, slit the abdominal skin just below the breastbone. The cut should be large enough to accommodate your hand. This is easiest done with the bird on its back. Do not plunge your knife blade deep into the abdomen where it will cut the intestines and make a proper mess. Rather, use just the knife tip and cut as shallowly as possible. Your hand enters the cavity and feels for the gizzard, identifiable by its hard, round shape. Pulling it toward the hole will remove most of the innards. Use an index finger to extract the livers from against the base of the spine, and the lung tissue from against the spine near the ribs. Save the giblets — livers, heart and kidneys for separate cooking. Rinse all blood from the heart and strip away the thin, tough, pericardium — a transparent layer of skin surrounding the organ — before cooking. Surplus fat should be trimmed and saved for rendering. You may also wish to remove the bird's oil sac near its tail, or the entire "Pope's nose" as it's irreverently called. Some, however, love this piece — and it may taste lovely if you're really hungry!

When you remove the feet, take the tough leg tendons out with them; they're inedible and get quite large in bigger birds like turkeys. To remove them and the feet in one motion, first cut around the leg about 1½ inches up from the knee joint. Be careful not to sever the tendons we're going to try to extract. Position the leg atop a counter or table, and hang the lower leg over the edge with the knee joint at the edge of the table. Snap the foot down sharply, which will break the leg at the knee joint and should withdraw the unwanted tendons with continuous steady pressure. If not, run your knife blade under them one at a time and pull them out.

There are several methods of preserving poultry, discussed in this chapter: raw pack with bone, raw pack without bone, hot pack with bone, and hot pack without bone. Even using quart jars, you'll be forced to bone turkey and goose before canning.

Boning for canning isn't so complicated or delicate as in preparing haute cuisine, since a whole boned bird won't fit into a quart jar — you've got to cut it up into chunks for loose packing. Therefore, cutting the bird into traditional pieces and then removing meat form those pieces is a simple way to go.

It seems everyone has a preference for cutting up chickens and each feels he gets maximum meat doing it his way. What follows, as illustrated in the text, is how a butcher showed me to cut up chickens:

First, remove the bag of giblets from the abdominal

You must cook the chicken, either in an oven or in jars, until half-done. This is required even with so-called raw pack. Use a good pressure canner here.

cavity — if you bought the bird at the store, as most of you will. Normally the oil gland near the tail will already have been removed; if not, do so now, or chop off the "Pope's nose" entirely with cleaver or knife.

With a sharp knife cut through the flank skin of a leg as the chicken lays on its back. Snapping the leg toward the cutting board and away from the body will snap the hip joint ball socket so the leg and thigh lay flat. Detach from carcass by cutting through the exposed joint. Repeat with other leg and thigh.

Feel with your index finger for the knee joint on the severed leg. You'll feel a hollow spot or valley and cut through this hollow with your knife to separate the dark, juicy drumstick from its thigh.

Next are the wings. Cut into the breast near the base of the limb in a circular stroke. Snap the wing's ball socket,

Using hot-pack method, partially cooked chicken pieces are fitted into sterile jars (above). Try to pack as tightly as possible, whether bone-in or boneless. Below: Broth is poured into jars until meat is covered. Free bubbles, wipe rim, then seal.

ALTITUDE ADJUSTMENTS

If your pressure canner gauge is more than five pounds off, replace it with a new one.

If four pounds or less, the following U.S. Department of Agriculture chart should be used to compensate. Attach some type of permanent tag to the canner telling which reading to use to get the correct pressure. If the food is to be processed at ten pounds of steam pressure:

Gauge Reads High
1 pound high .... process at 11 pounds
2 pounds high .... process at 12 pounds
3 pounds high .... process at 13 pounds
4 pounds high .... process at 14 pounds

Gauge Reads Low
1 pound low .... process at 9 pounds
2 pounds low .... process at 8 pounds
3 pounds low .... process at 7 pounds
4 pounds low .... process at 6 pounds

Keep in mind that pressure charts given are rated at sea level, and you must adjust for altitudes over one thousand feet. Add one-half pound of pressure to your processing requirements for each one thousand feet above sea level. For example, if processing requires ten pounds pressure at sea level, at two thousand feet you should process at eleven pounds on the gauge; four thousand feet calls for a twelve-pound gauge reading during processing; and so forth.

If you're using the boiling-water bath at elevations above sea level, use the guide following to help ensure sufficient processing. If your processing time is twenty minutes or less, add one minute per thousand feet of altitude. Example: If processing time is ten minutes at sea level and you're at five thousand feet, you should add five minutes to the processing time for a total of fifteen minutes. If your processing time is for more than twenty minutes, add two minutes per thousand feet. Example: If processing time is thirty minutes at sea level and you're at five thousand feet, add ten minutes to your processing time for a total of forty minutes.

HOW TO MAKE SYRUP

Classified as Light, Medium or Heavy, syrup is used to pack many fruits. Light Syrup is a solution of one cup (227g) sugar to three cups (720ml) water. Medium Syrup is one cup (227g) sugar to two cups (480ml) water, and Heavy Syrup is one cup (227g) to one cup (240ml) water. Heat until sugar is dissolved.

You can use light corn syrup or mild-flavored honey to replace as much as half the sugar. Do not use brown sugar or molasses, sorghum or other strong-flavored syrups; their flavor overpowers fruit flavor and may darken fruit.

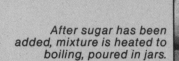

Author prefers light syrup for Bartlett pears, and here pours three cups of water into pot.

Amount of sugar dictates whether it's light, medium, or heavy syrup.

After sugar has been added, mixture is heated to boiling, poured in jars.

then cut through the exposed joint. Some cooks now prefer to sever the wingtip portion of the wing, then open the forearm and arm into another pair of "legs." (The wingtips can be chucked into the soup pot with other bony portions like the back, which take up valuable space in your canning jars.) Slit through the skin at the elbow juncture to keep the limb straightened. If you prefer, separate the forearm from the upper arm for better space utilization inside canning jars.

Separate the breast from the back by either slicing through the ribs and cleaving down through the shoulders, or by slicing straight through the back at the base of the rib cage. Cut the breast into two or four pieces first by slicing through the gristle of the breastbone. This enables you to expose and extricate its keel-shaped breastbone. Now halve the breast with your sharp knife and the pieces will fit much easier into your jars. Cooking will be described presently.

CANNING MEATS

The secret to good-tasting canned meat is to start with good-quality meat or poultry, whether home-grown or purchased. By watching for sales, you can put aside great amounts when prices are low. And if the prices get lower still, then you can eat some of your canned meat and replace with the cheaper food.

If you're slaughtering your own stock (see Chapter 11, which deals with killing, cleaning and slaughtering large animals), chill if possible right after cleaning. Chilling animal flesh at maximum 40F (5C) degrees starts the tenderizing process and makes meat easier to handle. Refrigeration for a few days is okay, but if you won't be process-

ing the meat for longer periods, the USDA recommends freezing; saw the meat when processing time comes, and begin canning when thawed or when ice crystals are pretty well gone.

Once you begin cooking and canning, move rapidly. Handle the meat as little as possible and take pains to keep it clean. For poultry, chill as above and rinse in cold water before draining and processing.

The methods for preserving in the accompanying text are suitable for beef, veal, mutton, lamb, pork, rabbit, both large and small game, game birds, chicken, duck, goose, guinea, squab and turkey.

As stated earlier, there are two methods of packing meat: hot pack or raw pack. Hot pack requires precooking of the meat, which then is packed loosely into jars and covered with boiling broth or boiling water. The reason for loose packing is because the jars will lose liquid during processing if packed too tightly. The food still should be at least 170F (77C) degrees at time of packing, so you must be quick.

Why 170F (77C) degrees? Because meat heated to this temperature contains no air — heating exhausts or drives out air so that a vacuum will be formed in the jars after processing and cooling. This also prevents changes in the flavor of canned meat.

Trim away as much fat from the meat before canning as you can without slashing into the lean. Be sure to carefully wipe jar lips free of grease before putting on your lids or you may not get airtight seals.

Before securing your lid and processing, most people add one tablespoon of salt per quart jar; one teaspoon for a pint jar. This is simply for flavoring, not for preserving meat.

How much meat goes into a jar? The three-pound (1.5kg) chicken I'm photographed cutting up and processing fit into two one-pint jars, with a little left over. You can figure on getting 3½ to 4¼ pounds (1.5 to 2kg) of bone-in chicken to the quart. Removing bone before packing increases yield to 5½ to 6¼ pounds (2.5 to 3kg) of chicken to the quart. Using fresh, untrimmed beef with bone, figure you can get 3 to 3½ pounds (1.25 to 1.5kg) of meat from the round, or 5 to 5½ pounds (2.5 to 2.75kg) of beef rump. You'll get 5 to 5½ pounds (2.5 to 2.75kg) of fresh, untrimmed pork loin with bone to the quart.

USING THE PRESSURE CANNER

Follow the manufacturer's directions, which should go something like this: First, prepare your meat according to directions given earlier in this chapter. Put two or three inches (5 to 7.5cm) of water into the canner, which should be enough that the canner doesn't run dry during processing.

Put your jars on a rack, separated from each other, so steam circulates freely. I've never seen or used a two-layer pressure canner, but the USDA says you should stagger the top layer if using this type of equipment, along with putting a rack between layers.

Now, affix the cover tightly; these usually lock by twisting the two handles toward each other. Heat to boiling and check that steam is escaping freely from the vent or petcock. If there's any obstruction, abnormal pressure could build inside the canner, as mentioned earlier. If steam is escaping from somewhere other than the petcock, your cooker isn't closed properly; remove from heat, allow pres-

Pint jars are frequently used for canning meats and poultry, since you can get more capacity into your pressure canner or cooker. Jars must not touch.

Some of liquid may boil out of jars during cooking process (right jar above), but this doesn't affect taste or safety. It may discolor somewhat, though.

sure to subside, then open and reclose the container. If you've noted a problem with the petcock, immediately remove from heat, allow pressure to abate, then open and clean petcock with pipe cleaner, cloth or string.

Most meat and non-acid foods are processed at ten pounds of pressure (see chart for altitude adjustments). Begin timing when the cooker reaches this level, the equivalent of 240F (116C) degrees. Follow the time charts and watch that the pressure remains constant throughout; fluctuating pressure will force liquid from jars. When time is up, immediately remove cooker from heat source and allow pressure to abate to zero before opening the canner's lid. Don't try to speed cooling time by running cold water over the cooker — you could rupture the canner and perhaps be scalded by escaping steam. Tip the canner away from you so that escaping steam (when you open the top) won't burn your arms.

SUGGESTED READING

1. *Joy Of Cooking,* by Irma S. Rombauer and Marion Rombauer Becker; published by The Bobbs-Merrill Company, Inc., 4300 West 62nd Street, Indianapolis, IN 46268.

2. *Better Homes and Gardens Cookbook,* Meredith Corporation, 1716 Locust Street, Des Moines, IA 50336.

3. *Home Canning of Fruits and Vegetables,* by Science and Education Administration for the United States Department of Agriculture (Home and Garden Bulletin #8); published by Superintendent of Documents, U.S. Government Printing Office, Washington, D.C. 20402. Price: $2.50.

4. *Home Canning of Meat and Poultry,* by Consumer Nutrition Center/Human Nutrition Information Service for the United States Department of Agriculture (Home and Garden Bulletin #106); published by Superintendent of Documents, U.S. Government Printing Office, Washington, D.C. 20402. Price: $2.25.

SMOKING YOUR OWN

Learn To Preserve All Manner Of Meats, Fish & Fowl In Gourmet Fashion

By Louis Bignami

Fred Bear and Bob Evrett smile in anticipation of smoked venison this plump forkie can become.

IN A survival scenario, a hunter who's successful must look to preserve his bag without the aid of refrigeration, unless there's ice and snow about. As discussed, canning is one way, but another to consider is smoking. In this way, I make my deer, pig, turkey or other gourmet delights last over a year.

Even without a survival need, you can use a smoker to gourmetize inexpensive store-bought meats like 79¢-a-pound turkey into gourmet delights such as smoked turkey breast that tops $3 a pound in most delicatessans.

Smoking is one of the oldest and easiest means of preparing and preserving food, so it seems odd that you pay such a premium for smoked foods from the deli. And it's so easy! All you need to do it yourself are basic skills, something smokable and minimal equipment. If you consider the flexibility of modern moist cookers and add a sausage option to tenderize the toughest trophy buck or long-bearded gobbler, you'll find smoking a superb way to beat today's tight food budgets, while honing a survival skill.

Basic to the process is a smoker, although you can use an open campfire. All sorts of commercial and homemade smokers work, some better than others, so it's useful to realize the advantages and drawbacks of each.

Commercial smokers come in three basic types: small,

The Smoke'N Pit line from Brinkmann has barbecue applications besides use as a smoker. Use charcoal or electric converter to use moist smoking method.

rectangular metal models such as Mirro Smoker or Luhr Jensen Little Chiefs; larger cylindrical electric or charcoal sportsman smokers such as those from Brinkmann; and the nifty Coleman smoker-grills with electric, propane or charcoal heat source options.

Of course, the smaller models are the most compact. Luhr Jensen even makes a model that folds flat for storage.

The Mirro Smokehouse has a forty-pound capacity, considerably larger than the Luhr Jensen. Using the Little Chief models to smoke fifty pounds of jerky or sausage could require 'round-the-clock operation. Water smokers by Brinkmann are large capacity and the moist-cooking method tenderizes even lean venison or autumn-bagged gobbler.

Electric smokers are reliable and convenient, but not suitable for field use. Propane smokers cost less to run and seem easiest to use at home or in the field. Charcoal smokers take more time to start. Except for the Coleman and Brinkmann charcoal models, most lack means of controlling smoking temperatures. We'll see later why this is important.

Homemade smokers are worth considering (see directions for making a garbage can model). Old ice boxes or refrigerators work well, too. The advantages of this smoker are large capacity and low cost.

Once you have either purchased or made your smoker, gather wood chips. Commercial chips work well, but chips from your own nut or fruit trees can add a special flavor. We use spring fruit tree prunings run through a clean mulching machine. To be avoided are pine chips or sawdust which make everything taste like moldy violin strings and chips or scraps of plywood which have foul-tasting glues. Try a couple of types of wood chips so you can compare results.

You will find that presoaking chips overnight in water saves bother during cooking because you get more smoke and need not reload your chip container as often. Some smokers add more flavor to the smoke by soaking chips in wine or beer. This makes sense with homemade, Luhr Jensen, Mirro or other smokers that don't have a waterbath. With waterbath, moist-cooking smokers like the Brinkmann or Coleman, flavoring additives seem more effective. How-

ever, you should start with plain chips and a plain brine to establish a taste base against which you can compare additions to brines and waterbaths.

Your next step is preparing fowl, meat or fish for smoking by cutting pieces of uniform thickness to assure even smoking. Realize that size doesn't affect smokiness so long as the thickness is consistent. Fish is usually best if filleted, and most meats should be chunked into inch-thick sections. If you are fortunate and bag a boar, smoke your bacon in slabs, rather than slices which, like most ultra-thin cuts, tend to dry out too much. However, if you like the chewy taste of smoked jerky, thin slices one-quarter-by-one-inch by any convenient length work well.

This isn't to say that you can't smoke whole turkeys, hams or venison haunches. Of course you can. But I have found that separating turkey breasts, thighs and drumsticks produces a more even result, as thinner pieces can be removed early. In smaller pieces your smokables go farther as well. Inch-thick pieces smoke in three or four hours with one loading of chips, while a whole ham or turkey might take eight to ten hours or longer.

Consider sausage making if you trim your own meat. By adding cheap pork fat to game, called larding, you stretch your game and use up the odds and ends that might otherwise be tossed out. This also reduces the gamey taste some find objectionable and is a good way to save tough meat.

Luhr Jensen sells sausage-making kits or you can use Julia Child's *Mastering The Art of French Cooking, Vol. 2,* which has a good sausage-making section. Rytek Kutas' *Great Sausage Recipes and Meat Curing* has sold over sixty thousand copies and is the bible according to many food preservationists. Of course, sausages can be smoked after they are made.

Once your smokables are cut to suit, brine them in a solution made with two cups of coarse, un-iodized salt and a

Brinkmann's Smoke 'N Grill smokes, barbecues, steams or roasts, depending on your wish. Author advises fruit tree wood be used in your smoker.

Sportsman's Smoker is Brinkmann's line designed for electric or charcoal smoking. Self-basting is a feature that eliminates charred or overcooked meat.

Many racks inside Mirro Smokehouse make for increased capacity. Firm's electric heat source could be a problem if power was interrupted, but it'll work now.

cup of brown sugar per gallon (4.55 liters) of liquid to cover. You'll need a stainless steel or glass bowl: brine discolors aluminum containers. Use enough room-temperature liquid to cover and turn inch-thick pieces every hour for four hours. Or, if you'd rather, brine overnight in the ice box.

Additives in the brine enrich the taste. We use tarragon with salmon, black pepper with roasts and cardamom with venison, but I recommend doing a batch plain to start. If

Electric version of Sportsman Smoker is useful today, but is dependent upon electricity that in crisis might not be available. Prepare today.

you like, split the brine into two batches. You can compare to fine-tune your taste results.

Draining and drying is a vital step. Turn out the brined meat, rinse it quickly with cold water, pat dry with a towel and rack dry. We load directly onto our smoker racks when possible. This increases sticking, but cuts handling time. A shot of Pam cooking spray or oil helps avoid the former problem.

Space your cut-up smokables on the racks so they are not touching. Stacked or touching pieces stick to each other and smoke unevenly. If you leave on the skin, start with the skin-side down for a moister, more succulent result.

Drying usually takes one to four hours, depending on humidity. You'll know when drying is done when a shiny, dry film, or pelicle, forms.

DRYING MEAT

For those who, for whatever reason, can't make a long fire, you may air-dry one-inch strips of freshly killed meat. Build a small fire with dry wood. In the thin blue smoke produced, suspend your meat. Thread it onto a stick, string or wire and ensure the meat isn't touching. Leave it in the smoke until the meat surface is dry, then remove and hang for at least one day. The smoke treatment dries the surface to prevent blowflies from laying eggs that soon turn into maggots — females won't lay eggs on dry flesh. In dry, cool weather, your well-ventilated strips of meat are dry in a day; increase or decrease drying time for humidity and temperature differences. When dry, don't wrap in plastic or cellophane. The meat may sweat and begin to decay.

If you have access to electricity, you can use any of the dehydrators offered in the marketplace. These are fast and easy to use, reducing size of your rations once water is removed.

Start the smoker a half-hour before you're ready to add the contents so it's smoking well. Charcoal smokers may need more lead time. In any case, don't use more — or fewer — chips than the manufacturer suggests; this avoids too much or too little smoke.

A product for every budget and desire is hallmark of Coleman patio products. Optional smoking kit converts "Sunday cookers" into survivor tools.

Smoking overcomes the gamey flavor many people find distasteful, and this stringy big bear will benefit from moist cooking methods discussed in the text.

I found the Luhr Jensen and Mirro Smokehouse removable rack holders convenient because they let you load the racks directly from the brine and dry them. Then it is easy to carry the whole works to the smoker, open the top and set the rack-holding frame inside the smoker without the delay required to load one rack at a time. The Coleman Smoker-Grill and the Brinkmann models with raised handles on the racks are also easy to load.

Once everything is going, racks can be left in place for two to three hours, or until the amount of smoke produced drops and you need to add chips. Rotate top and bottom racks for more even smoking when you do this.

Smoking time depends on your smoker type, the temperature and your personal taste. Tasting is, by the way, the best means of assuring desired results (My wife claims tasting is a good way to pig out, too!) So you can expect to lose most of your first batch's top rack to samplers.

Inch-thick fish fillets usually take four to six hours; game takes longer. Six to ten hours is typical for smaller fowl and, if you either like a drier, smokier result or want to smoke whole turkeys or other large pieces, increase the time to twelve to fifteen hours.

Smoking temperature is important and wood or charcoal waterbath moist smokers like the Brinkmann are somewhat self-regulating. The Coleman is also able to be regulated with a closure over the charcoal. Temperature control is more convenient with electric or propane models. If your commercial smoker lacks a thermometer, see "Building a Garbage Can Smoker" later in this chapter for a thermometer modification you can add yourself.

I find fish smokes best at 115F (46C) degrees for two hours, then raise the temperature to 160 or 170F (71 to 77C) degrees until it's finished. Meat temperatures should run a bit higher to start — 130 to 140F (55 to 57C) degrees — in the first stage.

All smokers come with directions keyed to their particular operation. Heed those directions.

Once food is smoked, it should be completely cooled on racks. Draconian penalties may be needed here if your buddies drop by to help out. I recently ended up with a sandwich bag of smoked venison left from ten pounds of jerky, not to mention the beer I supplied to wash things down!

When in the field and often smoking game alfresco, I use plastic bags transported in coolers before freezing at home. In the refrigerator most smoked meats and fish will store for several weeks. Check cookbooks supplied with commercial smokers for exact keeping dates, or refer to *The Art of Smokecooking* by Jack Sleight and Ray Hull for this and other information.

Of course, you can smoke a lot more than meat. Gamefish can also be smoked. Those a bit oily are especially good smoked as the process removes excess oil. Salmon, steelhead, striped and black bass, crappie, panfish, bluefish and albacore smoke beautifully. Brining and smoking also improve bland fish like cod. Even carp do well. These abundant trash fish need to be killed, gutted, skinned and iced as soon as possible. Like shad they have a lot of bones, but these are easy to remove after smoking fish steaks cut along the ribs.

All upland birds, ducks, deer, elk, and other species smoke well. The taste of extremely dry birds, like tough old pheasants, is improved if one-quarter cup of oil is added to each quart of brine. Dry game also can be converted to sausage if it is mixed with pork fat and cased. Or you can find a larding needle that lets you insert thin strips of fat (see any gourmet cookbook for directions) smoked in fillets. Water bath cookers that steam cook meat are effective here.

Bear and wild pig should be commercially frozen — home freezers do not always get cold enough — after smoking and must be well cooked because of trichinosis problems.

Those who shore-harvest clams, oysters, shrimp or crayfish will find smoking produces a fine result. Tongue also is improved in taste and texture by smoking, and smoked liver pate is delicious. Monterey jack and cheddar cheeses

Cutaway drawing of Smoker-Grill from Coleman (opposite page) reveals the twin grids capable of holding fifty pounds of meat. Bake, barbecue, steam, roast or smoke following maker's directions. Above is shown entire Coleman line: Smoker-Grill, Tabletop Grill, and kettle-type grill. All can use charcoal or propane fuel.

smoke especially well, and sausage lets you get mileage from meat scraps. Almonds, especially if brushed with vegetable oil and dusted with garlic just before smoking, are extremely good.

Smoking concentrates flavor and nutrients per ounce so smoked foods go much farther than fresh. Heavily smoked meat like jerky is excellent trail food and when sauced is delicious over rice or noodles. Cold smoked fowl is superb when sliced on hot summer days, and most smoked fish is delightful when thinly sliced and served with cream cheese on bagels. Various other smoked items are delicious finger food, and the biggest problem with smoking your own will doubtless be midnight snackers who deplete stocks.

BUILDING A GARBAGE CAN SMOKER*

Materials
1 large new galvanized garbage can with lid
4 pieces of reinforcing rod longer than the can's diameter
1 steel or cast iron pot or frying pan (to hold chips)
1 electric hot plate or hibachi
1 dial-type roast thermometer
2 oven racks
1 wire coat hanger
Small spool with hole larger than thermometer stem diameter (this insulates stem from can to offer a reliable temperature reading)

Tools
Tin snips or saber saw with metal-cutting blade
Electric drill and bit larger than reinforcing rod diameter
Pliers with wire cutters

Construction
1. Cut oven racks to fit inside can.
2. Cut a rectangular door at the bottom of the can just large enough so the pan can be removed for easy chip additions during cooking at the bottom of the can. Drill first to start sawing or snipping.
3. Drill two holes in door and two in can and add wire hanger hinges. You can use pop rivets and hinges instead for a professional result.
4. Drill four holes for each rod rack support one-third and two-thirds up side of can.
5. Drill two or three holes in can lid for ventilation and, if using a hot plate, drill a small hole near the door for the cord. (Hot plate sits on bottom of can, with chip pan on burner.)
6. Insert spool in top hole and add thermometer.

*Given adjustments in rack size, just about any other smoke-tight container also will work.

GROWING YOUR OWN
NOW'S THE TIME TO LEARN

With A Backyard Garden You Can Learn Basics Of Food Production Before You Need Them — And Save Money, Too!

By Grace Calcagno

Author's backyard garden produced corn, onions, tomatoes, cucumbers, zucchini, peppers, potatoes, and more

HAVING LIVED in the country, I can say from experience that country folk know how to raise and preserve produce from a vegetable garden. Now, as a city dweller, I want to prove that everyone today can have a vegetable garden, regardless of where you live or how much space you have. Whether it's indoor hydroponic growing, herbs in a flower pot or such things as patio tomatoes, there's nothing that equals the flavor and satisfaction derived from "growing your own." Time was when I would shudder at dirt under a manicured nail, but today finding earthworms in my soil is like finding a cache of diamonds!

Your public library has a wealth of information on all types of gardening, and now is the time to acquire the skills. Not only can raising vegetables or fruits provide economic relief, mastering the techniques could keep you alive if we ever face long-term interruption of normal food chains.

I am the average backyard type of gardener and what

Strawberries are easily cultivated in window boxes or other odd-shaped containers, but watch for birds.

A wire cage acts to support tomato plants during growth and especially when heavy with large fruit.

Tomatoes are among the easier vegetables to grow, even if the patio variety. Save money and learn!

Cluster of dusky Concord grapes are bonus to having vine that gives shade, privacy from outside eyes.

Fruit leather, in this case apricot, is produced by rendering fruit in blender and pouring into a pan covered with cheesecloth that then air dries.

Finished product can be rolled in cellophane, as you find in the stores, but is thicker and usually tastes fruitier, because only best-quality fruit is used.

I've gleaned by trial and error to be most important are: (1) a knowledge of how plants grow; (2) an understanding of your type of soil; and (3) a working knowledge of watering and fertilizing.

Once you know what type of soil you have, you can enhance it with proper mulches and nutrients. I got good results in my garden by adding twenty-five percent rotted sawdust (simply wet a pile of sawdust and leave it for several weeks) to seventy-five percent garden soil, as well as working in about a four-inch-deep layer of potting soil. (My garden bed measures four feet wide by forty-five feet long, which required ten twenty-pound sacks of potting soil. I watched for sales and picked up my stock at a special price of eighty-eight cents per bag.)

I am a firm believer in returning nutrients to the soil every time I take something out of the garden. Consequent-ly, I bury all of my edible kitchen garbage, except meats or fat which the dogs or cats would unearth, directly into the soil. At certain times of the year when my garden bed is full of growing plants, I'll use my electric blender to grind up all peelings, rinds, coffee grounds and the like with a little water and pour this nutrient-rich liquid into the soil. Don't be surprised to see new tomato plants and peppers coming up from the planted refuse. In fact, I read of a Florida man who used fertilizer from a local human waste disposal plant for his lawn. He was chagrined to find ten thousand tomato plants emerging from his grass!

Some seedlings may have to be transplanted, as all vegetables do not make good neighbors. Carrots, peas and beans get along well, but of these only carrots should be planted near onions and garlic. Plant a few marigolds in the vegetable garden, too — both flower and root contain

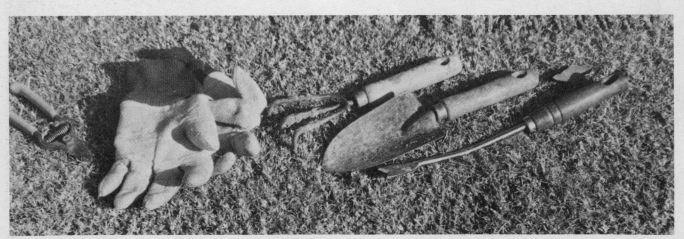

The backyard gardener does need some tools, but not many, especially if the plot is a tiny one.

If you have a larger area in which to grow, you'll need commensurate increase in your hardware. All shown above find application in garden situations.

pyrethrins that repel insects both above ground and in the soil. Learn more about this and compatibility of vegetables from charts found free at most nurseries or libraries.

In my four-foot by forty-five-foot summer garden, I last year grew radishes, carrots, bell peppers, jalapeno peppers, tomatoes, corn, peas, onions, garlic, parsley, and, just for fun, six large sunflowers next to the fence. Strawberries planted in a window box yielded sufficient for jam as well as the fresh we consumed daily, not counting what the birds beat me to. A six-foot by four-foot garden of corn gave us three ears per stalk — excellent yield. From my backyard garden I produced — not counting what my family consumed fresh or what I gave away to friends — four quarts of frozen carrots, four quarts of pickled pep-

Tomato plant nearly six feet tall is loaded with produce. Make sauces, catsup, canned tomatoes, etc.

Author's belief is that something should be put into soil each time something else is taken from it. In this photo, she's covering some wet garbage.

Wet garbage like potato peelings, carrot tops, pear skins, etc., are buried in garden to enrich soil. You'll probably find plants growing from your scrap!

Variety of peppers can be grown with little trouble. These do wonders to spice up drab, ordinary meals.

A secret to growing Italian squash is to keep it producing squash, and not growing big leaves!

That's one huge sunflower! Seeds were harvested, salted, then dried to be consumed as snack foods.

Zucchini harvested before getting too large helps the paint continues producing, not just growing.

Louis Calcagno, author's husband, discourages bird with nylon netting over figs. They're sweet dessert.

Strawberries can be picked at height of sweetness — if you can keep birds away! Below: Tiny tomatoes have emerged from flowers and now will grow rapidly. If you learn techniques now, you'll be ready when!

A relatively young bell pepper can be kept insect-free by planting marigolds throughout the garden, borders.

pers, twelve quarts of canned tomatoes, twenty-four ears of frozen corn, and a good supply of dried onions and garlic. The sunflower seeds were salted and dried for snacking.

One word on planting when temperatures outdoors are warm enough: Sow seed and transplant only with a waxing, never a waning, moon. I have found this old wives' tale to be true by planting two sets of vegetables at the opposite times. The difference in growth was phenomenal. Scientists now agree that the lunar rhythms on the earth's magnetic field affect growth.

By following simple basic instructions, you too can have fresh produce with extra to preserve so you can enjoy your vegetables when they are out of season and priced high at the market. A well-stocked larder is not only a rewarding accomplishment — it might mean survival!

Rene Lagasse has unpacked Katadyn Pocket Filter, shipped in heavy bubble packaging to prevent any breakage. Directions accompany each Swiss unit.

producing germs transmitted in water generally come from animal matter more than vegetable matter.

Therefore, it's safest to purify water being stored if uncertain of the safety of the source. There are several ways of purifying water, and your shelter should be adequately stocked with required chemicals or equipment. One way to purify water — providing you have access to a heat source, is to boil it. A rolling boil (212F or 100C degrees) for three minutes (experts argue between one to twenty minutes) will sterilize most water, although boiling leaves it tasting flat. Restore "life" by pouring it back and forth between drinking cups just before imbibing. Of course, make sure that your cups are clean.

An old method of water purification is use of Halazone tablets. These are easy to carry and take up little space in your storage facility. Follow the maker's directions, since there are several varieties available. Shelf life averages two to five years.

Water can be purified using common household bleach containing hypochlorite in 5.25 percent solution. If your water is clear, use eight drops per gallon (4.5 L); if water is cloudy, use sixteen drops per gallon. Stir or shake thoroughly, then let stand for half an hour before tasting. Yuck! It tastes like chlorine! But that's the way it's supposed to taste and if you can't smell and taste the chlorine, add another eight or sixteen drops of bleach per gallon (4.5 L). Wait another fifteen minutes and taste another sip. If you still can't smell and taste the chlorine, figure that the bleach is out-of-date and unable to purify your water. Obviously, don't drink the treated solution.

Any properly stocked first-aid kit will contain tincture of iodine in two-percent solution. This can be used at twelve drops per gallon (4.5 L) of clear water, or twenty-four drops per gallon for cloudy water. Stir well to mix the iodine thoroughly. The water may taste a little odd, but it's usually safe to imbibe. Check the date on your iodine bottle. This method is not suitable for individuals with thyroid disturbances.

But preferable by far is mechanical purification, and chemicals are advised only when you have no filter available.

I N THE ideal, you should know that the source of your water is pure and that your storage vessels are sterile. This is easier satisfied before a disaster or catastrophe, since safe water is generally available from the existing water source and you can sterilize your storage jars or jugs before filling. Following a nuclear accident or incident, for example, you wouldn't know by sight whether or not the water has been contaminated by radioactive fallout. Many miles from a flood site, you won't know whether or not raw sewage has contaminated your drinking water.

Color of water isn't indicative of purity. A bayou may be purer than a sapphire-colored mountain lake, since disease-

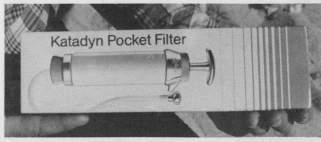

Katadyn Pocket Filter

Choice of relief agencies, governments, airlines, even armies is this Katadyn, distributed in the U.S. by Provisions Unlimited, of Oakland, Maine.

The Swiss-made Katadyn Pocket Filter is a high-volume purifier using no chemicals that has been tested in outdoor conditions all over the world. It's perfect for survivalists, too. The Katadyn Pocket Filter is used by armies of eight nations (Colombia, India, Portugal, Rhodesia, South Africa, Sweden, Switzerland and West Germany); three international organizations (Food and Agriculture Organization [FAO] of the United Nations, United Nations Children's Emergency Fund [UNICEF], and the World Meteorological Organization); six national relief associations, including the Dutch and Swiss Red Cross; and it's even found in use at Harvard University in Cambridge, Massachusetts.

The portable twenty-three-ounce filter has been used for nearly every Himalayan expedition, but also in desert conditions such as Henry Maurice Berney's trans-Australia expedition. Expeditions into southern Iraq and Africa have also taken along the pocket purifier, and it's in daily use by railroad firms in Nigeria, Mexico, Sweden, Colombia, Germany, Italy and East Africa. No less than sixteen oil companies use the filter in the fields of Basrah, Netherlands, East Africa, Colombia, Iran, Mexico, Turkey and Bolivia. Even the World Health Organization and Pan American Health Organization, respectively, have bought the filter. State or national health departments in Australia, Sweden, the Philippines, Finland, Hong Kong, Colombia, Northern Ireland, Switzerland, Venezuela, Peru, El Salvador, Spain, Rhodesia, Guatemala, Burma, the Bahamas, Egypt, the Sudan and Iowa and Wisconisn in the U.S. use it. Thirteen universities, five commercial laboratories and even the International Red Cross use the filter.

So what is it, anyway? As its name suggests, it's a filter that uses the principle of absolute microfiltration to strain all known bacteriological contaminants from wild or contaminated water. "The filter element is a microporous ceramic material with a pore diameter of less than 0.2 micron," explains Peter Gut, president of the family-owned Swiss firm that has made water disinfection filters for a half-century. "The filter element acts as a microfine sieve on water forced through it, straining out bacteriological contaminants. Since all known single-cell bacteria dangerous to health are considerably larger than 0.2 micron, and since the chemically very resistant cysts of *Giardia lamblia* and the amoebic and *Shigella* dysenteries are far larger still, ALL such pathogens are physically prevented from passing through the Katadyn Pocket Filter."

There are no chemicals involved with the Katadyn purification system. Because they are based on the simple mechanical principle of microfiltration, the filter works equally well on all types of raw water, regardless of its temperature and level or type of contaminants.

"Chemical methods of water disinfection — including both chemicals added to water and all water filters based on chemical disinfection principles involving chlorine or iodine compounds — can be shown to work very well under carefully controlled laboratory conditions, but will vary greatly in their effectiveness under practical field conditions," Gut explains. "Factors bearing importantly on the effectiveness of chemical sterilization schemes include the type and concentration of the pathogen, turbidity of the water including the nature and quantity of the suspended

The Katadyn filter will work in both running streams or standing water. Rene deposits induction tube with coarse strainer on end into California desert creek.

Prevalence of Giardia lamblia *is much more widespread than previously assumed. Clear running streams far from civilization aren't free of sickening spores.*

Rene Lagasse demonstrates the push-pull action of Katadyn that produces a stream of safe water.

materials, the water's temperature and pH (acidity), whether and how much organic matter may be in the water (such as humic acid from decaying vegetation), and the contact time between the chemical sterilant and the pathogens.

"Also to be considered is whether or not and how vigorously and how long the chemical/water mixture is agitated, and what plastics may be present that might react with and consume the chemicals," Gut says, building his product's case for the survivalist. "You also must think of the storage history of the chemical sterilant. Is it old, been stored too long at too high a temperature and hence become stale or ineffective?"

When sterilizing water, he suggests, a 99 or even a 99.999 percent effectiveness isn't good enough. "In the case of *Giardia lamblia,* as few as half a dozen ingested cysts can infect you," he explains. "Badly contaminated water may contain a million cysts per liter of raw water."

These are problems exclusive to Asia or disease-plagued Africa, right? Wrong! Even in the remotest areas of North America, contamination of wild water is a problem. The most serious health risk from water in areas remote to civilization, according to the Center for Disease Control in Atlanta, is the same *G. lamblia.* It's only recently been

recognized as a major health hazard that's spread through rivers, streams, lakes, and ponds by feces of beaver, muskrats, dogs, cats, coyotes, humans, and livestock.

G. lamblia has recently been recognized as the most common intestinal parasite in the U.S. by the Center for Disease Control. An estimated three to seven percent of all Americans are plagued by chronic diarrhea, cramping and gas. Colorado has the highest incidence of Giardiasis, with seven to ten percent of the populace passing *G. lamblia* cysts in their stool, followed by Utah, Oregon, Washington, New Hampshire and New York. Outbreaks tied to *G. lamblia* from sewage-contaminated drinking water have occurred in Aspen, Colorado: eleven percent of the skiers in '65-66 were infected — Rome, New York: ten percent of the town's population contracted giardiasis — and other outbreaks have been reported in New Hampshire and Kentucky.

"The cyst form in which it moves from one host to another is very resistant to chemical disinfection," explains Peter Gut, whose sixty-man factory has produced 75,000 Katadyn Pocket Filters since the product debuted twenty-five years ago. "Scientific literature shows no consensus on how to effectively kill *Giardia* in the field with chemical

With a little practice, one can produce a substantial volume of water per minute, stored in canteen here.

methods. According to some experiments, even boiling the water for several minutes cannot be relied on."

Infection with *Giardia lamblia* leads to many months of stomach trouble including chronic diarrhea, abdominal pains and severe weight loss. The cysts have an incubation period of several weeks, which makes it difficult to pinpoint the site of infection. Treatment after a difficult diagnosis is with the drugs Quinacrine hydrochloride, Metronidaze and Furazolidone, which have serious side-effects for many people.

"But the *Giardia* cysts are very large by microbiological standards," continues Peter Gut, who's firm produced its one-millionth filter in 1970. "The cysts are over four microns in their smallest dimension, which is twenty times larger than the pore size of the Katadyn filters, and hence are totally removed."

Muddy or algae-populated water present no problem for the Pocket Filter, or other industrial-size filters made by Katadyn Products Limited and distributed in the U.S. by Provisions Unlimited in Oakland, Maine. "Guides on the Colorado and Green rivers use Katadyn filters on water so muddy you can't see your fingertips if you dip your hand in the water," notes Peter Gut. "Because of the large surface area and depth filter action of the microporous ceramic element, you can work with raw water laden with mud and algae. Plugging is seldom a problem, and if you do manage to plug it up, full flow can normally be restored merely by wiping off the filter element. Under very difficult conditions, such as water loaded with microfine clays, the top surface of the filter element can be scraped away using a stiff brush included with each filter to expose a fresh. unobstructed surface. This can be repeated hundreds of times if necessary "

Because there are no chemicals to replace, there's almost no maintenance. "You must be careful when cleaning the exposed ceramic filter element," cautions Peter Gut.

"Were you to drop the exposed element on a sharp rock when you had it apart for cleaning, you could break the ceramic. With reasonable care, this should never happen." Still, it's a good idea to pack away several spare filters in your retreat and slip a spare into your pack when you go afield.

Won't mud or contaminants harm the filter element if the unit is put away uncleaned? "The ceramic filter element is factory-impregnated with silver to prevent algae and bacteria from colonizing the surface of the filter and plugging it up," answers Gut, whose product is used by international airline crews so they can keep flying high, wherever they take a drink. "This might otherwise happen if you put a wet and dirty filter away for several weeks after using it. Silver is in no way involved in the Katadyn Pocket Filter's sterilization process."

The process, as defined by the Swiss manufacturer, is mechanical, pure and simple. "Basically, the Pocket Filter contains three concentric chambers," explains Gut. "The outermost chamber is the 'raw water' cavity and the surface of the ceramic filter you see when you remove the outer case is the 'dirty' side of the filter element. In the center of the filter is a pump cylinder with a reciprocating piston connected to the pump handle. The pump sucks raw water into the cylinder through a check valve on the upstroke, and then on the downstroke routes the raw water through a second check valve to the outermost chamber. Here the raw water is forced into the outer surface of the ceramic filter, through the body thickness of the ceramic filter, and into a hidden inner 'clean water' chamber. The

Without water, man can't last long in a desert environment. Fine sand driven by hot winds here covered a road. Dry heat saps your body moisture.

'clean water' chamber is a little difficult to visualize as it's hermetically sealed and connected to the outside world only through the output spout. The 'clean water' chamber is concentric with and is between the outermost 'dirty water' chamber and the pump cylinder."

The pump easily develops pressures of fifty pounds per square inch (psi) that are needed to achieve good flow rates through the very fine pores of the ceramic filter element.

SURVIVABILITY WITH RATIONED WATER
NO WALKING AT ALL

Maximum Daily Temperature (°F) In Shade	Available Water Per Man, U.S. Quarts					
	0	1	2	4	10	20
	Days of Expected Survival					
120	2	2	2	2½	3	4½
110	3	3	3½	4	5	7
100	5	5½	6	7	9½	13½
90	7	8	9	10½	15	23
80	9	10	11	13	19	29
70	10	11	12	14	20½	32
60	10	11	12	14	21	32
50	10	11	12	14½	21	32

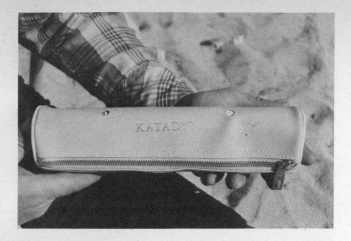

Portability of Katadyn Pocket Filter is plus for sportsmen/survivalists who prefer safe drinking water to risk of infection with G. lamblia.

The intake hose has a strainer on the end to keep coarse particles out of the filter, which might interfere with the seating of the ball check valve.

Instructions packed with Pocket Filters distributed in the U.S. warn against use with chlorinated water. This, explains Peter Gut, is to satisfy an arbitrary requirement of the Environmental Protection Agency. "User instructions included with every Pocket Filter sold in every other country of the free world include no limitation on using chlori-nated raw water input," Gut says. "Tests by more than fifty government agencies and laboratories in other countries have approved Katadyn Pocket Filters without any chlorinated water limitations. The reason the prohibition is included in the U.S. user instructions is due to another technical requirement of the EPA based on their arbitrary standard limiting silver content of drinking water to fifty parts per billion.

"As I've said, Katadyn filter elements are impregnated with silver to keep algae and bacteria from colonizing the filter surface and plugging it up if it's put away wet," he continues. "Chlorinated water has very slight solvent properties for silver and especially for the first few liters of heavily chlorinated water passed through a new Pocket Filter, it's possible to exceed the EPA's fifty parts per billion silver limit by a small amount. This is ,in no way, harmful to health. Many Rocky Mountain area municipal water supplies have more than fifty parts per billion of silver in them from natural sources. Silver in water has not been shown to be harmful to health at far higher concentrations than the EPA's limit — and silver nitrate solutions have long been used to sterilize burns and to bathe the eyes of newborn babies to prevent loss of eyesight as a result of the mother having any form of venereal disease at the time of birth."

One Pocket Filter — the smallest in the firm's line of water disinfection products — is capable of producing a half-liter of safe water per minute with moderate pumping action, and can service the water requirements of several individuals. To keep the unit, which sells for about $150

SURVIVABILITY WITH RATIONED WATER
WALKING AT NIGHT UNTIL EXHAUSTED AND RESTING THEREAFTER

Maximum Daily Temperature (°F) In Shade	Available Water Per Man, U.S. Quarts					
	0	1	2	4	10	20
	Days of Expected Survival					
120	1	2	2	2½	3	
110	2	2	2½	3	3½	
100	3	3½	3½	4½	5½	
90	5	5½	5½	6½	8	
80	7	7½	8	9½	11½	
70	7½	8	9	10½	13½	
60	8	8½	9	11	14	
50	8	8½	9	11	14	

Tabletop water purification system suitable for camp or retreat is the New World Distiller line. Models can produce up to five gallons in twelve hours.

a quart of water or other fluid per day would sustain life, but such a limited amount would prevent just about all work or movement, especially in a hot climate. If you're working in a cool climate, a more accurate daily estimate is 1½ to 2 gallons (6.8 to 9 L). And if the temperature is up over 80F (25C) degrees, you will probably consume about three gallons (13.7L) per day. Small children may not consume their entire ration, but you may find their shortfall offset by adult consumption. But one thing is certain: You can't have enough water.

It's doubtful we'll continue to receive and squander the 326,000 gallons the average Southern California family requires per year. According to the Metropolitan Water District, about half of that amount is used in and around the home — hygiene, cooking, yard maintenance. The other half is used in manufacturing the goods we use, in growing the family's food at the farm level, building the house, and to keep the company you work for producing.

While the hot water heater, or toilet bowl tank or water softener can be drained to provide potable water in an emergency of short duration, storing water is cheap insurance. You can store water for long periods in glass, plastic or metal containers, but plastic is by far the most practical. Glass can be broken and exposure to heat or light may accelerate growth of algae present and render the water less desirable. Plastic, normally gallon-sized milk jugs that are thoroughly rinsed of all traces of fat, are normally used for water storage. They're light, unbreakable, and made of a plastic that's safe for contact with human food. Some polyethylene-type plastics are not recommended for food storage because they could contribute harmful chemicals to the contents. (Most plastics used in waterbeds are not approved food storage plastics — always use plastics which have previously been used for food storage, or which are being advertised as suitable for storing food.) Since plastic is permeable to certain vapors, do not store your water near petroleum products or pesticides, and away form heat sources that could melt the plastic. Keep out of direct sunlight.

Many survivalists pack a five-gallon (22¾L) collapsible, plastic water storage container in their immediate survival kit. Retailing around the $5 range from companies like American Survival Products, Inc., of Sharon Center, Ohio, these have a carrying handle attached, with a secure, threaded cap. Olive drab in color, they are airtight and suitable for storing grain.

Long-term storage containers of blue plastic in five- or fifteen-gallon sizes are also available from Noah in Palo Alto, California. These are earthquake-proof and water will store safely for a year, the makers claim.

A stackable-design, long-term water storage container from The Survival Center in Ravenna, Ohio, is of polypropylene with the handle and lid fitted with a resealable gasket. A plus with this design is a sealed pour spout, and the containers can be used to store grains and honey. The Survival Center and others also market thick plastic poly buckets in sizes from one to six gallons (4.5 to 27L) capacity. All have special gasket lid for sure seal and have carry handles. They can be used for water or food storage.

Metal is also used for storing water, but the container must be rust-resistant (stainless steel, for example). Oftentimes a metallic taste is transferred to the water, and a suit-

from Provisions Unlimited, operating easily just wash and dry thoroughly after use. Store as you would a pair of binoculars, away from heat sources that might damage its seals. "Aside from that, you'll want to lubricate the pump piston O-ring occasionally with Vaseline," Peter Gut concludes. "That's about it!"

The EPA currently classifies filters in three categories: Category 1 do not prevent, destroy, or repel microorganisms. They merely remove large debris like dirt or rust. Category 2 filters are similar to Category 1 filters, but also contain a chemical that inhibits the growth of bacteria inside the filter. Only Category 3 filters can be classed "water purifiers." Intended for use on contaminated waters, besides the Katadyn, are the Seagull IV (filters particles down to .5 microns), an iodine-based purifier called the Walbro, and a Pocket Purifier form Survival Factor, Inc. The latter is a portable, straw-like device eight inches long through which water is inspired. It's been found ninety-nine-percent-plus effective against *Giardia*.

How much water should you store? That obviously depends on the number of people for whom you're preparing, their stages of maturity, and your environment. It's stated that you can get by on two quarts per day (about seven gallons or thirty-two liters for two weeks), plus another seven gallons for hygiene per two weeks. The Department of Defense's Office of Civil Defense says that

Difficulty of accurately diagnosing infection with G.lamblia has led to idea that areas of country are "pure." Unfortunately, this appears not to be so, and why risk lengthy illness?

able metal container should not be used to store water treated with chlorine. Chlorine is corrosive to most metals.

Inspect stored water frequently and replace if cloudy.

Several firms offer large volume distillers that could be suitable for retreat use, thus freeing portable filters for use away from the base camp, as during hunting or scouting forays. Most, unfortunately, require electricity to heat water to the boiling point, to create steam that when condensed back to liquid is purified of contaminants and safe to drink. Still, Provisions Unlimited, distributor of the New World line of distillers, says the product will produce pure drinking water for a fraction of the cost of bottled water.

Essentially, the distillers work like this: Raw water is introduced from a hose or continuous source via water pressure. This new water is routed through a condensation chamber, which helps cool steam present while being warmed in the process. The new water then flows to the heating vat, where 110-volt electricity heats the water to boiling. Steam rises about two feet inside the sealed chamber, which frees contaminants and ensures only the purest steam is vented into the condensation chamber. As it's cooled by new water flowing in, the steam condenses into purified water that's captured in a receptacle. Capacity is five gallons (22¾L) in about twelve hours. The units cost from $450 to $700 from Provisions Unlimited.

Another unit with survival applicability is offered by Stow-A-Way Industries of Cohasset, Maine. Its the Clean Water Machine, a distiller which operates either on electric power or using any available heat source — stove top,

hot plate or camp stove. It weighs just seventeen pounds (7.8 kg) which makes it portable, but its capacity is three gallons (13.7L) in twenty-four hours. Stow-A-Way's Midi Still D uses electricity to heat the water to steam, and has a four-gallon (18.2L) optional storage tank. At maximum capacity, it will purify seven gallons (31.9L) every twenty-four hours.

If you figure to remain where you have piped-in water, you can ensure the potability of what comes out of the tap by using a countertop model Water Washer. Using a filtration system of silver-impregnated filters with charcoal, the Water Washer eliminates most undesirable odors, colors, tastes, sediment and chlorine, without removing beneficial minerals. A thousand-gallon capacity is sufficient for a year, according to Stow-A-Way, and replacement filters are available. The firm also markets a portable version of the water washer, suitable for field use and weighing one pound (454 g). It has been tested and approved by the Environmental Protection Agency.

The Survival Center in Ravenna, Ohio, markets a wide range of water purifiers, including the portable Traveler-30 which uses a three-stage filtration process powered by standard 115-volt AC current or automobile cigarette lighter outlet. Stage One is a prefiltration step that removes sediment, rust, dirt or silt from the pressurized water source. Stage Two uses organic chemical filtration to eliminate odors, taste, pesticides, herbicides, and other chemicals. The final stage uses ultraviolet sterilization to destroy bacteria, viruses, algae, yeast organisms and many mold spores. Capacity is one gallon (4.5L) every three minutes.

Chapter 15

EMERGENCY FIRST-AID

Restore Breathing, Heartbeat And Stop The Blood Flow — Immediate Attention Required

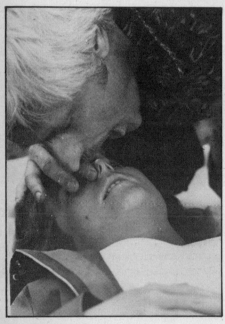 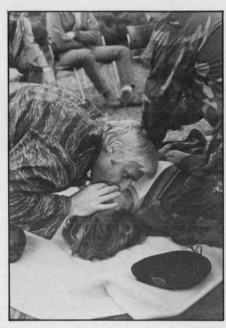 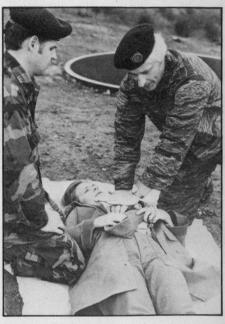

Rescue breathing, as demonstrated by Bill Ungerman of California Survival Training Center, is lifesaving art that should be mastered by all. Sequence begins as Ungerman, having cleared and opened airway, pinches nostrils closed and prepares to form airtight seal around patient's mouth (above left). He blows into the victim's mouth (center), inflating the lungs, then watches for exhalation before continuing. Often artificial respiration is coupled with cardiac massage (above right). Ungerman uses heels of both hands to press hard.

THE AMERICAN Red Cross and other relief agencies tell us that accidents are the number one cause of death for people less than 38 years old. Accidents are one of the leading causes of death for people over this age, too. In fact, more than 100,-000 Americans die each year from accidents, while ten million sustain disabling injuries. To put this latter statistic into perspective: one of every twenty Americans suffers disabling injuries, a great many needlessly; for had proper medical attention or first-aid been administered immediately, the victims would have recovered.

In a survival situation as when natural disaster strikes, you must assume that medical attention will be delayed.

Hospitals may be overcrowded with victims more seriously injured than your wounded. As the Red Cross says: "Knowing what to do in an emergency helps to avoid the panic and disorganized behavior which is characteristic of unprepared persons at such times. Knowledge of first aid is a civic responsibility. It not only helps to save lives and prevent complications from injuries, but also helps in setting up an orderly method of handling emergency problems according to their priority for treatment so that the greatest possible good may be accomplished for the greatest number of people."

Because there are books like the *American Red Cross Advanced First Aid and Emergency Care,* this chapter

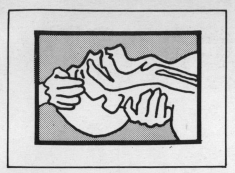

Lifting neck while tipping forehead backs opens airway unless clogged. This is your first step.

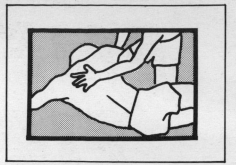

If choking victim is prostrate, roll his chest against your leg and smack between shoulder blades.

won't plow the same ground. Rather, it's recommended that you purchase a copy of this excellent paperback and store it with your first aid supplies.

This chapter simply covers the emergency treatment required to alleviate major trauma: resumption of cardiopulmonary function and staunching blood flow. These conditions require immediate action. If a person stops breathing, death could result in six minutes or less. One could bleed to death in fifteen minutes. Other injuries or illnesses listed in the aforementioned first aid manual, while painful, aren't so serious. You may refer to the Red Cross book for treatment required.

There are any number of causes for interrupted respiration: electric shock, drowning, choking, head injury, heart attack, and so forth. Whatever the cause, you must try to restore breathing as rapidly as possible.

If you approach an unconscious victim, see if the cause of the accident is visible. You may find the victim is in contact with high-tension or electrical wiring and touching him could likewise shock you. Either turn off the electricity before touching the individual, or separate him from contact with the wire by moving the wire with a limb or other wooden shaft.

Classic signs of lack of oxygen through interrupted respiration include a bluish pallor of tongue, lips, and fingernails. The Office of Emergency Services recommends you first try shaking the unconscious victim and shouting, "Are you all right?" If there's no response or evidence of breathing, quickly follow these steps:

● Position the victim on his back.

● Loosen clothing around the neck and chest.

● Open the airway by slipping one hand under the victim's neck and lifting up, at the same time pressing downward, with your other hand on the victim's forehead.

● Listen for breathing with your ear close to the victim's now-open mouth. If you can't detect breathing, watch his chest for signs of movement. If you have a mirror — in a makeup case, for instance — putting it close to the victim's mouth will cause fogging if the victim is breathing at all.

Choking victim needing assistance should be draped forward, then whacked smartly between shoulder blades to dislodge foreign matter.

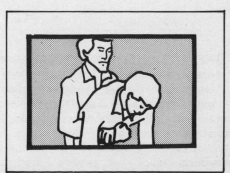

Upright victim often is helped by grabbing from behind as shown, then sharply driving balled fists into abdomen to dislodge choking cause.

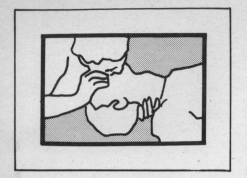 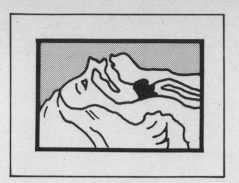

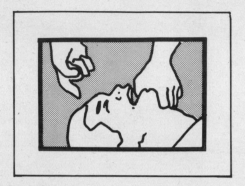 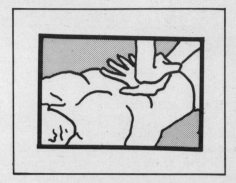

If victim is a child (top left), you should cover mouth and nose with your own while performing artificial respiration. If victim has regurgitated and matter blocks airway, your rescue breathing is ineffective. First step, therefore is to clear airway (top right). Use your finger or, if victim is semi-conscious, stick or toothbrush (to avoid convulsive bite). Hold tongue down with other thumb (above left). Attempt to use diaphragm pressure to expire air in lungs and, hopefully, unblock airway (above right).

● If there's no indication of breathing, begin artificial respiration by pinching shut the victim's nostrils. Lifting slightly under his neck, take a deep breath, cover his mouth completely with your own, and blow into the victim's mouth noting the rise of the victim's chest. Remove your mouth and listen for air escaping from the victim's mouth; the chest should also fall. Repeat the cycle five seconds, or twelve breaths per minute.

● If your victim is a child, you'll probably find it more convenient to cover both mouth and nose with your mouth. Blow into the lungs, keeping in mind that a child requires less oxygen. Watch for escaping air and fall of the chest, then repeat every three seconds, or twenty times per minute.

● If you suspect air isn't reaching the lungs, there may be something obstructing the airway. In this case, roll the victim on his side facing you, his chest against your knee. Give four sharp blows on the back between the shoulder blades then check for signs of breathing. If that doesn't work, turn the victim onto his back and place the heel of one hand in the center of the abdomen, above the navel. Position the heel of your other hand atop the first, then press down hard four separate times. This pressures the diaphragm upward, perhaps dislodging the foreign body in the airway. These thrusts should be short and sharp, and not to either side.

● Clear the airway holding down the victim's tongue with your thumb then searching at the back of the throat with a crooked index finger. Caution: If the victim is convulsive, hold down the tongue with a stick or other hard object that won't be severed — as would your finger — should he bite down.

● Try again to inflate the lungs with artificial respiration. Continue the back blows/thrusts/probing/respiration until the victim is breathing on his own. Then transport to hospital as soon as possible.

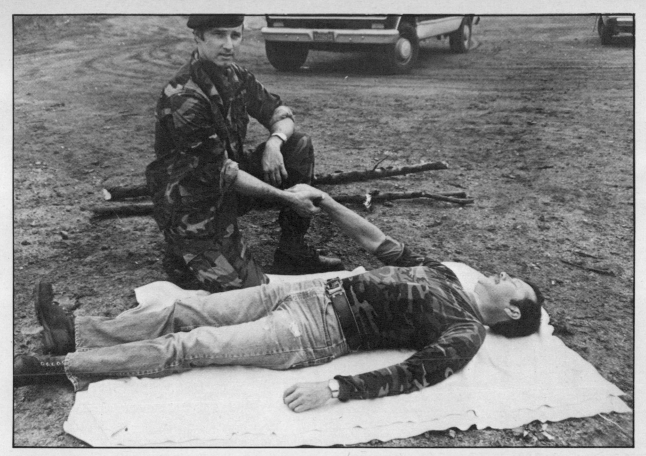

Steve Henson of California Survival Training Center shows how application of direct pressure is used to stop bleeding. CSTC's Phil Snyder has scrounged emergency crutch from woods. Cut to desired length.

The Office of Emergency Services notes that it may take several hours to revive a victim, but you can't stop until help arrives. If you quit, even for six minutes, the victim could die.

Conscious victims also may die from asphyxiation — up to two thousand die per year, many below age 4. The problem usually is a foreign body that lodges in the esophagus or base of the throat. Young children discover their world through their mouths — hence the problem with choking. Adults can choke over food, also.

The American Red Cross recommends that you don't interfere with a choking victim who can speak, cough or breathe. If the victim can't, render immediate aid in this manner:

● Standing just behind and to the side of the victim, bend him forward at the waist slightly, while supporting him with one arm across the chest. Administer four sharp blows between the shoulder blades. This may free the debris.

Need an emergency stretcher? Use your imagination! Steven Henson and Phil Snyder chop downed limbs into selected length (left). Robin Anderson and Snyder lay out blanket that will form carrying space (below).

Two limbs are placed about one-third of the way in on each end...

...then sides are folded atop one another (left). Students observe steps from background seats.

● If not, stand behind the victim and wrap your arms around his chest, just above the navel. Clasp your hands together in a double fist. Press in and up in quick thrusts, driving the diaphragm and air within the lungs against the lodged matter. Repeat both steps as needed. If the victim still can't breathe, he'll become unconscious and you should then follow the instructions given previously.

Heart attacks sometimes combine respiratory interruption with lack of heartbeat. You must act fast by administering CPR — cardiopulmonary resuscitation — which combines artificial respiration by one helper with cardiac massage by another. This forces the heart to continue pumping the oxygen you're introducing, hopefully eliminating brain damage or death. CPR is somewhat specialized. The American Red Cross offers four, one-hour courses open to all individuals age 13 and over. Your attendance is encouraged.

The other major trauma that requires instantaneous treatment involves bleeding. You must control bleeding and there is one main method: direct pressure.

You can stop most severe bleeding by pressing the wound site hard for five to fifteen minutes. First, elevate the limb

Robin and Phil smooth out the wrinkles and remove slack from stretcher, which would impair function.

Blanket sags but holds, enabling evacuation of injured with much less effort and less chance of further injury.

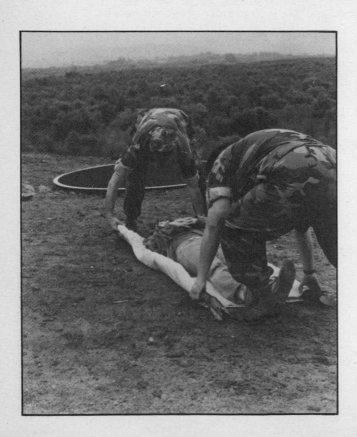

(if possible) higher than heart level. This reduces blood flow to the injury site. Use a clean gauze bandage, handkerchief, sanitary napkin or even your bare hand if needed and press down firmly against the wound site. Be careful when applying pressure to a head wound, since a mild skull fracture can be worsened by too much enthusiasm.

Get medical help as quickly as possible. You may have to reapply pressure several times en route to medical attention.

STOCKING THE FIRST-AID KIT

There are many readily available kits at drug stores ranging from auto travel kits to fully-stocked industrial first aid kits. You can then purchase supplies to stock your own. Most are stocked in either rugged plastic cases or nylon carry bags. You can buy dental emergency kits and even childbirth supplies.

Volunteer positioned on the blanket, two instructors from CSTC prepare to lift and evacuate to medical site.

THE COMPLETE SURVIVAL GUIDE

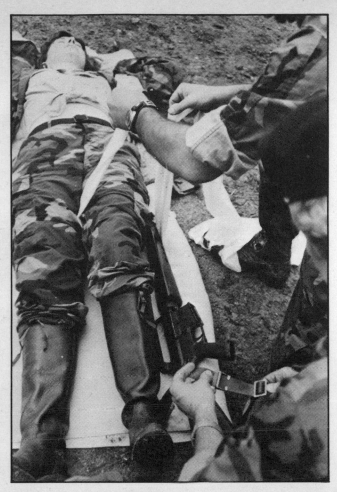

In a pinch, two rifles can be used as sides of makeshift splint. A handkerchief, sock, torn shirt, etc., is used to bind muzzle or forend to leg, while sling is used to immobilize ankle (above left). Steve Henson grimaces as he slides sling adjustment clips tight against ankle, around stock of second weapon.

What you should buy will be determined by your perception of future need: If medical emergency will exist only for a short time, then perhaps a kit designed for six to ten people will suffice — and certainly cost less. If you see a disaster of prolonged duration, you might be wiser to purchase a bigger kit or assemble your own. You'll want to add unqiue medicines preferred by your family — aspirin-free pain relievers or specific brand of birth control pills, for example. If possible, try to buy medicines and items in individual sterile packages; this reduces contamination of the entire supply for a single treatment.

Major suppliers include Surgical Company, Incorporated, Garden City, New York; Just In Case, Inc., Windsor, California; and North Star Survival Systems, Inc., Fort Smith, Arkansas.

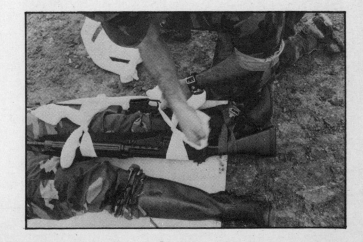

A few more rags tied around both rifles and limb is immobilized. Get to proper medical facility soonest.

Chapter 16
TOOLS FOR TOMORROW

Having An Assortment Of Tools On Hand, And Knowledge of Their Use, Is Smart Planning!

THE WELL-STOCKED workbench of today may be your passport to survival tomorrow — or be virtually worthless. Most modern workbenches are equipped with inexpensive power tools, labor savers that considerably speed completion of projects by average handymen or do-it-yourselfers. But power tools are worthless without electricity. So here, as in other parts of the book, your evaluation of future need will dictate the degree of preparedness to which you aspire.

For example, one learned author recently wrote of caching wood-, stone-, metal- and woodworking tools, along with plumbing supplies. Clearly, he was anticipating the worst — a society forced to rebuild, not one simply dis-

Above: Most of us have tools on hand, and some common ones are these. Ensure you buy only top-quality tools, which last longer and work better.
Right: Farming on this scale requires heavy equipment like tractors, but the basics of growing food are the same for backyard plots. Shown is wheat at harvest time in Australia.

Photo: J. Tanner, Australian Information Service

THE COMPLETE SURVIVAL GUIDE

turbed by short-lived interruption of essential services. Other writers talk of storing a modest selection of wood-working and agricultural tools, anticipating resumption of skilled trades and commerce relatively soon after "the end."

Which way you go will depend upon your personal evaluation of the risks ahead. But however you feel, there's no argument over the need for skill in using the tools. Without the knowledge of how to use them, tools are worthless.

Obviously, this means that you should devote thought to your major hazards, and put reasoned thought into the tools you'll require, then begin to assemble and become familiar with them. At the same time, you may find great personal satisfaction and monetary reward from tackling projects around the home that you've put off because you didn't have the tools or the knowledge to use them! The money you save today can be used to purchase other tools or for the never-ending list of materials you'd like to stock-pile today, for use if needed tomorrow.

Speaking of purchasing tools, a cardinal rule you'd be wise to observe is to purchase the best-quality tools you can afford. Don't opt for the bargain counters at your nearest hardware store: The tools are marked down to $1 or less because they didn't sell at full price. They didn't sell at full price because tool-buyers recognized the inferior materials and workmanship inherent with them. Save your money for the best brand names you can find.

Poor-quality tools that are unreliable are equivalent to no tools at all. Good tools are made of better raw materials — hardwoods, strong synthetics, top-quality steels —

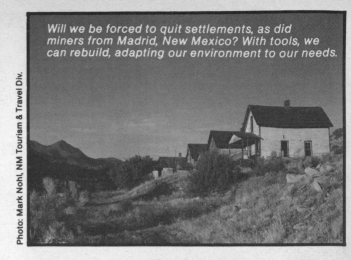

Will we be forced to quit settlements, as did miners from Madrid, New Mexico? With tools, we can rebuild, adapting our environment to our needs.

hence the higher price. Some are of stainless or are chrome-plated to fight rust. Remember, better-made tools last longer and if you're faced with not having a corner hardware store for replacing a broken tool, this is vitally important.

It is unrealistic to expect that every person with a penchant for preparedness will stockpile all of the tools needed to establish a blacksmithing operation, for woodworking, plumbing, machining, and stone masonry. Not only could you go broke purchasing them, but you'd never have the time to acquire skill in each facet. If your mindset tells you that society will need rebuilding from the foundation up, you probably have joined or will find a survival group among whom these important trades will be distributed. Each retreatist will be charged with procuring the tools and skills with them for each of the trades listed. If needed, you therefore have the nucleus for new civilization — or at least continuation of the old civilization in civilized conditions!

Let's learn from history what Mr. Average and his family will require. There were, during this country's early years, a handful of mountain men who walked solo trails. They were skilled in woods lore and were able to live off the land. For the most part, these trappers and explorers weren't encumbered by wife and children, though, and these pioneering homesteaders came to raw land equipped with skills we may need tomorrow: The ability to construct a shelter, heat it, and make the ground produce food. Naturally, some were also able to use existing vegetation for food and medicine, but the homesteaders were largely an agrarian society.

As Ray Dorr of Adobe Fort says in the chapter on Survival Schools, frontier communities were for the most part built around the general store. "The trading patterns or commerce during a 'New Civilization' period as we had during settlement of the American West involved the store-keeper at the hub, with eight tradesmen at the ends of the spokes," says Dorr, who conducts schools throughout the year that teach pioneer skills. "Your blacksmith would create tools, kitchen utensils, wagon parts and traps, which he'd furnish to the general store for sale. In exchange, he'd get coal, food, clothing, firewood and hay from the store. Your spinner/weaver fashioned blankets and woolen clothing, which would go to the store. This person would purchase wool, scissors, needles, shoes, food and firewood

Best-quality hardwood handles for these tools will keep them usable for years. Hat keeps off hot sun.

If you consider life without nails, you'll surely stockpile a supply of various sizes! Right: The blacksmith can manufacture some tools, but not of quality available at low cost at hardware stores.

from the store. The pattern was the same for the miller: He'd sell flour to the general store, and buy grain, food, clothing, firewood and hay. Your woodsman — woodcutter, hunter, trapper, or fisherman — would sell his firewood, hides, pelts, fish and meat to the store, buying in return traps, ammunition, tools, saddles, wagons, food and clothing.

"The fifth essential trade is the tanner/saddlemaker," continues Dorr, based in Colorado Springs. "He'd make tanned leather, saddles, harness, shoes and leather clothing. He'd buy new hides, battery acid, animal brains, food, clothing, firewood and hay from the storekeeper. The raw hides he requires would be furnished by the rancher/farmer, who also sold through the general store horses, beef, wool, potatoes, and hay. He'd receive in exchange the goods he needed: saddles, tools, harness, and clothing."

Essential to the program, says Dorr, was the teamster or trader, who furnished many of the goods not made locally.

If you have no car or horse, a bicycle beats walking! Consider even children's bikes when accumulating tools and equipment. Right: Low-cost nylon rope can be purchased by the coil well before it's needed. Uses are innumerable.

Photo: Arkansas Dept. of Parks & Tourism

"He would haul in salt, soda, wool, fresh fruits and vegetables, coal and grain, then would buy local trade goods, harness, wagons, food and clothing," Dorr says. "These local trade goods would be sold in other areas where they were needed, and in exchange the trader would procure products specific to that geographic area."

The last spoke was the service professional — that individual like the doctor, dentist, peace officer or lawyer who contributed professional services in exchange for monetary compensation that was in turn used to purchase food, clothing, blankets, horses, saddles, firewood and hay from the general store.

While each of these eight tradesmen require some specialization of equipment, for the most part the tools they require are woodworking or agricultural in nature. Therefore, what follows is a suggested list for following in the path of our pioneering forefathers. Remember that they had little storage space and made do, at least at the begin-

ning, with limited tools. The point is, you can do all facets of carpentry with the following tools, but it takes longer than if you had other tools.

WOODWORKING TOOLS
Ax, single bit, 36-inch
Splitting maul
Sledgehammer
Splitting wedges
Rip saw, 6-point, 26-inch
Crosscut saw, 26-inch
Bowsaw, 30-inch
Claw hammer, 16-ounce
Framing (carpenter's) square, 16x24-inch
Tape measure, steel, 10- and 50-foot
Level, spirit-filled, 2-foot
Screwdrivers, slotted head, assorted sizes
Screwdrivers, Phillips head, assorted sizes
Hand drill, ratchet brace, with set of bits
Plane, block or jack
Chisels, assorted sizes
Files, tapered, round and half-round
Whetstone
Nails, nuts, screws, bolts, etc.

AGRICULTURAL TOOLS
Shovel, round-point
Pickax
Mattock
Hoe, long-handled
Rake, metal
Spading fork
Scythe
Cultivator

MISCELLANEOUS EXTRAS
Wrenches
Socket sets
Pliers, regular and needlenose
Crowbar, 36-inch
Vegetable seeds
Fertilizer
Soil test kit
Insecticides/pesticides

A few safety precaution notes that could keep you out of trouble:

Hammer — Use the correct hammer for the job — a sixteen-ounce is best for overall carpentry, but a twenty-ounce framing hammer is designed for heavier use like demolition. Never use a hammer with a loose head — on the downswing it could separate from the handle and injure someone. Hammers aren't designed to hit other hammers, so don't use them that way. Likewise, don't use a hammer

Livestock production is vital to national well-being today, and will take on larger roll in survival setting. Horse is a tool that makes work easier.

Photo: Arkansas Dept. of Parks & Tourism

Youngsters outfitted with proper tools can help in food gathering, whether shooting or gardening.

where a prybar or crowbar is required — you could break the hardwood handle and it mightn't be easy to replace. Hammer on stable, braced surfaces that won't tip upon impact of the hammer. To start a nail, hold it between your middle and index fingers, palm up. Once it's started, remove your hand. This'll keep you pounding happily.

Photo: Wyoming Travel Commission

Wrenches — Never strike a wrench with a hammer. This could cause it to fly off in an unknown direction and cause injury. Don't use any form of extender like a length of pipe to increase torque. You could ruin the tool by bending it or breakage. A common cause of trouble when using a crescent wrench is improper adjustment. This puts the force against the adjustable jaw, not against the objective.

Pliers — You'll skin your knuckles if you use pliers where you should be using a wrench, as on bolts.

Screwdrivers — Use the proper shape and size for the work being turned, and never hold the work in one hand while the screwdriver applies force with the other. I can confirm that the tool will inevitably jump the slot and stab through a finger or palm. Screwdrivers are meant to be screwdrivers, not chisels. Hitting the handles with your hammer could destroy the tool.

Hand saws — Keep them sharp and oiled, which helps the tool cut. Tools stay sharp longer if used as intended — crosscut for cutting across the grain, rip sawing with the grain. Use force only on the pushing stroke — the pulling

Photo: Arkansas Dept. of Parks & Tourism

Photo: Tenn. Tourist Dev.

Photo: Bureau of Land Management

Left: Spinning is a pioneer industry that will return if electricity disappears. Above: With tools and technology, you can duplicate pioneer housing. Below: Source of woolen fabric is valuable.

Photo: Oklahoma City Tourist Development

If we can't extract oil like Oklahoma gusher in 1930 (left), how can we produce oils, grease? Perhaps we'd better stockpile some while we have it!

stroke cleans the channel of sawdust. To keep from cutting your hand, keep it above the saw's teeth, and hold the work being cut in a vise, Workmate or other clamp. Let the cut-off end extend into space where it can drop cleanly, thus preventing binding pressure on the saw blade. When starting a cut, use three or four pull strokes to establish the cutting channel, also called a kerf, before using pressure on the pushing thrust. This keeps from marring the surface of the work as the saw blade will want to jump around. If your hand is holding the work, guess where the teeth will cut?

Chisels — These work best if sharp, and use them for intended task only; no cold chisels for wood, or wood chisels for metal. It's safest to put the work in a vise or clamp, and keep your free hand out of the cutting path.

Ax — Don't use the back or flat side of the ax head for a hammer. Before using an ax on cold days, many woodcutters warmed the blade; this prevents structural damage due to concussion that could eventually break the head. Keep ax sharp — use whetstone often and properly.

Plane — Hold the work in a clamp or vise and use only sharp tools. Retract the iron when not in use and keep your hand out of the plane's path when cutting.

With any tool, you're wise to care for it properly. Keep cutting tools sharp. You'll find it easiest to resharpen before putting the tools away after use; that way, they're sharp for your next use without delay. Metal parts subject to rust should be inspected frequently and never put away wet.

You're wise to stockpile as many tools as you can reasonably afford. Consider them barter items more valuable than gold if there's an extended social breakdown. Your familiarity with them may also keep you alive in a situation where only those with useful skills are permitted to remain.

So consider now the tools you may need in a survival scenario. Procure them and learn their use. You may derive immense pleasure and budget savings by completing home repairs yourself, while gaining needed familiarity with your tools of tomorrow.

Demolition or construction are just two uses for an eight-pound sledgehammer.

Chapter 17

SURVIVAL SOURCES

ARCHERY TACKLE

Allen Archery, 200 Washington St., Billings, MO 65610 (bows, accessories)
American Archery, P.O. Box 100 Indus. Park, Oconto Falls, WI 54154 (bows, accessories)
Bear Archery, RR 4, 4600 Southwest 41st Blvd., Gainesville, FL 32601
Bingham Archery, Box 3013, Ogden, UT 84403 (bows, accessories)
Browning, Rt. 1,Morgan, UT 84050 (bows, accessories)
Carroll's Archery Products, 59½ South Main, Moab, UT 84532 (bows, accessories)
Cravotta Brothers, Inc., Third St., E. McKeesport, PA 15132 (bows)
Darton, Inc., Archery Division, 3261 Flushing Rd., Flint, MI 48504 (bows)
East Side Archery Ltd., 3711 E. 106th St., Chicago, IL 60617 (longbows, accessories)
Golden Eagle Archery Co., Inc., P.O. Box 310, 104 S. Mill St., Creswell, OR 97426 (bows)
Graham's Custom Bows, P.O. Box 1312, Fontana, CA 92335 (bows, accessories)
Harvard Sports, Inc., 2640 E. Del Amo Blvd., Compton, CA 90221
Herter's Inc., RR1, Waseca, MN 56093 (bows, accessories)
Howard Hill Archery, Rt. 1, Box 1397, Hamilton, MT 59840 (longbows, accessories)
Damon Howatt (Martin Archery), Rt. 5, Box 127, Walla Walla, WA 99362 (bows)
Jack Howard, Washington Star Rt., Nevada City, CA 95959 (bows, accessories)
Hoyt Archery Co., 11510 Natural Bridge Rd., Bridgeton, MO 63044 (bows, accessories)
Indian Archery, 817 Maxwell Ave., Evansville, IN 47717 (bows, accessories)
Jeffery Enterprises, Inc., 821 Pepper St., Columbia, SC 29209 (bows)
Jennings Compound Bow Inc., 28756 N. Castaic Cyn. Rd., Valencia, CA 91355 (bows, accessories)
Kittredge Bow Hut, P.O. Box 598, Mammoth Lakes, CA 93546 (bows, accessories)
Bill Lookabaugh, Inc., 716 E. Mission Dr., San Gabriel, CA 91776
Martin Archery, Rt. 5, Box 127, Walla Walla, WA 99362 (bows, accessories)
Mohawk Archery, 228 Bridge St., E. Syracuse, NY 13057 (bows, accessories)
Dick Palmer Archery, 932 N. College, Fayetteville, AR 72702-1632 (longbows, accessories)
Ben Pearson Archery, P.O. Box 7465, Pine Bluff, AR 71611
Plas/Steel Products, Inc., Walkerton, IN 46574
Precision Shooting Equipment, 2550 N. 14th Ave., Tucson, AZ 85705 (bows, accessories)
Pro-Line Co., 1843 Gun Lake Rd., Box 370, Hastings, MI 49058 (bows, accessories)
Stemmler Archery, 984 Southford Rd., Middleburg, CT 06762 (bows, accessories)
Survival Outfitters (see Food)
Total Shooting Systems, Inc., 419 Van Dyne Rd., N. Fond du Lac, WI 54935
Woodcraft Equip. Co./York Archery, P.O. Box 110, Independence, MO 64051
Yamaha International Corp., 6600 Orangethorpe Ave., Buena Park, CA 90620 (bows)
Zebra Long Bow Mfg. Co., 231 E. Meuse St., Blue Grass, IA 52756 (longbows)

ATTIRE

Academy Broadway Corp., 5 Plant Ave., Smithtown, NY 11788
Acorn Products Co., Inc., Box 1257, Lewiston, ME 04240 (socks)
Because It's There (see Camping)
Bellweather, 1161 Mission St., San Francisco, CA 94103
Black Ice, 2310 Laurel St., Napa, CA 94559
Blue Puma (see Camping)
Brigade Quartermasters, Ltd., 266-N6 Roswell St., Marietta, GA 30060
Camel Mfg. Co., Box 835, Knoxville, Tn 37901
Chouinard Equip., Box 160, Ventura, CA 93002
Columbia Sportswear Co., 6600 N. Baltimore, Portland, OR 97203
Danner Shoe Mfg. Co., Box 22204, Portland, OR 97222 (boots)
Donner Mountain Corp., 2110 Fifth St., Berkeley, CA 94710 (boots, outerwear)
Duofold, Inc., P.O. Drawer A, Mohawk, NY 13407
Expeditions International, Box 1040, Hamilton, MT 59840 (boots)
Fabiano, 850 Summer St., S. Boston, MA 02127 (boots)
Famous Trails, 3602 Kurtz St., San Diego, CA 92138
Force 10, 4304 W. Jefferson Blvd., Los Angeles, CA 90016
Fox River Mills, Inc., 227 Poplar St., Osage, IA 50461 (socks)
G&M Sales, Inc., 1667 Market St., San Francisco, CA 94103 (boots)
GEE Corp., 323 Geary St., San Francisco, CA 94102
Georgia Boot, Box 10, Franklin, TN 37064
Gerry Mfg., 6260 Downing St., Denver, CO 80216
Granite Stairway Mountaineering, 4620 Alvarado Canyon Rd., San Diego, CA 92120
Handsome Enterprises, Inc., 1131 Monterey Pass Rd., Monterey Park, CA 91754 (boots)
Inter-Footwear USA, Inc., 2923 A. Nicholas Way, Modesto, CA 95351 (boots)
Landav, Box 4724, Portland, OR 97208
Merell Boot Co., Rt. 1, Box 105, Waitsfield, VT 05673 (boots)
Nelson Recreational Products, Inc. (boots — see Camping)
Pleasure-Knit Corp., Box 126, Boston, MA 02134
Rockford Textile Mills, Inc., 200 Mulberry St., McMinnville, TN 37110
Rocky Boots, 45 Canal St., Nelsonville, OH 45764
Walls Industries, Inc., Box 98, Cleburne, TX 76031
Wigwam Mills, Inc., 3402 Crocker Ave., Sheboygan, WI 53081
Wolverine World Wide, Inc., Rockford, MI 49351 (boots)

BOOKS

Alaska Northwest Publishing Co., 130 2nd Ave., S., Edmonds, WA 98020
Anchor Press/Doubleday, 501 Franklin Ave., Garden City, NY 11530
At Home Everywhere, Rt. 2, Box 269, Aurora, Co 87002
Atlan J Formularies, Box 327, Harrison, AR 72601
Ballinger Publishing Co., 17 Dunster St., Harvard Square, Cambridge, MA 02138
Clayton Survival Services, 5056 Hwy. 140, Mariposa, CA 95338
Cloverleaf Books, Box 440259, Aurora, CO 80044
Contemporary Sports Books, 180 N. Michigan Ave., Ste. 2110, Chicago, IL 60601
DBI Books, Inc., One Northfield Plaza, Northfield, IL 60093
Desert Publications, Cornville, AZ 86325
East Woods Press, 429 E. Boulevard, Charlotte NC 28203
Everyman's Guide to Better Home Security, by Vincent Joseph Guarino, Paladin Press, Box 1307, Boulder, CO 80306
Garden Way Publishing, Charlotte, VT 05445
Harper & Row Publishers, Inc., Scranton, PA 18512
ICS Books, Box 8002, Merrillville, IN 46410
Kephart Communications, Inc., 901 N. Washington, Alexandria, VA 22314
Long Survival Newsletter, Box 163, Wamego, KS 66547
Bill Lookabaugh, Inc. (see Archery)
Mother's Bookshelf, Box 70, Hendersonville, NC 28739
New Alchemy Institute, Box 432, Woods Hole, MA 02543
Paladin Press, Box 1307, Boulder, CO 80306
Personal Security, Petersen Publishing Co., Specialty Publications, 8490 Sunset Blvd., Los Angeles, CA 90069
Personal Survival Letter, Box 598, Rogue River, OR 97537
Portola Institute, 540 Santa Cruz Ave., Menlo Park, CA 94024
Prepare, Inc., 7155 E. Thomas Rd., Ste. 103, Scottsdale, AZ 85251
Rodale Press, 33 E. Minor St., Emmanus, PA 18049
Scarecrow Press, Inc., 52 Liberty St., Metuchen, NJ 08840
Survival Books, 11106 Magnolia Blvd., North Hollywood, CA 91601
Survival Cards (see Camping)
Survival Outfitters (see Food)
The Anglers Art, RD 9, Box 204, Carlisle, PA 17013
The Mountaineers Books, 715 Pike St., Seattle, WA 98101
The Survival Center, 5555 Newton Falls Rd., Ravenna, OH 44266
U.S. Government Printing Office, Superintendent of Documents, Washington, D.C. 20402
Van Nostrand Reinhold, 135 W. 50th St., New York, NY 10020

CAMPING SUPPLIES & ACCESSORIES

Academy Broadway Corp. (tents, packs — see Attire)
Ajay Sports, 1501 E. Wisconsin St., Delavan, WI 53115 (misc.)
Allison Forge Co., Box 404, Belmont, MA 01178 (life tool)
Alpenlite Packs, 3891 N. Ventura Ave., Ventura, CA 93001 (packs)
Alpine Research, Inc., 765 Indian Peaks Rd., Golden, CO 80403 (tools)
Aussie Campa Champ Pty. Ltd., Box 1461, Canberra, ACT, Australia 2601 (tents)
Basic Designs, Inc., Box 479, Muir Beach, Sausalito, CA 94965 (misc.)
Eddie Bauer, Box 3700, Seattle, WA 98124
Because It's There, 1000 First Ave., S., Seattle, WA 98134 (sleeping bags, tents)
Black Ice (sleeping bags, tents, packs — see Attire)
Blue Puma, 650 Tenth St., Arcata, CA 95501
Brunton Compasses, 620 E. Monroe Ave., Riverton, WY 82501
Bushwalker, Box 1630, Flagstaff, AZ 86001 (packs)
Camel Mfg. Co., Box 835, Knoxville, TN 37901 (tents)
Camp Time, East 12505 Skyview, Spokane, WA 99216 (tables, chairs)
Camp-Ways, 12915 S. Spring St., Los Angeles, CA 90061 (tents, packs, misc.)
Century Tool & Mfg. Co., Box 188, Herry Valley, IL 61016 (Primus kitchens)
Champion Industries, 34 E. Opolar St., Philadelphia, PA 19123 (packs)
Coghlan's Ltd., 121 Irene St., Winnipeg, Canada R3T 4C7 (misc.)
Coleman Canvas Products Div., 250 N. St. Francis St., Wichita, KS 67201 (tents, sleeping bags)
Diamond Brand, Hwy. 25, Naples, NC 28760 (tents, packs)
Dolt of California, 10455 W. Jefferson Blvd., Culver City, CA 90230 (packs)
Dorcy International, Inc., 7382 Lampson Ave., Garden Grove, CA 92641 (misc.)
East-Pak, 17 Locust St., Haverhill, MA 01830 (packs)
Ero Leisure Industries, 5950 W. Touhy Ave., Chicago, IL 60648 (sleeping bags, packs)
Esbit, 8311 Westminster Ave., Westminster, CA 92683 (fire starters)
Family Camping Products, Inc., 329 S. Main St., Canandaigua, NY 14424 (heaters, stoves)
Famous Trails (tents, packs, misc. — see Attire)
GEE Corp. (sleeping bags — see Attire)
Gladding Corp., Athletic Bag Div., Box 187, Syracuse, NY 13204 (packs)
Granite Stairway Mountaineering (see Attire)
Gutmann Cutlery, Inc., 900 S. Columbus Ave., Mt. Vernon, NY 10550 (misc.)
Hoffman Associates, 16542 Burke Lane, Huntington Beach, CA 92647 (sleeping bags, tents, packs)
Igloo Corp., Box 19322, Houston, TX 77024 (misc.)
Illexim Foreign Trade Co., 13 Decembrie St., Bucharest, Romania (tents, packs)
Imax Industries, Inc., USA, 13810 Bentley Pl., Cerritos, CA 90701 (packs)
Innovative Things, 5959 Adobe Falls Rd., San Diego, CA 92120 (misc.)
Jansport, 2425 W. Packard, Appleton, WI 54911 (packs, tents)
Johnson Camping, Inc., Box 966, Binghamton, NY 13902 (tents, compasses, packs)
KBR Investments, Ltd., Box 3598, Long Beach, CA 90803 (emergency blanket)
King Seeley Thermos Co., 37 East St., Winchester, MA 01890 (emergency blankets)
Leisure Sales South, Inc., Box 3532, City of Industry, CA 91744 (misc.)
Liberty Organization, Inc., Box 306, Montrose, CA 91020 (packs, cutlery)
Bill Lookabaugh, Inc. (see Archery)
Lowe Alpine Systems, 802 S. Public Rd., Lafayette, CO 80026 (packs)
Madden Mountaineering, 2400 Central Ave., Boulder, CO 80303 (packs)
Mirro Corp., 1512 Washington St., Manitowoc, WI 54220
Moss Tent Works, Camden, ME 04843 (tents)
MZH Sleeping Bags, 230 5th Ave., New York, NY 10001 (sleeping bags)
Nelson Recreation Products, Inc., 14760 Santa Fe Trail Dr., Lenexa, KS 66215 (packs, misc.)
Outdoor Products, 533 S. Los Angeles St., Los Angeles, CA 90013 (packs)
Outdoorstuff, Div. of F&L Packing Corp., 681 Main St., Belleville, NJ 07109 (misc.)
Outdoor Venture Corp., Box 337, Stearns, KY 42647 (tents, sleeping bags)
Pacific Mountain Sports, Inc., 910 Foothill Blvd., La Canada, CA 91011 (misc.)
Sew-Town USA, Inc., 42 Ladd St., Warwick, RI 02886 (packs)
Shelter Systems, Box 308, Carmel Valley, CA 93924 (tents)
SierraWest, 6 E. Yanonali St., Santa Barbara, CA 93101 (packs)
Slumberjack, Inc., Box 31405, Los Angles, CA 90031 (sleeping bags)
Southwind Mfg., 230 5th Ave., New York, NY 10001 (sleeping bags)
Sportsmaster, Inc., 1355 Market St., San Francisco, CA 94103 (packs, tents)
Standard Sales, Inc., 4611 Pacific Blvd., Vernon, CA 90058 (misc.)
Summit Products Inc., 43 Park Ln., Brisbane, CA 94005 (misc.)
Sunbeam Leisure Products Co., Box 622, Neosho, MO 64850 (misc.)
Surplus Center, 1000 W. "O" St., Lincoln, NE 68528 (misc.)
Survival Cards, Box 1805, Bloomington, IN 47402

The Wenzel Co., Box 12434, St. Louis, MO 63132 (tents, sleeping bags)
Tough Traveler, Ltd., 1012 State St., Schenectady, NY 12307 (packs)
T.P. Manufacturing, 12752 Monarch St., Garden Grove, CA 92641 (sleeping bags, packs, camouflage clothing)
Trailwise, 221 W. 1st St., Kewanee, IL 61443 (packs)
Wave Products, 11 E. Kensington, Salt Lake City, UT 84115 (packs)
Winnebago Industries, Inc., Box 152, Forest City, IA 50436 (tents, sleeping bags, kitchens, misc.)
White Stag Camping, 300 W. Washington St., Chicago, IL 60606 (tents, sleeping bags, packs)
Zypher International Co., 6231 Truckee Ct., Newark, CA 94560 (sleeping bags)

FIREARMS & ACCESSORIES

Alberts Corp., 12 Commerce Rd., Fairfield, NJ 07006
Allen Fire Arms Mfg., 950 W. Cordova Rd., Santa Fe, NM 87501
American Derringer Corp., Box 8393, Waco, TX 76701
Arcadia Machine & Tool, 536 N. Vincent Ave., Covina, CA 91722
Armament Systems & Procedures, Box 356, Appleton, WI 54912
Arminex, 7882 E. Gray Rd., Scottsdale Airpark, Scottsdale, AZ 85260
Armsport, Inc., 3590 N.W. 49th St., Miami, FL 33142
Barnett International, Inc., Box 226, Port Huron, MI 48060
Beeman, Inc., 47-SV9 Paul, San Rafael, CA 94903
Browning, Route 1, Morgan, UT 84050
C-H Tool & Die Corp., 106 N. Harding St., Owen, WI 54460 (reloading)
Cash Manufacturing Co., 816 S. Division St., Waunakee, WI 53597
Charter Arms, 430 Sniffens Lane, Stratford, CT 06497
Choate Machine & Tool, Box 218, Bald Knob, AR 72010
Colt Firearms Division, Box 1868, Hartford, CT 06102
Connecticut Valley Arms, Saybrook Road, Haddam, CT 06438
Coonan Arms, Inc., 1163 Old Fort Road, St. Paul, MN 55102
Corbin Mfg. & Supply, Box 758, Phoenix, OR 97535
Daisy, Box 220, Rogers, AR 72756
Denver Bullet Company, 11355 West 46 Place, Wheat Ridge, CO 80033
Detonics .45 Associates, 2500 Seattle Tower, Seattle, WA 98101
Dixie Gun Works, P.O. Box 130, Union City, TN 38261
EMF Co., 1900 E. Warner Ave., Suite 1-D, Santa Ana, CA 92705
Euroarms of America, P.O. Box 3277, Winchester, VA 22601
Feather Ent., 2500 Central Ave., Boulder, CO 80301
Forster Products, Division of Wiebers, 82 E. Lanark Ave., Lanark, IL 61046
Freedom Arms, Box 1776, Freedom, WY 83120
Garrett Arms & Imports, Inc., 24 Southern Shopping Center, Norfolk, VA 23505
H. Geisser, Inc., 347 W. Main St., Waukesha, WI 53186
Goex, Inc., Belin Plant, Moosic, PA 18507
Green Mountain Barrel Company, RFD 1, Box 184, Center Ossipee, NH 03814
Hatfield Rifle Works, 2028 Frederick Ave., St. Joseph, MO 64501
Heckler & Koch, 933 N. Kenmore St., Suite 218, Arlington, VA 22201
Hodgdon Powder Co., P.O. Box 2905, 7710 W. 50 Hiway, Shawnee Mission, KS 66202
Hopkins & Allen Arms, P.O. Box 217, Hawthorne, NJ 07507
Hoppe's, Penguin Industries, Airport Industrial Mall, Coatsville, PA 19320
Hornady Manufacturing Co., P.O. Box 1848, Grand Island, NE 68801
Interarms, 10 Prince St., Alexandria, VA 22313
Liberty Cartridge Co., 1360 Willow Point Terr., Marietta, GA 30067
Bill Lookabaugh, Inc. (see Archery)
Lyman Products Corp., Rt. 147, Middlefield, CT 06455
Marlin Firearms Co., 100 Kenna Dr., North Haven, CT 06473
Midway Arms, Inc., Rt. 5, Box 298, Columbia, MO 65201
Mowrey Gun Works, FM 368, Box 28, Iowa Park, TX 76367
Navy Arms Company, 689 Bergen Blvd., Ridgefield, NJ 07657

N.E. Industrial, Inc., 2516 Wyoming St., El Paso, TX 79903
Nu-Brite Labs, 1050 W. Katella, Unit D, Orange, CA 92667
Numrich Arms Corp., Box 9, W. Hurley, NY 12401
Odin Intl. Ltd., 818 Slaters Ln., Alexandria, VA 22314
Ox-Yoke Originals, 130 Griffen Road, West Suffield, CT 06093
Ozark Mountain Arms, S.R. 4, Box 4000W, Branson, MO 65616
Product Development Corp., 540 N.E. 21st Terrace, Ocala, FL 32670 (lubricants)
R&R Enterprises, Box 385, Jefferson, SD 57038
Randall Firearms Mfg. Corp., Box 728, Sun Valley, CA 91352 (magazines, cases)
Remington Arms Co., Bridgeport, CT 06601
Richland Arms Co., 321 W. Adrian St., Blissfield, MI 49228
S-R Industries, Inc., 2133 Dominguez St., Torrance, CA 90509 (air guns)
S&S Precision Bullets, Box 1133, San Juan Capistrano, CA 92693
C. Sharps Arms Co., Inc., P.O. Box 885, Big Timber, MT 59011
Sile, Inc., 7 Centre Market Place, New York, NY 10013
Smith & Wesson, Inc., Box 520, Springfield, MA 01101
Speer, Omark Industries, P.O. Box 856, Lewiston, ID 83501
Sporting Arms Div., Steyr Daimler Puch of America Corp., 8685 Metro Way, Sea-caucus, NJ 07094
Springfield Armory, 420 W. Main St., Geneseo, IL 61254
Stocking Systems Div., DWM, Inc., 113 N. 2nd St., Whitewater, WI 53190
Stoeger Industries, 55 Ruta Ct., South Hackensack, NJ 07606
Sturm, Ruger & Co., Inc., 1 Lacey Place, Southport, CT 06490
Survival Outfitters (see Food)
Tasco Sales, Inc. (scopes — see Optics)
Texas Contender Firearms, 4127 Weslow St., Houston, TX 77087
The Hawken Shop, 3028 N. Lindbergh Blvd., St. Louis, MO 63074
Thompson/Center Arms, Box 2405 Rochester, NH 03867
Uncle Mike, Michaels of Oregon, P.O. Box 13010, Portland, OR 97231
U.S. Repeating Arms, 255 Winchester Ave., New Haven, CT 06511
Valor Corp., 5555 N.W. 36th Ave., Miami, FL 33142 (black powder guns)
Weatherby, Inc., 2781 Firestone Blvd., South Gate, CA 90280
Wilkinson Arms, Rt. 2, Box 2166, Parma, ID 83660
Winchester, 120 Long Ridge Rd., Stamford, CT 06904
Winchester Group, Olin Corp., East Alton, IL 62024

FISHING TACKLE & ACCESSORIES

Abu-Garcia, Inc., 21 Law Dr., Fairfield, NJ 07006
Academy Broadway Corp. (see Attire)
American Import Co., 1167 Mission St., San Francisco, CA 94103
Fred Arbogast Co., 313 W. North St., Akron, OH 44303 (lures)
Jim Bagley Bait Co., Inc., Box 110, Winter Haven, FL 33880 (lures)
Dan Bailey Flies & Tackle, Box 1019, Livingston, MT 59047
Bass Buster, Inc., Box 118, Amsterdam, MO 64723 (lures)
L.L. Bean, 936 Main St., Freeport, ME 04033
Berkley Rods, Trilene Drive, Spirit Lake, IA 51360
Blue Fox Tackle Co., 645 N. Emerson, Cambridge, MN 55009 (lures)
Bomber Bait Co., Box 1058, Gainesville, TX 76240 (lures)
Browning, Rt. 1, Morgan, UT 84050
Buck Knives (see Knives)
Burnside Originals, Inc., 7472 Old Highway 78, Olive Branch, MS 38654
Camp Time (see Camping)
Lew Childre & Sons, 110 E. Azalea Ave., Foley, AL 36535
Cordell Tackle, Box 1452, Fort Smith, AR 72902 (lures)
Cortland Line Co., 67 E. Court St., Cortland, NY 13045
Crankbait Corp., 23500 Mercantile Rd., Beachwood, OH 44122
Daiwa Corp., 14011 S. Normandie Ave., Gardena, CA 90249
Dolphin Tackle Co., 2100 E. Howell Ave., Ste. 303, Anaheim, CA 92806
Eagle Electronics, Box 6690, Catoosa, OK 74015 (fish finders)
Early Winters, 110 Prefontaine Pl. S., Seattle, WA 98104
Eppinger Mfg. Co., 6340 Schaefer Highway, Dearborn, MI 48126 (lures)
Eze-Lap Diamond Knife Sharpeners (see Knives)
Fenwick/Woodstream, Box 729, Westminster, CA 92683
Gapen's World of Fishin' Inc., Big Lake, MN 55309
Gold-N-West Flyfishers Ltd., 6812 Radisson St., Vancouver, B.C., Canada V5S 3W9
Harrich International, Industrial Rowe, Gardner, MA 01440

James Heddon's Sons, 414 West St., Dowagiac, MI 49047 (lures)
Hook & Hackle Co., Box 1003, Plattsburgh, NY 12901
Huffy Corp., 2018 S. First St., Milwaukee, WI 53207
Johnson Fishing, Inc., 1531 Madison Ave., Mankato, MN 56001 (lures)
Kirsch Enterprises, 1720 N. Casimir Rd., Stevens Point, WI 54481
Knight Mfg. Co., Box 6162, Tyler, TX 75711 (lures)
Kodiak Corp., P.O. Box 137, 100 Mill St., Bessemer, MI 49911
Korkers, Inc., Box 166, Grants Pass, OR 97526
Kunnan Tackle Co., 7282 Bolsa Ave., Westminster, CA 92683
H.L. Leonard Rod Co., Laurel Lane, Central Valley, NY 10917
Lindy-Little Joe, Inc., Box C, 1110 Wright St., Brainerd, MN 56401 (lures)
Lowrance Electronics, Inc., 12000 E. Skelly Dr., Tulsa, OK 74128 (fish finders)
Mann's Bait Co., Box 604, Eufala, AL 36027 (lures)
Merrick Tackle, 2655 Merrick Rd., Bellmore, NY 11710
Meter Fishing Tackle, Box 1882, Bismarck, ND 58502 (lures)
Mister Twister, Inc., P.O. Drawer 1152, Minden, LA 71055 (lures)
Miya Epoch, 1634 Crenshaw Blvd., Torrance, CA 90501
O. Mustad & Son, USA Inc., Box 838, Auburn, NY 13021
Normark Corp., 1710 E. 78th St., Minneapolis, MN 55423 (Rapala lures)
Northwoods, Box 609, Menomonee Falls, WI 53051-0609 (lures)
Orbex, Inc., 620 S. 8th St., Minneapolis, MN 55404
Orvis, 9 River Rd., Manchester, VT 05254
Plano Molding Co., Plano, IL 60545
Quick, 620 Terminal Way, Costa Mesa, CA 92627
Rebel Lures, Box 1452, Fort Smith, AR 72902 (lures)
Reliance Rods, Box 703, Columbus, MS 39701
Rodon Mfg. Co., 123 Sylvan Ave., Newark, NJ 07104
Ryobi America Corp., 1555 Carmen Dr., Elk Grove, IL 60007
St. Croix of Park Falls, Ltd., Park Falls, WI 54552
Sampo, Div. Rome Specialty Co., Inc., Barneveld, NY 13304 (swivels)
Scientific Anglers/3M Co., Box 33984, St. Paul, MN 55133
Scott PowR-Ply Co., 765 Clementina St., San Francisco, CA 94103
Seal-Dri/Cantex Supply, Inc., 2945 South Kansas, Wichita, KS 67216
Shakespeare Fishing Tackle Division, P.O. Drawer S, Columbia, SC 29260
Sheldon's, Inc., CS 1400, Antigo, WI 54409 (lures)
Shimano American Corp., 205 Jefferson Rd., Parsippany, NJ 07054
Simms, Box 3330, Jackson Hole, WY 83001
Techsonic Industries, Inc., One Humminbird Lane, Eufala, AL 36027 (fish finders)
The Angler's Supply House, Inc., Box 996, Williamsport, PA 17703
The Lynn Co., Inc., 313 Mill St., Occoquan, VA 22125
Uncle Josh Bait Co., Box 130, Fort Atkinson, WI 53538 (lures)
Val-Craft, Inc., 67 N. Worcester St., Chartley, MA 02712
Zebco Division, Brunswick Corp., P.O. Box 270, Tulsa, OK 74101
Zypher International Co. (see Camping)

FOOD PRODUCTS & EQUIPMENT

Academy Broadway (cooking — see Attire)
Adobe Fort, 35 E. Ramona Ave., Colorado Springs, CO 80906 (instruction)
Aqua-Ponics, Inc., 17221 E. 17th St., Santa Ana, CA 92701 (food growing)
ASURP Corp., 1818 Wilbur Rd., Medina, OH 44256 (food, storage equipment)
Back Country Foods, Box 2457, Missoula, MT 59806
Barth-Spencer Corp., 270 W. Merrick Rd., Valley Stream, NY 11582 (vitamins)
Bemm Enterprises, Box 108, Gelview, IL 60025 (cooking)
Bolton Farms, 780 N. Clinton Ave., Trenton, NJ 08638 (food)
California Survival Training Center, 15751 Brookhurst St., Ste. 207, Westminster, CA 92683
Camplite Outdoor Foods, 5490 Brooks St., Montclair, CA 91763 (dehydrated foods)
Camp-Ways (cooking — see Camping)
Century Tool & Mfg. Co. (cooking — see Camping)
Cumberland General Store, Rt. 3, Crossville, TN 38555
Esbit (cooking — see Camping)
Family Camping Products, Inc. (see Camping)
Family Products, Inc., 65 Middlesex Rd., Tyngsboro, MA 01879 (food storage containers)
Famous Trails (cooking — see Attire)
Fisher Century Corp., Box 10605, Eugene, OR 97440-2605 (stoves)
Food Reserves, 710 S.E. 17th St. Causeway, Ft. Lauderdale, FL 33316 (food, storage equipment)
Food Storage Sales, Box 15985, Salt Lake City, UT 84115 (food, equipment)
Granite Stairway Mountaineering (cooking — see Attire)
Grover's Supplies & Equipment, 330 W. University Dr., Tempe, AZ 85281
Key Survival Grains, Clay Center, KS 67432 (food, storage equipment)
Magna American Corp., Box 90, Raymond, MS 39154 (duck pickers)
McKendree Products Co., 1893 Del Moro, Klamath Falls, OR 97601 (duck picker)
Mirro Corp. (cooking, smoking, water storage — see Camping)
Moore Supply Co., 3000 S. Main St., Salt Lake City, UT 84115 (deer field dressing kit)
New England Cheesemaking Supply Co., Box 84, Ashfield, MA 01330 (equipment)
Noah Catalog, Box 51656, Palo Alto, CA 94303 (food, water storage)
Optimus, Inc., Box 1950, Bridgeport, CT 06601 (stoves)
Oregon Freeze Dry Foods, Inc., Box 1048, Albany, OR 97321 (Mountain House foods)
Provisions Unlimited, Pond Rd., RFD 1, Oakland, ME 04963 (food, water storage, equipment)
Pyramid Environmental Systems, Inc., 12901 Saratoga Ave., Ste. 8, Saratoga, CA 95070 (stove)
R&R Mill Co., 45 W. First N., Smithfield, UT 84335 (equipment)
Reliance Products, Ltd., 1830 Dublin Ave., Winnipeg, Canada R3H 0H3 (water storage)
Remco Mfg., Inc., 459 S.W. 9th, Dundee, OR 97115 (Pyramid stove)
Solar Mfg. Corp., 14110 Bldg. A, Marquessa Way, Marina del Rey, CA 90292 (cooking)
Sportcraft International Corp., 2318 2nd Ave., Seattle, WA 98121 (cooking)
Stow-A-Way Industries, 166 Cushing Hiway, Rt. 3A, Cohasset, MA 02025 (food, storage equipment)
Survival Outfitters, Box 594, Festus, MO 63028 (bulk grains, dehydrators, grinding mills, misc.)
The Brinkmann Corp., 4215 McEwen Rd., Dallas, TX 75234 (cookers, smokers)
The Family Preparedness Institute, Box 1035, Roxboro, NC 27573 (food, plans)
The Sausage Maker, 177 Military Rd., Valley Stream, NY 11582 (vitamins)
The Survival Center, 5555 Newton Falls Rd., Ravenna, OH 44266
Totem Plastics, 1841 E. Acacia St., Ontario, CA 91761 (water containers)

HOME SECURITY PRODUCTS

A&A Sheet Metal Products, Inc., Box 547, LaPorte, IN 46350 (gun cases)
Academy Broadway Corp. (gun racks — see Attire)
ADA-LARM Co., 26022 A Cape Dr., Laguna Niguel, CA 92677 (auto alarm)
Burbank Enterprises, Inc., 950-D N. Rengstorff Ave., Mountain View, CA 94043 (Audio-Safe car stereo lock)
Cal Custom Hawk, 23011 S. Wilmington Ave., Carson, CA 90745 (auto alarm)
Cemco Security Systems, Box 1113, Yuba City, CA 95991 (gun cases)

Clark Mfg., 9156 Rose St., Suite P, Bellflower, CA 90706 (auto disabler)
Colorado Electro Optics, 2200 Central, Boulder, CO 80301
Communication Control Systems, Ltd., 633 Third Ave., New York, NY 10017 (security blanket system)
Crimestopper Security, 9620 Topanga Canyon Pl., Unit E, Chatsworth, CA 91311
Elpac Automotive Systems, 3131 S. Standard Ave., Santa Ana, CA 92705
Fisher Century Corp. (gun lockers — see Food)
Gard-A-Car, Box 294, Grosse Ile, MI 48138
Guardian Electronics, Inc., 31117 W. Via Colinas, Westlake Village, CA 91362 (Guardex system)
Imperial Screen Co., 5336 W. 145th St., Lawndale, CA 90260
International Safe Manufacturing, 510 W. Washington Blvd., Montebello, CA 90604
Bill Lookabaugh, Inc. (see Archery)
Major Safe Co., 3600 E. Olympic Blvd., Los Angeles, CA 90223 (safes)
Master Lock Co., 2600 N. 32nd, Milwaukee, WI 53216 (alarm products, locks)
Maxwell Alarm Screens, 2326 Sawtelle Ave., W. Los Angeles, CA 90064 (alarms)
Meilink Safe Co., Box 2458, Whitehouse, OH 43571 (safes)
Microlert Systems International, 1755 Cosmic Way, Glendale, CA 91201 (alarms)
B.E. Myers & Co., Inc., 17525 N.E. 67th Ct., Redmond, WA 98052 (Omicron-4 system)
Norton Co., Box 7500, Cerritos, CA 90701 (air space devices)
Pease Industries, Inc., 7100 Dixie Highway, Fairfield, OH 45014 (vault door)
PRP Industries, 1201 Sesame Dr., Sunnyvale, CA 94087 (gun cases)
Saf-T-Case, Box 5472, Irving, TX 75062 (vault door)
Scramco, 832 W. 1st St., Birdsboro, PA 19508 (BurglarMist system)
Security Systems Co., Box 1005, Modesto, CA 95353 (gun lockers)
Sunshine Express, 4357 Chase Ave., Los Angeles, CA 90066 (electrical equipment alarm)
Survival Outfitters (gun vaults — see Food)
Survival Sports, Box 18206, Irvine, CA 92713-8206 (burial vault)
Thrush Enterprises, 1626 N. Wilcox, Suite 130, Los Angeles, CA 90028 (Camp-alert)
Travel Sentry, 3621 W. MacArthur Blvd., Suite 109, Santa Ana, CA 92704 (smoke/fire detector)
Tread Corp., Box 5497, Roanoke, VA 24010 (gun lockers)
Tri-Star Corp., 730 Independent Ave., Grand Junction, CO 81501 (car disabler)
Wall-It, Inc., 230 Fifth Ave., New York, NY 10001 (vaults)
Westfield Sheet Metal Works, Inc., Monroe Ave. & Eighth St., Kenilworth, NJ 07033 (gun cases)
York Safe & Lock, Canton, OH 44711 (safes)

KNIVES & EQUIPMENT
Advent Sales Co., Box 11795, Ft. Lauderdale, FL 33339
Al Mar Knives, 8600 S.W. Salish Lane, Wilsonville, OR 97070
American Blade, P.O. Box 21809, Chattanooga, TN 37421
Atlanta Cutlery Corp., Box 839, Conyers, GA 30207
Bali-Song, 3039 Roswell St., Los Angeles, CA 90065
Ballard Cutlery, P.O. Box 97, Golf, IL 60092
Benchmark Knives, P.O. Box 998, Gastonia, NC 28052
Bianchi, 100 Calle Cortez, Temecula, CA 92390
Bingham Projects, Box 3013, Ogden, UT 84409
Boker, The Cooper Group, P.O. Box 728, Apex, NC 27502
Brigade Quartermasters, Ltd. (see Attire)
Browning, Rt. 1, Morgan, UT 84050
Buck Knives, Box 1267, El Cajon, CA 92022
Buckle & Blade, 150 Nassau St., New York, NY 10038
CAM III Ent., 713-D Merchant St., Vacaville, CA 95688
Camillus Cutlery, P.O. Box 38, 52-54 W. Genesee St., Camillus, NY 13031
W.R. Case & Sons, 20 Russell Blvd., Bradford, PA 16701
Crosman Blades, The Coleman Co., Inc., 250 N. St. Francis, Wichita, KS 67201
Dixie Gun Works, Gunpowder Lane, Union City, TN 38261
DMT, 34 Tower St., Hudson, MA 01749
Easy Climbers, 3900 60th St., Kenosha, WI 53142
Ensign Company, Gunnison, UT 84634
Eze-Lap Diamond Knife Sharpeners, 15164 Weststate St., Westminster, CA 92683
Firearms Import & Export, P.O. Box 520691, Miami, FL 33142
Frost Cutlery Co., P.O. Box 21353, Chattanooga, TN 37421
Geier Enterp., Inc., 1607 S. Chicago Ave., Freeport, IL 61032
Gerber Legendary Blades, 14200 S.W. 72nd Ave., Portland, OR 97223
Gurkha Knives, 4535 Huntington Dr. South, Los Angeles, CA 90032
Gutmann Cutlery, 900 S. Columbus Ave., Mt. Vernon, NY 10550
Imperial Knife Co., 1776 Broadway, New York, NY 10019
Jet-Aer Corp., 100 Sixth Ave., Paterson, NJ 07514
Ka-Bar Cutlery, 5777 Grant Ave., Cleveland, OH 44105
Kershaw Knives, 6024 Jean Road, Lake Oswego, OR 97034
Liberty Organization, Inc. (knives — see Camping)
Jay Luttrull Enterprises, 26255 Walker Rd., Bend, OR 97701
Olsen Knife Co., Howard City, MI 49329
Precise, 3 Chestnut St., Suffern, NY 10901
Precision Sports, P.O. Box 30-06, 798 Cascadilla St., Ithaca, NY 14850
Rigid Knives, P.O. Box 186, Hiway 290E, Lake Hamilton, AR 71951
S&S Industries, Inc., 9212 W. Grand Ave., Franklin Park, IL 60131 (travel carver)
Schrade Cutlery, 26-30 Canal St., Ellenville, NY 12428-0590 (knives)
Smith & Wesson, P.O. Box 2208, Springfield, MA 01101
Swiss Army Knives Victorinox, 14 Progress Dr., Shelton, CT 06484
Taylor Cutlery Co., 806 E. Center St., Kingsport, TN 37662
Tekna, 3549 Haven Ave., Menlo Park, CA 94025
Toledo Armas, S.A., P.O. Box 430435, So. Miami, FL 33143
Tru-Balance Knife Co., 2155 Tremont Blvd., N.W., Grand Rapids, MI 49504
Valor Corp. (knives — see Firearms)
Westbury Sales Co., 373 Maple Ave., Westbury, NY 11590
Western Cutlery, 1800 Pike Rd., Longmont, CO 80501

ARTIFICIAL LIGHTING DEVICES
Aerospace Logistics, Inc., Box 1026, Sun Valley, CA 91352

ALH, Inc., Box 100255, Nashville, TN 37210
Brigade Quartermasters, 226 Roswell St., Marietta, GA 30060
Brinkmann Corp., 4125 McEwen Rd., Dallas, TX 75234
Century Tool & Mfg. Co. (see Camping)
Coleman Company, Inc., Box 1762, Wichita, KS 67201
Dawn To Dusk Co., Box 118, Florence, CO 81226
Diamond, Inc., 16612 Burke St., Huntington Beach, CA 92647
Dorcy International, Inc. (see Camping)
Family Camping Products, Inc. (see Camping)
Hoffmann Associates (lanterns — see Camping)
Lighting Systems, Inc., 6410 W. Ridge Rd., Erie, PA 16506
Mag Instrument, Box 1840, Ontario, CA 91762
Sportcraft International Corp. (lanterns — see Food)
Survival Outfitters (see Food)
Tekna, 3549 Haven Ave., Menlo Park, CA 94025

MEDICAL SUPPLIES & EQUIPMENT
Steve Arnold's Gun Room, 2515 W. Orangethorpe Ave., Fullerton, CA 92633
Just In Case Survival Preparedness Products, Inc., P.O. Box 731, Windsor, CA 95492
King Seeley Thermos Co. (see Camping)
North Star Survival Systems, Inc., P.O. Box 3304, Fort Smith, AR 72913
Outdoor Research, 17423 Beach Dr., N.E., Seattle, WA 98155
Physicians & Nurses Mfg. Corp., Box 68, Larchmont, NY 10538
Surgical Company, Inc., 2 South St., Garden City, NY 11530

NUCLEAR
Biosphere Corp., National Marketing Div., Box 300, Elk River, MN 55330
Core Resource, Box 4526, Mountain View, CA 94040
GO Services, Box 39085, Chicago IL 60639 (nuclear attack analysis)
Just In Case, Box 731, Windsor, CA 95492
Life Science Systems, 4049 First St., Livermore, CA 94550
Prepare, Inc., 7155 E. Thomas, Scottsdale, AZ 85251
Provisions Unlimited (see Camping)
Survivaid Co., 4810 Airport Center, Charlotte, NC 28219
Survival, Inc., 17019 Kingsview Ave., Carson, CA 90746
Survival Outfitters (shelters, radiation meters, misc. — see Food)
Total Survival, Box 1315, Port Arthur, TX 77640

OPTICS
Aerospace Logistics, Inc. (night vision — see Artificial Lighting)
Aimpoint USA, 201 Elden St., Ste. 203R, Herndon, VA 22070
Bausch & Lomb, 1400 N. Goodman, Rochester, NY 14602
Brunton Co., 620 E. Monroe, Riverton, WY 82501
Foster Grant Corp., 517 Oak Lake Ave., Santa Rosa, CA 95405 (sunglasses)
Hoffmann Associates (binoculars — see Camping)
JPM Sales, Box 593, Mansfield, TX 76063
Leupold & Stevens, Box 688, Beaverton, OR 97075
Pentax Binoculars, 35 Inverness Dr. East, Englewood, CO 80112
Redfield, 5800 E. Jewell Ave., Denver, CO 80224
Survival Outfitters (scopes, sights — see Food)
Tasco Sales, Inc., 7600 N.W. 26th St., Miami, FL 33122
Thompson/Center Arms (see Firearms)
Traq, Inc., 8601 N.E. Underground Dr., Kansas City, MO 64161
W.R. Weaver Co., 7125 Industrial Ave., El Paso, TX 79915
Williams Guide Line Products, 6811 Lapeer Rd., Davison, MI 48423
Zeiss Service Center, Box 2010, Petersburg, VA 23803

POWER SOURCES
Core Research, Box 4526, Mountain View, CA 94040 (generators)
Enerlite Products Corp., 550 Stephenson Hwy., Troy, MI 48084 (recharger)
Marlow Associates, Box 42, Rogue River, OR 97537 (alcohol still)
Ruvel & Co., 3037 N. Clark St., Chicago, IL 60657 (generators)
The Survival Center, 5555 Newton Falls Rd., Ravenna, OH 44266 (wind generator)